Automation in Welding Industry

Scrivener Publishing
100 Cummings Center, Suite 541J
Beverly, MA 01915-6106

Industry 5.0 Transformation Applications

Series Editor: Dr. S. Balamurugan and Dr. Sheng-Lung Peng

Scope: The increase in technological advancements in the areas of artificial intelligence (AI), machine learning (ML) and data analytics has led to the next industrial revolution, "Industry 5.0". The transformation to Industry 5.0 collaborates human intelligence with machines to customize efficient solutions. This book series aims to cover various subjects under promising application areas of Industry 5.0 such as smart manufacturing, green ecology, digital medicine, supply chain management, smart textiles, intelligent traffic, innovation ecosystem, cloud manufacturing, digital marketing, real-time productivity optimization, augmented reality and virtual reality, smart energy consumption, predictive maintenance, smart additive manufacturing, hyper customization and cyber physical cognitive systems. The book series will also cover titles supporting technologies for promoting potential applications of Industry 5.0, such as collaborative robots (Cobots), edge computing, Internet of Everything, big data analytics, digital twins, 6G and beyond, blockchain, quantum computing and hyper intelligent networks.

Publishers at Scrivener
Martin Scrivener (martin@scrivenerpublishing.com)
Phillip Carmical (pcarmical@scrivenerpublishing.com)

Automation in Welding Industry

Incorporating Artificial Intelligence, Machine Learning and Other Technologies

Edited by
Syed Quadir Moinuddin
Shaik Himam Saheb
Ashok Kumar Dewangan
Murali Mohan Cheepu
and
S. Balamurugan

Scrivener Publishing

WILEY

This edition first published 2024 by John Wiley & Sons, Inc., 111 River Street, Hoboken, NJ 07030, USA and Scrivener Publishing LLC, 100 Cummings Center, Suite 541J, Beverly, MA 01915, USA

For more information about Scrivener publications please visit www.scrivenerpublishing.com.

Wiley Global Headquarters
111 River Street, Hoboken, NJ 07030, USA

For details of our global editorial offices, customer services, and more information about Wiley products visit us at www.wiley.com.

Library of Congress Cataloging-in-Publication Data

ISBN 978-1-394-17241-2

Cover image: Pixabay.Com
Cover design by Russell Richardson

Set in size of 11pt and Minion Pro by Manila Typesetting Company, Makati, Philippines

Printed in the USA

10 9 8 7 6 5 4 3 2 1

Dedication

Dedicated to all editors' parents, teachers, Almighty God and the welding fraternity.

Contents

Preface **xv**

Acknowledgments **xix**

1 Introduction to Industry 5.0 **1**
Muralimohan Cheepu, Syed Quadir Moinuddin and Ashok Kumar Dewangan
1.1 Introduction 2
1.2 Industry 4.0 8
1.3 Industry 5.0 9
References 11

2 Advancements in Welding Technologies **13**
Pavan Meena, Ansari Mohd Farhan, Ramkishor Anant and Shaik Himam Saheb
2.1 Introduction 13
2.2 Quality of Weld Joint 15
2.3 Pulsed Current GMAW 16
2.4 P-GMAW Process Stability Factors 18
2.5 Suitable Pulse Parameters of Selection 18
2.6 Effect of Pulse Parameters 19
2.6.1 Weld Bead Geometry 19
2.6.2 Weld Dilution 20
2.6.3 Weld Microstructure 20
2.7 Pulsed Current GMAW Advances 22
2.8 Double-Pulsed GMAW 23
2.9 Synergic Control 24
2.10 Self-Regulating Control 25
2.11 Microcomputer Control 26
2.12 GMAW Shielding Gas Flow 27
2.13 Particle Image Velocimetry (PIV) 27
2.14 The Measurement of Oxygen (O_2) Concentration 31

2.15 Spectroscopic Measurements of Plasma Temperature 31
2.16 P-GMAW Numeric Simulation 32
2.16.1 Approach-1 32
2.16.2 Approach-II 33
References 34

3 Automation in Welding Industries 37
Deepak Kumar Naik, Ved Prakash Sharma and Dinesh Kumar R.
3.1 Introduction 38
3.1.1 Types of Automatic Welding 39
3.1.2 Challenges of Automatic Welding 40
3.1.3 Benefits of Automatic Welding 40
3.2 Automation Trends 41
3.2.1 Production Monitoring 41
3.2.2 Adaptive Welding Advancements 42
3.2.3 Upstream Practices 42
3.2.4 Collaborative Technology 42
3.2.5 Easier Programming of Automation Systems 42
3.3 Plasma Welding 42
3.4 Laser Welding 44
3.5 Arc Welding 45
3.6 MIG Welding 45
3.7 Resistance Welding 46
3.8 Conclusions 47
References 48

4 Digitalization of Welding Processes 49
Atla Sridhar, K. Prasanna Lakshmi, Shaik Himam Saheb and M. Siva Surya
4.1 Introduction 49
4.2 Techniques for Process Monitoring 51
4.2.1 Electrical Process Tests: Voltage and Current for Welding 51
4.2.2 Thermal Measurement 54
4.2.3 Optical Measurement 56
4.2.4 Acoustic Measurement 58
4.2.5 Measurement of Displacement and Velocity 59
4.2.6 Measurement of Force 59
4.3 Process Monitoring Applications 61
4.3.1 Measurement of Current and Voltage 61
4.3.2 Thermal Measurement 63

4.3.3 Optical Measurement 64
4.3.4 Acoustic Measurement 65
4.3.5 Displacement and Velocity Measurement 66
4.3.6 Measurement of Force 67
4.3.7 EMF Measurement 67
4.4 Future Directions 67
References 69

5 AI and ML in Welding Technologies 73
Suresh Goka, Gorle Shanmukha Narayana, Divya Jyothi G., Himam Saheb Shaik and Syed Quadir Moinuddin
Nomenclature 74
5.1 Introduction 74
5.2 Enhancing the Welding Industry 76
5.3 Machine Learning Algorithm Types 80
5.4 Background of AI and ML 81
5.5 Weld Defects 82
5.6 Level of Weld Quality 83
5.6.1 Mining Industry 84
5.6.2 Challenges in ML Practice 85
5.7 Case Studies 86
5.7.1 Use of AI Programs to Obtain CCT Welding Diagrams 86
5.7.2 Use of Algorithms to Predict the Penetration Depth in Friction Stir Spot Welding 86
5.8 Feasibility of Online Inspection of Ultrasonic Weld Quality 88
5.9 Conclusions 89
References 89

6 Digital Twin in Welding 91
Syam Kumar Chokka, M. Nagaraju and K. Nagabushan Kumar
6.1 Introduction 91
6.2 Friction Stir Welding 92
6.2.1 FSW Parameters 94
6.3 Defects in Friction Stir Welding 96
6.3.1 DT for FSW 99
6.4 Laser Welding 102
6.4.1 Heat Conduction Welding 103
6.4.2 Deep Penetration or Keyhole Welding 103
6.4.3 Weld Process Parameters 104
6.4.3 DT for Laser Welding 104

6.5 Summary 106
References 106

7 IoT in Welding Industries 111
Harisivasri Phanindra K., S. Venukumar, Muralimohan Cheepu and Venkata Charan Kantumuchu
7.1 Introduction 111
7.2 Sensing and Analyzing Welding Data via the Internet of Things (IoT) 113
7.2.1 Electrical Information 113
7.2.2 Optical Information 113
7.3 Welding Manufacture Based on IoT 114
7.3.1 Example 1: Arc Quality Management with IoT 115
7.3.2 Example 2: Case Study on IoT-Enabled Molten Metal Temperature Sensing System for Welding 117
7.3.3 Example 3: IoT-Based Safety Monitoring System During Welding Operations 119
7.3.4 Example 4: IoT-Based Monitoring of Submerged Arc Welding Process 122
7.4 Conclusion 127
References 128

8 VR and AR in Welding Technologies 129
Veningston K. and Dinesh Kumar Rajendran
8.1 Introduction 129
8.1.1 Virtual Reality (VR) 130
8.1.2 Augmented Reality (AR) 131
8.1.3 Artificial Intelligence (AI) 131
8.1.4 Machine Learning (ML) 131
8.2 How Intelligent is AI When Coupled with VR/AR? 132
8.3 VR/AR Architecture 132
8.4 Welding Processes 132
8.5 Intelligent Welding Technology 133
8.6 Types of Intelligent Welding Processes 134
8.6.1 Types of Welding Positions 135
8.7 Automated Welding Examples 135
8.7.1 Computer Interface of Automated Welding Processes 135
8.8 Applications of VR and AR in Automated Welding 136
8.9 AI and ML for Visual Inspection of Welds 138
8.9.1 AI in Arc Welding 138

8.9.2 AI Detection of Welding Defects 138
8.9.3 VR/AR Welding Simulator 139
8.10 Limitations in the Existing State-of-the-Art Welding Techniques 140
8.10.1 Advantages of AR/VR 140
8.11 Conclusions 141
References 141

9 Intelligent, Clean Cobot Arc Welding Cell 143
E. Schubert, S. Rose, M. Bender, N. Spietz and T. Weber
9.1 Chances for SMEs 143
9.1.1 Introduction and Goals 144
9.2 Parameters and Consumption Data 146
9.3 CO_2 Footprint Methodology 148
9.4 Result Presentation 149
9.5 Conclusion 154
Acknowledgments 154
References 155

10 Welding-Based 3D, 4D, 5D Printing 157
Suresh Goka, Satish Narayana Srirama, Divya Jyothi G., Syed Quadir Moinuddin and Himam Saheb Shaik
Nomenclature 158
10.1 Introduction 158
10.2 Differences Among 3DP, 4DP and 5DP 160
10.3 Materials Used in 3DP, 4DP and 5DP Processes 162
10.3.1 Additive Manufactured Metallic Components 163
10.4 Machinability of Welded Components 168
10.5 Concept of 4D and 5D Printing 169
10.6 FEM-Based Analysis 172
10.7 Applications 174
10.7.1 4D Printing Applications 174
10.7.2 3D Printing in the Aerospace Industry 175
10.7.3 3D Printing in Electronics 176
10.7.4 3D Printing in Electrochemical Industries 176
10.7.5 5D Printing in Dentistry 176
10.7.6 5D Printing in Orthopedics 176
10.8 Conclusions 177
References 178

11 Welding and Joining of Novel Materials **183**
Rajendra Goud, Poonam S. Deshmukh, Bhavesh Jain, G. Dan Sathiaraj and Kodli Basanth Kumar
11.1 Introduction 184
11.1.1 Concept of High Entropy Alloys (HEAs) 184
11.2 Core Effects 184
11.2.1 High Entropy Effect 185
11.2.2 Sluggish Diffusion Effect 186
11.2.3 Severe Lattice Distortion Effect 186
11.2.4 Cocktail Effect 186
11.2.5 Current Status of HEAs 186
11.3 Arc Welding Techniques for HEAs 186
11.4 Solid State Welding 192
11.4.1 Friction Stir Welding (FSW) 193
11.5 Explosive Welding 197
11.5.1 Soldering and Brazing 199
11.6 EBW and EBC of HEAs 200
11.7 Laser Welding of HEAs 202
11.8 Laser Cladding of HEAs 206
11.9 Conclusion and Summary 208
References 208

12 Sustainability in Welding Industries **215**
Y.G. Bala, Santhi B. and Dinesh Kumar R.
12.1 Introduction 215
12.2 Critical Factors for Sustainability of Welding 216
12.3 Adoptability of Sustainable Welding 218
12.4 New Welding Standards for Sustainability 218
12.5 Resource-Conserving Techniques 219
12.5.1 Sustainable Welding in Practice 220
12.5.2 Boosting Efficiency with Special Welding Processes 220
12.6 Sustainability in Welding Training 220
12.6.1 Sustainable Technologies for Thick Metal Plate Welding 221
12.7 5S Lean Strategy for a Sustainable Welding Process 221
12.7.1 Sustainability Assessment of Shielded Metal Arc Welding (SMAW) Process 222
12.8 A-TIG Welding: A Small Step Towards Sustainable Manufacturing 223
12.8.1 Weight Space Partitions-Based Sustainable Welding 223
12.8.2 Sustainability Assessment of Welding Processes 223

12.8.3 Sustainability in Manufacturing 226
12.9 Sustainability Indices 227
12.10 Conclusion 227
References 228

13 Global Welding Market Growth 229
Y.G. Bala and Dinesh Kumar Rajendran
13.1 Introduction 229
13.1.1 Overview of Global Welding Products Market 231
13.2 Patrons of Global Welding Market 233
13.3 Welding Technologies in the Global Welding Market 236
13.4 Fluxes, Wires, Electrodes, and Fillers 237
13.5 Welding Market Dynamics 238
13.6 Manpower and Labor Challenges in Global Market 239
13.7 COVID-19's Impact on Global Welding Materials Market 240
13.8 New Opportunity in the Welding Market and Advanced Applications 241
13.9 Conclusions 241
References 242

14 Quality Assurance and Control in Welding and Additive Manufacturing 245
Venkata Charan Kantumchu, Syed Quadir Moinuddin, Ashok Kumar Dewangan and Muralimohan Cheepu
14.1 Introduction 246
14.2 Quality Issues in Welding 247
14.3 Quality Issues in 3D Printing 255
14.4 Conclusion 259
References 259

15 Welding Practices in Industry 5.0: Opportunities, Challenges, and Applications 263
Suresh Goka, Syed Quadir Moinuddin, Muralimohan Cheepu and Ashok Kumar Dewangan
15.1 Introduction 264
15.2 Manufacturing Trends 264
15.3 Welding Technology 265
15.3.1 Classification of Welding 267
15.4 Variety of Materials Used by Welding for Industry 5.0 267
15.4.1 Advantages of Welding 269
15.4.2 Applications 269
15.4.3 Automation 269

15.4.4 Welding-Based AM 271
15.4.5 Welding Trends in Aeronautic Industry 271
15.4.6 Robotic and Automated Welding 272
15.5 Virtual Reality (VR) for Welders 274
15.6 Challenges and Opportunities in Nuclear Reactor 275
15.7 Challenges of AM-Based Functionally Graded Materials Through LDED 276
15.8 Conclusion 277
References 277

Index **281**

Preface

In the era of modern manufacturing, industries have evolved from automation to digitization and mass personalization to fulfill consumer demands. To this end, Industry 5.0 provides mass personalization along with effective human–machine interaction for efficient and faster outcomes in the manufacturing sector. Among the different manufacturing industries, the welding industry is dominant because of its wide-ranging applications in the healthcare, automotive, construction, pipeline, shipping, and aerospace industries, among others. Although the implementation of Industry 4.0 has digitized the welding industries, there is still a lack of welding knowledge, which affects, for example, productivity, product quality, material compatibility, and, ultimately, the industrial economy. To overcome these limitations, the need has arisen for the integration of Industry 5.0 technologies in the welding industry, wherein human–machine interaction through critical components, such as artificial intelligence (AI), machine learning (ML), the internet of things (IoT), augmented and virtual reality (AR & VR), and collaborative robots (Cobots), can perform efficient welding with less human effort.

The objective of this book is to provide in-depth knowledge on welding technologies, including advancements, challenges, and opportunities, in relation to Industry 5.0. Over the decades, the use of revolutionary methods has grown simultaneously in industries and manufacturing technologies because of the proven value they offer in the constantly changing global market. Unlike other industries, there is still a need for development in welding industries towards automation to address welding issues, which will require more experimentation. In particular, there is a need to bridge the gap between industries and welding professionals to pave the way from conventional methods to digitization to cobot welding, and Industry 5.0 presents the opportunity for this to occur. Industry 4.0 has already provided a platform for Industry 5.0 with the integration of AI, ML, IoT, AR and VR, cobots, digital twins, and cloud technologies in developing intelligent welding systems. Furthermore, welding technologies along with

Industry 5.0, could be extended to the joining of novel materials and metal additive manufacturing (AM), which has wide-ranging applications over traditional manufacturing techniques. Upon implementation of Industry 5.0 in welding technologies, the welding and AM industries will be able to better meet the supply and demand in the global market, thereby contributing to the world economy.

This book introduces the concepts of Industry 5.0 in welding technologies, wherein human brain–robot collaboration is employed to achieve rapid growth in productivity and economic efficiency. It has been organized into 15 chapters, wherein each chapter comprehensively discusses the prospects of each component of Industry 5.0 on welding technologies. Therefore, it will enlighten the reader's knowledge of Industry 5.0 in relation to manufacturing, welding technologies, and computation, and will encourage entrepreneurship that enhances the global economy. The following is a brief description of the information contained in each chapter of the book:

Chapter 1 introduces Industry 5.0 and its importance in the manufacturing industry and welding technologies. This chapter briefly discusses the evolution that has taken place in industry through various generations over the years. The purpose of Industry 5.0 is to advance the technologies of Industry 4.0 and leverage modern technologies of artificial intelligence, machine learning, blockchain, digital twins, and the internet of things to create smarter and more efficient manufacturing processes.

Chapter 2 comprehensively addresses the advancements in welding technologies, especially fusion welding technologies, owing to their widespread applications in various manufacturing industries. Advancements include process stability through V-I characteristics, power sources, and weld bead geometry; the microstructure and its corresponding numerical modeling techniques are also discussed.

Chapter 3 explores the extent of advancements in the automation of welding technologies, wherein the productivity and economic efficiency are increased. It also addresses the challenges faced in welding automation, along with its benefits and drawbacks, which are addressed to control arc processes and thereby, weld quality.

Chapter 4 introduces the utilization of sensors in welding processes that allow the independent monitoring and control of each variable independently, leading to the digitization of welding processes. In addition, sensors can be integrated with welding systems to facilitate the digitalization of welding processes.

Chapter 5 briefly describes emerging tools, such as machine learning and artificial intelligence and their importance in welding technologies.

It also addresses how the implementation of AI and ML enhances welding technologies by training digitized data, resulting in less material wastage and defect-free quality welds. This chapter concludes with real-world case studies and future research directions.

Chapter 6 describes the implementation of digital twin in welding technologies to design a model that can perform simulations using computerized digital technologies. The authors of this chapter specifically approached the digital twin role in two welding processes: friction stir welding and laser welding.

Chapter 7 discusses the use of IoT for better quality management and provides suitable examples for arc quality management and molten metal temperature-sensing systems for welding operations and monitoring of the submerged arc welding process. In addition, the critical hazards confronting the welder during confined space and hot work operations, and IoT-based solutions to alleviate their risks.

Chapter 8 describes the importance of augmented reality and virtual reality in welding technologies. In addition, the coupling of AI and ML, along with the contribution of AR and VR to intelligent welding systems, was addressed. This chapter concludes with a brief examination of contemporary issues related to cobots discussed in the next chapter.

Chapter 9 stresses the importance of a clean robotic arc-welding environment aided by cobots. The authors present experimental results from their project, wherein a novel clean cell is developed that minimizes fumes, and shields gas and energy consumption, thereby monitoring ecological footprints and productivity.

Chapter 10 explores the extent of welding technologies in the field of additive manufacturing, wherein three-, four-, and five-dimensional complex structures can be generated. Additionally, the authors addressed the concepts of multidimensional printing, materials, and applications.

Chapter 11 discusses the start of the art in different welding and joining processes of novel materials, such as HEAs, including friction stir welding, explosive welding, soldering, and brazing.

Chapter 12 offers a broad framework for evaluating sustainability, which was later modified to offer a tool for precisely evaluating the sustainability performance of the welding processes.

Chapter 13 provides insight into the current global welding market and future growth trends among other manufacturing industries. It addresses the use of welding consumables, welding market dynamics, manpower challenges, COVID-19 impact, and new opportunities in the global welding market.

Chapter 14 discusses the importance of quality in fabrication, particularly in welding technologies. The necessity of quality is addressed in a few case studies, wherein welding failures damaged the entire structure. The authors also addressed the solutions that could have been achieved with more research and utilization of artificial intelligence, which reduces costs and enhances the quality of the welds.

Chapter 15 reports the challenges, opportunities, and applications related to welding practices in Industry 5.0. It also summarizes the complete book and concludes with directions for future research.

Syed Quadir Moinuddin
Department of Mechanical Engineering, College of Engineering,
King Faisal University, Al-Hofuf, Kingdom of Saudi Arabia

Acknowledgments

The preparation of this edited book was like a journey that we had undertaken for several months. We wish to express our heartfelt gratitude to Director Prof. (Dr.) K. L. Narayana, Faculty of Science and Technology, ICFAI Foundation for Higher Education, Hyderabad, Telangana, India, ICFAI Society, our families, friends, colleagues, and well-wishers for their constant support throughout this journey. We express our gratitude to all the chapter contributors who have allowed us to quote their remarks and work in this book. In particular, we would like to acknowledge the hard work of authors and their cooperation during the revisions of their chapters. We would also like to acknowledge the valuable comments of the reviewers which have enabled us to select these chapters out of the so many chapters we received and also improve the quality of the chapters. We wish to acknowledge and appreciate the Scrivener team, especially Martin, for their continuous support throughout the entire process of publication. Our gratitude is extended to the readers, who gave us their trust, and we hope this work guides and inspires them.

1

Introduction to Industry 5.0

Muralimohan Cheepu[1], Syed Quadir Moinuddin[2*] and Ashok Kumar Dewangan[3]

[1]STARWELDS Inc., Busan, South Korea
[2]Department of Mechanical Engineering, College of Engineering, King Faisal University, Al-Hofuf, Kingdom of Saudi Arabia
[3]Department of Mechanical Engineering, National Institute of Technology, Delhi, India

Abstract
Industry 5.0 is the next generation of industrial manufacturing that is expected to combine efficiency and automation for a human-centric approach. The goal of Industry 5.0 is human-machine collaboration for the creation of customized products, reducing waste, enhancing efficiency, and prioritizing environmental responsibility in manufacturing industries. The purpose of Industry 5.0 is to advance the technologies of Industry 4.0 and leverage the modern technologies of artificial intelligence, machine learning, blockchain, digital twins, and the internet of things to create smarter and more efficient manufacturing processes. Along with modern techniques, Industry 5.0 also highlights the importance of human skills and creativity and without damaging the environment. The manufacturing industry is expected to need advanced technologies to deal with critical joints and compensate for the shortage of welders. The modern era of Industry 5.0 in welding technology brings more creative methods than conventional ones. This chapter introduces Industry 5.0, its importance in the manufacturing industry, and welding technologies.

***Keywords*:** Internet of Things, artificial intelligence, Industry 5.0, manufacturing industries, welding technologies, digital twin

**Corresponding author*: syedquadirmoinuddin@gmail.com

Syed Quadir Moinuddin, Shaik Himam Saheb, Ashok Kumar Dewangan, Murali Mohan Cheepu and S. Balamurugan (eds.) Automation in Welding Industry: Incorporating Artificial Intelligence, Machine Learning and Other Technologies, (1–12) © 2024 Scrivener Publishing LLC

1.1 Introduction

The Industrial Revolution was a period of intense social and economic transformation that took place from the late 18th to the mid-19th centuries in Europe and North America. It began because of complex and multifaceted advancements. Technological advancements enabled the development of new machines that were used to power locomotives by steam engines and spinning jennies for attaining goods in a faster and more efficient manner [1]. Secondly, accessing resources such as the ease of use of natural resources like coal and iron, was considered an important source material for industrial production. Also, since economic incentives became important to evaluate the growth of nations, the growth of entrepreneurship and the aspiration for profits led industrialists to seek out different ways to improve industrial goods production and efficiency [2]. After that, social and political policies slowly began to change. The evolution of cities and the development of trade were directed towards new prospects for business and industry. Finally, scientific advancements in science and engineering, along with new developments in chemistry and metallurgy, empowered new extraction methods and processes to produce various goods [3]. Inclusively, the industrial revolution was a complex and interconnected phenomenon that arose from a combination of factors, among which were technological advancements, access to resources, economic incentives, social and political changes, and scientific advancements.

The second phase of the Industrial Revolution (Industry 2.0) started in the middle of the 19th century and continued until the early 20th century. During this period, there was major progress in technology, in particular in the production of iron and steel, textile industries, telecommunications, and advanced transportation facilities [4, 5]. Some of the key achievements in the period of Industry 2.0 were the generation of steam and its usage for the driving of machinery, ships, and engines. Moreover, mass production methods were introduced by advancing machinery technologies for various industries. Communication became easier between continents and within countries. In order to transport both mass-produced goods and passengers, railroads and steamships were developed. At the same time, interchangeable machinery parts were also developed. Due to this revolution, there were tremendous developments in innovative production methods, resulting in economic growth [6]. The living standards and facilities of many people were enhanced by advanced technologies. Conversely, the advancements had significant impacts on social and environmental fields by increasing the displacement of workers, urbanization, pollution, and the utilization of natural resources. Inclusively, Industry 2.0 paved the way for additional technological advancements and industrialization in the 20th century and beyond.

The third Industrial Revolution (Industry 3.0) encompasses the period of advancements in the manufacturing industry that commenced in the late 20th century and continued until the early 21st century. This period was defined by the extensive implementation of computerized and automated systems in factories and manufacturing processes [7]. Industry 3.0 saw the introduction of advanced methods, such as computer-aided manufacturing (CAM), automatic machinery, robotics, and programmable logic controllers, which became increasingly dominant in manufacturing, resulting in important increases in efficiency and productivity. Furthermore, improvements in communication technologies enabled greater collaboration and management between diverse stages of the manufacturing process [8].

Industry 3.0 had an insightful effect on the manufacturing industry and paved the way for further advancements in Industry 4.0, which is characterized by the combination of advanced technologies such as the internet of things (IoT), artificial intelligence (AI), and big data analytics. Moreover, sensors and computers became the main technology in the printing industry [9]. Step-and-repeat machines, digital viewers and type setters, color scanners, and workstations all relied on computer technology. Another major technology was the electronics industry, where controls and sensors are used to count accurately and allow more flexibility in folding and binding solutions. This technology was also utilized for sorting and labeling automatically and was programmable to ensure accuracy [10].

The Fourth Industrial Revolution is referred to as Industry 4.0, which includes and prioritizes the latest technological innovations. The term Industry 4.0 was coined in Germany in 2011 and refers to the technological changes related to advanced automation fields and connected with information technologies [11], with the goal of encouraging manufacturing automation and, accordingly, growing productivity through "smart factories." This means that the stagnant looming Fourth Industrial Revolution can be categorized by the integration between the Internet and production processes. This technology is widely used in controllable devices to enhance automation using small sensors and artificial intelligence in machines [12].

In 2014, German industries were already assessing their competitiveness with other parts of the world in terms of Industry 4.0's implementation. It was identified that 41% of the German companies were aware of the future revolution and had started some determined initiatives. Therefore, in most of the companies, about 20% of the equipment manufacturers implemented their technologies and sold them before other large-scale companies were aware of them [13]. With these technologies, a new level of socio-technical interaction was implemented by carrying out the planning processes for various organizations. Smart products are some of the things introduced, and the operating parameters of several production processes can be known and utilized for their optimized production, as illustrated in Figure 1.1.

Industry 5.0 is a term used to describe the future phase of the industrial revolution, which includes Industry 4.0 and builds on further developments in the industries. Industry 5.0, also known as the human-centric industrial revolution, places a transformed attention on the reputation of human workers in the manufacturing process [14]. This revolution highlights the incorporation of advanced technologies with the skills and creativity of humans to create a more efficient and effective production process. Industry 5.0 endeavors to produce a harmonious balance between the abilities of machines and the unique abilities of humans, encouraging a more sustainable and socially responsible industrial model. It is defined as a re-found and extended single-mindedness, going beyond manufacturing goods and services for profit. The extended single-mindedness establishes three core elements: human-centricity, sustainability, and resilience [15].

Figure 1.2 illustrates the development and overview of the industrial evolutions with the time frame between each industrial revolution. Taking into consideration all the developments from the Industrial Revolutions 1.0 to 4.0, the main motivation behind Industry 5.0 is to leverage the distinctive creativity of human experts to cooperate with powerful, smart, and perfect machinery. In keeping with the natural environment, it is expected

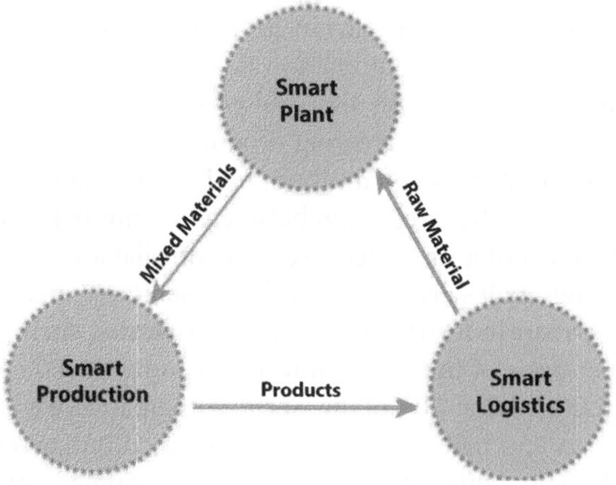

Figure 1.1 Key aspects of Industry 4.0.

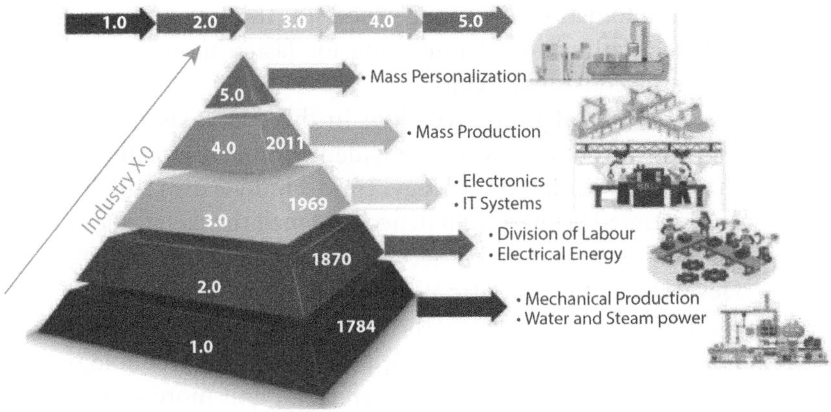

Figure 1.2 Overview of the industrial evolution.

that greener solutions will be used in Industry 5.0 to replace those of existing industrial systems. In other words, it can be said that Industry 5.0 will use predictive analytics and intelligence operations to create models for accurate outputs using the most reliable decisions. Moreover, in this evolution, most of the manufacturing process will be converted to automation; additionally, it will be able to use real-time data produced from the machines in collaboration with highly qualified experts.

The welding industry has undergone several revolutions over the years, from the introduction of new techniques and technologies to the adoption of new materials and the development of new applications. Following are some of the major revolutions in the welding industry:

1. **Introduction of Electric Arc Welding:** In the late 1800s, the introduction of electric arc welding provided a significant breakthrough in welding technology. This technique uses an electric arc to heat and melt the metal, allowing it to be fused together. This technique revolutionized welding and provided a faster, more efficient method for joining metals.
2. **Introduction of Gas Welding:** The introduction of gas welding in the early 1900s marked another revolution in the welding industry. This technique uses a flame produced by burning a mixture of oxygen and acetylene gas to heat and melt the metal. Gas welding is still widely used today in applications such as repairing automotive bodies and welding pipes.
3. **Development of Automatic Welding:** In the 1930s, automatic welding technology was introduced, which allowed

for the automation of welding processes. This revolutionized the welding industry by allowing for faster, more precise, and more consistent welding.
4. **Introduction of Laser Welding:** In the 1960s, laser welding was introduced, which provided another major breakthrough in welding technology. This technique uses a highly concentrated beam of light to heat and melt the metal, allowing for precise and highly accurate welding.
5. **Development of Robotic Welding:** In recent years, robotic welding has revolutionized the welding industry by allowing for the automation of welding processes. This technology has made welding faster, more efficient, and more consistent, while also reducing the risk of injury to human welders.

Overall, the welding industry has undergone several revolutions over the years, with each new development bringing faster, more efficient, and more precise welding techniques.

Welding, as a process of joining two pieces of metal or thermoplastic together, has been around for centuries. However, the modern form of welding, as we know it today, was developed in the 19th century.

The first welding process that was widely used was arc welding. It was invented by Auguste de Méritens in 1881. Arc welding involves using an electric arc to melt the metals that need to be joined and then allowing the metals to cool and solidify, forming a permanent bond.

Another major development in welding technology was the invention of oxyacetylene welding, which was developed by Edmund Davy in 1903. This method involves using a torch to heat the metals to be joined and then adding filler material to create a bond.

In the years that followed, various welding processes were developed, including gas tungsten arc welding, gas metal arc welding, and resistance welding. These methods allowed for greater precision and efficiency in welding, making it possible to join a wider variety of materials and create stronger bonds.

Today, welding technology continues to evolve with the development of new methods like laser welding and friction stir welding. These advancements have made welding a vital part of many industries, from construction and manufacturing to aerospace and automotive engineering.

Welding has been an essential aspect of manufacturing and construction for centuries. However, with the advent of Industry 1.0, also known as the Industrial Revolution, welding began to be used in mass production and other large-scale manufacturing processes. The introduction of steam power, mechanization, and mass production techniques allowed for more efficient and effective welding processes.

During this period, welding was primarily performed using the forge welding process, which involved heating metal pieces in a forge and hammering them together to create a bond. This process was time-consuming and required skilled laborers to perform it.

However, with the rise of Industry 1.0, welding techniques were revolutionized with the introduction of electric welding. In 1881, the first electric arc welding process was developed by Nikolai Benardos and Stanisław Olszewski, and it was later improved upon by Charles L. Coffin and Elihu Thomson in the United States.

This new welding technology allowed for faster and more efficient welding processes, which led to increased productivity and lower production costs. Welding began to be used in a wider range of industries, including shipbuilding, railroad construction, and the manufacturing of automobiles and other machinery.

Welding played an important role in the development of Industry 1.0, as it enabled the efficient and effective production of goods on a large scale.

Welding is an important process in many industries, and it has evolved significantly with the advent of Industry 2.0, which is characterized by the widespread use of automation, digitization, and the internet of things (IoT). In the context of welding, Industry 2.0 has enabled the development of new technologies and techniques that have made welding faster, safer, and more efficient.

One of the key benefits of Industry 2.0 in welding is the use of automation. Automation can be used to perform repetitive welding tasks, which reduces the risk of human error and increases productivity. Automation can also be used to improve the quality of welds, as it can ensure consistent welds every time.

Another important aspect of Industry 2.0 in welding is the use of digitization. Digital technologies can be used to monitor the welding process in real time, which allows for more precise control of the process. This can lead to better quality-welds and fewer defects.

The IoT also plays a role in Industry 2.0 welding, as it allows for greater connectivity between different parts of the welding process. For example, sensors can be used to monitor the condition of welding equipment and send alerts when maintenance is required. This can help prevent equipment breakdowns and reduce downtime.

In addition to these technological advancements, Industry 2.0 has also led to the development of new welding techniques, such as friction stir welding and laser welding. These techniques offer benefits such as improved speed and precision, as well as the ability to weld materials that were previously difficult to weld.

Industry 2.0 has had a significant impact on the welding industry, enabling the development of new technologies and techniques that have improved productivity, quality, and safety. As the industry continues to evolve, we can expect to see further advancements in welding technology that will continue to enhance the efficiency and effectiveness of the welding process.

Welding has been a crucial process in the manufacturing industry for many years, and with the advent of Industry 3.0, it has become even more important. Industry 3.0 refers to the use of automation, data exchange, and other advanced technologies in manufacturing processes.

One of the key benefits of Industry 3.0 for welding is the increased use of robots and automation in the welding process. Welding robots can perform repetitive welding tasks with high precision and consistency, reducing the need for human welders and improving overall quality and productivity.

Another advantage of Industry 3.0 in welding is the use of data and analytics to optimize the welding process. By collecting and analyzing data from welding machines, manufacturers can identify trends and patterns that can be used to optimize welding parameters, reduce defects, and improve overall quality.

Industry 3.0 also enables greater connectivity and collaboration between different parts of the welding process, from design and engineering to production and quality control. This can lead to faster and more efficient welding processes, as well as better communication and collaboration between different teams and departments.

Overall, welding with Industry 3.0 offers a range of benefits, from increased efficiency and productivity to higher quality and consistency. As manufacturers continue to adopt new technologies and automation, the role of welding in the manufacturing process will only become more important.

1.2 Industry 4.0

Industry 4.0 refers to the Fourth Industrial Revolution, which has brought about the integration of advanced technologies such as artificial intelligence, the internet of things (IoT), robotics, and big data analytics into industrial processes. Welding, being an essential industrial process in many manufacturing industries, can also benefit from the integration of Industry

4.0 technologies. Here are some ways that welding can be improved with Industry 4.0:

1. **Welding Automation:** With the integration of robotics and automation, welding can be automated, making it more efficient, consistent, and precise. Welding robots can perform repetitive tasks more accurately, and with the use of sensors and machine learning, they can adapt to changing conditions.
2. **Predictive Maintenance:** Welding machines are subject to wear and tear, which can lead to breakdowns and production downtime. With Industry 4.0 technologies, sensors can be used to monitor the condition of welding machines and predict when maintenance is required. This approach can help reduce downtime, increase productivity, and extend the lifespan of welding equipment.
3. **Quality Control:** Welding defects can occur due to factors such as improper welding technique, material defects, or environmental conditions. With the use of sensors and big data analytics, welding defects can be identified and corrected in real time. This approach can help improve the quality of welded products, reduce rework, and improve customer satisfaction.
4. **Remote Monitoring:** Welding processes can be monitored remotely using IoT devices and cloud-based software. This approach can help manufacturers monitor the welding process in real time, optimize performance, and reduce the need for manual intervention.

Overall, the integration of Industry 4.0 technologies into welding processes can help manufacturers improve efficiency, reduce costs, increase productivity, and enhance the quality of welded products.

1.3 Industry 5.0

Industry 5.0 is a new paradigm in manufacturing that focuses on the integration of advanced technologies, such as artificial intelligence (AI), the internet of things (IoT), and robotics, with human skills and expertise. Welding is one area where Industry 5.0 can have a significant impact.

Welding is a critical process in many manufacturing industries, including automotive, aerospace, and construction. Welding with Industry 5.0 can help improve productivity, efficiency, and quality while also reducing costs and improving safety.

Here are some ways welding with Industry 5.0 can be implemented:

1. **Automated Welding:** Industry 5.0 can enable the automation of welding processes using robotics and advanced sensors. This can improve consistency and accuracy in welding, reduce cycle times, and reduce the need for human intervention.
2. **Welding Process Optimization:** AI algorithms can be used to optimize welding processes by analyzing data from sensors, cameras, and other sources. This can help identify areas for improvement, reduce waste, and improve product quality.
3. **Collaborative Welding:** Industry 5.0 can enable human and robotic workers to work together in a collaborative environment. This can improve safety and efficiency by allowing humans to focus on complex tasks while robots handle repetitive or dangerous tasks.
4. **Virtual Welding:** Industry 5.0 can enable virtual training and simulation of welding processes. This can help reduce the time and cost of training while also improving safety by allowing trainees to practice in a virtual environment.
5. **Welding Quality Control:** Industry 5.0 can enable real-time monitoring of welding quality using sensors and analytics. This can help identify defects and improve product quality, while also reducing the need for post-weld inspections.

Overall, welding with Industry 5.0 has the potential to revolutionize the welding industry by improving efficiency, quality, and safety. By leveraging advanced technologies and human expertise, welding with Industry 5.0 can help manufacturers meet the demands of a rapidly changing market.

References

1. De Vries, J., The industrial revolution and the industrious revolution. *J. Econ. Hist.*, 54, 2, 249–70, Jun. 1994.
2. Ashton, T.S., *The Industrial Revolution 1760-1830*, OUP Catalogue, OUP-Oxford University Press-UK, 1997.
3. Berg, M. and Hudson, P., Rehabilitating the industrial revolution 1. *Econ. Hist. Rev.*, 45, 1, 24–50, Feb. 1992.
4. Xu, M., David, J.M., Kim, S.H., The fourth industrial revolution: Opportunities and challenges. *IJFR*, 9, 2, 90–5, Feb. 5, 2018.
5. Hudson, P., *The Industrial Revolution*, Bloomsbury Publishing, India, Sep. 29, 2014.
6. Shahi, A.S., Pandey, S., Gill, J.S., Effect of auxiliary preheating of filler wire on dilution in gas metal arc stainless steel surfacing using RSM. *Surf. Eng.*, 23, 5, 384–390, 2007.
7. Lin, Y.C. and Lee, K.H., Effect of preheating on the residual stress in type 304 stainless steel weldment. *J. Mater. Process. Technol.*, 63, 1–3, 797–801, 1997.
8. Nakamura, T. and Hiraoka, K., Ultra narrow GMAW process with newly developed wire melting control system. *Sci. Technol. Weld. Join.*, 6, 6, 355–362, 2001.
9. Tong, H., Ueyama, T., Harada, S., Ushio, M., Quality and productivity improvement in aluminium alloy thin sheet welding using alternating current pulsed metal inert gas welding system. *Sci. Technol. Weld. Join.*, 6, 4, 203–208, 2001.
10. Stanzel, K., Pulsed GMAW cuts cycle time by 600 percent. *Weld. Des. Fabr.*, 85–87, April 2001.
11. Tippins, J., Box beam fabrication using the pulsed MIG process. *Mater. Construct. Br. Weld. J.*, 14, 547–550, December 1970.
12. Harvey, R.C., Gas metal arc welding fume generation using pulsed current. *Weld. J.*, 74, 11, 59s–68s, 1995.
13. Thamodharan, M., Beck, H.P., Wolf, A., Steady and pulsed direct current welding with a single converter. *Weld. J.*, 78, 3, 75s–79s, 1999.
14. Amin, M., Pulsed current parameters for arc stability and controlled metal transfer in arc welding. *Met. Construct.*, 15, 272–278, 1983.
15. Allum, C.J., Welding technology data: Pulsed MIG welding weld. *Met. Fabr.*, 53, 24–30, 1985.

2

Advancements in Welding Technologies

Pavan Meena[1], Ansari Mohd Farhan[1], Ramkishor Anant[1*] and Shaik Himam Saheb[2†]

[1]*Department of Materials and Metallurgical Engineering, Maulana Azad National Institute of Technology, Bhopal, India*
[2]*Department of Mechanical Engineering, Faculty of Science and Technology, ICFAI Foundation for Higher Education, Hyderabad, India*

Abstract
Due to the many advantages of advanced welding processes, including their cost-effectiveness, welding engineers have recently become more interested in using advanced welding technologies rather than conventional (older) welding processes. The use of an advanced welding technique has been found to enhance the weld's conservative qualities over those seen with a weld created using a conventional welding procedure, primarily because it has a positive impact on the microstructure, heat-affected zone (HAZ), or bonding strength of the weld. One of the most frequently utilized procedures is fusion welding, which is also frequently used to combine metals of different types. There are several options for fusion welding processes; depending on the rate of weld deposition, shielding environment, and welding conditions, every operation has a unique weld thermal cycle. In order to obtain good weld characteristics, some cutting-edge welding procedures have been created, and these techniques are covered in this chapter.

Keywords: P-GMAW, advances in welding technologies, heat affected zone, microstructure

2.1 Introduction

Pulsed gas metal arc welding (P-GMAW), which has various special benefits for making high-quality welds where a current in pulsation is employed

**Corresponding author*: ram.met@gmail.com
†*Corresponding author*: himamsaheb@ifheindia.org

Syed Quadir Moinuddin, Shaik Himam Saheb, Ashok Kumar Dewangan, Murali Mohan Cheepu and S. Balamurugan (eds.) Automation in Welding Industry: Incorporating Artificial Intelligence, Machine Learning and Other Technologies, (13–36) © 2024 Scrivener Publishing LLC

to produce the welding arc, has become quite popular in weld production. Yet, the shielding gas plasma's complex arc properties still make it uncomfortable to use this method to its full potential. In this study, an effort is to be made to deepen our understanding of numerous fluid dynamics phenomena related to plasma shielding under the P-GMAW process' variable arc characteristics. By examining many aspects of the arc and plasma flow of inert shielding gas, including the behavior of metal transfer impacting the kind and quality of weld bead on plate deposition, the main goal of the work will be addressed.

In gas metal arc welding (GMAW), the current is supplied by melting the wire, i.e., the electrode. GMAW is often used in the industrial sector to combine a variety of ferrous and non-ferrous materials. The metal coalescence is achieved via GMAW, as seen in Figure 2.1.

The GMAW functions in the spherical metal transfer mode when the energy is relatively low. The process switches to spray mode as the current is raised. The periodic formation of enormous droplets detaches due to gravity pushing inside the welding pool. These are described by a lack of control over molten droplets and arc instability, which is known as globular mode. Spray mode allows for high deposition rates, but there are some

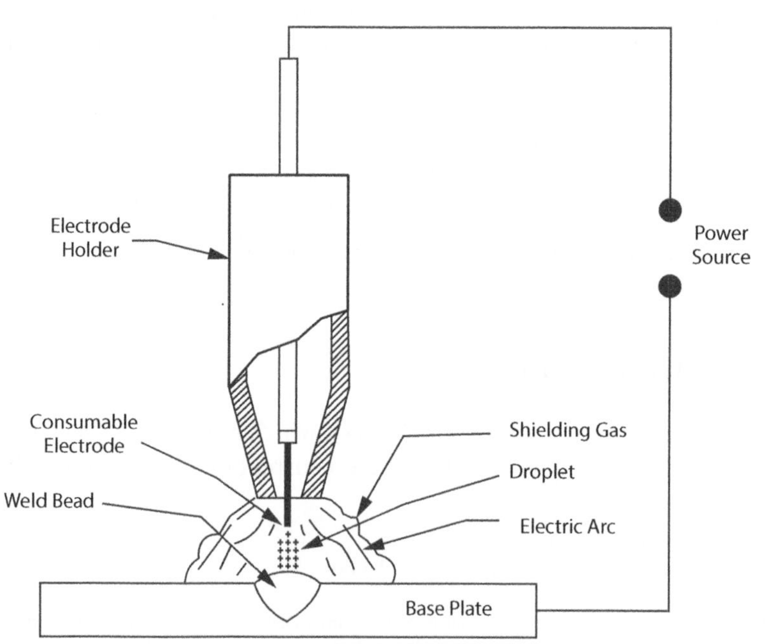

Figure 2.1 Gas metal arc welding process [1].

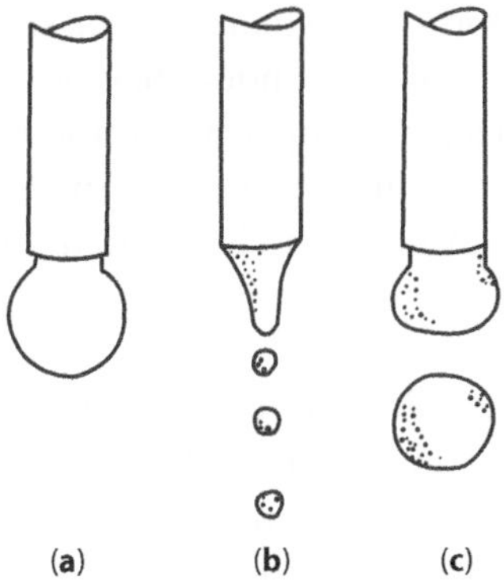

Figure 2.2 Various techniques in GMAW: (a) globular metal transfer, (b) spray metal transfer, and (c) pulse metal transfer [2].

restrictions, such as a large bead, a significant heat contribution to the work piece, and constrained downward movement options. Figure 2.2 displays various metal transfer methods.

2.2 Quality of Weld Joint

The superiority of a weld joint is a crucial aspect that determines the strength, durability, and safety of the welded structure. A high-quality weld joint should have the following characteristics:

Strong bond: The weld joint should have a strong bond with no cracks or voids, which can weaken the joint.

Consistent size and shape: The size and shape of the weld should be consistent throughout the joint. This ensures that the joint can withstand the applied load.

Proper penetration: The weld should penetrate both the base material and the filler material, ensuring a strong and durable joint.

Smooth surface finish: A smooth surface finish indicates that the weld has been properly fused and that there are no surface defects that could weaken the joint.

Proper alignment: The pieces being welded should be properly aligned to ensure that the joint is strong and durable.

Minimal distortion: The welding process can cause distortion, which can weaken the joint. Therefore, minimizing distortion is important to maintain the strength of the joint. A high-quality weld joint should have a strong bond, a consistent size and shape, proper penetration, a smooth surface finish, proper alignment, and minimal distortion. These characteristics ensure that the welded structure is strong, durable, and safe.

The heat-affected zone (HAZ) microstructure is principally affected by cooling pace, base metal composition, filler metal composition, and a suitable protective atmosphere. The structure of the grains inside the fusion zone can be changed by differences in heat input caused by different solidification processes [4]. When welding stainless steel, argon and nitrogen (N2) can also be used to fortify the bonds (Ar). The main factors causing cracks in the weld zone of high-strength steel are residual stresses generated during the welding process, a harder microstructure, and widespread hydrogen inclusion. The GMAW process has surpassed other welding technologies [5]. However, the coarse weld microstructure, larger HAZ brought on by increasing heat input, and poorer weld incursion with more reinforcement severely limit the weld strength and its service life. When two different ferrous metals are joined together with welding, carbon diffusion from a high- to low-carbon alloy causes variations in the thermal coefficient of expansion, which in turn causes the weld to have poor joint quality because of residual stresses.

2.3 Pulsed Current GMAW

The P-GMAW process uses pulsed direct current to produce a weld. This process is a variation of the conventional GMAW process, also known as MIG welding, which uses continuous direct current. As shown in Figure 2.3, in pulsed current GMAW, the welding current is pulsed at a controlled frequency and amplitude, which produces a series of overlapping weld droplets that create the weld bead. The pulsed current can be adjusted to provide precise control of the weld pool, which can lead to improved weld quality and reduced distortion.

The advantages of pulse-current GMAW are as follows:

Improved control of heat input: The pulsed current allows for precise control of the heat input, which can be especially beneficial when welding thin materials or in areas with tight tolerances.

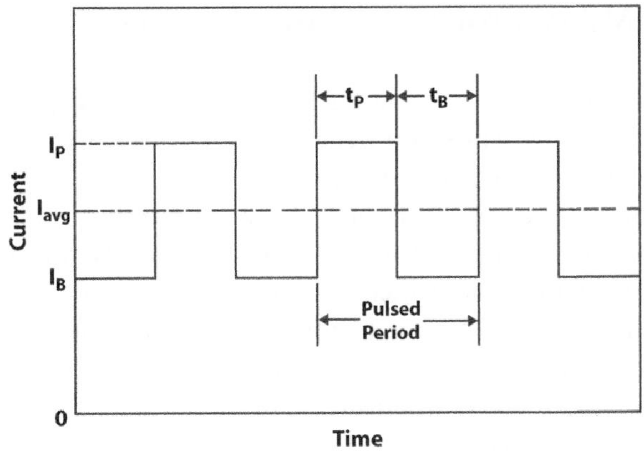

Figure 2.3 P-GMAW current-time diagram [1].

Reduced spatter: The pulsed current can also reduce spatter, which is a common problem in conventional GMAW.
Improved weld quality: The precise control of the weld pool can lead to improved weld quality, particularly in applications where the weld needs to be made in difficult-to-weld materials or in areas with complex geometries.
Increased productivity: Pulsed-current GMAW can also increase productivity, as the controlled heat input and reduced spatter can result in faster welding speeds and less time spent cleaning up after welding. Pulsed-current GMAW is used in a variety of industries, including aerospace, automotive, and manufacturing. It is particularly useful for welding aluminum and stainless steel, which can be difficult to weld using conventional GMAW. Pulsed GMAW is another alternative technique that provides a superior resolution for these weld quality difficulties. It is frequently used to weld thin sheet metals in various sectors to boost output and joint quality [3].

Several process variables, like welding speed, pulse generating parameters, welding source voltage, and electrode characteristics like feed rate and extension of electrode, have an impact on the welding behavior in P-GMAW. The peak current magnitude and detachment time are inversely related. The plate distortion is decreased because the current pulsing reduces total heat input with no splatter, which results in a narrower HAZ [10, 11]. P-GMAW has the advantage of improving weld properties that can be seen in conventional welding.

2.4 P-GMAW Process Stability Factors

The process stability of the welding process is mostly dependent on arc variations and metal deposition behavior, or the steady transfer of metal without spatter. It is more challenging to show arc stability in P-GMAW due to the abundance of control variables. If the pulse concentration is insufficient and the droplet does not separate from the pulses in time, the metal transfer becomes unstable, which can increase the production of spatter and lower the weld quality due to uneven metal transfer [6]. P-GMAW uses a pulsed current to improve control overheat input, reduce distortion, and improve weld quality. To ensure stability during the process, several factors need to be considered:

Welding Parameters: The welding parameters, such as current, voltage, wire feed rate, and pulse duration, should be set correctly based on the material being welded and the desired weld quality. Any deviation from the optimal settings can lead to instability in the welding process.
Welding Equipment: The welding equipment used for P-GMAW should be in good condition and maintained regularly. Any malfunctioning or faulty equipment can cause instability in the welding process.
Welding Technique: The welding technique used in P-GMAW should be consistent and controlled. The welding gun should be held at the correct angle, and the distance between the gun and the workpiece should be maintained.
Material Preparation: The material being welded should be prepared properly, with any surface contaminants removed. The fit-up should be precise, with the correct gap and alignment between the work pieces. By ensuring that these factors are taken care of, the P-GMAW process can be stabilized, leading to consistent and high-quality welds.

2.5 Suitable Pulse Parameters of Selection

The difficulties in choosing the right pulse parameter to manage all of these occurrences commonly limit the general implementation of this technology in the production of welds from a variety of materials. Burn-off rate, arc stability, droplet detachment, and shielding gas stability have always been the major determinants of selecting an adequate variety of pulse

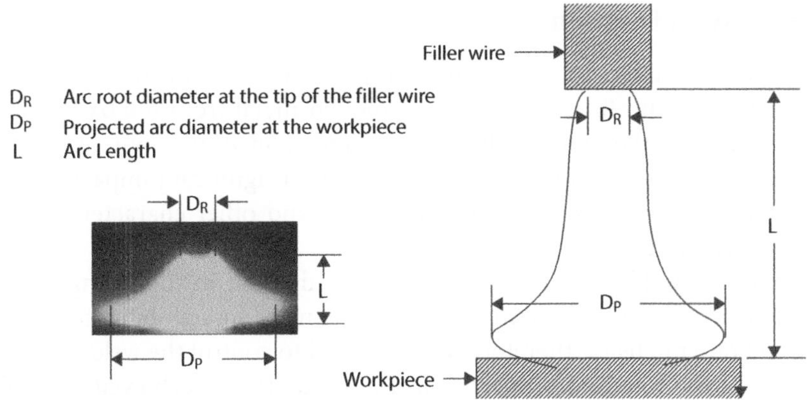

Figure 2.4 Measurement technique of arc characteristics [8].

parameters in P-GMAW. S. Subramaniam and White [7] used experimental techniques to select the pulsed GMAW's pulsing settings. Comparatively fewer experiments are required with conventional techniques.

Nevertheless, the idea of this dimensionless parameter is only applicable to the traditional rectangular pulse form in P-GMAW, where this process is controlled with fewer parameters than those shown in the Figure 2.3. Nevertheless, since we are now exploring advanced pulse waveforms, which include four major and six secondary adjustable factors, we are unable to use the notion to examine the arc characteristics shown in Figure 2.4, metal transfer behavior, and stability in the protection of arc environments; thus, we no longer need to manually input the pulse parameters into the modern power source.

2.6 Effect of Pulse Parameters

2.6.1 Weld Bead Geometry

The geometry of a weld bead refers to the shape and dimensions of the weld metal deposited by a welding process. It is an important aspect of welding as it affects the strength, appearance, and functionality of the welded joint. Because heat content rises as speed drops, weld bead penetration is improved by electrode diameter, arc voltage, welding current, and less welding speed. Weld penetration is greatly impacted by welding current, 2.5 times more than by arc voltage; however, it is not significantly impacted by shielding gas.

2.6.2 Weld Dilution

Weld dilution refers to the mixing of the base metal with the filler metal in a welded joint. It occurs when the molten metal from the base material mixes with the molten filler material and changes the composition of the weld. The extent of weld dilution can have a significant impact on the mechanical properties, corrosion resistance, and other characteristics of the welded joint.

Excessive weld dilution can result in a reduction in the strength and toughness of the weld, as well as an increase in the susceptibility to cracking and other defects. Therefore, welders need to control the weld dilution to ensure the required properties in the weld. This is achieved through various techniques, such as adjusting the welding parameters, using different welding processes, or selecting appropriate filler materials. Weld dilution is a critical factor that affects the quality and performance of welded joints, and it requires careful consideration and control during the welding process.

2.6.3 Weld Microstructure

Weld microstructure refers to the structure of the metal that forms as the result of the welding process. The microstructure of a weld can have a significant impact on its properties, such as strength, toughness, and ductility. During welding, the metal is heated to a high temperature, causing it to melt and fuse together. As the metal cools, it solidifies and forms a distinct microstructure. The microstructure of a weld can be divided into several zones, including the fusion zone, HAZ, and base metal, as shown in Figure 2.5.

The fusion zone is where the metal has melted and fused together. The microstructure of this zone is usually made up of dendrites, which are tree-like structures that form as the metal solidifies. The size and shape of the dendrites are affected by factors such as the cooling rate and the composition of the metal. The heat-affected zone is the area surrounding the fusion zone that has been heated by the welding process but not melted. The microstructure of this zone can be altered by the heat, which can cause changes in grain structure and hardness. The base metal is the metal that was present before welding. The microstructure of this zone can also be affected by the welding process, particularly in areas that have been heated by the welding process. The microstructure of a weld is complex and can be influenced by many factors. Understanding the microstructure of a weld

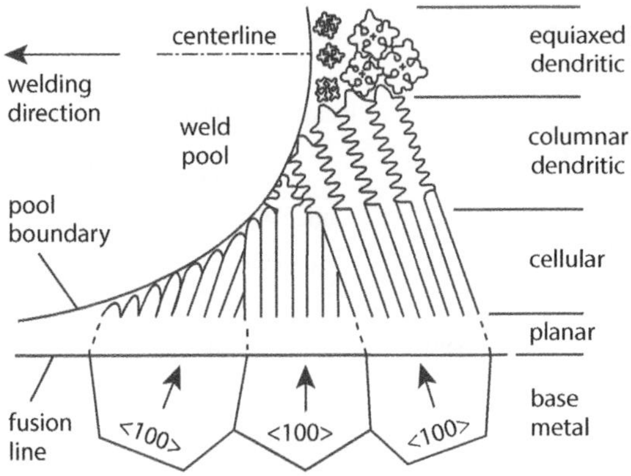

Figure 2.5 Solidification mode across the FZ [9].

can help welders choose the right welding technique, filler metal, and other variables to produce a weld with the desired properties.

Particularly when using incompatible metals, the impoverished weld microstructure lowers the weld's quality. The connection between the weld zone and HAZ is set up to be the weak zone in the majority of ferrous weldments (HAZ). The coarse-grained microstructure in non-ferrous alloys may cause failure. Several post-process quench techniques can improve the mechanical and metallurgical properties of the welds by providing a homogeneous microstructure.

Figure 2.6 represents the CCT standard diagram for low-carbon steel [1, 9]. Due to the extremely fast cooling rate, bainite (B) and martensite (M) may also form during high energy density welding (EBW, LBW, etc.). Except for AF, the phases in weld metal share the same phase production mechanism as HAZ. The resulting conversion of the pearlite colonies to austenite causes them to somewhat expand into the former ferrite matrix during heating (from 1 to 2) and cooling (from 2 to 3) before disintegrating into tiny ferrite-pearlite grains.

These materials degrade the weld's properties. The pulse parameters, which also indirectly affect the weld microstructure, have a significant impact on the weld heat cycle and arc characteristics in P-GMAW. Current pulses cause regular arc-force fluctuations. Due to the forces created, some additional fluid may flow, which could lower the temperature on the solidifying surface [10–12]. The weld pool thermal oscillations' amplitude increases as the ratio of peak to base currents rises and decreases as the pulse frequency rises. Thus, the P-GMAW welds showed evidence of grain refining.

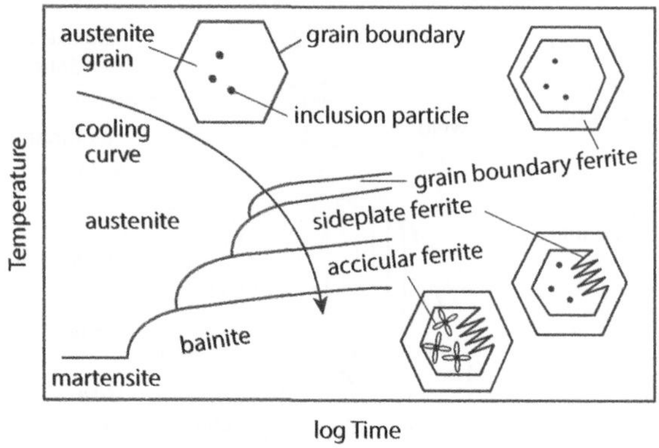

Figure 2.6 Weld metal CCT diagram [9].

2.7 Pulsed Current GMAW Advances

Pulsed-current gas metal arc welding (GMAW) is a welding process that uses a pulsating direct current to produce a weld. The pulsed current can be adjusted to provide precise control of the weld pool, which can lead to improved weld quality and reduced distortion. In recent years, there have been several advances in pulsed current GMAW technology:

Waveform control: The latest pulsed-current GMAW systems offer greater control over the waveform of the current, allowing for more precise control over the welding process. This can lead to improved weld quality, particularly in applications where the weld needs to be made in thin materials or in areas with tight tolerances.

Enhanced pulsing: Some pulsed-current GMAW systems now offer enhanced pulsing capabilities, which can further improve the control of the weld pool. These systems allow the user to adjust the frequency, amplitude, and duration of the pulses, providing even greater control over the welding process.

Improved arc stability: Advances in pulsed-current GMAW technology have also led to improved arc stability, which can help reduce spatter and improve weld quality. This is particularly important in high-speed welding applications, where spatter can be a significant issue.

Greater efficiency: The latest pulsed-current GMAW systems are also more energy efficient than older models, thanks to advances in power supply technology. This means that they require less energy to operate, which can result in lower operating costs and a reduced environmental impact.

These advances in pulsed-current GMAW technology have led to improved welding quality, greater efficiency, and increased flexibility in a range of welding applications. As a result, pulsed-current GMAW is becoming an increasingly popular welding process in many industries.

Good metal conductivity has the drawback of excessive heating of the base metal while welding. To get around this, welding methods are used that don't require as much heat, like P-GMAW; this creates spray transfer issues at small mean currents.

2.8 Double-Pulsed GMAW

Double-pulsed gas metal arc welding (GMAW) is a welding technique that utilizes two pulses of welding current during the welding cycle. It is a modified version of the traditional GMAW process that allows for improved control over the heat input and deposition rate, leading to better-quality welds. During the double-pulsed GMAW process, two pulses of current are applied to the welding wire for each welding cycle. The first pulse is a high-current pulse that provides the heat necessary for melting of base metal and filler material. The second pulse is a lower-current pulse that helps control the weld pool and reduce spatter.

The advantages of double-pulsed GMAW are as follows:

- Improved control overheat input and deposition rate, leading to better-quality welds.
- Reduced spatter and fumes, resulting in a cleaner welding environment.
- Reduced heat input, which can reduce distortion and improve welding speed.
- Improved weld bead appearance due to better control over the weld pool.
- Better control over penetration, which can improve joint strength.

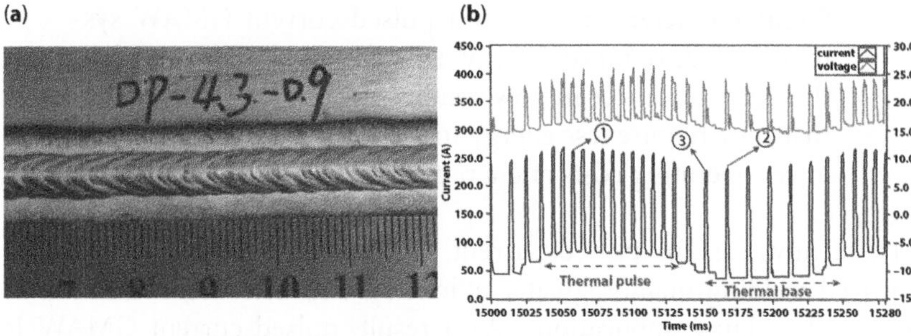

Figure 2.7 (a) Weld joint; (b) Welding electrical signal waveform [13].

Double-pulsed GMAW is commonly used in the automotive, aerospace, and construction industries, among others, for welding diverse materials like aluminum and steel. The properties of Al alloys' double-pulsed GMAW arc profile were investigated by Liu and Tang [13]. They have demonstrated that the arc profile is matched with a high-frequency pulse and a thermal pulse in double-pulse mode, as shown in Figure 2.7. The high-frequency pulse cycle is always present when using the "one drop per pulse" droplet transmission technique. The arc profile and droplet transmission of the thermal base are less variable than those of the thermal peak. During the thermal peak, as opposed to the thermal base, droplet transfer occurs more frequently. After the droplet split, a serial-type arc developed between the "wire-droplet-pool." High current densities are dispersed at the top and bottom of the moving droplets, forming a bright zone. The cathode spot effect is produced at the weld pool's surface as a result of the droplet's interaction with it. Arc force varies with thermal pulse frequency because the thermal base arc size variance is greater than the thermal peak variance. The periodic alteration of the arc force increases the mobility of the weld pool.

2.9 Synergic Control

Mean current wire-feed speed control is another name for this mode. A straight connection between the power source and wire feeder, in which the wire feeder makes the current dependent on the rate of wire feed, ensures a stable arc. The circuitry of the system and pulse waveform are shown in Figures 2.8 and 2.9, respectively.

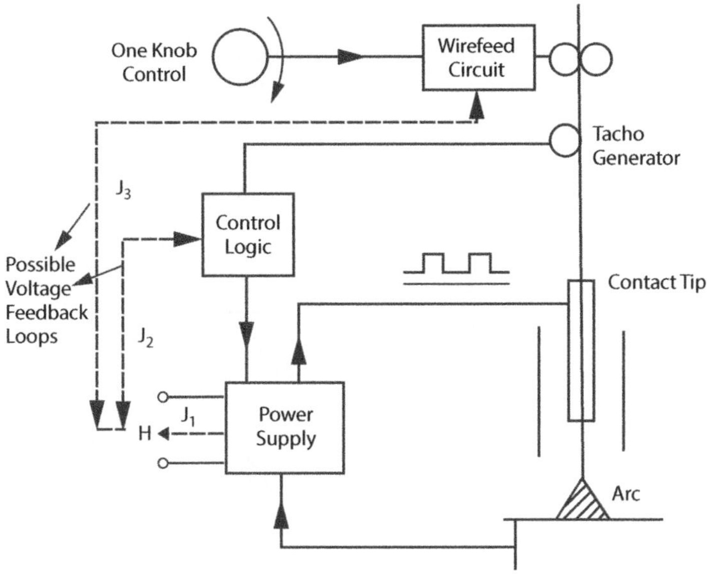

Figure 2.8 Synergic control [14].

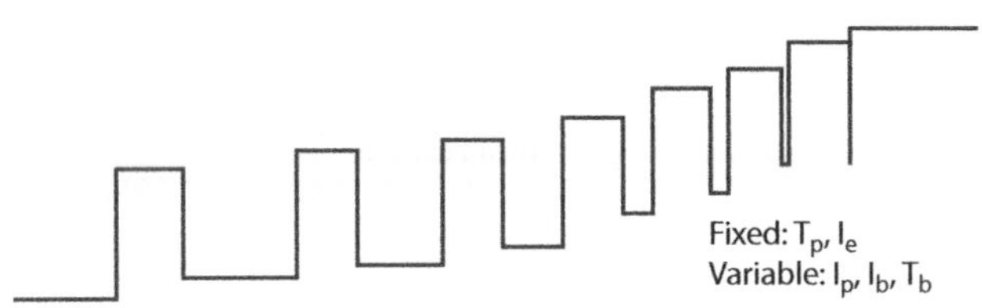

Figure 2.9 Pulse waveform of synergic control [15].

2.10 Self-Regulating Control

This technique is also known as an error voltage system or a mean current voltage control. The welding voltage in GMAW changes according to the length of the arc. In order to return the arc length to the predetermined reference voltage, this technology automatically alters the burn-off rate. The circuitry of the system is depicted in Figure 2.10.

The sole variable pulse parameter is the base current duration, as shown in Figure 2.11. Its control logic is unclear because base current influences droplet size and calls for routine electrical stick-out adjustment (or arc length).

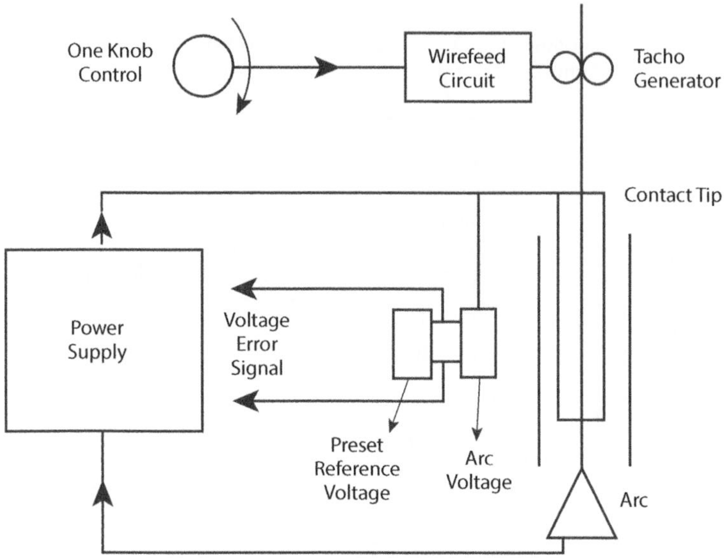

Figure 2.10 Self-regulating control [14].

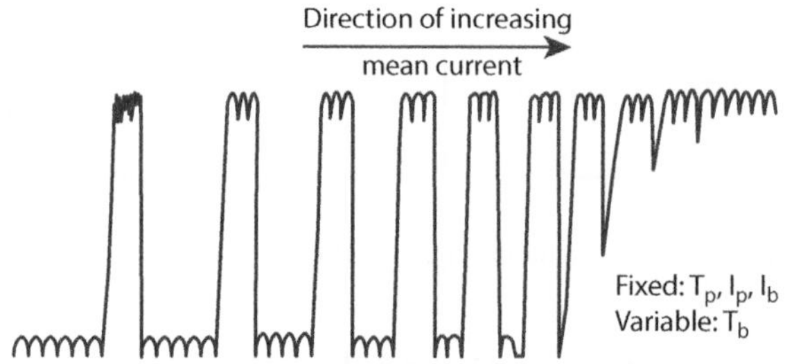

Figure 2.11 Pulse waveform of self-regulating control [15].

2.11 Microcomputer Control

Microprocessors, or microcontrollers, are used to operate the advanced power sources used in modern electronics. To get the best outcomes, they have engaged the conservative hard-wired systems for controlling, scheduling, and timing processes. By storing algorithms that calculate relationships among multiple pulse variables and rapidly retrieving the relevant process parameters, microprocessors increase adaptability.

2.12 GMAW Shielding Gas Flow

A protective gas with a cover is essential in GMA welding technique using titanium, high alloy steels, or aluminum to either guarantee a low concentration of oxygen (O_2) at the joint or prevent ambient contamination (oxidation). The arc is controlled and maintained by shielding gas flow, which also helps to cool the torch. The negative effects that lessen the weld's efficiency and quality are spatters, oxidation, gases, and porosity. So, it is necessary to investigate and describe how shielding gas moves around the arc. The most common gases used for shielding in GMAW are argon, carbon dioxide, and a mixture of both. The flow rate of the shielding gas is also important, as it determines the level of protection provided to the weld pool. The flow rate of the shielding gas should be sufficient to provide complete coverage of the weld pool and prevent atmospheric contamination.

Typically, the recommended flow rate for GMAW shielding gas is between 20 and30 cubic feet per hour (CFH) for argon and 20 to 40 CFH for carbon dioxide. However, the optimal flow rate can vary depending on factors such as the diameter of the welding wire, the welding current, the welding position, and the joint design. It is important to ensure that the flow rate of the shielding gas is adjusted correctly before welding to avoid issues such as porosity, contamination, and poor weld quality. The shielding gas flow rate should be monitored throughout the welding process to ensure that it remains constant and provides adequate protection to the weld pool.

The gas flow must therefore be carefully monitored and evaluated both inside the torch and at the workpiece. The shielding gas flow in GMAW and GTAW was analyzed using ANSYS CFX by Dreher and Schick. Also, they employed particle-based diagnostic methods like the Schlieren technique, particle image velocimetry (PIV), and laser doppler anemometry (LDA). To determine if PIV or LDA experimental methods were suitable for producing flow profiles for protection gas flow analysis in GMA welding, Zschetzsche *et al.* studied them [16, 17]. Due to the very transient flow state, it was suggested that the PIV 2D full-field measurement approach is particularly appropriate.

2.13 Particle Image Velocimetry (PIV)

The PIV analysis consists of a double-pulse laser that double-irradiates tracer particles before injecting them into the protective gas that follows the flow. A little plane in which this laser light expands is synchronized with a double-pulse laser and placed orthogonally to the laser light plane, as shown in Figure 2.12. Continuous P-GMAW recording typically uses a resolution of 768 × 512 pixels at a frame rate of 10,000 frames per second [18]. Particle image velocimetry (PIV) is a non-intrusive optical flow measurement technique that is used to measure and visualize the velocity of fluid or gas flows, as shown in Figure 2.13. It is widely used in fluid mechanics research to investigate the characteristics of turbulent and laminar flows, boundary layers, and other fluid dynamics phenomena.

The PIV technique works by seeding the fluid or gas with small particles that are illuminated by a laser light sheet. A camera captures images of the particles as they move through the flow. The displacement of the particles between two images captured at a specific time interval is used to calculate the velocity vector at that location. This process is repeated across the entire region of interest, generating a velocity field that can be used to visualize the flow patterns and calculate relevant flow parameters. There are two types of PIV techniques, namely, 2D-PIV and 3D-PIV. 2D-PIV

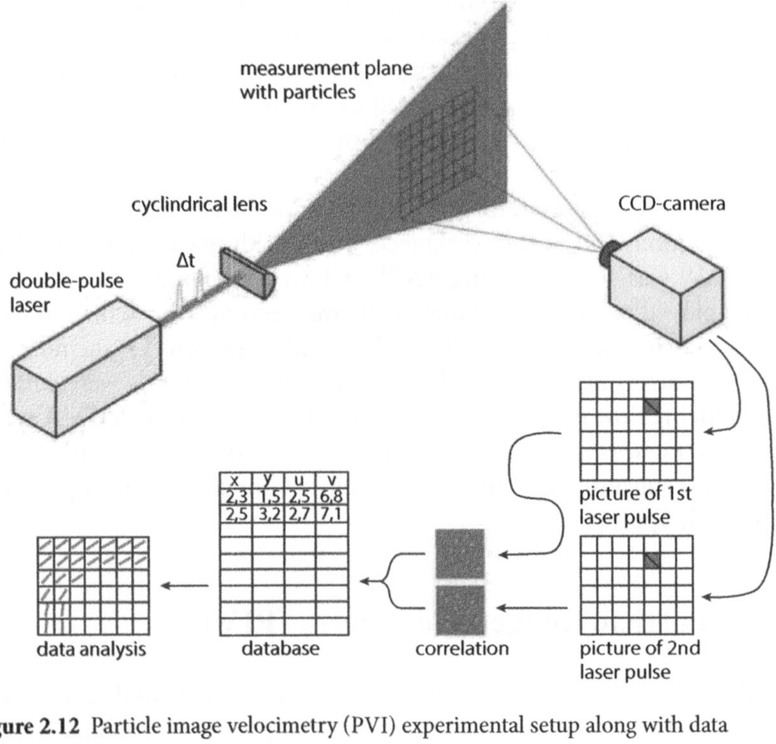

Figure 2.12 Particle image velocimetry (PVI) experimental setup along with data processing [19].

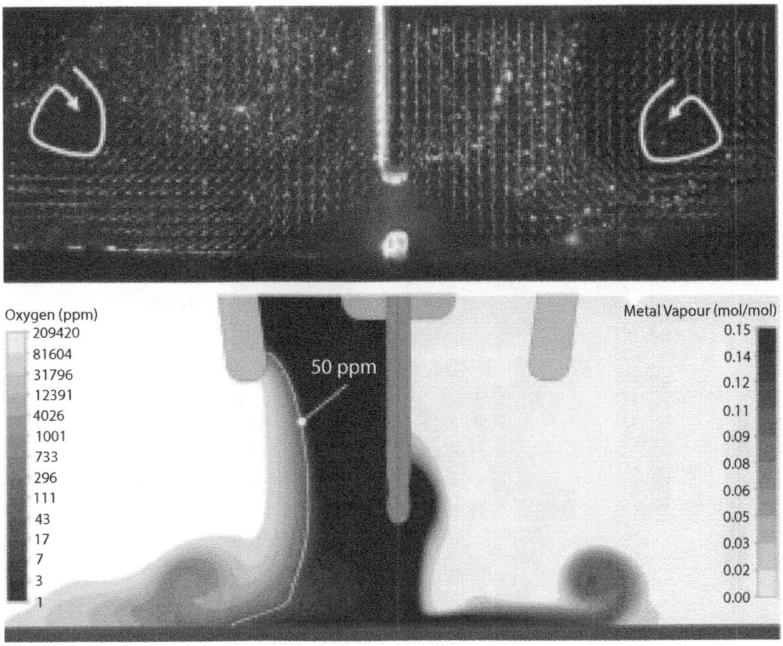

Figure 2.13 PIV measurement and simulation of a pulse process [20].

measures the flow in two dimensions, typically in the plane perpendicular to the laser light sheet, while 3D-PIV extends the measurement to three dimensions by using multiple cameras and laser light sheets to capture the flow field.

This technique is a powerful tool for investigating complex fluid dynamics problems because it provides detailed information about the flow field that cannot be obtained through other methods. It has been used in a wide range of applications, including aerodynamics, hydrodynamics, combustion, biomedical engineering, and environmental science.

Based on an experimental setup by Zschetzsche [16], a funnel-shaped storage vessel with the protective gas intake at a tiny diameter was placed on a vibration plate as the dosage unit, and the particles were added using a unique mix device to the shielding gas flow. Dreher *et al.* calculated the flow field using commercial DANTEC software flow management 4.7 and programs built using MATLAB and LabVIEW. In conclusion, PIV is effective for quantitatively defining the flow field in the shielding gas-free jet and the vicinity of the arc with high temporal and spatial precision. In addition to the flow map, you can also gather eddies from the rotation of pixel groups. It is not possible for diffusion and oxygen content (see Figure 2.14), and

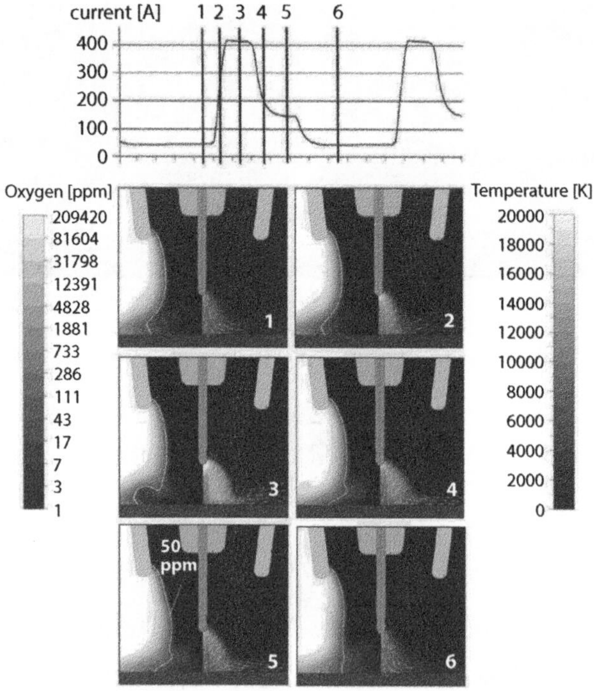

Figure 2.14 A 400 A pulse process: Content of oxygen (left side) and temperature (right side) [20].

flow field analysis can be done regardless of the chemical composition of the shielding gas [19]. PIV's correlation program only displays the primary flow instructions while mapping turbulence, as shown in Figure 2.15. The flow field external to the free jet cannot be studied since there are no particles there or inside the arc.

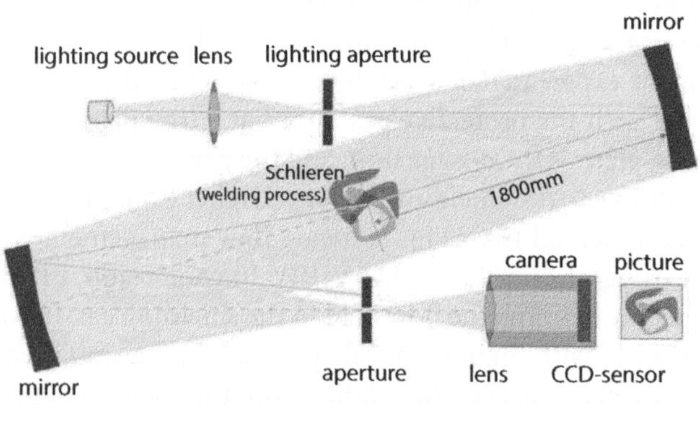

Figure 2.15 Measurement setup of compact Toepler-Z [19].

2.14 The Measurement of Oxygen (O_2) Concentration

The lambda sensor idea-based configuration is used by Fuentes Muñoz [21] for the quantitative capacity of the oxygen deliberation, as shown in Figure 2.16. Through the measuring borehole, a small partial flow of 0.15 L/min may be extracted thanks to this arrangement, and it is evaluated by a maximum-performance lambda sensor, allowing measurements of PP. The method was previously only used for TIG welding. Conversely, Dreher *et al.* suggested a few techniques for measuring oxygen concentration during the GMAW procedure [18].

2.15 Spectroscopic Measurements of Plasma Temperature

Spectroscopic measurements are a common method for determining the temperature of plasma. The basic principle behind this method is that the emission or absorption spectra of certain atomic or molecular species in a plasma can be used to infer the plasma temperature.

When atoms or molecules in a plasma are excited to higher energy levels, they can emit or absorb photons of specific energies. The energies of these photons are related to the differences in energy between the excited and ground states of the atoms or molecules. By analyzing the emission or absorption spectra of these species, one can determine the energy levels involved and, hence, the temperature of the plasma.

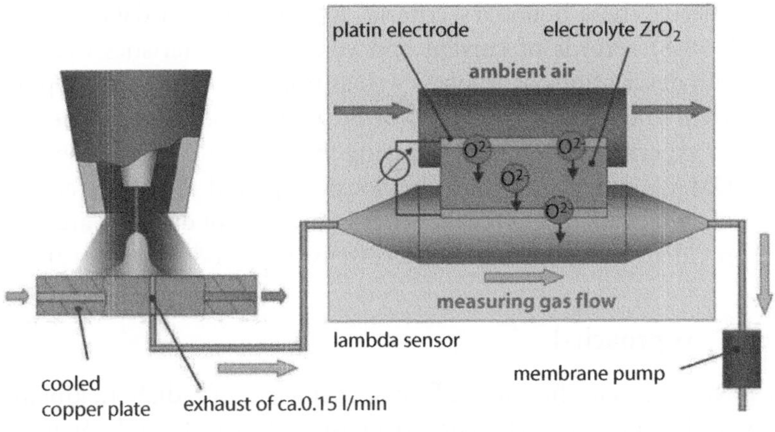

Figure 2.16 Lambda sensor principle used for oxygen measurement [19].

There are several spectroscopic techniques that can be used to measure the temperature of a plasma. One such technique is optical emission spectroscopy (OES), which involves analyzing the emission spectra of the plasma. Another technique is absorption spectroscopy, which involves analyzing the absorption spectra of the plasma. In OES, a spectrometer is used to measure the intensity of the light emitted by the plasma at various wavelengths. The intensity of the light at different wavelengths is related to the number of atoms or molecules emitting photons at those wavelengths. By analyzing the emission spectra of specific atomic or molecular species, the temperature of the plasma can be determined.

Absorption spectroscopy works in a similar way, but instead of measuring the emission spectra of the plasma, it measures the absorption spectra of the plasma. This technique involves passing a beam of light through the plasma and analyzing the wavelengths of the light that are absorbed by the plasma. By analyzing the absorption spectra of specific atomic or molecular species, the temperature of the plasma can be determined. Overall, spectroscopic measurements are a powerful tool for determining the temperature of a plasma. By analyzing the emission or absorption spectra of specific atomic or molecular species in the plasma, the temperature of the plasma can be determined with a high degree of accuracy.

2.16 P-GMAW Numeric Simulation

Hässler *et al.* [22] applied practically collected data on the time-dependent relative form of the wire and droplet for the numerical modeling of the P-GMAW process. Signals, images, and distinguishing patterns are examined to derive these boundary criteria. As experimental data, Dewetron (DEWE-30-8) records of current and voltage characteristics over time, along with descriptions of argon as well as iron radiation, were employed. The current and voltage runs used in the simulation were transient and based on experimental data. By applying the Physical Evaporation Model to the GMAW process, Schnick previously explored the appearance and effects of metal vapor. As a result, better knowledge of dynamic arc behavior is provided. The following models discuss two modeling strategies.

2.16.1 Approach-1

Due to variations in the wire's effectual coefficient of radiation, kinematic viscosity, dynamic viscosity, current density, electrical conductivity, and other properties, metal evaporation at the wire end has an impact on the practically observed structures in the arc. In the P-GMAW process, the evaporation rate changes along with the mass fraction of the iron vapor and the distribution of the vapor. The evaporation rate is at its maximum during the period of peak current. The wire feed rate is used to define the evaporation rate, which is often estimated to be between 1% and 5% of the wire feed rate (in the range of 6–30 mg/s).

2.16.2 Approach-II

We investigated the informational usefulness of numerical simulation regarding altering metal vapor distribution and the consequent dynamic arc behavior. As a result, the boundary condition is fixed based on the distribution of the metal vapor in the high-speed photographs. The spatial boundary is defined by the metal vapor's contour. Greifswald's spectroscopic data are used to calculate the iron vapor's mass fraction. The experimentally measured voltage run is found to be in excellent accord with Rose's transient model.

They concluded that, compared to earlier models with fixed geometries, the wire's and the droplet's changeable geometry made it possible to calculate more precise numbers for the regular density along with temperature circulation. These characteristics are difficult to measure experimentally, if not impossible. There are four main physical consequences that can be attributed to the distinctive pattern in the phase space of current voltage. Consequently, the arc length and metal evaporation can only be determined from these two electric signals. The outcomes of the numerical simulation further demonstrate that the diagnostically determined arc parameters require a constant increase in metal evaporation. The position of the metal vapor source at the wire tip has no bearing on how the metal vapor is distributed in the arc. The metal vapor has a big impact on the arc, and the influence on the current course can be seen during the whole transient pulse, with decreasing arc pressure due to rising evaporation at the wire lead.

The suggested methodology bridges the divide between the experimental and numerical approaches that were previously taken into consideration. The combination of diagnostics and simulation holds enormous promise for improving our comprehension of the arc as a crucial technical tool. It is possible to develop new control concepts and applications from this improved understanding. The understanding of evaporation can result in innovative GMAW processes with lower emissions.

References

1. Kou, S., *Welding Metallurgy*, 2nd ed., pp. 145–430, John Wiley & Sons, Inc., Hoboken, New Jersey, 2002.
2. Praveen, P., Yarlagadda, P.K., Kang, M.J., Advancements in pulse gas metal arc welding. *J. Mater. Process. Technol.*, 164, 1113–9, May 15, 2005.
3. Tong, H., Ueyama, T., Harada, S., Ushio, M., Quality and productivity improvement in aluminium alloy thin sheet welding using alternating current pulsed metal inert gas welding system. *Sci. Technol. Weld. Join.*, 6, 4, 203–208, 2001.
4. Murti, V.S.R., Srinivas, P.D., Banadeki, G.H.D., Raju, K.S., Effect of heat input on the metallurgical properties of HSLA steel in multi-pass MIG welding. *J. Mater. Process. Technol.*, 37, 1–4, 723–729, 1993.
5. Eroglu, M., Aksoy, M., Orhan, N., Effect of coarse initial grain size on microstructure and mechanical properties of weld metal and HAZ of a low carbon steel. *Mater. Sci. Eng. A*, 269, 1, 59–66, 1999.
6. Amin, M., Pulsed current parameters for arc stability and controlled metal transfer in arc welding. *Met. Construct.*, 15, 272–278, 1983.
7. Rajasekaran, S., Method of selecting the most suitable combination of parameters in pulsed current gas metal arc welding process. *Proceedings of International Conference on Advances in Mechanical and Industrial Engineering*, Roorkee, pp. 1115–1122, 1997.
8. Ghosh, P.K., Dorn, L., Hübner, M., Goyal, V.K., Arc characteristics and behaviour of metal transfer in pulsed current GMA welding of aluminium alloy. *J. Mater. Process. Technol.*, 194, 1–3, 163–75, Nov. 1, 2007.
9. Pouranvari, M., Khorramifar, M., Marashi, S.P.H., Ferritic–austenitic stainless steels dissimilar resistance spot welds: Metallurgical and failure characteristics. *Sci. Technol. Weld. Join.*, 21, 6, 438–445, 2016.
10. Stanzel, K., Pulsed GMAW cuts cycle time by 600 percent. *Weld. Des. Fabr.*, 85–87, April 2001.
11. Tippins, J., Box beam fabrication using the pulsed MIG process. *Mater. Construct. Br. Weld. J.*, 2, 12, 547–550, December 1970.
12. Young, K. and Pickin, C., Welding met. *Fabrication*, 11, 5, 14–15, 1999.
13. Liu, A., Tang, X., Lu, F., Arc profile characteristics of Al alloy in double-pulsed GMAW. *Int. J. Adv. Manuf. Technol.*, 65, 1–7, Mar. 2013.
14. Kumar, M., Moinuddin, S.Q., Surya, S., Sharma, A., Discrete wavelet analysis of mutually interfering co-existing welding signals in twin-wire robotic welding. *Int. J. Manuf. Process.*, 63, 139–151, 2020.
15. Moinuddin, S.Q., Hameed, S.S., Dewangan, A.K., Kumar, R., Kumari, S., A Study on weld defects classification in gas metal arc welding process using machine learning techniques. *Mater. Today: Proc.*, 43, 1, 623–628, 2020.
16. Zschetzsche, J., *Diagnostik von Schutzgas-Schweissprozessen, (Diagnostics of Gas-Shielded Welding Processes)*, Dissertation, Technical university of Dresden, Verlag der Wissenschaften, Dresden, 2007.

17. Fuessel, U., Zschetzsche, J., Zosel, J., Guth, U., *Stroemungsmessung in Lichtbogen- und Plasmaprozessen (Flow Measurement in Arc and Plasma Processes)*, Stiftung Industrieforschung, Forchungsvorhaben S 559, Abschlussbericht, 2005.
18. Dreher, M., Schnick, M., Fuessel, U., Rose, S., Hertel, M., Methods and results referring the shielding gas flow in GMAW. *65th Annual Assembly & International Conference of the International Institute of Welding Commission XII Arc Welding Processes and Production Systems.*
19. Schnick, M., Dreher, M., Zschetzsche, J. *et al.*, Visualization and optimization of shielding gas flows in arc welding. *Weld World*, 56, 54–61, 2012. https://doi.org/10.1007/BF03321146.
20. Dreher, M., Füssel, U., Schnick, M., Numerical optimisation of gas metal arc welding torches using ANSYS CFX. *63rd Annual Assembly & International Conference of the International Institute of Welding*, Istanbul, Turkey, July 11-17, 2010.
    a. Young, K. and Pickin, C., Welding met. *Fabrication*, 14–15, 1999.
    b. Liu, A., Tang, X. & Lu, F. Arc profile characteristics of Al alloy in double-pulsed GMAW. *Int. J. Adv. Manuf. Technol.*, 65, 1–7 (2013). https://doi.org/10.1007/s00170-012-4141-0.
21. Fuentes Munoz, J.E., *Einfluss der Brennergestaltung auf den WIG-Lichtbogen (Influence of Torch Design on the TIG Arc)*, Dissertation, Dresdner Fuegetechnische Berichte, Germany, ISBN: Band 22/2011, ISBN 978-3-942710-41-1, 2011.
22. Rose, S., Hässler, M., Füssel, U., Spille-Kohoff, A., Schnick, M., *Numerical Simulation of A Pulsed GMAW Processes by Using Experimental Data of the Time-Dependent Geometry of Wire and Droplet*, Technical University Dresden, Germany, 2011.

3

Automation in Welding Industries

Deepak Kumar Naik, Ved Prakash Sharma and Dinesh Kumar R.*

Department of Mechanical Engineering, National Institute of Technology Srinagar, Jammu and Kashmir, India

Abstract

Industrial automation plays a vital role in various fabrication units. Because of its numerous advantages over the traditional process, many welding industries use the automation process to join or weld different materials, especially thermoplastics and metals. Automatic welding is a process which refers to the welding process that utilizes various equipment to continue the welding process without any engagement of manpower. To improve the efficiency of mass production and processing time, welding industries require automation to replace the manual welding process. Therefore, in this chapter, along with the types of automatic welding, the challenges for automation in welding, its benefits and drawbacks are also addressed to control arc processes and maximize the productivity in factory automation. There are a total of five automation trends which influence automation in welding industries, i.e., adaptive welding advancement, collaborative technology, production monitoring, upstream practices and operation and easier programming of automation systems. The above-mentioned trends are also explained in this chapter. The various automatic welding techniques which could be integrated into automation with welding processes are plasma welding, laser welding, arc welding, spot welding, MIG welding and resistance welding. Various applications and welding methods for different automatic welding are also well described in this chapter.

Keywords: Automation, welding, productivity

**Corresponding author*: rdinesh@nitsri.net

Syed Quadir Moinuddin, Shaik Himam Saheb, Ashok Kumar Dewangan, Murali Mohan Cheepu and S. Balamurugan (eds.) Automation in Welding Industry: Incorporating Artificial Intelligence, Machine Learning and Other Technologies, (37–48) © 2024 Scrivener Publishing LLC

3.1 Introduction

The welding industry is proceeding with automation due to its enhanced adv antages over the traditional process. Nowadays, most industries are integrating the automation system with the existing equipment.

Welding automation is generally categorized as fully automatic welding and semi-automatic welding. Generally, loading and unloading of parts to be welded are managed by operators in semi-automatic cases. Only the process control and the motion of the torch are controlled by the controller. But, in fully automatic welding automation all the processes as well as monitoring of welded joints can be achieved. Many subprocesses, such as torch position, loading and unloading of the product, placing the final product in the appropriate place and quality inspection, are also included in the fully automation type.

Among the many advantages of automatic welding include factors such as increased output, improved weld quality, decreased labor cost and decreased scrap. Also, weld quality can be classified as two factors, i.e., repeatability and weld integrity. With the help of an electronic weld process controller, weld integrity can be enhanced in the automatic welding process. Combining automated motion control and mechanized torch results is far better than manual welding, which achieves higher quality control of the process. With this process, the defects are easily detectable as the welding is done only once with the automated process control feature. There must be a flaw in welding penetration during the manual process, whereas in automatic welding the penetration will be symmetrical. Furthermore, vision system and leak testing can be interspersed into a best automatic welding platform to bring enhanced quality control.

By eliminating the human error factor from the fabrication process, increased output can be achieved through fully automatic and semi-automatic welding process. The weld speed can be controlled by the controller which is integrated with the automatic welding system. A fully automatic mechanized welding process can very easily surpass a highly skilled manual welder with higher weld speeds and minimal set-up time. Automating the motion or torch of manual equipment will result in a high possibility of reducing human error. Also, in the case of manual welding the quality of weld depends on the effort taken by the welder to achieve the goal. The different types of automatic welding processes are shown in Table 3.1. The heavy target for welder would be fatigued for him. But it would be possible in automatic welding as all the input process parameters will be controlled by the controller of automatic welding.

Table 3.1 Types and application of automatic welding.

Types of automatic welding	Automatic fusion welding	Automatic pressure welding	Automatic brazing/ soldering
Application	Assembly of parts, bodies, frame of motorbikes and cars or building material	Pipes and tanks, floor material and outer panels of airplanes, cars and trains	Small parts of cars, motorbikes, valves, cooling equipment pipes
Welding method	Arc welding (MIG/TIG/ Plasma) and laser welding	Friction stir welding (FSW), Resistant spot welding and Seam welding	Electron beam soldering, Furnace brazing

3.1.1 Types of Automatic Welding

Automation in welding can be categorized into robotic welding and automatic welding. Automatic welding processes eliminate the manual processes with advanced integration of automation. Generally, robots are used to hold the torch and do the welding process with continuous path. Automatic welding is caused by the movement of the torch and robot welding is basically used for holding the torch. Also, the robotic welding is an advanced form of automatic welding in terms of flexibility and higher level of precision welding. The stages of automation in welding are shown in Figure 3.1.

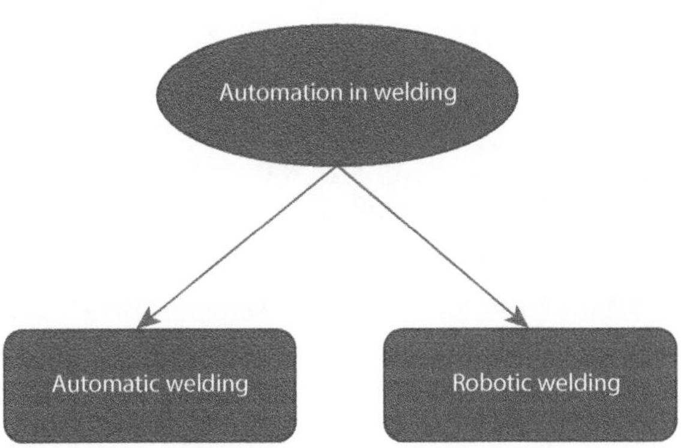

Figure 3.1 Automation in welding.

3.1.2 Challenges of Automatic Welding

- Time required is much more for fitting and handling of the machine.
- Lack of trained skilled manpower for automatic welding. Special training is required for welder.
- Cost is higher for purchasing, installation and handling of automatic welding.
- Higher volume of production can increase the storage cost of the product.
- Lack of volume of jobs can be justified.
- Lack of acceptance of change in welding methods by inspecting agencies.
- Special alloys cannot be welded until inspected properly as process parameters are already defined for previous material which is regular in industry.

3.1.3 Benefits of Automatic Welding

Following are the advantages of automation in welding, some of which are shown in Figure 3.2.

- **Multiple parameters for multiple weld run:** As the process parameters can be adjusted for each and every pass of welding, the required amount of precision can be achieved. Moreover, a microprocessor-based welding machine can

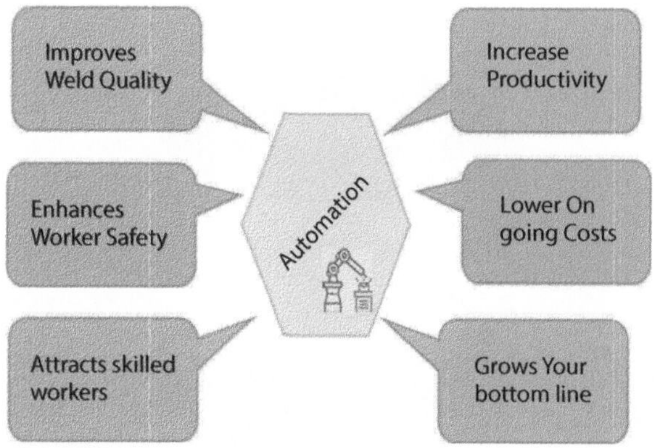

Figure 3.2 Advantages of automation in welding.

also change the program for weld passes, which results in superior advantages over other manual welding.

- **Quality control:** If the process parameter for welding falls outside the control limit of the welding machine, then an alarm notifies the weld operator. The parameters are most important factor for management of quality during welding.
- **Consistency in weld result:** Irregularity occurs during manual welding when a semi-skilled or less skilled welder does the welding. But, consistency of the weld result can be achieved during automatic welding as the welding speed is controlled by the automation process. Override and underpass welding also can be eliminated in welding automation.
- **Data storage and record:** The welding data, i.e., process parameter, can be stored and recorded by the welding machine processor and whenever it is required a printout can be taken of the data and can be shown to the customer.
- **Quicker weld-fault diagnostics:** The fault can be analyzed at any time during the welding process due to the integration of automation. If the weld pass goes beyond the limit, then the machine should stop immediately to prevent the fault without wasting time and material.
- **Shortage of skilled labor:** There is a shortage of skilled and trained labor available in the market nowadays. Automation in the welding process eliminates this labor shortage and time savings can be realized due to idle trained welders.

3.2 Automation Trends

There are a total five automation trends which influence automation in welding industries, which are given below.

3.2.1 Production Monitoring

Production monitoring system increases part quality, manages processes more efficiently and achieves much more accurate measurement compared to manual welding processes. It results in higher production speed. The quality of the weld process is monitored though microprocessor and can be seen in product output. This offers huge time savings in the line production system without neglecting the quality.

3.2.2 Adaptive Welding Advancements

Sensors can be integrated with automatic welding machine for more flexibility, good welding speed and user-friendliness. With the help of sensors, robots sense the target and distance to be covered at uniform speed. This helps to communicate with the microprocessor and robotic torch to make quality welding.

3.2.3 Upstream Practices

Upstream practices employ the availability of the right quantity of parts at the right time on the shop floor during automatic welding. This mutual dependence between weld cell and availability of material at weld cell reduces the material handling time, saves resources and space on the floor. Moreover, upstream practices ensure that the operation (automatic welding) is running very smoothly without wasting resources as well as time.

3.2.4 Collaborative Technology

Having a robot and human welder in close proximity to one another on a shop floor ensures efficient operations and safety. The new age of collaborative techniques enhances the gesture of operators that can be understood by the robot and work on that particular command/program.

3.2.5 Easier Programming of Automation Systems

Programmers employed to operate the system need special training to smoothly conduct the processes. Programming includes what exactly needs to be done in the weld cell and controlling the process parameters. Many systems now offer elements like wireless communication systems, sensor technologies and offline programming to integrate with automation in welding.

3.3 Plasma Welding

Plasma arc welding (PAW) is an arc welding process where an electric arc is formed between an electrode and the work pieces to be welded [1–4]. It uses a torch having an internal plasma gas nozzle with a non-consumable tungsten electrode at the center. The PAW can be used for joining metals such as steels.

The PAW process is generally preferred over other arc welding processes because of its good welding speed, better weld penetration and weld quality. It is better suited for joining similar materials as a stable, controlled arc is formed with low current. This enhances the electrode life. In recent years, a lot of advancements have been made in arc welding to improve the weld quality by stabilizing the welding process and improving the depth of penetration. To join thicker steels (9.5 mm–12.5 mm), generally pulsed plasma gas welding (PPGW), variable polarity plasma arc welding (VPPAW) process, and double-pulsed plasma arc welding (DPPAW) processes are widely used. The PPGW provides better process stability and weld quality over VPPAW. Some other PAW are soft plasma arc welding, plasma spot welding, laser-assisted plasma arc welding, and PAW-MIG hybrid welding, and these are generally used for specific industrial application [2]. The heat affected zone is less in the PAW process than that of the traditional welding process. The PAW has more energy density than gas tungsten arc welding (GTAW); however, it is less than that of the electron beam welding (EBW) process. The PAW and GTAW both use non-consumable tungsten electrode for the arc generation. A schematic diagram of automation in plasma arc welding is shown in Figure 3.3.

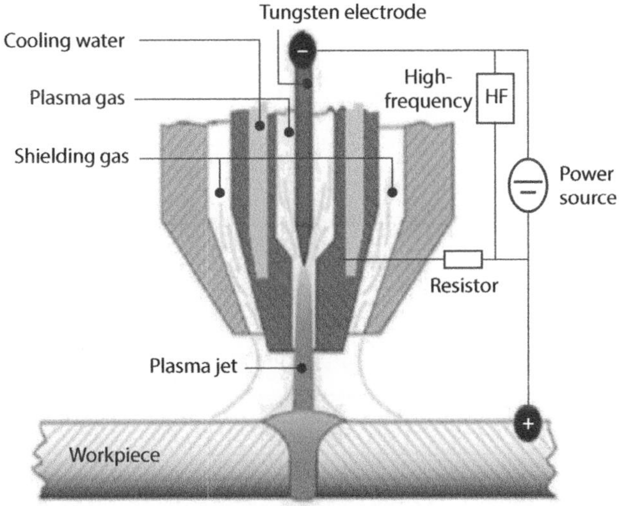

Figure 3.3 Automation in plasma arc welding [2].

3.4 Laser Welding

In laser beam welding (LBW), a laser providing a concentrated heat source is used to join two metal or polymer pieces by focusing the laser at the cavity between the two pieces [5–8]. It is based on keyhole or penetration mode of welding. The LBW is commonly used for mass fabrication such as in the automation industry. One of the most important facts about LBW is that the laser is concentrated and has high energy density, due to which it melts the area at the joint without affecting the other areas of the component. The heat affected zone and the thermal distortions are comparatively less in LBW than that in the case of other conventional arc welding processes. In addition, as the heat source is concentrated, the welding speed for thin plates is quite high and for thicker plates it can produce deep and narrow welds between square-edged parts. The principle of automation in laser beam welding is shown in Figure 3.4. This welding type is done out of a vacuum, which makes it a very suitable candidate for the fabrication of metallic aerospace parts. A laser beam is also commonly used as a heat source to join metal matrix composites [9].

Laser beam welding is very commonly used in the automotive industry for high-volume applications because of its concentrated heat source [10]. The speed of welding is dependent on the power supplied and thickness of the workpieces. It is capable of welding titanium, aluminum, stainless

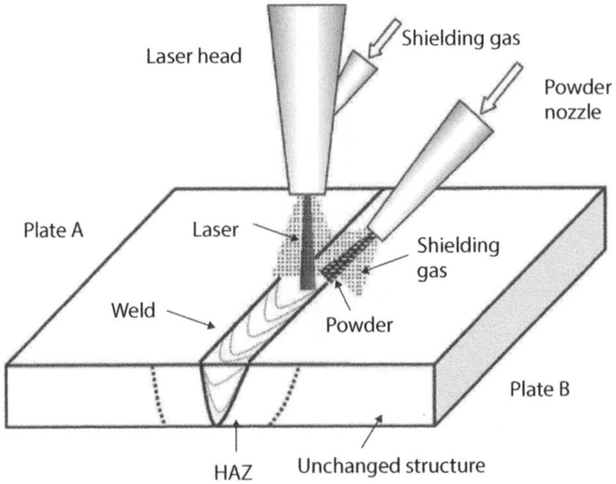

Figure 3.4 Automation in laser beam welding [11].

steel, and carbon steels. The weld quality is quite high and similar to that of electron beam welding. However, due to high cooling rates, weld cracking is a concern in high carbon steels.

3.5 Arc Welding

Arc welding is a welding process that joins metals by using electricity to create an arc between the metal pieces to generate heat. This heat melts metals and when these metals cool it results in binding of the metal pieces. It uses a metal stick known as an electrode. The arc is in between the electrode and the metal pieces. The electrode could either be consumable or non-consumable. In this, both the direct and alternating currents can be used. The arc welding with consumable electrode and non-consumable electrode are termed as gas metal arc welding (GMAW) or sometimes metal inert gas arc welding (MIG) and tungsten inert gas arc welding (TIG), respectively. A shielding gas (inert gas), vapor, or slag is generally used to protect the welding area. The arc welding can be done in manual, automatic and semi-automatic mode. Arc welding was developed in the late 19th century and became popular for shipbuilding during the Second World War. Nowadays, it is very commonly used for joining steel structures.

3.6 MIG Welding

The metal inert gas (MIG) welding process uses consumable electrode. This electrode is a continuous solid wire which is fed into the weld pool by a welding gun. The two base materials melt together at the joining site to form a joint. A shielding gas is also supplied by the welding gun to protect the weld pool from any contamination.

The MIG process was first developed to join the aluminum and helium was the shielding gas used. MIG can be used to join both thin and thick sections. The electrode serves two purposes, i.e., the heat source and the filler material for making the joint. The shielding gas used in MIG depends on the material to be welded. The electrode may be solid or flux cored. The automation in MIG welding is depicted in Figure 3.5.

In the manual MIG process, the travel speed and the wire position are manually controlled; however; the power source is used to control the electrode feed rate and the arc length. Therefore, often the manual MIG process is also referred to as semi-automatic. When all these parameters

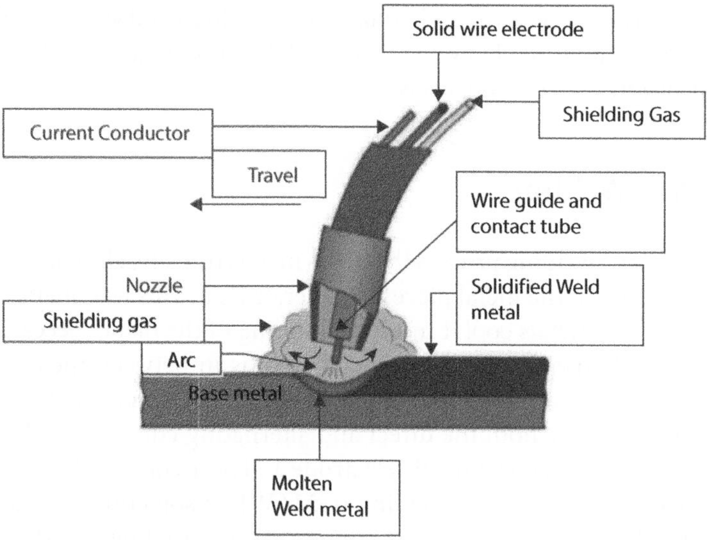

Figure 3.5 Automation in MIG welding [12].

are controlled without any manual intervention, it is known as a fully automatic process. In the welding process, power with constant voltage is supplied to the electrode. The welding current is generally determined by electrode diameter and electrode feed rate.

3.7 Resistance Welding

In resistance welding, the components join each other by supplying the continuing current through them due to the melting of the materials at the interface. The filler material is not required to make a joint. The current, time and resistance are the important factors for heat generation. The resistivity, parent material surface condition, material, size and shape of electrodes, and the applied pressure are the main functions of resistance developed at the interface. A clamping force (hold the components) also plays an important role during the heating process to get the solidification of the joint. Spot welding, flash welding and induction welding are types of resistance welding. Among these, spot welding is a common type of welding which is shown in Figure 3.6.

The joints or sample made by this welding gives a higher strength and soundness similar to rivet joint. The resistance spot welding process is very

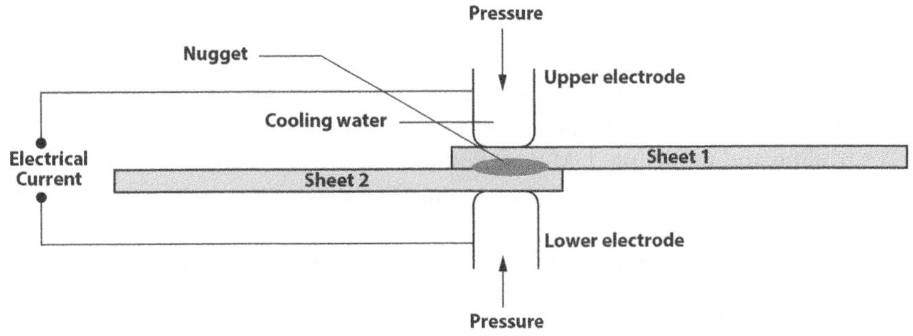

Figure 3.6 Resistance spot welding [13].

effective for fabricating sheet metal samples with high production rate. For this reason, the automotive industry mostly prefers spot welding for the joining of steel and also in aerospace and other appliance industries for fabricating aluminum alloys in airframe components, thin section components, etc. [14]. However, the applications of seam welding is used to produce thin sheet, fuel tanks, etc., and for securing nuts onto plate fabricated by projection welding. As per the previous studies, the use of resistance welding for aluminum creates more difficulties than steel due to its characteristics, i.e., high electrical conductivity and large capacity equipment requiring high welding currents. In addition, copper with aluminum alloys electrodes produces rapid wear and a short electrode life. Oxide entrapment and hot cracking are the major issues in resistance welding which produces cracks and porosity in the welded components [15].

3.8 Conclusions

This chapter covered the various levels of automation used in arc welding processes, ranging from manual (non-automated) processes to adaptive controls. Studying certain factors, such as financial viability and the quantity and variability of welds, is necessary before deciding which level of automation should be used in a process. If the process is highly variable, there should be no automation at all since the setup and programming would take longer than the actual welding. On the other hand, a robotic system with a preprogrammed task would ensure repeatability and productivity to the process if it is a repeated operation with proper preparation of the pieces to be welded.

References

1. Liu, Z.M., Cui, S.L., Luo, Z., Zhang, C.Z., Wang, Z.M., Zhang, Y.C., Plasma arc welding: Process variants and its recent developments of sensing, controlling and modeling. *J. Manuf. Process.*, 23, 315–327, 2016.
2. Sahoo, A. and Tripathy, S., Development in plasma arc welding process: A review. *Mater. Today Proc.*, 41, 363–368, 2019.
3. Prasad, K.S. and Rao, C.S., Advances in plasma arc welding: A review. *J. Mech. Eng. Technol.*, 4, 1, 35–60, 2012.
4. Wu, C.S., Wang, L., Ren, W.J., Zhang, X.Y., Plasma arc welding: Process, sensing, control and modeling. *J. Manuf. Process.*, 16, 1, 74–85, 2014.
5. Auwal, S.T., Ramesh, S., Yusof, F., Manladan, S.M., A review on laser beam welding of copper alloys. *Int. J. Adv. Manuf. Technol.*, 96, 1–4, 475–490, 2018.
6. Sarila, V.K., Moinuddin, S.Q., Cheepu, M.M., Rajendran, H., Kantumuchu, V.C., Characterization of microstructural anisotropy in 17-4PH stainless steel fabricated by DMLS additive manufacturing and laser shot peening. *Trans. Indian Inst. Met.*, 76, 2, 403–410, 2023.
7. Svenungsson, J., Choquet, I., Kaplan, A.F.H., Laser welding process-A review of keyhole welding modelling. *Phys. Proc.*, 78, 182–191, 2015.
8. Wang, P., Chen, X., Pan, Q., Madigan, B., Long, J., Laser welding dissimilar materials of aluminum to steel: An overview. *Int. J. Adv. Manuf. Technol.*, 87, 9–12, 3081–3090, 2016.
9. Guo, J. and Chen, X.G., Study on laser welding of AA1100-16 vol.% B 4C metal-matrix composites. *Compos. B Eng.*, 43, 5, 2012.
10. Cieslak, M.J. and Fuerschbach, P.W., On the weldability, composition, and hardness of pulsed and continuous Nd: YAG laser welds in aluminum alloys 6061, 5456, and 5086. *Metall. Trans. B*, 19, 1, 319–329, 1988.
11. Czerwinski, F., Welding and joining of magnesium alloys, in: *Magnesium Alloys-Design, Processing and Properties*, 2011.
12. Moinuddin, S.Q., Dewangan, A.K., Roshan, S., Chapter 2 Direct metal laser sintering, in: *Advances in Additive Manufacturing Processes*, pp. 55–79, Bentham Science Publishers, United Arab Emirates, 2021.
13. Dewangan, A.K., Moinuddin, S.Q., Cheepu, M.M., Sajjan, S.K., Dutt, N., Chapter 15 Thermal energy storage devices: opportunities, challenges and future scope, in: *Thermal Energy Systems: Design, Computational Techniques and Applications*, CRC Press, Taylor and Francis Publications, Boca Raton, 2022.
14. Moinuddin, S.Q., Kumar, M., Kumar, S., Sharma, A., Assessment of twin-wire GMAW as a candidate for large scale arc based additive manufacturing, in: *The 10th International Conference on Trends in Welding Research and 9th Japan Welding Society (9WS)*, Hitotsubashi Hall, Tokyo, Japan, 2016.
15. Mathers, G., Introduction to the welding of aluminium, in: *Woodhead Publishing Series in Welding and Other Joining Technologies, The Welding of Aluminium and its Alloys*, pp. 1–9, Woodhead Publishing, United Kingdom, 2002.

4

Digitalization of Welding Processes

Atla Sridhar[1]*, K. Prasanna Lakshmi[2], Shaik Himam Saheb[3] and M. Siva Surya[1]

[1]Department of Mechanical Engineering, GITAM Deemed to be University Hyderabad, Telangana, India
[2]Department of Mechanical Engineering, Jawaharlal Nehru Technological University Hyderabad, Telangana, India
[3]Department of Mechanical Engineering, ICFAI Foundation for Higher Education, Donthanapally, Hyderabad, India

Abstract
Processes for welding provide a special competence with several industrial uses. Additive manufacturing on a large scale has gained recognition as a prominent application of welding in recent times. Process monitoring techniques, especially, must be integrated with current welding and additive manufacturing processes to ensure the quality and repeatability of welding. They are a good candidate for digitization since welding processes create process-specific information such as welding current variations, temperatures, and acoustics. The methods of process monitoring applicable to welding and additive manufacturing are thoroughly covered in this chapter. First, the design and operation of several welding sensors are presented. The specific uses of the sensors in digitizing welding operations are then discussed.

***Keywords*:** Digitalization of welding, Industry 5.0, process monitoring, digital twins, additive manufacturing and sensors

4.1 Introduction

Welding must be managed and monitored to achieve the appropriate standards because it is a complex and unpredictable, dynamic process. Recent

**Corresponding author*: atla.sridhar9@gmail.com

Syed Quadir Moinuddin, Shaik Himam Saheb, Ashok Kumar Dewangan, Murali Mohan Cheepu and S. Balamurugan (eds.) Automation in Welding Industry: Incorporating Artificial Intelligence, Machine Learning and Other Technologies, (49–72) © 2024 Scrivener Publishing LLC

improvements in power source technology have led to the regulation of several input parameters to reduce disruptions and enhance output quality, which has increased the welding system's complexity. By breaking down the welding process into a few smaller operations, the complicated system of welding may be controlled [1]. As seen in Figure 4.1, each subprocess may be watched for inputs, outputs, and disturbances.

These subsystems and procedures may be observed for a broad range of signals, including welding voltages and currents, temperatures, spark, type of metal transfer, electric arc between the electrode, weld seams, weld penetrating, rate of flow of gas, deficiencies, and more. The monitoring classifications for prior, during, and after the process can also be used to organize these subsystems and procedures. Level of a melt pool scales, single level scales, and developing level scales may all be effectively used for monitoring and controlling the process in additive manufacturing (AM) [1].

The weld pool parameters and HAZ, where they impact the process's uniformity and the component's standard, are monitored on the first scale. The secondary stage keeps track of the dimensions, thickness, flaws,

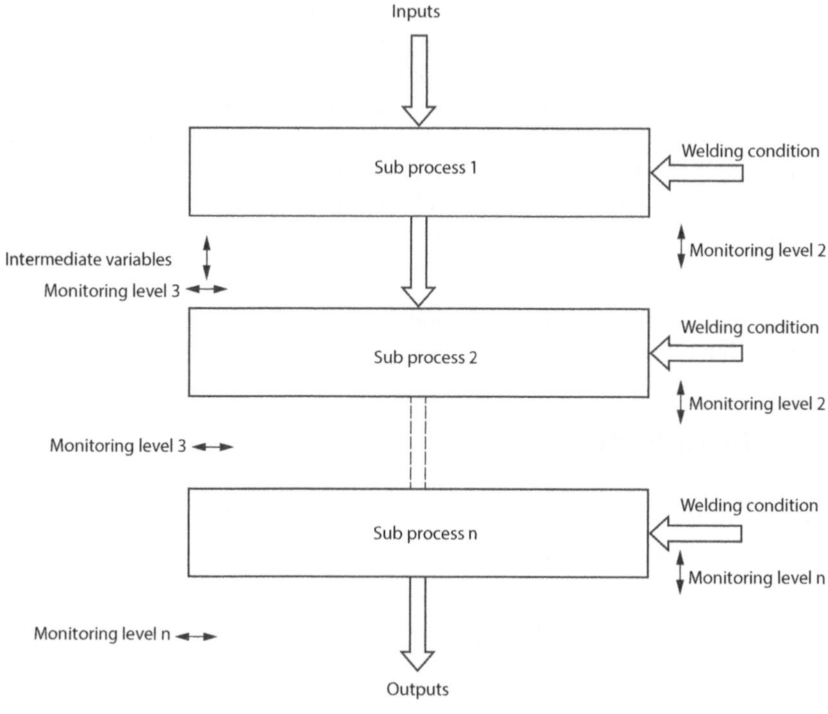

Figure 4.1 Monitoring welding procedures (adapted from [1]).

morphology and structure, heat transfer characteristics, and melted behavior of a single layer. These elements determine each layer's stability and quality. The final scale keeps track of the process stability and quantitative increase of the element in the construction track. In monitoring processes, various types of contact and non-contact sensors are commonly employed to convert process events into signals.

In order to achieve impeccable welds or components with the desired mechanical characteristics and metallurgical attributes, it is imperative to employ a range of monitoring sensors during the fusion and additive manufacturing processes. However, as of right now, setting up the sensors requires a lot of human labor, which makes the monitoring activity error-prone and time-sensitive. Numerous methods are used by modern industry on the same grounds.

The whole process chain must be digitalized through the development of technologies like artificial intelligence, data science, machine learning, etc. Since a few years ago, the phrase "digital twin" has often been used to describe the digitization process. The idea of "Industry 5.0," or next-generation smart manufacturing, is related to digitalization and has the potential to greatly enhance welding and AM processes. The internet of things (IoT) and machine-to-machine (M2M) connectivity will increase automation, which will enhance self-monitoring and communication. The implementation of a multi-sensor network might improve the manufactured components' temperature management and property homogeneity.

This chapter discusses various process monitoring methods with special purposes for the sensors utilized in welding and additive manufacturing (AM) practices considering current advancements in smart sensor usage in welding monitoring and its control.

4.2 Techniques for Process Monitoring

4.2.1 Electrical Process Tests: Voltage and Current for Welding

Welding current and voltage control the amount of heat that is input into the welding process, which affects the way the weld bead forms and the microstructure of the metal. The welding voltage is directly proportional to the length of the arc, and the welding current is directly related to the feed speed. Stable current and voltage are the two most common main power parameters [2, 3] used in arc welding. Depending on the application, both DC and AC currents are utilized [4]. Due to ongoing and constant variations in arc resistance, the effective voltage and current of welding vary when using consumable electrodes. The molten droplet expands and then separates at the electrodes' tips simultaneously. Different probes, such as Hall effect sensing devices and shunt resistor-based probes, are used to measure the welding current.

Both alternating and direct currents can be measured by a current measuring instrument (such as a clamp meter). The clamp meter consists of two independently coiling clamps made of ferrite iron. The alternative and direct current clamp meters function on somewhat different principals. As seen in Figure 4.2, the AC clamp meter functions as a current transformer. The transformer picks up the primary current (IP), or magnetic flux produced by a conductor's current flowing through it. Electromagnetic induction causes a secondary current (I_S) to be induced in the transformer's winding, which is directly proportional to the primary current (I_P/N), where N represents the number of turns in the transformer's winding.

A Hall effect device can be utilized in DC applications to sense the magnetic flux by producing a voltage that is perpendicular to the magnetic field

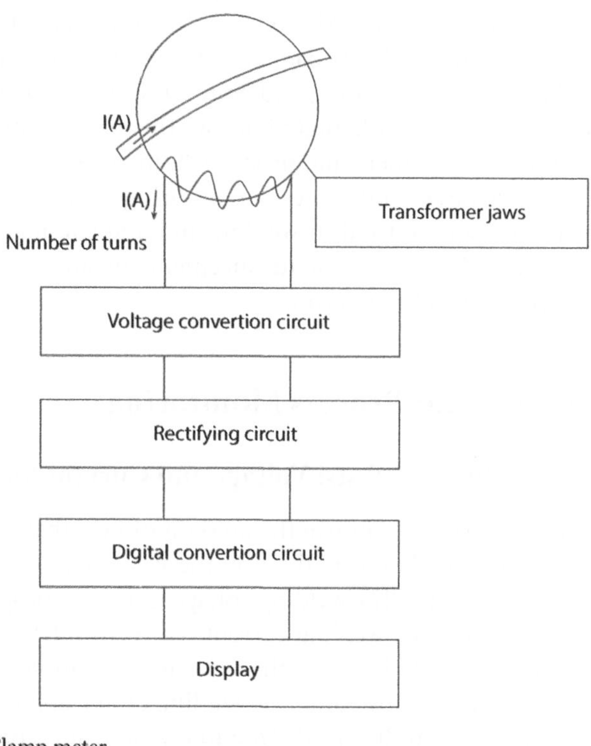

Figure 4.2 Clamp meter.

and the current flow when a conductor is positioned in a magnetic field. The Hall effect is the name of this concept. To determine the current, a Hall effect element is placed between the two clamps. The Hall sensor then identifies the electromagnetic flux caused by the current passing through the transformer jaws, resulting in the production of a voltage.

This sensor's benefits include dependability and lower costs when compared to other sensing methods. An electrical resistive element is attached between two terminals to make up the current shunt resistor. Manganin is a substance that is utilized as a resistive element because of its increased output power, poor resistivity, and superior conduction characteristics. According to Figure 4.3, the welding apparatus is linked in series with the current shunt resistor; allowing the resistor to conduct current results in a decrease in power supply across the entire resistor, which measures the flow of electric current.

Using sensors of the capacitor or resistive type, the welding voltage is monitored. Depending on the power supply parameters, voltage is being monitored at any output terminals or between the work material and the welding flame. Measuring the welding voltage closer to the welding torch is not practical. Two conductors and an insulator make up the capacitor-type voltage sensor. As seen in Figure 4.4(a), the insulator is positioned in a series connection between the two conductors. The electricity will start flowing through the condensers. when the voltage is applied across the conductors. The corresponding output levels are determined by the variations in electrical capacity.

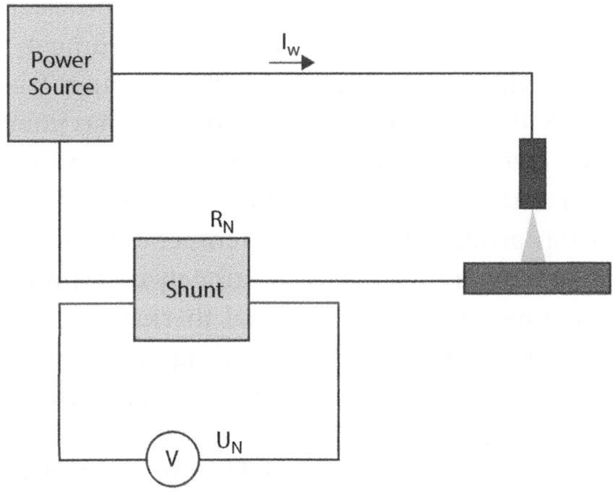

Figure 4.3 Shunt resistor operation.

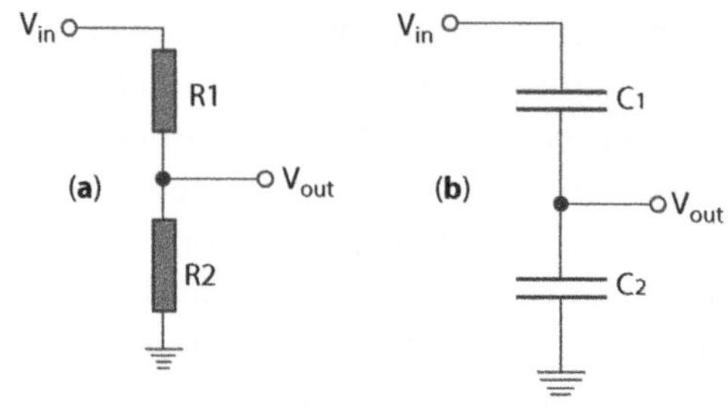

Figure 4.4 Types of voltage sensors: (a) capacitive (b) resistive.

Resistive voltage sensors can be categorized into two types: bridge circuits and voltage dividers. As illustrated in Figure 4.4(b), the voltage divider circuit consists of a pair of resistors, with one resistor acting as the reference voltage and the other as the sensing element. In the bridge circuit, there are four resistors, one of which serves as a voltage detector. It amplifies and monitors how much voltage changes as resistance varies.

4.2.2 Thermal Measurement

Thermal management, or regulating the temperature that determines the quality of the weld, is another crucial component of welding and AM. The solidifying of workpiece material and its mechanical characteristics are strongly influenced by temperature. As illustrated in Figure 4.4, touch-type and non-touch-type sensors are two main groups of sensors that may be used to monitor temperature.

The three other categories for contact-type sensors are electrical-resistive devices, electro-mechanical devices, and thermo-electrical devices. The thermocouple, a type of thermo-electrical instrument, is principally used to monitor welding temperatures, which may range from −200 °C to 3000 °C. Figure 4.5 illustrates that the thermocouple has junctions made of different metals, in which one junction behaves as the measuring connection and the other as the reference (cold/hot) junction. By taking advantage of the voltage drop produced due to the temperature difference between two junctions, the temperature can be accurately determined. Depending on the various temperature ranges, several thermocouple material combinations are possible. Due to its outstanding sensitivity and ability to withstand high temperatures, the K-type thermocouple is well-suited for additive manufacturing and welding applications.

Radiation as well as convection are used by non-contact sensing devices to track temperature variations. The three types of radiation detectors are

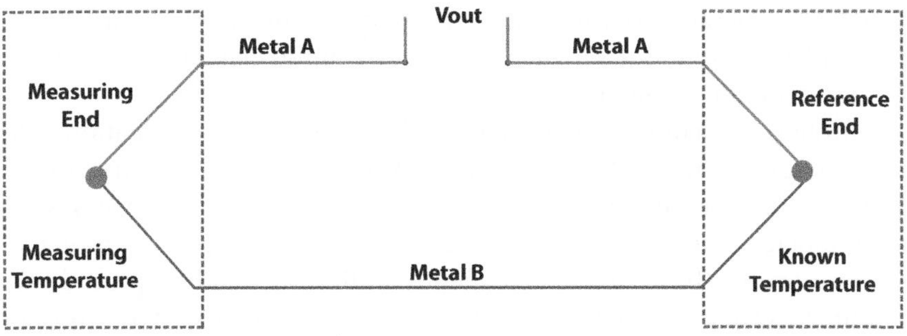

Figure 4.5 Thermocouple.

thermal, optical pyrometers, and photon or quantum detectors. According to Figure 4.6, the brightness of the reference lamp and the emitting source are compared to determine the temperature using an optical pyrometer. The radiation released from the source is captured by the objective optical lens. A lens directs the heat radiation onto the reference light. The reference lamp's current and intensity fluctuate as the observer modifies the rheostat parameters. Calibrating the current on the temperature scale to prevent the optical differentiation between the brightness of the temperature source and the lamp filament when they are at the same level enables the accurate determination of temperature. A lower brightness of the filament indicates

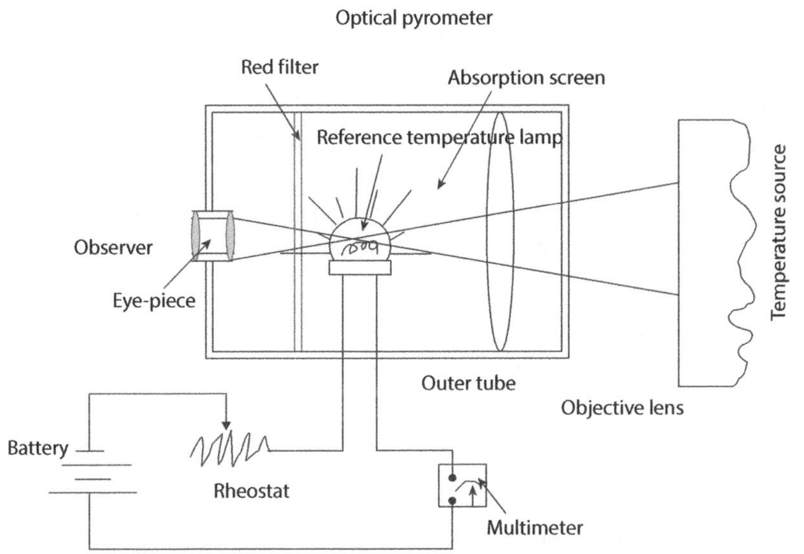

Figure 4.6 Optical pyrometer.

a higher temperature of the temperature source, while a higher brightness of the filament signifies a higher temperature of the filament as compared to the temperature source.

Through the conversion of absorbed electromagnetic radiation into heat energy, thermal detectors can effectively raise the temperature of the detector. The resulting heat can then be detected by various devices, such as bolometers, thermopiles, and pyroelectric detectors. Pyroelectric detectors are one of those that are frequently utilized in welding procedures. Bolometers and thermopiles cannot match the response speed of pyroelectric detectors. Figure 4.7 illustrates the design and operation of a pyroelectric detector. Two electrodes covered in pyroelectric material, such as lithium tantalite or triglycine sulfate, make up the sensitive element. When radiation is absorbed by the sensitive element. The preamplifier is responsible for processing the signal produced by the detector.

The photo effect is the mechanism by which quantum detectors quantify the excitation of electrons into conduction states. By distributing carriers of electrical charge, quantum detectors, on the other hand, record each photon's reaction. Despite having greater sensitivity than thermal detectors, quantum detectors are less effective because excited electrons quickly return to their ground state.

4.2.3 Optical Measurement

To operate effectively, sensing devices rely on detecting light. These devices are capable of detecting and regulating various welding characteristics. They are primarily non-contact devices. The basic welding operation and controlling method shown in Figure 4.8 employ a photosensitive sensing device and utilize the outputs to regulate the welding procedure.

High-speed cameras, electro-optic and infrared sensors, CMOS, and CCD are the sensors that are frequently used in welding operations. The photodetector, also known as an electro-optic sensor, detects

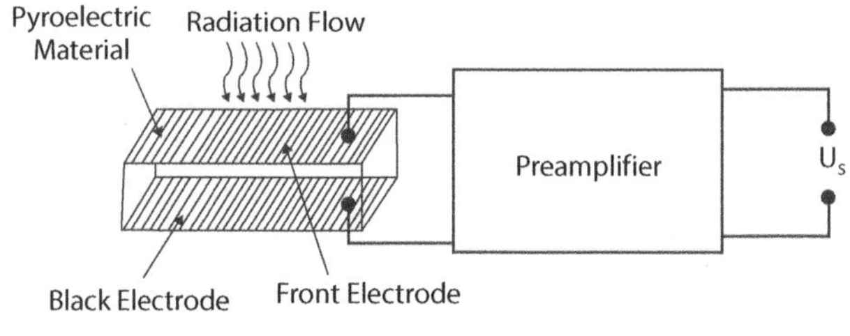

Figure 4.7 Design and operation of a pyroelectric detector.

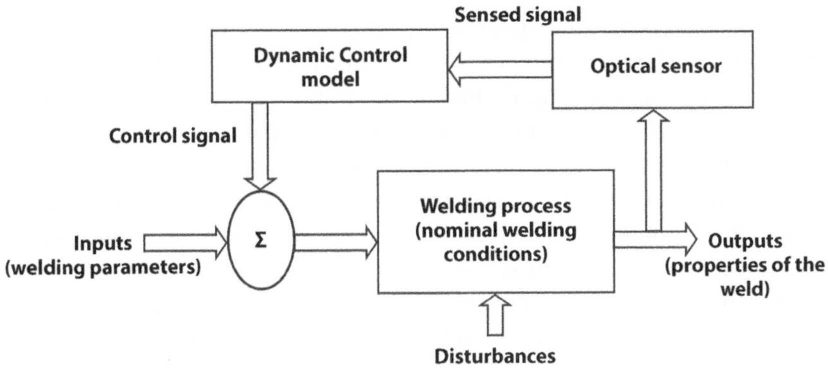

Figure 4.8 An optically sensing device used in the welding operation and controlling method (adapted from [1]).

electromagnetic radiation. These either function in photovoltaic or photoconductive modes. The conductivity of the detector material is altered by the photoconductivity absorption of electron-boosting lights. Figure 4.9(a) illustrates the biasing of the photoconductive detector via the load resistor. When there is no light present, photovoltaic detectors are sometimes referred to as photodiodes. The operation of the photovoltaic detector is shown in Figure 4.9(a). Photon interaction with the p-n junction generates an electron-hole pair in these detectors, producing a photocurrent that charges the capacitor in proportion to the amount of incident radiation. This process occurs without the need for an external bias as the photons are absorbed and converted into electrical energy.

Photodiodes are similar to CCD sensors. They are constructed from silicon, a substance frequently found in digital cameras. The near-infrared and visible light spectrums are both included in the sensitivity range. Light intensity is detected by the CCD sensor and afterwards recorded as a

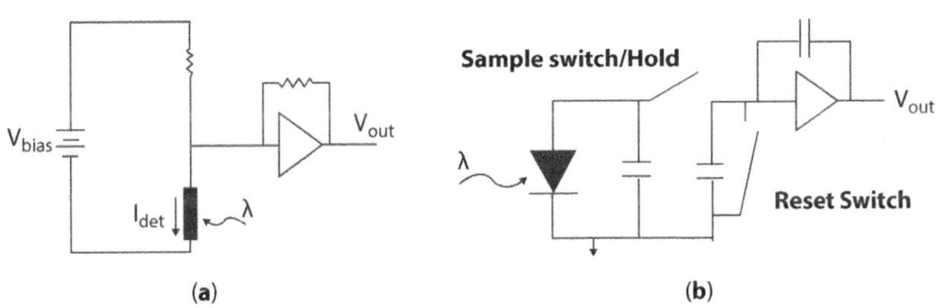

Figure 4.9 (a) Photoconductive detector; (b) Photovoltaic detector.

supply voltage indication. However, this charge-couple device (CCD) sensor is unable to detect the light's color, which may be corrected by applying color filters (red, green, and blue) to each pixel before identifying the missing data. There are three fundamental methods for scanning images: point, line, and area. The four types of transfer methods used by the CCD area image sensor are based on various designs (FIT), such as FT, FFT, IT, and FIT. The kinds of detectors used are MOS, photoconductive devices, and diodes. Photoconductive devices differentiate various transfer techniques. The transfer technique that is most frequently employed in the CCD sensor is either FFT or FT. The same basic idea underlies all of the various transfer techniques: for each pixel in the picture array, the light signal is transformed into an output voltage. According to Figure 4.10, the CCD image sensor functions in three steps. During the initial stages of an exposure, the conversion of light into an electric charge happens within an individual pixel. Charge transfer, the next phase, involves moving the charge to the silicon substrate. The charge must then be changed into an output voltage and amplified as a final step [1].

The fast-moving digicam that records slow motion in order to examine ephemeral events is another crucial optical tool. By passing the picture via a revolving prism or mirror rather than a shutter, high-speed cameras may capture images at speeds of up to 250,000 frames per second.

4.2.4 Acoustic Measurement

It is possible for acoustic sensors, such as microphones, to convert waves of acoustic pressure into electrical impulses. A few variables influence the

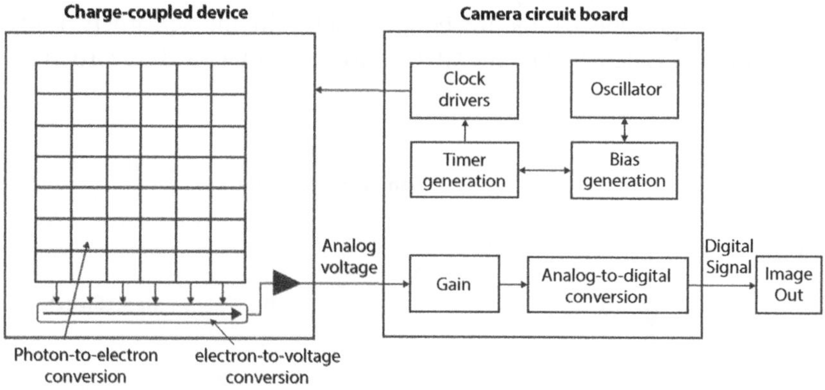

Figure 4.10 CCD sensors operation (adapted from [1]).

microphone choice for a variety of observed methods. The microphone detects the change in air pressure that is caused. Humans can perceive sound waves within the limits of 20 Hz and 20 kHz. Only a liquid medium allows the ultrasonic wave frequency to propagate effectively. Sound waves that have a frequency exceeding 20 kHz are known as ultrasound waves. The sound pressure levels (SPL) in welding and AM processes can forecast arc behavior, weld flaws, etc. Decibels are used to measure the SPL (dB). There are several varieties of microphones, including piezoelectric microphones and condenser microphones. Piezoelectric microphones are among the several types of microphones that are often utilized. To construct this microphone, piezoelectric ceramic material is utilized to create electrically conducting electrodes on both ends. Mechanical forces are converted into electrical charges by the piezoelectric crystal. Furthermore, this sensor is capable of capturing and analyzing the resulting acoustic emission (AE).

4.2.5 Measurement of Displacement and Velocity

A non-contact sensor known as a vibrometer is employed to measure an object's displacement and velocity. Depending on the application, this sensor employs either an infrared or helium laser. The single-point laser Doppler vibrometer (LDV) is the most used vibrometer type. The LDV is capable of measuring high frequencies with excellent amplitude resolution. Figure 4.11 illustrates that the LDV consists of a Mach-Zehnder interferometer, a laser source, two detectors, three beam splitters, and a lens. Using an interferometer and the Doppler effect, the LDV is able to measure the vibrations of objects in motion. The laser light emitted from the laser source is split into an object beam and a reference beam by the beam splitter (BS1). With the use of a lens, the object beam is focused on the moving item after passing through a beam splitter (BS3). Upon diverting the backscattered beam (reflected light) through BS3 and subsequently mixing it with the reference beam, a frequency shift/change occurs. This is due to the beam's interaction with BS2. The Doppler effect is what causes these changes in frequency. Two photodetectors are used to detect and convert the output optical signal to electrical signals (PD1 and PD2). Moreover, the signals obtained are demodulated to determine the moving object's displacement and velocity values.

4.2.6 Measurement of Force

As a passive contact-type transducer, the dynamometer transforms mechanical displacements into electrical impulses. Resistance and friction

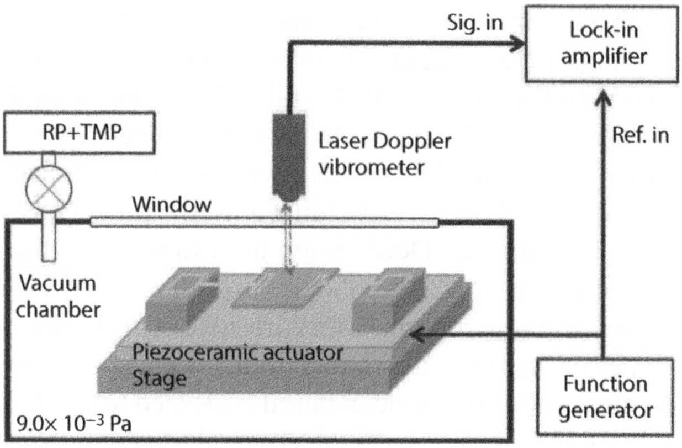

Figure 4.11 Vibratometer with laser doppler.

stir welding frequently employ a strain gauge-based dynamometer to measure the forces. A Wheatstone bridge and elastically flexible material make up the strain gauge. The strain gauge's wire length lengthens as a result of the load being applied, changing the resistance of the Wheatstone bridge. Arc pressure sensors are utilized for monitoring welding arc pressure. These sensors can transform pressure waves into electrical signals that are further amplified via processing circuits. Piezoresistive and piezoelectric sensors are frequently employed for measuring the pressure of the welding arc. These pressure sensors have a sensitive component for detecting pressure waves and a converter component for turning those waves into electric signals. According to Figure 4.12, silicon serves as the piezoresistive component of the piezoresistive sensor.

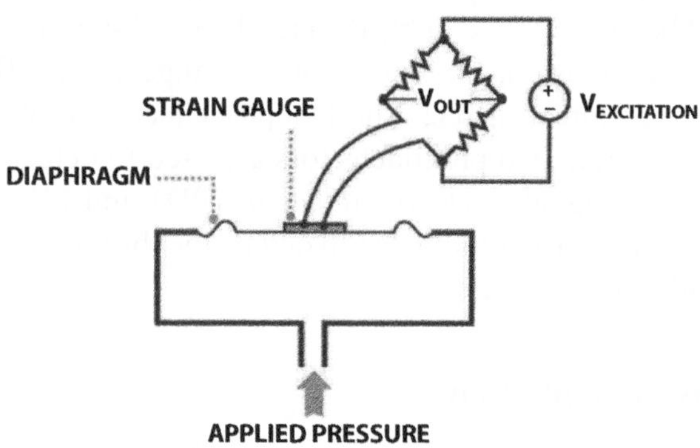

Figure 4.12 Piezoresistive pressure sensor.

In wire-based additive manufacturing (AM) and welding, there is a magnetic field present that surrounds the direction of the current flow. Different sensors, such as gaussmeters, webmasters, magnetometers, etc., can be used to record this EMF. In welding and additive manufacturing, gaussmeters with Hall effect probes are frequently used to detect EMF. The Hall effect component of this probe is linked to a circuit of electricity and a voltmeter. The strength of the magnetic field is directly proportional to the voltage fluctuations, which are then amplified, and the resulting voltage is measured by the Hall effect gaussmeter as an indicator of the magnetic field strength.

4.3 Process Monitoring Applications

4.3.1 Measurement of Current and Voltage

Real-time monitoring of welding methods, such as resistance, spot, LBW, and WAAM, involves the measurement of voltage and current. The heat input can be correlated with current and voltage. The melting efficiency is calculated using instantaneous current and voltage wherein determining the amount of energy utilized from the overall energy input for deposition and is crucial since it gives an estimate of how much energy was used to generate the deposit area (Ad) from the overall energy input.

$$HI = \int V(t)I(t)dt$$

$$E = Ad * 100$$

$$0.0854 * (HI)$$

where

S—Travel speed (mm/s),
E—Melting efficiency,
HI—Heat input (kJ/mm),
V(t)—Instantaneous voltage (V), and
I(t)—Instantaneous current (A).

By utilizing a current sensor and a data collection technique, the dynamic welding parameters of electric current and voltage are monitored and recorded. Figure 4.13(a) provides a standard representation of the current and voltage data variations. A study [5] analyzed the current and voltage data to examine arc instability within the anti-phase synchronized twin-wire GMAW process. Meanwhile, cyclogram analysis (Figure 4.13(b)) and PDD

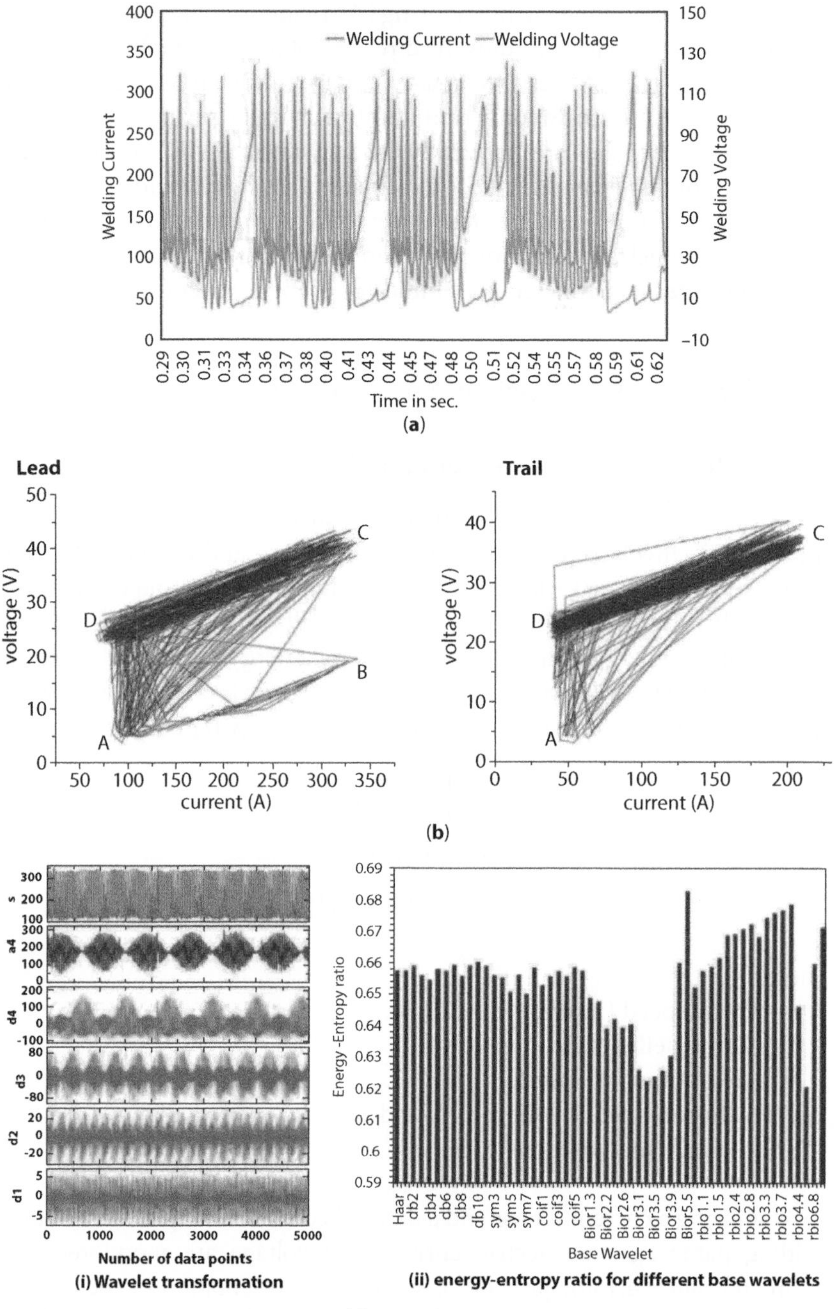

Figure 4.13 (a) A pulsed GMAW current–voltage signal [6], (b) twin-wire GMAW cyclogram stability analysis [5], and (c) (i) wavelet transformation (A), (ii) energy-entropy ratio for various wavelets [6].

(probability density distribution) are used to determine arc stability. Weld microstructure and form are related to the impact of arc stability. Wavelet energy entropy (WEE) and discrete wavelet transformation (DWT) [6] measurable analyses of the current data may also be used to evaluate arc stability.

Figure 4.13(a) shows the current-voltage signal, which is transformed into a wavelet in Figure 4.13(c (i)). In addition, Figure 4.13(c (ii)) displays the energy-entropy ratio for various base wavelets.

Voltage and current data can be employed to observe and analyze various welding procedures, such as welding and related wire arc additive manufacturing (WAAM), apart from arc welding. The dynamic resistance, an essential parameter in the resistance spot welding (RSW) process, is calculated using the measured current and voltage signals [7]. The current and voltage signals are crucial in analyzing and characterizing the welding process in several techniques, such as magnetic pulse welding (MPW) [8], vaporizing foil actuator welding (VFAW) [9], and various arc welding methods [10, 11]. In the case of MPW, analyzing the circuit's rise time using the current signal can provide valuable insights into important factors like impedance and overall efficiency. In VFAW, the energy deposition and process effectiveness are assessed using the current and voltage signals.

4.3.2 Thermal Measurement

In welding processes, monitoring the transient temperature or temperature change is crucial for producing strong and quality welds. Thermocouples are frequently employed to sense temperature fluctuations in the work piece and use them to compute heat source model parameters and the thermal cycle based on the welding conditions [12, 13]. The experimentally determined cooling rate significantly impacts the resultant microstructure, which in turn affects the mechanical characteristics of the weld [14, 15]. Welding operations sometimes involve thermographic process monitoring, which involves keeping an eye on the melt pool and the surrounding temperature field. The effects of the oscillation frequency and focal diameter on the weld pool and temperature field are examined using infrared thermography [16]. Thermal imaging is a useful tool to study the melt pool characteristics during welding and obtain information about its dimensions and solidification fronts. Different temperature sensing techniques have been used in laser welding to calculate the temperature of the molten or vapor pool, as described in the study by Gao *et al.* [17]. Additionally, infrared sensors have been utilized in friction stir welding (FSW) to monitor the weld pool and tool temperature in real time [18]. Through feedback control, accurate control of the tool pin temperature can be achieved.

4.3.3 Optical Measurement

Optical sensors, including CCD and CMOS image sensors, are widely used in several industrial applications, including monitoring arc behavior, detecting droplet detachment, tracking weld seams, and identifying defects. Shigeta *et al.* [19] conducted a study in which imaging spectroscopy was utilized to examine the impact of the CO_2 mixture GMAW. The researchers were able to observe the dynamic behavior and plasma properties of droplets by monitoring the temperature in the argon plasma and metal plasma areas. In situations where the behavior of one arc can impact the entire multiple-wire welding process, high-speed photography as shown in Figure 4.14 is even more crucial for understanding arc behavior [20].

Observing the droplet production and detachment is equally critical to detecting the arc's temperature distribution and its behavior. The temperature of the droplet was measured using a two-color temperature measuring technique in plasma MIG welding by Haribabu *et al.* [21]. A system to regulate the droplet temperature can be created based on the temperature observations. The shadowgraph technique and high-speed video camera observation may also be used to record the metal transfer behavior (color

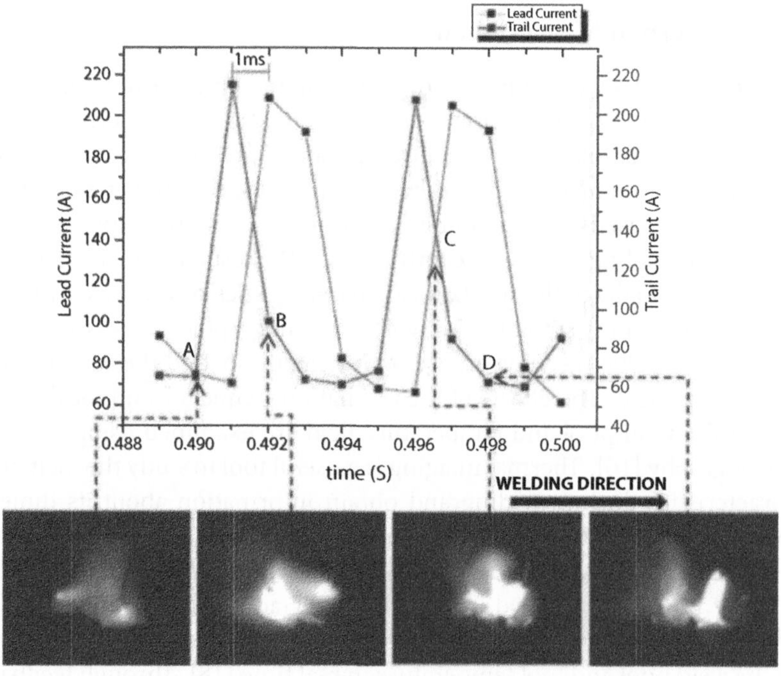

Figure 4.14 Arc behavior in twin-wire GMAW varies with current and voltage [20].

HSVC). High-speed imaging is utilized for visual examination to understand the dynamic behaviors of the arc, droplet, and weld pool, and it has also been used to study AM [22].

Segmenting the reflected laser lines allows for online weld pool monitoring in arc welding [23]. Segmentation and image processing methods work together to provide a reliable and precise way to measure the geometry of the weld pool surface. It is also possible to use a machine vision technique to identify and categorize weld defects in real production [24]. In the past ten years, DIC has become a more popular non-contact optical approach for characterizing the mechanical characteristics of welds. A deposited weld's various zones, including the fusion zone, HAZ, and BM, may be identified using DIC. The experimental setup for digital image correlation (DIC) can be observed in Figure 4.15(a), while Figure 4.15(b) displays the strain distribution data necessary for identifying different zones. Photodiodes, high-speed cameras, and spectrometers have been widely used as traditional optical sensors in laser welding. These sensors enable the detection of plasma-reflected laser energy or vapor plumes, as well as the observation of keyholes and molten pools and flaw identification, among other things [17].

4.3.4 Acoustic Measurement

Acoustic emission is a common method for monitoring the quality of welding and AM processes at different stages of the process and for detecting flaws [26]. To identify metal transfer modes, time and frequency domain analysis of the arc sound signal is performed together with voltage and current measurements. Statistical variables, such as root mean square (RMS)

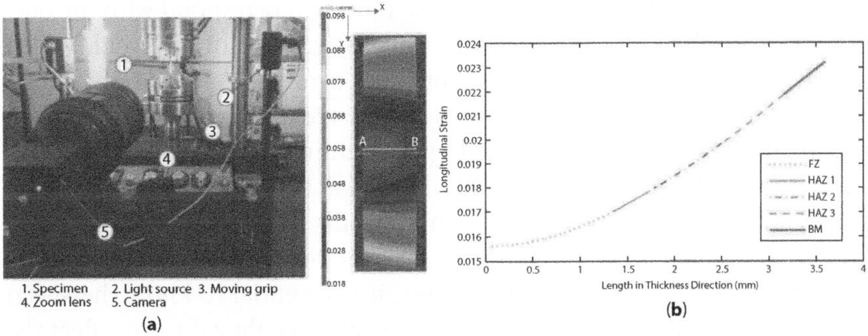

Figure 4.15 (a) Experimental setup for DIC, and (b) zone identification using strain distribution [25].

and kurtosis, can be used to analyze metal transfer behavior. The variation of arc sound kurtosis can help detect blowhole-like weld defects. Acoustic sensors have also been applied to laser welding, with studies conducted on fault detection using acoustic emissions from the workpiece or vapor plume [17]. However, the use of acoustic sensors in welding operations has some limitations, including difficulties in installing contacting sensors at industrial sites and interference from work noise in the case of non-contacting sensors. While acoustic monitoring can aid in evaluating welding results, it may not be the best choice for feedback or adaptive control due to the sound delay caused by the distance between the sound source and the detection location.

4.3.5 Displacement and Velocity Measurement

The grain fineness of the weld metal is influenced by vibrations given to the molten metal, which are crucial for dendritic formation and fragmentation [27]. Vibrations influence how well the molten weld flows, reducing imperfections. Monitoring the vibrations generated during the processes of vibration-assisted welding and ultrasonic welding is critical. When laser welding stainless steel, Moinuddin *et al.* [28] used laser Doppler vibrometry (LDV) to examine how the ultrasonic energy input affected the weld properties and microstructure. The LDV enables getting the velocities of the vibrations for the welded workpiece immediately. Photon Doppler velocimetry (PDV) has become an additional method that gives details on the movement and speed of moving objects. In a study conducted by Lu *et al.* [29], the PDV method was employed to monitor the ultrasonic welding (USW) of aluminum alloys. By analyzing the velocity profiles generated through PDV, researchers were able to gain a better understanding of the relative movement between the connecting sheets, sonotrode, and anvil during the USW process. The PDV findings correspond with the outcomes of mechanical testing and the microstructure of the weld, which aid in the comprehension and quantification of bond formation. When high-speed moving objects' velocities and related displacements need to be recorded, PDV is very helpful. In impact welding processes such as magnetic pulse welding (MPW) and vaporizing foil actuator welding (VFAW), the PDV method has been utilized in a specific manner. In this process, a weld is generated by colliding sheets at velocities between 300 and 1,000 m/s in this process. In such procedures, it is essential to know the speed and angle at which the sheets meet or impact since they directly affect the characteristics and structure of the resulting joint (and may be computed from speed data). In a recent research work [30], PDV was used to measure the speed of impacts during the collision process, which helped establish a connection between the welding process, the microstructure formed, and the final properties of impact spot welding.

4.3.6 Measurement of Force

The friction stir welding (FSW) tool's axial forces must be measured since they are a key factor in determining how the metal flows [31, 32]. It is feasible to build efficient tool pins by experimentally predicting tool failure zones using tool forces collected with a rotating component dynamometer for various welding situations. Su *et al.* [32] created a less expensive alternative to employing a dynamometer or load cell, allowing for the synchronized amount of torque and forces (both transversely as well as axially) operating on the FSW tool [33].

4.3.7 EMF Measurement

It is feasible to measure and numerically model the magnetic field that surrounds the welding arc since it is a necessary component of arc welding operations [34]. Any current-carrying object in the field's proximity is subject to an electromagnetic force (EMF). The characteristics of welded joints are influenced by the flow pattern of the weld pool, which is determined by the electromagnetic field (EMF) and is essential for both mechanical and metallurgical properties. Other functions of the EMF in various welding processes include the change of element distribution, management of welding hot cracks, and grain refining in gas tungsten arc welding, among others. Due to the potential health risks it poses, assessing EMF is also essential.

4.4 Future Directions

As technology develops quickly, there is a greater need to fulfill welding needs by creating new techniques, materials, and products. A multi-sensor-enabled welding system is necessary to bridge the gap between welding as an art and welding as a science. This system must extract, analyze, and integrate all kinds of information both during and after welding. Both stochastic and deterministic analyses of the signals are required. To prepare welding operations for Industry 5.0, the results of the welding process must be digitalized. For sustainable production with zero-defect output as the ultimate objective, it is advisable to adopt a centralized management approach for all machines, especially in situations where multiple welding sources using different techniques are functioning concurrently. The focus of research studies and manufacturers should be on automating welding torch and tool maintenance (tip, wire spool, gas cylinder, etc.), as well as fault detection and correction.

The adaptive control of welding processes, or the modification of process parameters in response to shifting circumstances, has recently attracted attention. The adaptive control will be quite advantageous for AM methods that use welding to deposit the layer. For the construction quality and characteristics to be maintained during such operations, it is essential to modify the method as the parameters vary with each layer that is deposited. It is necessary to combine welding techniques with other manufacturing methods where monitoring and control are vital. This is a result of the complexity of materials and part designs increasing. There are several prospects for process and product development in additive or layered manufacturing through close-loop control. These areas of research are depicted in Figure 4.16. Future research on layered manufacturing enabled by multi-sensor technology can explore various topics, such as residual stress management, adaptive processing that considers digital analysis of electrical, acoustic, and thermal responses, and consolidation of process feedback, among others.

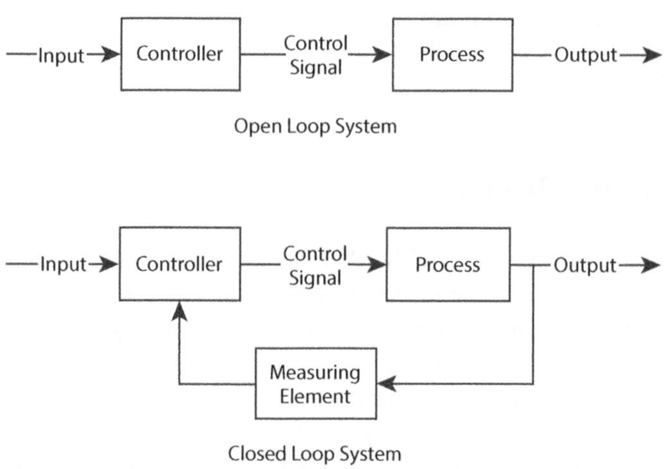

Figure 4.16 Monitoring and control system.

References

1. Zhang, Y. (Ed.), *Real-Time Weld Process Monitoring*, Elsevier, England, 2008.
2. Uhring, W. and Zlatanski, M., Ultrafast imaging in standard (Bi) CMOS technology, InTech, Croatia, 2012.
3. Moinuddin, S.Q. and Sharma, A., Melting efficiency in anti-phase synchronized twin-wire gas metal arc welding, in: *Proceedings of the 10th International Conference on Trends in Welding Research and 9th International Symposium Japan Welding Society (JWS)*, Tokyo, Japan, pp. 11–14, October 2016.
4. Mohanty, U.K., Abe, Y., Fujimoto, T., Nakatani, M., Kitagawa, A., Tanaka, M., Sharma, A., Performance evaluation of alternating current square waveform submerged arc welding as a candidate for fabrication of thick welds in 2.25 Cr-1Mo heat-resistant steel. *J. Press Vessel Technol.*, 142, 4, 041506, 11, 2020.
5. Moinuddin, S.Q. and Sharma, A., Arc stability and its impact on weld properties and microstructure in anti-phase synchronized synergic-pulsed twin-wire gas metal arc welding. *Mater. Des.*, 67, 293–302, 2015.
6. Kumar, M., Moinuddin, S.Q., Kumar, S.S., Sharma, A., Discrete wavelet analysis of mutually interfering co-existing welding signals in twin-wire robotic welding. *J. Manuf. Process.*, 63, 139–151, 2020.
7. Su, Z.W., Xia, Y.J., Shen, Y., Li, Y.B., A novel real-time measurement method for dynamic resistance signal in medium-frequency DC resistance spot welding. *Meas. Sci. Technol.*, 31, 5, 055011, 2020.
8. Kapil, A. and Sharma, A., Magnetic pulse welding: an efficient and environmentally friendly multi-material joining technique. *J. Clean. Prod.*, 100, 35–58, 2015.
9. Hansen, S.R., Vivek, A., Daehn, G.S., Vaporizing foil actuator: Controlling the pressure pulse for impulse metalworking, in: *International Manufacturing Science and Engineering Conference*, vol. 45813, American Society of Mechanical Engineers, p. V002T02A081, June 2014.
10. Moinuddin, S.Q., Hameed, S.S., Dewangan, A.K., Kumar, K.R., Kumari, A.S., A study on weld defects classification in gas metal arc welding process using machine learning techniques. *Mater. Today Proc.*, 43, 623–628, 2021.
11. Sumesh, A., Rameshkumar, K., Raja, A., Mohandas, K., Santhakumari, A., Shyambabu, R., Establishing correlation between current and voltage signatures of the arc and weld defects in GMAW process. *Arab. J. Sci. Eng.*, 42, 11, 4649–4665, 2017.
12. Sharma, A., Chaudhary, A.K., Arora, N., Mishra, B.K., Estimation of heat source model parameters for twin-wire submerged arc welding. *Int. J. Adv. Manuf. Technol.*, 45, 11-12, 1096, 2009.
13. Sharma, A., Arora, N., Mishra, B.K., Mathematical model of bead profile in high deposition welds. *J. Mater. Process. Technol.*, 220, 65–75, 2015.
14. Mohanty, U.K., Sharma, A., Abe, Y., Fujimoto, T., Nakatani, M., Kitagawa, A., Suga, T., Thermal modelling of alternating current square waveform arc welding. *Case Stud. Therm. Eng.*, 25, 100885, 2021.

15. Moinuddin, S.Q., Kapil, A., Kohama, K., Sharma, A., Ito, K., Tanaka, M., On process–structure–property interconnection in anti-phase synchronized twin-wire GMAW of low carbon steel. *Sci. Technol. Weld. Join.*, 21, 6, 452–459, 2016.
16. Mann, V., Hofmann, K., Schaumberger, K., Weigert, T., Schuster, S., Hafenecker, J., Schmidt, M., Influence of oscillation frequency and focal diameter on weld pool geometry and temperature field in laser beam welding of high strength steels. *Proc. CIRP*, 74, 470–474, 2018.
17. You, D.Y., Gao, X.D., Katayama, S., Review of laser welding monitoring. *Sci. Technol. Weld. Join.*, 19, 3, 181–201, 2014.
18. Vijendra, B. and Sharma, A., Induction heated tool assisted friction-stir welding (i-FSW): A novel hybrid process for joining of thermoplastics. *J. Manuf. Process.*, 20, 234–244, 2015.
19. Shigeta, M., Nakanishi, S., Tanaka, M., Murphy, A.B., Analysis of dynamic plasma behaviours in gas metal arc welding by imaging spectroscopy. *Weld. Int.*, 31, 9, 669–680, 2017.
20. Moinuddin, S.Q. and Sharma, A., *Effect of Welding Speed on Arc Stability and its Impact on Structure–Property in Anti-Phase Synchronized Twin-Wire GMAW Process*, .
21. Haribabu, S., Cheepu, M., Tammineni, L., Gurasala, N.K., Devuri, V., Kantumuchu, V.C., Dissimilar friction welding of AISI 304 austenitic stainless steel and AISI D3 tool steel: Mechanical properties and microstructural characterization, in: *Advances in Materials and Metallurgy*, pp. 271–281, 2018. https://doi.org/10.1007/978-981-13-1780-4_27.
22. Shiva, A., Cheepu, M., Kantumuchu, V.C., Ravi Kumar, K., Venkateswarlu, D., Srinivas, B., Jerome, S., Microstructure characterization of Al-TiC surface composite fabricated by friction stir processing. *IOP Conf. Ser. Mater. Sci. Eng.*, 330, 012060, 2018. https://doi.org/10.1088/1757-899x/330/1/012060.
23. Haribabu, S., Cheepu, M., Devuri, V., Kantumuchu, V.C., Optimization of welding parameters for friction welding of 304 stainless steel to D3Tool steel using response surface methodology. *Techno-Societal 2018*, pp. 427–437, 2019. https://doi.org/10.1007/978-3-030-16962-6_44.
24. Sun, J., Li, C., Wu, X.J., Palade, V., Fang, W., An effective method of weld defect detection and classification based on machine vision. *IEEE Trans. Industr. Inform.*, 15, 12, 6322–6333, 2019.
25. Saranath, K.M., Sharma, A., Ramji, M., Zone wise local characterization of welds using digital image correlation technique. *Opt. Lasers Eng.*, 63, 30–42, 2014.
26. Pal, K., Bhattacharya, S., Pal, S.K., Investigation on arc sound and metal transfer modes for on-line monitoring in pulsed gas metal arc welding. *J. Mater. Process. Technol.*, 210, 10, 1397–1410, 2010.
27. Jose, M.J., Kumar, S.S., Sharma, A., Vibration assisted welding processes and their influence on quality of welds. *Sci. Technol. Weld. Join.*, 21, 4, 243–258, 2016.

28. Moinuddin, S.Q., Hameed, S.S., Dewangan, A.K., Kumar, K.R., Kumari, A.S., A study on weld defects classification in gas metal arc welding process using machine learning techniques. *Mater. Today Proc.*, 43, 623–628, 2020, doi: 10.1016/j.matpr.2020.12.159.
29. Lu, Y., Song, H., Taber, G.A., Foster, D.R., Daehn, G.S., Zhang, W., *In-situ* measurement of relative motion during ultrasonic spot welding of aluminum alloy using photonic doppler velocimetry. *J. Mater. Process. Technol.*, 231, 431–440, 2016.
30. Kapil, A., Moinuddin, S.Q., Sharma, A., Chapter: 16 Digitization of welding processes, in: *Joining Processes for Dissimilar and Advanced Materials*, Elsevier-Woodhead Publishing Reviews: Mechanical Engineering Series, England, ISBN: 9780323853996, 2021.
31. Moinuddin, S.Q., Dewangan, A.K., Roshan, S., Chapter 2 Direct metal laser sintering, in: *Advances in Additive Manufacturing Processes*, pp. 55–79, Bentham Science Publishers, United Arab Emirates, 2021, doi: DOI:10.2174/978981503 63361210101.
32. Su, H., Wu, C.S., Pittner, A., Rethmeier, M., Simultaneous measurement of tool torque, traverse force and axial force in friction stir welding. *J. Manuf. Process.*, 15, 4, 495–500, 2013.
33. Moinuddin, S.Q., Machireddy, V.V., Immaneni, S.D., Kaniganti, T.B., Ponnappan, S.M., Sarila, V.K., Cheepu, M.M., Analysis on bonding interface during solid state additive manufacturing of high performance alloys between 18Cr-8Ni and 42CrMo4. *Metals*, 13, 488, 2023.
34. Dahiwale, N.B., Kapil, A., Sharma, A., Integrated model for assessment of electromagnetic force field due to arc welding. *Sci. Technol. Weld. Join.*, 20, 7, 563–570, 2015.

5

AI and ML in Welding Technologies

Suresh Goka[1], Gorle Shanmukha Narayana[2], Divya Jyothi G.[3], Himam Saheb Shaik[4] and Syed Quadir Moinuddin[4*]

[1]*National Institute of Technology, Warangal, Telangana, India*
[2]*Junior Cloud Developer, HCL Technologies, Hyderabad, India*
[3]*Centurion University, Paralakhemundi, India*
[4]*Department of Mechanical Engineering, College of Engineering, King Faisal University, Al-Hofuf, Kingdom of Saudi Arabia*

Abstract

Low accuracy of manual inspections, delay in detecting defects, and shortage of skilled resources are challenges in tracing the defects in welding technology. It is very expensive and wasteful to pull apart welded automobile bodies to check the welding quality using typical quality monitoring techniques. On the other hand, machine learning (ML)-based techniques will assist in minimizing waste and supporting a more profitable and sustainable manufacturing sector. Because they have robust modeling capabilities and don't require explicit programming, ML technologies are drawing significant growing interest in contemporary industrial industries. The development of computational learning methods and pattern recognition within artificial intelligence has led to the development of ML technology. The use of ML learning techniques has grown over the past few years for a variety of industries, including smart cities, finance, banking, and education. Because of numerous new cutting-edge computing approaches, today's machine learning differs from the machine learning of the past. Machine learning and data science techniques have been widely used in the manufacturing sector over decades to optimize the mechanical and microstructure properties of manufactured mechanical components.

Keywords: Welding, artificial intelligence, machine learning, deep learning, artificial neural network, friction stir welding

**Corresponding author*: syedquadirmoinuddin@gmail.com

Syed Quadir Moinuddin, Shaik Himam Saheb, Ashok Kumar Dewangan, Murali Mohan Cheepu and S. Balamurugan (eds.) Automation in Welding Industry: Incorporating Artificial Intelligence, Machine Learning and Other Technologies, (73–90) © 2024 Scrivener Publishing LLC

Nomenclature

AI	Artificial Intelligence
SWR	Spool Welding Robot
ML	Machine Learning
IoT	Internet of Things
Cobot	Collaborative Robot
IMS	Intelligent Manufacturing System
HAI	Hybrid Artificial Intelligence
TTT	Time Temperature Transformation
CCT	Continuous Cooling Transformation
FSW	Friction Stir Welding
FSSW	Friction Stir Spot Welding
CFRTP	Carbon Fiber Reinforced Thermoplastic
RF	Random Forest
QC	Quality Control
ANN	Artificial Neural Network
GBM	Gradient Boost Machine
PLS	Partial Least Square
RT	Regression Tree
GA	Genetic Algorithm
SVM	Support Vector Machine
IFR	International Federation of Robotics

5.1 Introduction

Machine learning, automation and robotics, machine vision, expert systems, data mining, and big data are some of the many good AI approaches that have been successfully applied in the manufacturing sector [1]. These AI approaches are being used more frequently to create extremely complicated relationships, enhance system controllability and raise product quality in the era of digital manufacturing. This is thanks to the advancements in data collecting technologies, robotic systems and computer science [2].

Welding is a complex manufacturing process, either manual or automated, which is sometimes prone to defects. Since these defects are a crucial factor when it comes to a final component being accepted for introduction into markets, the rejection of defective components is a costly affair. Therefore, there is a need to build a solution that could be a proven game changer for the industrial automation era. This solution can have a significant impact on lowering total waste and meeting the necessary quality standards, starting with early fault detection, cost reduction, and operation optimization. The introduction of artificial intelligence (AI) and machine learning (ML) are playing a vital role in creating solutions for the current automated manufacturing processes, especially in welding technology. Deep learning is subset of machine learning. In union, machine learning and deep learning are parts of AI as shown in Figure 5.1.

Every welder has an idea of how to set the basic parameters such as voltage, current, wire feed rate, gun travel speed, type of shield gas, and its flow rate, etc., depending on the type of material, type of welding, root gap and some other similar variables. However, for operations with higher turnover, total hand welding is just not an option; therefore, utilizing some level of automation is frequently necessary to submit competitive bids for new contracts.

What level of automation should be used? It depends, since it is unavoidable that not all the factors at play are covered by preprogramming weld settings. With the NovEye vision-based, AI-guided control system on its most recent spool welding robot (SWR), Novarc Technologies hopes to assist fabricators in mastering welding's inherent unpredictability rather than just quality assurance. Even though the SWR uses orbital welding, the AI and machine learning that Novarc uses to power the device are novel.

Fluctuations in the variables of the welding process randomly occur. Thus, it has a direct effect on the quality of the weld. When an operator preprograms something, then the weld produces some distortion. Sometimes, when the parts move from their original position during welding, there exists some deviation in the accuracy of the process. The longer the process continues, the more errors or defects occur with the progress in such processes. Thus, it is very hard to predict the deviation in welding geometry because of the diversion in the position of the original part to be welded.

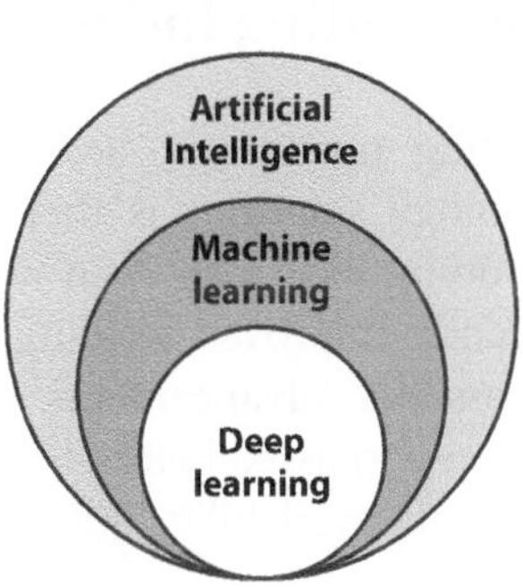

Figure 5.1 Relation between AI, ML, and DL [3].

Thus, the new technology offers different levels of automation from simple mechanized welding to automated systems to smart machines that can learn better procedures over time based on the recorded data.

The control system is also configured to detect the tack when the machine is set up. The vision system scans the groove and keeps track of the open root. The machine parameters are changed in real time to accommodate the tack when the vision system detects one going under the weld. The system shifts the recipe, so to speak, back to open-root settings once it has crossed the tack.

Furthermore, the need to make robots independent of their handler arose from the introduction of robots to welding. Additionally, the initial robotic welding process was designed for standard-sized products, thus any deviation from that size influenced productivity or impaired quality. As a result, it was necessary to develop an intelligent welding system to increase productivity, flexibility, and quality while lowering workers being exposed to dangers associated with difficult welding processes.

The development of advanced robotic systems made it possible for businesses in the internet of things (IoT), big data, AI, and also cloud computing to precisely track and optimize their manufacturing processes. The outcome is a current breakthrough that strengthens the welding system and advances the welding business by fusing cobots with artificial intelligence. These intelligent cobots powered by AI assist industries by enabling some non-redundant welding tasks to be completed with little to no supervision. Particularly in environments where human being's health/safety is at risk or in workplaces that require exact climatic or environmental control, AI-driven cobots enable complicated welding solutions. To improve the capabilities of the welding trade, AI is always developing. Following are a few instances of recent advancements in AI for welding.

5.2 Enhancing the Welding Industry

To perform steady welding operations, accuracy and consistency is expected. Finding technology solutions is therefore important to support the human arm in doing jobs with even more intelligence. Robots and cobots have significantly improved welding technology above what was originally thought possible. Advancements will continue to be made at a rate that has never been witnessed before thanks to machine learning algorithms and advanced data availability. All of these developments are advancing the welding sector.

There is a considerable demand for existing welding professionals to undergo retraining to comprehend and utilize cobots. With the introduction of these interesting curricula in welding education by welding technology institutions, welding technology students and experienced welders can make full use of the opportunity to develop into qualified welding professionals. Their careers will reach greater heights thanks to their knowledge of these welding techniques and experience with cutting-edge welding systems, making them in-demand welding specialists in the sector.

By taking advantage of welding technology technician programs, operators can advance their careers. In addition to theory, they will learn welding from specialists in the field through hands-on training and innovative technological breakthroughs, including virtual reality (VR) systems in welding education and gamification strategies. This exceptional experience is sure to prepare operators for a career in welding in a way and to a much higher degree than robotic welding services. It will also help them become sought-after, qualified, and certified welding specialists. Therefore, these programs provide countless opportunities to prepare for and create a better, brighter, and more stable future in the career of their choice with prospects for guaranteed employment.

- Sharing data through Ethernet
  In Industry 4.0, every industrial machinery is Ethernet-capable, and data is shared with a single source for analysis. This analysis aids in the surveillance of welding operations. For instance, the data sent can be used to keep track of the welding parameters and proactively flag any potential anomalies. This improves trouble prediction capabilities for systems and lowers production interruptions.
- Sensor capabilities
  Welding robots are becoming more valuable thanks to sensors. Without sensor systems that allow for performance analysis, a robot/cobot cannot produce good results. There are numerous sensors, including touch, laser, vision, and through-arc. Each sensor can be employed following welding requirements and industrial needs. Sensor innovation is essential for a better knowledge of how to support continued industrial advances with welding's ongoing progress.
- Arc welding robots
  Earlier arc welding robots used two-pass systems; the first pass was used to learn the specifications of the seam.

The analysis, tracking, and welding was done during the second run. Recent technological advancements, however, enable systems to weld concurrently and evaluate the correct procedure required for an optimal weld.

- Spool welding robots
  Fabrication of pipe spools now accommodates robotic technologies. With the new technology, the SWR's arm can be equipped with features like cameras, robotic welding services, and machine learning algorithms. The camera records several weld images that can be used as a guide to learning how to weld properly. By using this technique, a neural network is created that can recognize a new workspace and independently set up its procedures. This makes it possible for welders to approach robotic solutions as tools and trustworthy teammates for completing challenging industrial projects.

Machine learning is an application of AI, which is defined as the data analysis that automates the construction of analytical models. As models are shown to fresh datasets, the iterative component of learning algorithms plays a crucial role. They can adjust themselves well on their own. The findings of experiments are produced by the analysis of earlier computations, which is efficient, reproducible, and dependable. As a result, several smart application protections have been made using machine learning to guard against threats, attacks, and unlawful activity.

Machine learning is adept at picking up knowledge without using programs or code. In the words of Arthur Samuel, machine learning is a discipline that pushes the ability of computers to study with no programming. In contrast, Tom M. Mitchell provided a widely cited and more formal explanation, saying that a computer program is said to learn from experience E concerning performance P and some class of tasks T, in such a way that performance P at task T increases on behalf of experience E. This explanation stands out for using machine learning, which is fundamentally more effective than cognitive processes. Even though machine learning is directly related to AI, it is not a novel technique. Computers are capable of carrying out a wide range of machine learning operations, including sorting, prediction, regression, feature extraction, classification, pattern recognition, clustering, etc. To produce data-driven judgments or predictions, these sophisticated machine algorithms structure a model based on prior sample inputs.

Modern industries, like Bosch's welding monitoring, have seen the great expansion of ML-based data analytical applications as a result of the development and enlargement of Industry 4.0 technology. This has improved the quality and efficiency of welding monitoring. Industrial ML is, however, impacted by ML's lack of accessibility to non-ML professionals' needs. As ML methods are frequently generated on the fly for particular issues, the inability of domain experts to comprehend ML approaches hinders the deployment of ML techniques in industry and the reuse of existing ML pipelines [4]. In order to overcome these difficulties, the authors suggest the use of executable knowledge graphs (KGs), which specifically encode ML solutions and knowledge. For ML experts and non-ML experts, KGs can serve as a common language, enhancing communication and increasing the transparency of ML techniques. Bosch put their technology to a comprehensive test utilizing an industrial use case, and the results were promising.

Additionally, machine learning offered good options for maintaining the security of numerous sophisticated systems. According to IFI CLAIMS Patent Services, the machine learning sector experienced a 34% increase in patents between 2013 and 2017 [5]. Furthermore, 60% of businesses worldwide employ various learning algorithms/processes for a range of uses. We have gone to great lengths in this chapter to present effective, sophisticated, and ground-breaking machine learning in welding technologies.

Three key ML practices at Bosch are visual data analytics, statistical data analysis, and ML analytics, which involve professionals from various backgrounds, such as organizers and welders. They communicate differently but work collaboratively on ML development.

They need to communicate openly about machine learning (ML) practice (knowledge, solution, possibilities, etc.) so that people who aren't ML experts can grasp it and have faith that ML used in powerful, heavy robots can ensure product quality and worker safety. Bosch also has stringent guidelines for recording and reporting ML initiatives for a subsequent evaluation or audit. Consequently, the ML development process and the created ML solutions, understanding, and insights must be expertly documented by the specialists.

Around ten years ago, autonomous trucks served as the foundation for the introduction of AI, ML, and some autonomous technologies in the mining sector. The mining industry benefits economically from artificial intelligence, machine learning, and autonomous technology through cost savings, increased productivity, less worker exposure to dangerous circumstances, uninterrupted production, and enhanced safety. The use of the above-mentioned technologies, however, runs into issues with the economy, finances, technology, labor force, and society [6].

5.3 Machine Learning Algorithm Types

Artificial intelligence's machine learning techniques are made up of a variety of methods, including reinforcement learning, unsupervised learning, semi-supervised learning, and supervised learning, that can be used in real-world situations to prevent fraud and identify potential threats to various applications [2]. According to the learning input/signal available to a learning system, machine learning is traditionally divided into several major types. The Figure 5.2 shows the basic types of the technique/algorithms.

- **Supervised learning**
  It is good for labeled input data. The most prevalent method of learning in machine learning is supervised learning, which is based on labeled examples where output is determined based on input. A supervised algorithm that uses historical data to predict future events is employed in a variety of applications. Two phases of supervised learning are testing and training.
- Unsupervised learning
  It is good for unlabeled input data. This approach to unsupervised learning lacks any labels. Unsupervised trades stand in contrast to data without historical labeling. This method of learning utilizes training data that is not labeled.
- Semi-supervised learning
  It is good for both labeled and unlabeled data. This method of learning is essential for jobs that are related to it, such as supervised learning approaches. For training, it employs both labeled and unlabeled data. Regression, classification, and prediction all require a semi-supervised learning approach. In general, it is a collection of supervised and unsupervised learning strategies.

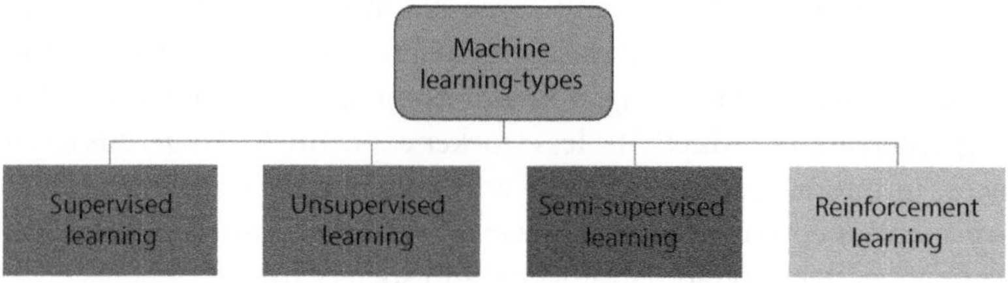

Figure 5.2 Algorithm types of machine learning.

- Reinforcement learning
  It is suitable where future action depends on current response. These learning strategies make use of trial-and-error notions. Based on the set of tuning restrictions, the problem's output has been projected. Agent, environment, and actions are the basic three elements.

5.4 Background of AI and ML

Artificial neural networks (ANN), expert systems, fuzzy systems, and the application of pattern recognition techniques in manufacturing can all be seen as successive steps in a process that began about three decades ago. Specially introduced and highlighted as viable options for handling complexity, changes, and disruptions in production systems are multi-strategy machine learning approaches and hybrid artificial intelligence (HAI). One of the most important characteristics of the current industrial systems is their increasing complexity. The systems function in a dynamic environment filled with uncertainty.

A tentative forecast by Hatvany and Nemes is the source of the term intelligent manufacturing system (IMS) [7]. It was described [8] as the following generation of manufacturing systems that, using the findings of AI research, were intended to, within certain bounds, address unexpected, unforeseeable challenges based on even insufficient and imprecise information The most popular definition of learning is attributed to Simon [9]. He said that learning is the process of making systemic changes that are adaptive in the sense that they enable the system to perform the same task—or tasks drawn from the same population—more successfully the following time.

New computer systems that not only generate, record, and retrieve information, but also digest and synthesize information into knowledge and accurately present this knowledge to support decision-making are required for advanced engineering automation [10]. It should be noted that intelligence and learning are closely related and that IMS must possess the capacity to learn [11].

However, artificial intelligence is a brand-new branch of technological research that studies and develops the concepts, procedures, tools, and software used to mimic, enhance, and supersede human intelligence. AI is credited with giving machines the ability to think and reason like humans do. Today, AI has a far broader meaning than it once had, making it a subject that cuts across many disciplines.

The goal of machine learning research is to make it possible for computers to mimic or replicate human learning processes and pick up new information and skills. Machine learning algorithms and processing systems create predictions mostly by finding hidden patterns in data. A significant area of AI is machine learning.

5.5 Weld Defects

Manufacturers want to steer clear of welding errors at any cost. When a robotic welder produces flaws during the welding process, the weld's integrity may be compromised, decreasing the product's quality.

The core of any manufacturing enterprise is welding. Traditionally, quality inspections are carried out in a different cell following welding. If any flaws are discovered throughout the quality control (QC) process, the assembly will be sent back to the welding cell to be fixed. There is a severe lack of qualified resources for both welding and QC, which leads to manual errors and greater costs and turnaround times for fixes. In addition, many QC processes are manual, making them vulnerable to these errors. To minimize delays, prevent material waste, and cut costs, it is essential to find any faults during the arc welding process as soon as possible.

Low accuracy of manual inspections, delay in detecting defects, and shortage of skilled resources are challenges in tracing the defects in welding technology.

One of the most prevalent welding defects is porosity, which is the presence of cavities in the weld metal brought on by the absorption of atmospheric gases (excess hydrogen, nitrogen, and oxygen) in the molten weld pool that escapes and leaves cavities upon cooling, potentially harming the corrosion and fatigue performance of the weld metal and making the welds less ductile and unable to pass inspection.

Factors causing porosity in welding are:

- Improper shielding of gas
- Improper welding process parameters
- Arc instability
- Presence of moisture
- Using longer arc and torch angles
- Deposited component variations
- Contamination of surfaces

As AI technology develops, manufacturers seek to use machine vision solutions to meet business issues, increase operational effectiveness, and enhance quality. This machine vision-based automated defect detection system attempts to address the costly, time-consuming issue of manual flaw detection in the robotic welding process. It enables manufacturers to spot defects early in the production process, whereas traditional manual inspection is a time-consuming technique that is inadequate to find flaws and depends on highly qualified inspectors, which results in production delays, material waste, and decreased efficiency.

To overcome their issues, increase operational effectiveness, and enhance quality, manufacturers are integrating machine vision technologies. These machine vision-based automated defect detection technologies enable businesses to identify flaws early in the manufacturing process and seeks to address the expensive, long-standing issue of manual defect identification in the robotic welding process.

5.6 Level of Weld Quality

The weld quality in CFRTPs can be divided into three categories: under, normal, and over welds. A typical weld is one that has an appropriate area (equal to or more than the nominal area) and has fibers pulled out of the polymer shattered through it. An over weld is a weld with voids or porosity. An under weld is a weld whose area is slightly less than the nominal area (horn tip area). The following Figure 5.3 depicts the under, normal, and over-weld looks in ultrasonic welding. Due to the striking differences between under, normal, and over-weld looks, the three levels can be distinguished visually.

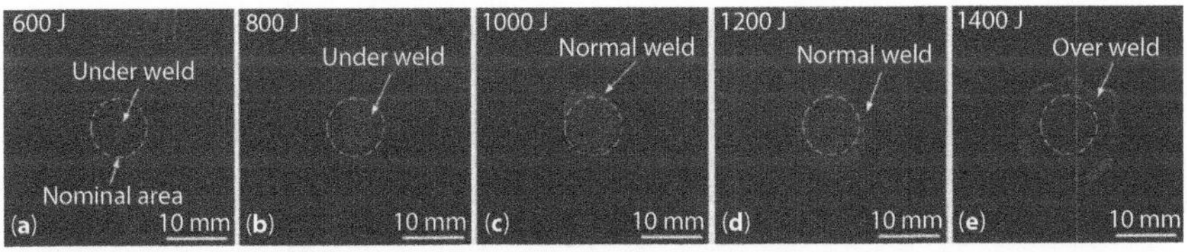

Figure 5.3 Various weld appearances under different energy values [12].

5.6.1 Mining Industry

The findings of interviews with some industry stakeholders are presented in the article by Hyder *et al.* [6], together with their perspectives on the risks, difficulties, advantages, and prospective effects of this cutting-edge technology. The essay also discusses their predictions for these technologies' future and outlines some of the procedures that must be taken for their successful adoption in this industry.

During welding operations, several metallurgical reactions and physical-chemical processes take place under the control of over 20 nonlinear variables, including the chemical makeup of the parent and filler materials, the dilution factor, heat energy, time, the design of the metallic structure, the welding order, the characteristics of the protective atmosphere, etc. Because of this, the analytical mathematical models used to describe welding phenomena are quite complex and have a narrow range of applicability due to beginning conditions, accuracy requirements, and applicability ranges for various material constants, etc. An ideal environment for AI applications is the correlation between the welding process parameters and the output data, such as the mechanical properties of the weld, the microstructural features in the deposited metal and HAZ, the behavior of the welded structure under load or under various working conditions, etc.

The content of published research work demonstrates the weight given to AI in welding as well as the range of offerings made by researchers using AI methods to address challenges and issues in welding. These difficulties include below par controlled welding settings and weld shape, which result in issues with the quality of the welded joint. Also included are case studies on the application and advancement of AI systems in the finish welding sector. The ability to forecast future scenarios for a 5 to 10-year duration period on the impact of AI on the welding industry throughout the Industry 4.0 era is provided by analyses of the findings. As a result of the changes brought on by AI, new technological, cost-effective, and societal policies will be required, along with modifications to educational curriculum and skill-building programs in the areas of sustainability and excellence of life. Both academics and businesses must take trends and scenarios into account, as these will influence how AI systems are researched and developed in the future.

Artificial intelligence systems are becoming more prevalent in our daily lives, but even more so in the cutting-edge technology of the present. When making decisions or controlling processes that are heavily defined by nonlinear factors, AI systems are the best options. The surroundings in which welding is done are well characterized by nonlinear characteristics such as the temperature at which a material's properties operate, process parameters and technological parameters, human factors, and others. Additionally, a software program created by the few Researchers for welding transformation diagrams, time temperature transformation (TTT) and continuous cooling transformation (CCT) diagrams, interpretation and implementation is described in the paper. AI and neural network analysis of data gathered from CCT scanned diagrams were used for this aim.

For more than 85% of products produced in the industrial sector, welding technologies are critical enabling technologies. About 22% of the workforce in Romania receives employment through the industry, which contributes 24.1% of the country's GDP (2019 national statistics). The International Federation of Robotics (IFR) indicated that the number of industrial robots increased by roughly 15% annually, and that by 2020 there will be an estimated 521 thousand industrial robots operating worldwide.

The study and classification of welding flaws using AI technologies consist of four steps: image collecting, image pre-processing, visual feature extraction, and data classification. An AI program's neural network is initially trained using hundreds or thousands of photos with various welding flaws. After that, when new, distinct photos are added to the network, the AI application can use ML algorithms to recognize and categorize the new welding flaws.

5.6.2 Challenges in ML Practice

Nevertheless, there are still some issues with ML practice in industry [13]. Modern industries frequently use interdisciplinary teams of professionals with varied backgrounds to complete ML projects. Since non-ML professionals didn't acquire the extensive training in ML that is frequently needed to comprehend the complex ML procedures and evaluate the ML outcomes, it can be difficult to make ML transparent to them [14]. Non-ML professionals must comprehend ML and have faith that its use in developing robots running on high electricity can guarantee product quality and worker safety. Additionally, in typical ML projects, the technical ML language used to explain the ML procedures, processes, handwritings, and judgments is heavily dependent on the author of the document. The lack of standardized descriptions and documentation of ML knowledge and solutions makes it difficult for subsequent reviews and retrospective comprehension of projects in large organizations like Bosch, which have tight reporting requirements for later audit and analysis.

Machine learning approaches were primarily used to examine the usage of artificial intelligence in the effective prediction of corrosion inhibitors [3].

Researchers employed the genetic algorithm-partial least squares (GA-PLS) and genetic algorithm-artificial neural network (GA-ANN) approaches to predict physiochemical and quantum variables pertinent to the surface absorption behavior of inhibitors. Using random forest (RF) and support vector machine (SVM) models, the prediction of benzimidazole derivatives as corrosion inhibitors was carried out. The gradient boosting machine (GBM), random forest (RF), and support vector machine are models for accurately predicting the corrosion inhibition efficacy of steel inhibitors. These techniques, help in predicting the pitting corrosion.

5.7 Case Studies

5.7.1 Use of AI Programs to Obtain CCT Welding Diagrams

The TTT diagrams are highly helpful in welding, but the CCT diagrams are particularly useful. Based on these figures, we can make an educated guess as to the microstructure and mechanical characteristics of the deposited metal in the HAZ under welding conditions. The various heat input energies used in welding processes, the dilution, which is typically between 10 and 35 percent, the chemical composition of the parent and filler materials, the characteristics of the protection atmosphere, the characteristics of the flux, etc., all contribute to the final chemical composition of the material that is deposited. The chemical composition of the substance has a significant impact on CCT diagrams; hence, we rarely have a CCT diagram for a certain composition. CCT diagrams can be created using AI systems for a wide variety of chemical compositions.

5.7.2 Use of Algorithms to Predict the Penetration Depth in Friction Stir Spot Welding

The use of these algorithms lowers the expense of experiments while also shortening their duration. The research work [15] focuses on the prediction of penetration depth utilizing supervised machine learning techniques, including the robust regression method, random forest algorithm, and support vector machines (SVM). The research project also emphasizes the use of image processing methods to identify the geometrical characteristics of weld production. Two components of the AA1230 aluminum alloy were fused using friction stir spot welding (FSSW). Rotational speed (in rpm), dwelling time (in seconds), and axial load (in KN) are the three input parameters that make up the dataset, which was used to train and evaluate machine learning models. With a coefficient of determination of 0.96, it was shown that the robust regression machine learning method performed better than the other algorithms.

Besides the work mentioned above, the AI methodology uses the AI/ML approaches in predicting and optimizing the process parameters of FSW [17] and classification of arc welding defects [18]. Therefore, high and economical expenditure can be obtained using the techniques summarized and reviewed in the research article by Eren *et al.* [19]. Figures 5.4 and 5.5 illustrate the complete idea of performing the friction stir welding (FSW) that incorporated the AI techniques.

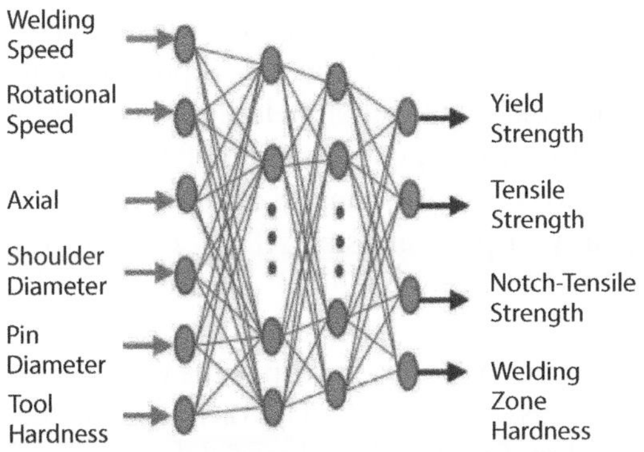

Figure 5.4 Structure of ANN model [16].

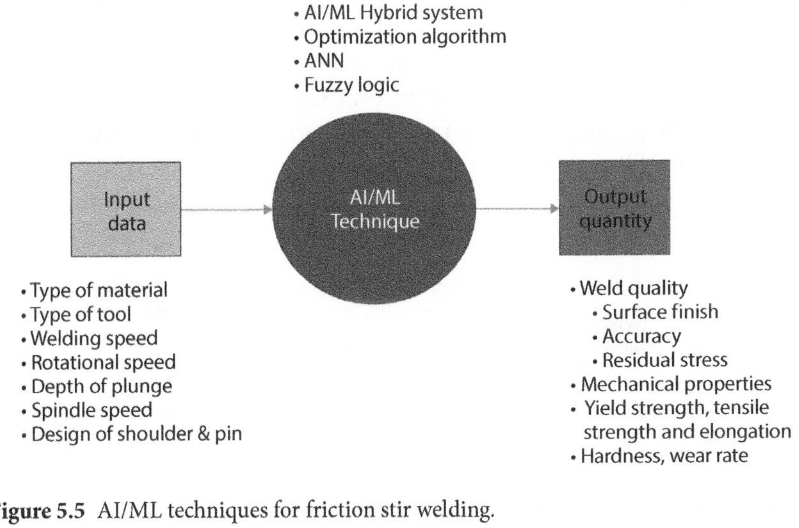

Figure 5.5 AI/ML techniques for friction stir welding.

To comprehend the impact of process variables on the mechanical properties of the friction stirred copper weld joint, different machine learning models are implemented [20]. The ANN predicted the main influencing parameter is ultimate tensile strength with an accuracy of 94%. The tool design variables, namely shoulder and pin diameter, have a significant impact on the joint strength.

5.8 Feasibility of Online Inspection of Ultrasonic Weld Quality

It is important to put multiple sensors on a welding machine to receive welding process signals to investigate weld quality utilizing AI technologies. For AI models, these signals serve as inputs. Due to the integrated monitoring systems that may gather welding process signatures in ultrasonic welders, ultrasonic composite welding offers a generic advantage for adopting AI technology. There is a dearth of literature on CFRTP ultrasonic welding weld quality inspection using AI. As a result, this work suggests an AI-based method for online CFRTP ultrasonic welding weld quality inspection [12].

A thorough and appropriate evaluation of the weld quality is made possible by the simultaneous employment of two artificial intelligence (AI) models, namely the random forest (RF) and artificial neural network (ANN), to predict the failure load and level of weld quality. The ANN and RF models are two well-known conventional AI techniques. In comparison to other AI technologies, ANN and RF are significantly more advanced, usable (mature programming), and suitable for industrial applications. Therefore, this research can aid in the creation of an intelligent, commercially viable weld-quality checking system for ultrasonic composite welding. This work investigates the prediction of the failure load and weld quality level during ultrasonic CRFTP welding using AI technologies, such as ANN and RF models. The findings of this work may be useful for additional commercial

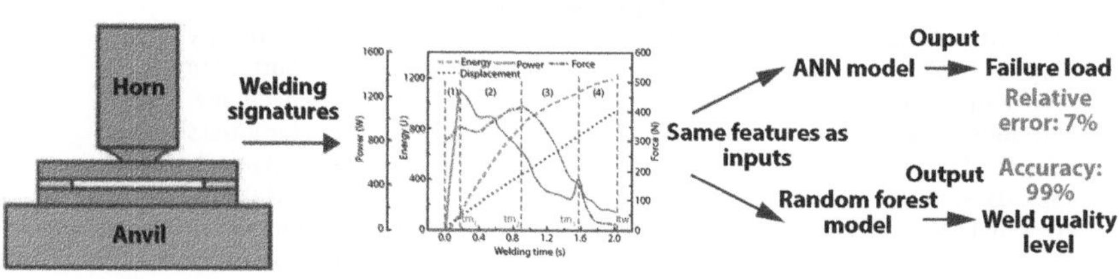

Figure 5.6 Graphical view of AI models used for ultrasonic welding quality inspection [12].

applications, including online quality monitoring of ultrasonic composite welding, as shown in Figure 5.6.

5.9 Conclusions

The use of AI in manufacturing, especially in welding, has the immense potential to revolutionize performance throughout the depth and breadth of operations, as major international manufacturers have begun to do. Only if manufacturers concentrate their efforts on generating the most value and then push the solutions to scale will this new industrial era recognize AI as a game-changer. A potential and essential prerequisite for improving mining productivity and maintaining environmental protection is the application of machine learning technology in the mining sector. Machine learning technologies can be utilized for a variety of activities, including choosing the best process flow diagram for mining operations, choosing the best complex of stripping and mining equipment, choosing the best mining operation planning, and monitoring the performance of mining equipment. Nevertheless, despite the potential of machine learning technology, this development is currently little understood and needs more investigation. Nevertheless, in this way AI and ML approaches appear to be effective tools to optimize the welding process parameters and can also predict the mechanical properties like tensile strength, elongation, fatigue life, and even microstructure and grain size.

References

1. Sarker, I.H., AI-based modeling: Techniques, applications and research issues towards automation, intelligent and smart systems. *SN Comput. Sci.*, 3, 2, 1–20, 2022, doi: 10.1007/s42979-022-01043-x.
2. Zhang, Y., Gao, X., Katayama, S., Weld appearance prediction with BP neural network improved by genetic algorithm during disk laser welding. *J. Manuf. Syst.*, 34, 53–59, Jan. 2015, doi: 10.1016/j.jmsy.2014.10.005.
3. Rajendran, D. *et al.*, Application of machine learning in corrosion inhibition study. *Mater. Prot.*, 63, 3, 280–290, 2022, doi: 10.5937/zasmat2203280R.
4. Zheng, Z., Zhou, B., Zhou, D., Soylu, A., Kharlamov, E., *Executable Knowledge Graph for Transparent Machine Learning in Welding Monitoring at Bosch*, vol. 1, Association for Computing Machinery, 2022, doi: 10.1145/3511808.3557512.
5. Zeba, S., Haque, A., Alhazmi, S.A., *Advanced Topics in Machine Learning*, pp. 1–16, Bentham Science Publishers, Singapore, 2022.

6. Hyder, Z., Siau, K., Nah, F., Artificial intelligence, machine learning, and autonomous technologies in mining industry. *J. Database Manage.*, 30, 2, 67–79, Apr. 2019, doi: 10.4018/JDM.2019040104.
7. Hatvany, J. and Nemes, L., Intelligent manufacturing systems—A tentative forecast. *IFAC Proc.*, 11, 1, 895–899, 1978, doi: 10.1016/S1474-6670(17)66031-2.
8. Hatvany, J. and Lettner, F.J., The efficient use of deficient knowledge. *CIRP Ann.*, 32, 1, 423–425, 1983, doi: 10.1016/S0007-8506(07)63433-7.
9. Simon, H.A., Why should machinnes learn?, in: *Machine Learning*, pp. 25–37, Elsevier, United States, 1983, doi: 10.1016/B978-0-08-051054-5.50006-6.
10. Lu, S.C.-Y., Machine learning approaches to knowledge synthesis and integration tasks for advanced engineering automation. *Comput. Ind.*, 15, 1–2, 105–120, Jan. 1990, doi: 10.1016/0166-3615(90)90088-7.
11. Monostori, L., Markus, A., Van Brussel, H., Westkämpfer, E., Machine learning approaches to manufacturing. *CIRP Ann.*, 45, 2, 675–712, 1996, doi: 10.1016/S0007-8506(18)30216-6.
12. Li, Y., Yu, B., Wang, B., Lee, T.H., Banu, M., Online quality inspection of ultrasonic composite welding by combining artificial intelligence technologies with welding process signatures. *Mater. Des.*, 194, 1–10, 2020, doi: 10.1016/j.matdes.2020.108912.
13. Zheng, Z. *et al.*, *Executable Knowledge Graphs for Machine Learning: A Bosch Case of Welding Monitoring*, pp. 791–809, 2022, doi: 10.1007/978-3-031-19433-7_45.
14. Saheb, S.H., Experimental study on influence of filler rods in gas tungsten arc welding. *AIP Conference Proceedings*, vol. 2166, AIP Publishing LLC, 2019.
15. Bahedh, A.S., Mishra, A., Al-Sabur, R., Jassim, A.K., Machine learning algorithms for prediction of penetration depth and geometrical analysis of weld in friction stir spot welding process. *Metall. Res. Technol.*, 119, 3, 1–11, 2022, doi: 10.1051/metal/2022032.
16. Yousif, Y.K., Daws, K.M., Kazem, B., II, Prediction of friction stir welding characteristic using neural network. *Jordan J. Mech. Ind. Eng.*, 2, 3, 1048–1058, 2008.
17. Moinuddin, S.Q. and Sharma, A., Arc stability and its impact on weld properties and microstructure in anti-phase synchronized twin-wire gas metal arc welding. *Mater. Des.*, 67, 293–302, 2015.
18. Moinuddin, S.Q., Hameed, S.S., Dewangan, A.K., Kumar, R., Kumari, S., A study on weld defects classification in gas metal arc welding process using machine learning techniques. *Mater. Today Proc.*, 43, 1, 623–628, 2020.
19. Eren, B., Guvenc, M.A., Mistikoglu, S., Artificial intelligence applications for friction stir welding: A review. *Met. Mater. Int.*, 27, 2, 193–219, Feb. 2021.
20. Thapliyal, S. and Mishra, A., Machine learning classification-based approach for mechanical properties of friction stir welding of copper. *Manuf. Lett.*, 29, 52–55, Aug. 2021, doi: 10.1016/j.mfglet.2021.05.010.

6
Digital Twin in Welding

Syam Kumar Chokka[1]*, M. Nagaraju[2] and K. Nagabushan Kumar[1]

[1]Keshav Memorial Engineering College, Hyderabad, India
[2]Circuits & Systems, Hyderabad, India

Abstract
A digital twin (DT) is created through simulation and other computerized digital technologies. It is a virtual version of a real-world thing, system, or process. In order to react to changes, enhance flexibility, optimize operations, refine quality, save time, decrease costs, and create value, a system or a process can be analyzed and replicated in real-world settings using a digital twin. In this chapter, an introduction to friction stir welding (FSW) is presented and the role of DT in quality control of the FSW process is discussed. An introduction to laser welding is also presented along with the DT's role in the production phase for the optimal production plan of laser welding.

Keywords: Digital twin, friction stir welding, laser welding, process optimization

6.1 Introduction

The change in production processes is referred to as an "industrial revolution." The Fourth Industrial Revolution, or Industry 4.0, is all about bringing the manufacturing process into the digital age. The traditional manufacturing processes are transitioning into smart manufacturing with the support of advancements in information technology such as cyber-physical systems (CPS), the internet of things (IoT), and artificial intelligence (AI). Digitalization or cyber-physical systems are an architectural framework that brings together the physical and virtual worlds, which creates new opportunities for substantial productivity and

**Corresponding author*: chokka.syamkumar@gmail.com

Syed Quadir Moinuddin, Shaik Himam Saheb, Ashok Kumar Dewangan, Murali Mohan Cheepu and S. Balamurugan (eds.) Automation in Welding Industry: Incorporating Artificial Intelligence, Machine Learning and Other Technologies, (91–110) © 2024 Scrivener Publishing LLC

effectiveness gains in complex manufacturing systems. Undoubtedly, achieving the fusion of cyber-physical systems is a crucial step towards the practical implementation of smart manufacturing. While CPS provides a framework and mechanism for the seamless interaction of physical and cyber components, its primary focus is on validating scientific principles rather than optimizing engineering applications in practice. The concept of DT and its accompanying models will revolutionize the current industrial landscape. It tries to refine the present concept of product design, manufacturing, and sales management. Applying DT on a shop floor performing manufacturing activities enables the identification of immediate data regarding the entities on the production floor, ongoing operations, and emerging faults. Thus, the ongoing procedures will be continuously visualized, and control can be exercised over them in the event of an error. In addition, it will allow engineers to simulate the system using data gathered in real time from sensors attached to the physical device, which will aid in predicting and preventing downtime. With the passage of time, the DT will gain intelligence by mimicking its physical counterpart and will have access to historical information that will enable it to predict how long it will be useful. All of these factors will ultimately result in a greater degree of machine availability by decreasing downtime and increasing production unit efficiency and profit. DTs offer a setting for examining the impact that deviations have on a system's performance in addition to monitoring and evaluating it. After a DT has been developed for a physical item or service, it is possible to project the errors or defects that will occur in the real world [1]. This enables the adoption of the appropriate adjustments to stop any errors or defects from occurring.

6.2 Friction Stir Welding

Welding is a fabrication method that joins materials by causing intense heat to melt the pieces together to form the physical bond. The materials joined are commonly metals or thermoplastics. Welding can be classified into two types [2]. Primarily as fusion welding that fuses the boundary of an element to the liquid phase, and later on condenses for the joining of the materials. Different welding processes of fusion welding are tungsten inert gas arc welding (TIG), laser beam welding (LBW), shield metal arc welding (SMAW), electron beam welding (EBW), etc. [2].

Secondarily, solid-phase welding heats the material above the recrystallization temperature or plasticizing phase (not beyond the melting point), and later on by applying pressure to combine both materials by quick diffusion at high temperatures. Fusion processes generally have eutectic phases and are frequently exposed to pores that influence the joining process's final characteristics. Additionally, the fusion procedure further dissolves the precipitates in the main matrix and reduces the actual strength by reinforcing materials from precipitation [2].

Friction stir welding (FSW) is one of the solid-state welding processes. The process was invented by The Welding Institute (TWI) and TWI Ltd. of Cambridge, England, patented it in 1991 [3]. It emerged as an extremely popular joining process for welding non-ferrous-based metals such as Cu, Al, and their alloys. Joining happens below the solidification temperature of the welded metal. Not only does FSW result in superior quality with high strength, but it is also cost-effective. During the process, non-generation fumes are additional predominant features of FSW.

The FSW process does not require any filler compound like conventional welding methods and is relatively easy to do. Processing speeds can be controlled by securing the work sample tightly. In addition, the process eliminates the unwanted intermetallic phase formation, which may have an impact on the properties of the joint or welded portion and efficiency. Also, the FSW process did not allow the formation of any kind of imperfections, such as porosity. It is, therefore, possible to use FSW comfortably to weld copper and its alloys [4].

The FSW process is an imitative method of traditional friction welding techniques. It provides the benefits of solid-state welding for generating lengthy butt as well as lap joints [5]. In this method, a revolving tool pin that is non-consumable having good wear-resistance gets stuck inside the space between the two specimens which are being joined. The shoulder creates a rigid connection with a top facet of the work specimen in such a way that, because of friction, heat is generated through the tool shoulder. The heat generated through friction softens the metal surface and pushes the tool to go forward along the weld center region [6]. The metal gets plasticized and moves across the joining line [7]. FSW is very much preferable for butt welds, as an extent of the pin approximation to the weld specimen thickness. The FSW process schematics are shown in Figure 6.1.

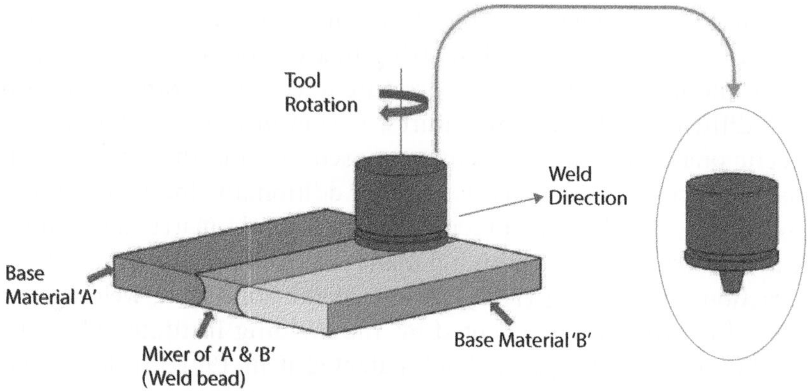

Figure 6.1 Schematic sketch of FSW process.

6.2.1 FSW Parameters

The optimal processing parameters must be chosen for any welding process in order to generate a high-quality weld joint. For the FSW, the most crucial process variables are:

(i) Rotational Speed (W)
The rotational speed mainly influences the mixing of two alloys by producing sufficient heat to sweep the deformed material from the advancing side to retrieving side during the welding process.
(ii) Welding Speed (V)
Welding speed mainly influences the time the alloy is exposed to high temperatures. Low welding speeds provide an escalation in the heat input because the rotating tool is subjected to more contact time with the materials, thereby generating more heat.

Numerous investigations have been taken up to scrutinize the outcome of joining speed and probe rotation upon the weldability of alloys, specifically of Mg. These criteria are crucial to producing superior-quality joints because they control the energy input and also the transfer of plastic metal. The energy contribution per unit extent is given by Eq. 6.1.

$$Heat\ Input = \frac{Q}{V} \tag{6.1}$$

where V is welding speed and Q is energy produced due to friction.

The energy produced due to friction rises with the probe's rate of rotation, yet not in the monotonic path, because the coefficient of friction at interlock also differs from the probe's rate of rotation. Hence, escalating the probe's rotation rate or de-escalating the joining speed impels a greater temperature and effortless transfer and improves the weld ability. This observation was uniform with each and every investigation undertaken previously [8, 9].

Investigations showed that, for a uniform joining speed, a reduced probe's rotation rate that led to the generation of internal voids caused by the frictional energy was not enough to encourage metal transfer. These imperfections can be eliminated by escalating the probe's rotation rate (W). At extremely high probe rotation rates, interior imperfections, a lacuna of bonding, and facet fissures commenced, which caused extra expulsion of the metal produced [10].

Investigations carried out at a uniform probe rotation rate displayed that escalating joining speed caused interior imperfections and lacuna in bonding, resulting in not enough metal transfer. Yan *et al.* [11] noticed that a lesser joining speed can give regulated dynamic recrystallization, encouraging fine-grain microstructure.

Gharacheh *et al.* [12] utilized the weight by volume ratio as operation criteria, and increasing the ratio has been observed to result in higher energy input, improved metal transfer, and a joint nugget that is both deeper and more extensive. The hardness escalated through escalating traverse speed. The ultimate tensile strength (UTS) was shown to decline as traverse speed increased over a certain limit, although the yield strength remained constant.

Gharacheh *et al.* observed that the tensile characteristics de-escalated as the W/V ratio increased. Escalating the probe rate of rotation results in an increase in strength, especially tensile strength. An escalation in traverse speed over a critical value results in decreasing ultimate tensile strength (UTS), whereas yield strength was observed to be unchanged.

For FSW of Mg alloys [13–15], modern investigations demonstrated that the weld quality was sensitive to the rate of rotation of the probe and traverse speed. Nakata *et al.* [16] showed that the FSW of the square butt was carried out flourishingly by utilizing a narrow scale of FSW criteria with huge probe rates of rotation and reduced traverse speeds. Larger probe traverse speeds and lesser rates of rotation than that of optimum criteria permitted the origination of interior imperfections caused by lacuna in bonding. FSW of Mg alloy has been found better between 800 to 1600 rpm probe rotation rate and 50 to 500 mm/min [17–20].

(iii) Tool Tilt Angle

The angle at which the tool is positioned in relation to the work surface is called the tilt angle, which is crucial to the quality of the welded blank. When the tilt angle is small, a gap is created between the tool and the blanks, which can make it easier to remove the material from the tool's shoulder. However, if the tilt angle is too high, the gap increases, causing the deformed material to escape from the shoulder of the tool, resulting in defects in the weldment. The tool's forging force enables homogenized material flow in the weld region, resulting in better weld zone properties. Therefore, selecting the appropriate tilt angle is critical for obtaining high-quality weldments.

A satisfactory angle of tilt for the probe must be chosen for optimum productivity of the probe. It predominantly relies on the geometry of the shoulder. It's traditionally set to 3° for a plain shoulder, further altered up to 1.5° for a concave shoulder, and 0° to 1° for a scroll shoulder [21].

(iv) Welding Pressure

In a study conducted by Zhang *et al.* [15], the effect of joining pressure on the quality of welds was examined while maintaining a constant tool travel speed and rotation speed. The results indicated that the joining pressure had a significant impact on the amount of heat generated by friction. Increasing the joining pressure quickly led to higher-quality welds, whereas low pressure resulted in the formation of pores [22].

(v) Insertion Depth

When utilizing probe shoulders of even sizes, it is essential to regulate the depth of insertion correctly. Excessive depth can result in a significant amount of flash generation, which can cause local thinning of the joined plates due to the shoulder perforating through the metal. On the other hand, insufficient depth can lead to incomplete mixing and the formation of surface grooves due to no contact between the shoulder and specimen surface [23].

(vi) Preheating or Cooling

The materials with a higher melting point, such as Ti and steel, or high thermal conductivity like Cu, should be preheated primarily, as the energy generated by the operation might not be enough. When joining materials with lower melting points, such as Mg and Al, cooling can play a vital role in preventing the enlargement of grains and the dissolution of precipitates [24].

6.3 Defects in Friction Stir Welding

Wayne *et al.* categorized the 3 types of defects or flaws that arise in FSW, namely lack of penetration, joint line remnants, and voids. Imperfections are furthermore categorized as maintained by codes into tolerable and intolerable imperfections. Imperfections inside the joint can be produced if inappropriate welding criteria were applied. The usage of the spoiled tool-tip, a tiny tool, a low or high rate of rotation, insufficient traversing speed, and lesser pressure can tend to the unacceptable quality of the weldment [25–28]. W. Abreast reviewed the possible imperfections/defects caused due to the improper regulation of the FSW criteria, as displayed in Figure 6.2. The welding parameters, such as rotation rate (W) vs friction stir welding speed (V), manifest the operative method in attaining a suitable weld in the case of Al alloys. Minor alterations in the speed of welding or rotation speed may generate imperfections which include lack of penetration, wormhole flaw, nugget collapse, lack of fusion, root flaw imperfection, scalloping, etc., normally observed in the metallographic investigations of the FSW microstructures [26].

(i) Voids

This class of imperfections is produced within the weld when there is a huge traverse speed, very low rotation speed [27–30], inappropriate pressure [31], as well as improper joint gap [31, 32]. Applying a lesser shoulder may also tend to lack metal transfer. Normally, the void origin is seen on the advancing side [25]. If the correct welding pressure is not used, the forging behavior will be quite different from the probe shoulder in attaining complete joining [31]. Under the combination of high traversing speeds and low probe rotation rates during FSW, the metal requires less work per unit

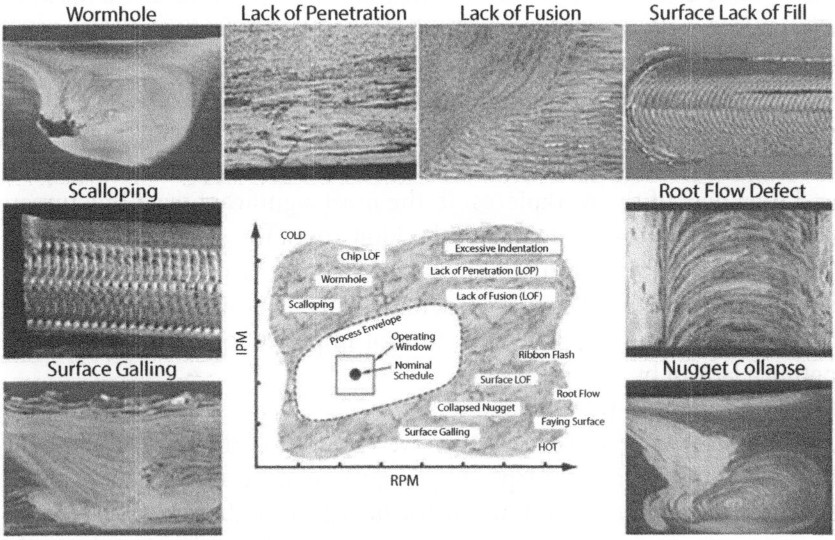

Figure 6.2 Characteristic defect types that occur with different FSW parameters [25].

of joint length, meaning fewer probe rotations per mm. However, under such parameters, in the plastically deformed metal, the temperature may not reach a high enough level [30]. Usually, voids have variable sizes and are oriented at any angle, and don't have any specific morphology.

(ii) Joint Line Remnants

Non-continuous regions can form in FSW joints due to inappropriate plastic deformation of the metal, which is caused by the absence of the necessary pressure to break down the metal. This can also result from inadequate dispersion of oxides, which can be attributed to poor surface cleaning and preheat treatment that leads to improper bonding [33]. The non-continuity in FSW joints has traditionally been observed to occur either at the joint's root or the interface, and the remnants of the joint line are commonly known as lazy S, a zigzag line, or kissing bond, and they should be diagnosed with a lot of care during the metallographic analysis, destructive inspection utilizing bend inspection and/or in worse parameters, can be noticed in the joint root by visual inspection [34]. It may also be an oxide that gets accumulated within the joint line. Metallographic studies can reveal oxide particles scattered across the actual joint line semi-continuously. The morphology of oxide particles plays a crucial role in determining the effectiveness of the structure coherence and the severity of this flaw [31, 34, 35]. Employing huge traverse speed and a shoulder with large diameter, as well as inappropriate probe arrangement with the weld line, may tend to the creation of such imperfections. Suitable regulation of the welding criteria and oxides elimination through the facet via machining, preliminarily to joining can diminish such imperfections [34].

(iii) Lack of Penetration/Root Flaw

To avoid root imperfections and insufficient penetration observed in the weld line, it is crucial to use properly designed and well-maintained tools, ensure proper depth of plunge, and carefully plan the joint arrangement and thickness of the workpieces. In the most significant weld line imperfections are habitually situated at the joint root. The suitable penetration depth of the probe is required to guarantee that stirring takes place above the complete plate thickness. A lacuna in precision in whichever of the over-considered conditions tends to root imperfection formation, designating a lack of binding [36].

(iv) Other Flaw Types

The characteristics of the flash type were found on the top facet, usually because of the enormous depth of plunges. To achieve adequate penetration, particularly in the joint where the fit is poor, additional flash features were sometimes included. Despite the recurrent discussions on the topic, local melting in FSW remains a challenging issue that requires further investigation and development of new techniques to overcome it. In addition, the FSW of 7050-T7451, produced at TWI [37], displayed the TMAZ area below the sample, providing the appropriate liquidation confirmation. In addition, the scarcity of phenomenon occurring in FSW somewhat in the scrutiny of Al arc welded joints, as per the various cases examined regarding liquation fissuring. Johnson [38] manifested liquidation happening in the TMAZ section during the FSW alloy of ZK60 Mg, which can be removed by optimizing FSW liquation, as investigated by Sato *et al.* [39]. Throughout the non-similar AA 1050 to Mg alloy FSW, the cause of intermetallic melting ($Mg_{17}Al_{12}$) process, the temperature passes through the secondary melting point in the Mg alloy during the FSW method.

6.3.1 DT for FSW

Researchers are developing many strategies for the monitoring of the FSW process for weld defects, spindle speed, feed, forces acting, etc. The absence of a comprehensive framework that can oversee the FSW procedure in conjunction with the equipment and propose corrective actions in real time has been identified, and the present section describes the DT model created by Rohan Basu Roy and his team to supervise the FSW apparatus [40]. The real-time monitoring provided by the cloud-based DT enhances the FSW device's operational efficiency and enables prompt identification and resolution of any issues. It processes and analyzes sensory data received as input before displaying important information about the machine and process on a dashboard in real time. Predictions of weld quality, machine health, and correction actions are included in the information. Real-time feedback from the user to the twin's proposal is transmitted back to the FSW machine.

Rohan Basu Roy *et al.* conducted experiments on FSW in order to show the effect of tool health on joint strength. The work pieces are sheets of AA6061 aluminum alloy, which are 3 mm thick. The choice of H13 tool steel was made as tool due to its high heat resistance, toughness, and ability to maintain its hardness even at elevated temperatures. Five distinct tools were chosen for the investigation, including one with weld material stuck on it, one without a pin, one with a partially damaged pin, one shattered, and one in good shape (healthy condition) with identical dimensions as shown in Figure 6.3. These five tools were used to create the welds at 1200 rpm tool rotation, 50 mm/min welding speed, 2° tilt angle, and 0.1 mm plunge depth. The weldments fabricated with different health conditions of

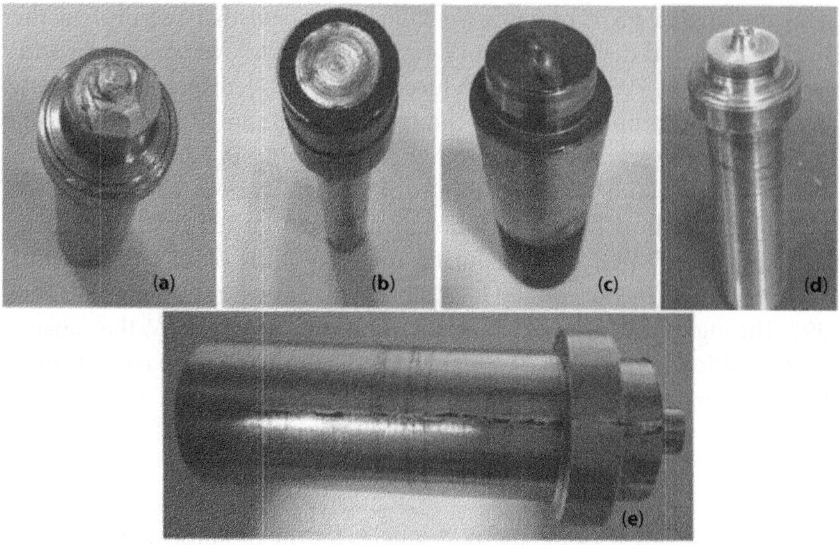

Figure 6.3 Tool profiles: (a) weld material adhered to the tool; (b) pinless tool; (c) tool with half-damaged pin; (d) standard tool; (e) cracked tool [40].

the tool can be seen in Figure 6.4. In order to deploy DT, different sensors are attached to monitor the oil level, weld tool RPM, weld velocity, force and power sensors, turbidity, temperature, and flow rate. The designed DT's workflow can be seen in Figure 6.5. The twin for the well-being and optimal output level of the FSW machine has been achieved through four distinct phases of work:

1. **Data acquisition phase:** The data is collected from all sensors attached to the FSW machine.
2. **Fault detection phase:** The twin predicts the potential flaws or errors that could arise in the FSW machine. Several machine learning and signal processing approaches are used to detect faults in signals obtained from the FSW process.
3. **Suggestion phase:** Once the problem has been located or identified, the twin proposes remedies to enhance the welding quality and maintain the well-being of the FSW machine components. The suggestion may be given as voice output or through a graphical user interface (GUI).
4. **Cooperation phase:** Based on the suggestion given, the working parameters were varied and the optimal output will be obtained. That is, in order to reduce overall health damage

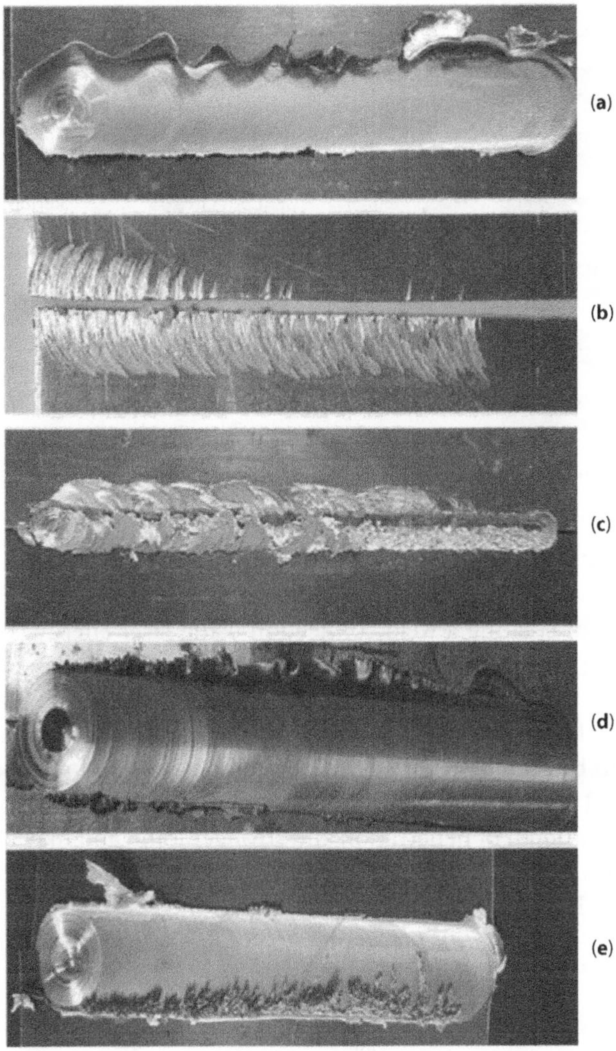

Figure 6.4 Welded joints with different tool health conditions: (a) weld material adhered to the tool; (b) pinless tool; (c) tool with half-damaged pin; (d) standard tool; (e) cracked tool [40].

and maximize output level, the workload is allocated across different equipment in the industry through optimization. This approach is based on the principle of preventive maintenance, where regular and consistent machine operation can help to identify potential issues early on and minimize the risk of costly downtime.

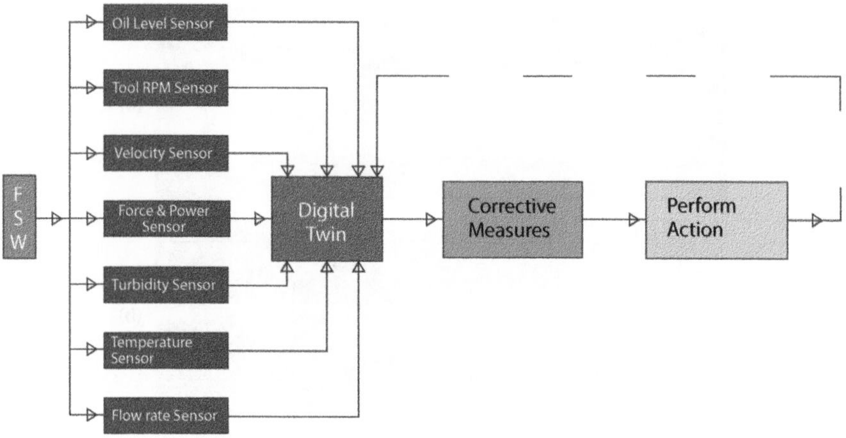

Figure 6.5 Developed DT workflow [40].

6.4 Laser Welding

The process of creating a weld connection using laser energy is known as laser welding (LW), also known as laser beam welding. The laser light from the source is diverted to the work piece through a system of glass lenses, mirrors, or a fiber-optic cable. A schematic representation of the laser beam welding can be seen in Figure 6.6. This method is a good replacement for conventional resistance spot welding as it provides the smallest weld zone with a greater depth of penetration and stronger joint, and may not require the other side of the material [41]. The LW is of two types: Heat conduction welding and Keyhole or Deep penetration welding.

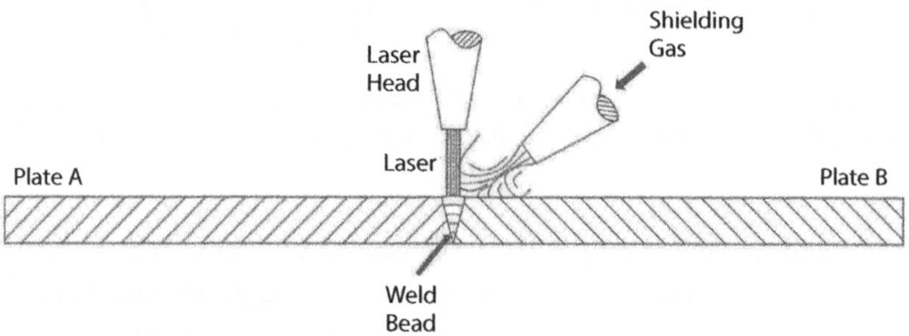

Figure 6.6 Schematic representation of laser weld.

6.4.1 Heat Conduction Welding

Heat conduction welding (HCW) utilizes low-intensity lasers or higher weld speeds. It is a process in which the energy is only transferred to the work piece via heat conduction. The material's surface is quickly heated to its melting point, and thus the laser beam is absorbed only at the material's surface rather than penetrating through the material, as depicted in Figure 6.7(a). Due to the surface tension-induced fluid flow within the weld pool, these welds often have a high width-to-depth ratio, which is typically governed by the thermal conduction. As the temperature of the weld zone increases, the surface tension of the molten metal flows outwards and increases the width of the weld [42]. The depth of the weld can be controlled by adjusting the speed of the weld and pulsation energy. Typically, materials with thicknesses less than 1 mm are welded using this method at energy densities around 105 W/cm2 and laser powers in the range of hundreds of watts.

6.4.2 Deep Penetration or Keyhole Welding

The deep penetration method is used where thicker and stronger joints are required. In this, the energy source is used to heat the material to its vaporization temperature (it can go up to 10,000K). Through the use of a high-energy laser beam during the welding process, the metal on the workpiece is vaporized, resulting in the creation of a hole or keyhole. The formation of a keyhole during laser welding is a crucial aspect that facilitates the penetration of the laser beam into the metal and creates a narrow, deep melt pool as shown in Figure 6.7(b). The formation of the keyhole results in numerous reflections inside the hole, thereby enhancing the laser beam's

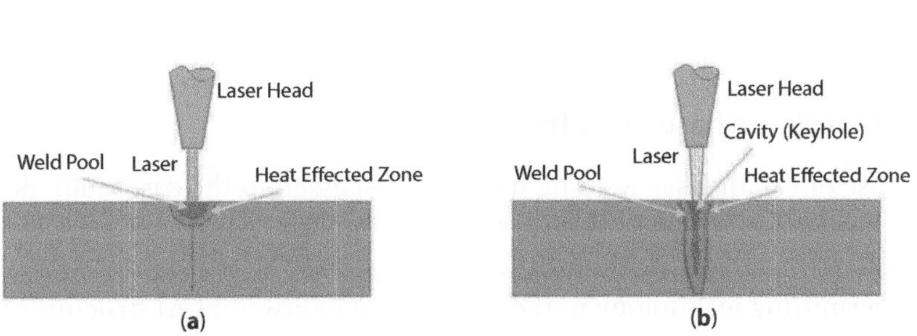

Figure 6.7 Penetration depth for (a) conductive welding and (b) keyhole welding.

absorption by the metal. Welding can be accomplished by either rotating the joint concerning the laser beam or by traversing the keyhole along the joint to be welded. Surface tension plays a vital role in the process, where the molten material at the leading edge of the keyhole flows around the cavity to the back and solidifies to form the weld. Only a fraction of the absorbed energy typically between 0.5 and 0.8 causes metal to melt; the remainder is lost through thermal conduction in the base metal, while the rest is radiated or convected within the weld pool [43, 44]. Typically, these welds are done at energy densities on the order of 10^6 to 10^7 W/cm^{2,} and laser powers on the order of kilowatts. This method is preferable for materials with greater than 1-mm thickness.

6.4.3 Weld Process Parameters

Various process parameters have an impact on the quality, size, and other characteristics of laser welds. Both pulsed and continuous wave (CW) lasers were employed during the studies. Pulsed lasers generate a sequence of pulses with specific pulse width and frequency until stopped, while CW lasers emit a constant laser beam. For CW lasers, several factors, such as laser power, beam size and shape, focal plane location, power density, wavelength, beam divergence, and intensity distribution, can influence the laser beam. Pulsed lasers have additional parameters like pulse length, pulse energy, pulse repetition rate, mean laser power, average peak power, pulse shape, and welding speed, welding time, and length of the weld. Material properties, such as melting temperature, thickness, heat capacity, and surface reflectivity, are also significant considerations that affect the welding process. The features of the generated melted weld pool depend on the material's heat capacity and flow characteristics. Other considerations include the type of shielding gas used, flow rate, gas angle, and nozzle designs.

6.4.4 DT for Laser Welding

The use of DT in laser welding has been discussed in the case study done by Franciosa *et al.* [40]. In this study, aluminum (Al) doors are welded using a remote laser welding (RLW) technique. RLW is regarded as a crucial permitting technology in the assembly of lightweight Al structures for automobiles. Non-contact and single-sided joining have several benefits over tactile welding, including faster welding, a smaller heat affected zone, lower weight, and lower operational costs. Given that one head may weld numerous items, it offers considerable versatility. However, difficulties choosing process parameters related to flaws (hot cracking, pores, or other significant faults) and sensitivity to product and process uncertainties develop throughout the new production introduction (NPI) phase in Al assemblies using RLW.

The DT adopted for this process is divided into three phases: concept stage, scale-up stage, and production pilot stage. As these phases are required to consider the implementation of a closed loop in process (CLIP) system as part of the DT, the concept stage (S1) of the NPI begins with the specification of the requirements for the product and the process as well as the identification of workable sets of the design configurations. The following scale-up stage (S2) involves the comprehensive design of the product and process, as well as the overall system prototyping utilizing pre-production equipment. Based on a small number (a few tens) of physically representative products, it improves the parameters and engineers the process. At (S3), the production pilot stage, a full-scale manufacturing system is put into place at the manufacturing facility to physically validate design requirements and assess the correctness of the process. Pre-volume production, the start of production, and full production come next. This research is concentrated on the initial three stages, namely S1 to S3, as these are critical steps that must be completed before the commencement of mass production. These stages are essential to understand and develop the CLIP system, which has been integrated as part of the digital twin. In order to produce parts that are almost defect-free, the current study uses a structured CLIP quality control system. In order to meet predetermined quality criteria, the overall structure for CLIP is shown in Figure 6.8 and is based on two main streams: process monitoring (forward process) and process control and adjustment (feedback process). Gap Bridging Loop (QL [1]) and Weld Quality Loop (QL [2]), which aim to control the integrity of the weld quality, such as seams roughness, penetration, convexity/concavity, etc., are two quality loops that have been found. In reality, any problems left unresolved at stages S1 through S3 will result in engineering revisions that will postpone the introduction of the product as well as a considerable cost increase. Most engineering modifications required for implementing RLW pertain to adjusting clamps, choosing and configuring laser parameters, and building a robot program that is collision-free and operates within the desired cycle time. For example, it can take more than two weeks to manually set the clamps for a door assembly fixture after design release, and up to four weeks to develop a workable process window that meets all joint criteria. Additionally, it may take up to four weeks to create a collision-free robot program that

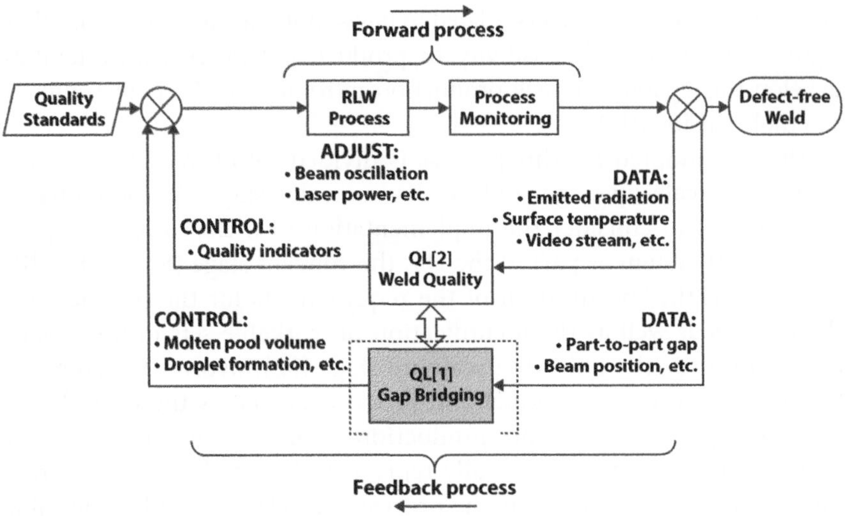

Figure 6.8 Closed-loop quality control system [40].

operates within the desired cycle time. In order to save time the DT model is first implemented in the process in virtual mode. Based on the feedback from the loops QL [1] and QL [2], the necessary actions will be implemented in the real-time environment. This makes the difference in performance between the system with DT and without DT.

6.5 Summary

The digital twin is a virtual illustration of the physical model that mimics actions, behaviors, and alterations in the real world. To create a thorough, intelligent digital twin, the relevant methods and technologies must be combined due to the diversity, complexity, and volume of data and information present in manufacturing processes. This chapter presented the basics of the friction stir welding process and laser welding process, and the application of DT for friction stir welding and laser welding with a case study.

References

1. Franciosa, P., Sokolov, M., Sinha, S., Sun, T., Ceglarek, D., Deep learning enhanced digital twin for closed-loop in-process quality improvement. *CIRP Ann.*, 69, 1, 369–372, 2020.

2. Marya, M., Edwards, G., Marya, S., Olson, D.L., Fundamentals in the fusion welding of magnesium and its alloys. *Proceedings of the Seventh JWS International Symposium*, Kobe, pp. 597–602, 2001.
3. W.M. Thomas, Improvements relating to friction welding. European Patent Specifications 0615 48 B1, 1995.
4. Ouyang, J., Yarrapareddy, E., Kovacevic, R., Microstructural evolution in the friction stir welded 6061 aluminum alloy (T6-temper condition) to copper. *J. Mater. Process. Technol.*, 172, 110–122, 2006.
5. Dawes, C.J., Woodward, R., Leroy, C., *Friction Stir Welding-Training in Aluminium Application Technologies*, TALAT Lecture 4410, TWI, 1999.
6. Esmaeili, A., Besharati Givi, M.K., Rajani, H.R.Z., A metallurgical and mechanical study on dissimilar Friction Stir welding of aluminum 1050 to brass (CuZn30). *Mater. Sci. Eng. A*, 528, 23, 7093–7102, 2011.
7. Bakesh, H., Benjamin, D., Kirkpatrick, C.W., *Metals Handbook*, vol. 2, pp. 3–23, ASM Metals, Park, OH, 1979.
8. Xunhong, W. and Kuaishe, W., Microstructure and properties of friction stir butt-welded AZ31 magnesium alloy. *Mater. Sci. Eng A*, 431, 117, 2006.
9. Johnson, R., Friction stir welding of magnesium alloys. *Indian Foundary J.*, 48, 37, 2002.
10. Johnson, R., Friction stir welding of magnesium alloys. *Materials Science Forum*, vol. 419, Trans Tech Publications Ltd., p. 370, 2003.
11. Yan, M., Wang, C., Sui, X., Liu, J., Lu, Y., Hao, J., Liu, W., Effect of substrate rotational speed during deposition on the microstructure, mechanical and tribological properties of aC: Ta coatings. *Ceram. Int.*, 49, 7, 10722–10730, 2023.
12. Gharacheh, M.A., Kokabi, A.H., Daneshi, G.H., Shalchi, B., Sarrafi, R., The influence of the ratio of "rotational speed/traverse speed" (ω/v) on mechanical properties of AZ31 friction stir welds. *Int. J. Mach. Tools Manuf.*, 46, 15, 1983–1987, 2006.
13. Esparza, J.A., Davis, W.C., Murr, L.E., Microstructure-property studies in friction-stir welded, thixomolded magnesium alloy AM60. *J. Mater. Sci.*, 38, 5, 941–952, 2003.
14. Esparza, J.A., Davis, W.C., Trillo, E.A., Lawrence, E.M., Friction-stir welding of magnesium alloy AZ31B. *J. Mater. Sci. Lett.*, 21, 917–920, 2002.
15. Zhang, H., Lin, S.B., Wu, L., Feng, J.C., Ma, S.L., Defects formation procedure and mathematic model for defect free friction stir welding of magnesium alloy. *Mater. Des.*, 27, 9, 805–809, 2006.
16. Nakata, K., Kim, Y.G., Ushio, M., Friction Stir Welding of Mg-Al-Zn alloys (Physics, Processes, Instruments & Measurements). *Trans. JWRI*, 31, 2, 141–146, 2002.
17. Lee, W.B., Yeon, Y.M., Kim, S.K., Jung, S.B., Microstructure and mechanical properties of friction stir welded AZ31 Mg alloy. *Proc. Magnesium Technology*, vol. 21, p. 17, 2002.

18. Zettler, R., Blanco, A.C., dos Santos, J.F., Marya, S., The effect of process parameters and tool geometry on thermal field development and weld formation in friction stir welding of the alloys AZ31 and AZ61. *Essential Readings in Magnesium Technology*, 529–543, 2016.
19. Threadgill, P.L., *Friction Stir Welds in Aluminium Alloys-Preliminary Microstructural Assessment*, pp. 30–33, TWI Bulletin, United Kingdom, 1997.
20. Norman, A.F., Brough, I., Prangnell, P.B., High resolution EBSD analysis of the grain structure in an AA2024 friction stir weld. *Mater. Sci. Forum*, 331, 1718, 2000.
21. Karlsen, M., Tangen, S., Hjelen, J., Friggard, O., Grong, O., Advances in FSW. *Proceedings of III International Symposium on Friction Stir Welding*, Kobe, Japan, Sept. 2001.
22. Lee, W.B., Kim, J.W., Yeon, Y.M., Jung, S.B., The joint characteristics of friction stir welded AZ91D magnesium alloy. *Mater. Trans.*, 44, 5, 917–923, 2003.
23. Nakata, K., Inoki, S., Nagano, Y., Hashimoto, T., Johgan, S., Ushio, M., Friction stir welding of AZ91D thixomolded sheet. *Proceedings of the Third International Symposium on Friction Stir Welding*, Kobe, Japan, September 2001.
24. Lee, W.B., Yeon, Y.M., Jung, S.B., Joint properties of friction stir welded AZ31B–H24 magnesium alloy. *Mater. Sci. Technol.*, 19, 6, 785–790, 2003.
25. Yang, B., Yan, J., Sutton, M.A., Reynols, A.P., Residual stress and microstructure effects on fatigue crack growth in AA2050 friction stir welds. *Mater. Sci. Eng. A*, 1, 364, 2004.
26. Mishra, R.S. and Mahoney., M.W., *Friction Stir Welding and Processing*, ASM International, The Materials Information Society, Material Park, Ohio, 2007.
27. Fratini, L. and Gianluca, B., CDRX modelling in friction stir welding of aluminium alloys. *Int. J. Mach. Tools Manuf.*, 45, 10, 1188–1194, 2005.
28. Guerra, M., Schmidt, C., McClure, J.C., Murr, L.E., Nunes, A.C., Flow patterns during friction stir welding. *Mater. Charact.*, 49, 2, 95–101, 2002.
29. Hashimoto, T., Jyogan, S., Nakada, K., Kim, Y.G., Ushio, M., FSW joints of high strength aluminum alloy. *Proceedings of the First International Symposium on Friction Stir Welding*, CA, USA, TWI Ltd, pp. Paper No. S9–P3, 1999.
30. Sato, Y.S., Urata, M., Kokawa, H., Parameters controlling microstructure and hardness during friction-stir welding of precipitation-hardenable aluminum alloy 6063. *Metall. Mater. Trans. A*, 33, 3, 625–635, 2002.
31. Leonard, A.J. and Lockyer, S.A., Flaws in friction stir welds. *4th International Symposium on Friction Stir Welding*, USA, 2003.
32. Christner, B.K. and Sylva, G.D., Friction stir weld development for aerospace applications. *Proceedings of ICAWT*, pp. 311–320, 1996.
33. Dickerson, T., Shi, Q., Shercliff, H.R., Validation of friction stir welding process models. *4th International Symposium on Friction Stir Welding*, USA, 2003.

34. Okamura, H.K., Aota, M., Sakamoto, M.E., Ikeuchi, K., Behaviour of oxides during friction stir welding of aluminium alloy and their effect on its mechanical properties. *Weld. Int.*, 16, 4, 266–275, 2002.
35. Palm, F., Henneboehle, U., Erofeev, V., Karpuchin, E., Zaitzev, O., Improved verification of FSW-process modelling relating to the origin of material plasticity. *4th International Symposium on Friction Stir Welding*, TWI Ltd., Metz, France, 2004.
36. Zhou, C., Yang, X., Luan, G., Effect of oxide array on the fatigue property of friction stir welds. *Scr. Mater.*, 54, 8, 1515–1520, 2006.
37. Lemos, G.V.B., Hanke, S., Dos Santos, J.F., L. Reguly, B.A., Strohaecker, T.R., Progress in friction stir welding of Ni alloys. *Sci. Technol. Weld. Join.*, 22, 8, 1–15, 2017.
38. Konkol, P.J., Mathers, J.A., Johnson, R., Pickens, J.R., Friction stir welding of HSLA-65 steel for shipbuilding. *J. Ship Prod.*, 19, 03, 159–164, 2003.
39. Sato, Y.S., Park, S.H.C., Michiuchi, M., Kokawa, H., Constitutional liquation during dissimilar friction stir welding of Al and Mg alloys. *Scr. Mater.*, 50, 9, 1233–1236, 2004.
40. Roy, R.B., Mishra, D., Pal, S.K., Chakravarty, T., Panda, S., Chandra, M.G., Pal, A., Misra, P., Chakravarty, D., Misra, S., Digital twin: Current scenario and a case study on a manufacturing process. *Int. J. Adv. Manuf. Technol.*, 107, 9, 3691–3714, 2020.
41. Franciosa, P., Serino, A., Botros, R.A., Ceglarek, D., Closed-loop gap bridging control for remote laser welding of aluminium components based on first principle energy and mass balance. *J. Laser Appl.*, 31, 2, 2019.
42. Yang, Y.S. and Lee, S.H., A study on the joining strength of laser spot welding for automotive applications. *J. Mater. Process. Technol.*, 94, 3, 151–156, 1999.
43. Graham, M.P., Hirak, D.M., Kerr, H.W., Weckman, D.C., Nd: YAG laser welding of coated sheet steel. *J. Laser Appl.*, 6, 4, 212–222, 1994.
44. Chiang, S. and Albright, C.E., The limit of joint penetration in high energy density beam welding. *Weld. J. New York*, 72, 1993, 1993.

7

IoT in Welding Industries

Harisivasri Phanindra K.[1]*, S. Venukumar[2], Muralimohan Cheepu[3] and Venkata Charan Kantumuchu[4]

[1]Department of Mechanical Engineering, Vel Tech Rangarajan Dr. Sagunthala R&D Institute of Science and Technology, Avadi, Chennai, Tamil Nadu, India
[2]Department of Mechanical Engineering, Vardhaman College of Engineering, Telangana, India
[3]STARWELDS Inc., Busan, Republic of Korea
[4]Electrex Inc., Hutchinson, Kansas, USA

Abstract
Due to rapid industrialization, the internet of things (IoT) has been introduced into the welding process. The four layers of the IoT system include the physical resource layer, the industrial network layer (sensors at work locations), the cloud layer, and the layer for supervision and control terminals. This chapter discusses the use of IoT for better quality management as per ISO 3834, along with suitable examples for arc quality management and molten metal temperature sensing systems for welding operations and monitoring of submerged arc welding processes. This chapter also discusses the critical hazards facing welders in confined spaces and hot work operations and IoT-based solutions to mitigate the risks presented by them.

***Keywords*:** IoT, sensing devices, arc quality management, weld quality, confined space, hot work

7.1 Introduction

Recently developed technologies have had a greater influence on the changes in the manufacturing sector. Presently, development of the manufacturing

**Corresponding author*: khssphanindra@gmail.com

Syed Quadir Moinuddin, Shaik Himam Saheb, Ashok Kumar Dewangan, Murali Mohan Cheepu and S. Balamurugan (eds.) Automation in Welding Industry: Incorporating Artificial Intelligence, Machine Learning and Other Technologies, (111–128) © 2024 Scrivener Publishing LLC

sector is mainly based on the following technologies [1]: a) big data and analytics; b) the internet of things (IoT) [2–4]; c) additive manufacturing; d) integration of horizontal and vertical systems; e) autonomous robots; f) simulation; g) augmented reality; and h) cyber security. Due to the stated emerging technologies, major changes have arrived in the manufacturing sector [1]. Welding plays a vital role in manufacturing, namely in the automotive, large fabrication, shipbuilding, electronics, and marine engineering sectors [5]. Figure 7.1 shows the evolution of welding operations [6]. Initially, the welding operation used to be carried out manually using workers' hands. During this stage, quality welding was highly influenced by the skills of the welders based on past awareness and practice. The instability and inconsistency of weld join quality are among the problems that arose from this situation. The introduction of industrial robot welding represents the next stage of automated welding evolution, and as robot technology has advanced, it has increasingly replaced manual welding in welding production [5]. This advanced technology not only enhances the quality of welding but also improves adaptability and production efficiency, and it allows for effective welding in hard-to-reach areas that human welders cannot access. But the majority of welding robots continue to operate in "teach and playback" mode. There is still a significant chance of mispositioning, and flaw detection still requires manual inspection.

Modern enhanced sensing technology has recently been developed for welding operations [6]. The sensors are being used for identifying welding environments, monitoring the welding process, and identifying welding defects. The sensing technology being used by the latest welding operations

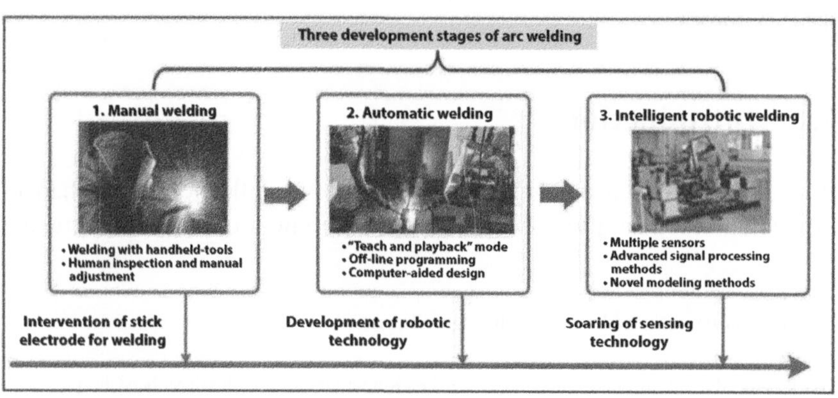

Figure 7.1 The evolution of welding operations [6].

is based upon the functional reproduction of welders' brains and senses [7]. By watching the welding work piece and the welding process phenomenon, the welder could first gather enough knowledge about the welding environment. After analyzing the inputs and drawing on their collective expertise and knowledge, the welding process characteristics can be identified, and an assessment of welding quality can then be made. The intelligent welding manufacturing system then recommends three technological solutions, which are outlined below:

- Utilizing cutting-edge sensors will enable you to collect accurate information about the welding process.
- Using efficient signal processing and characterization algorithms will enable you to extract the right amount of required information.

7.2 Sensing and Analyzing Welding Data via the Internet of Things (IoT)

The growth of the IoT has made it simpler to gather and combine data on the welding process. Numerous studies have been conducted on welding information sensing technology. Following is a list of welding information sensing techniques and their details [1].

7.2.1 Electrical Information

Welding current and arc voltage are the most frequently seen metrics in terms of electrical information. Both of them are adept at spotting unusual welding conditions, including an improper welding feed rate, an excess or shortage of welding gas, and others. Despite this, it is still challenging to identify the precise parameters that affect the normal welding condition simply by using the welding current and arc voltage as indicators [8, 9].

7.2.2 Optical Information

Welding utilizes different types of optical information, such as visual data and optical spectrum emissions, to carry out the process effectively.

- Optical spectrum emission
  There are numerous advantages to obtaining information on optical spectrum emissions, as it provides a wealth of

knowledge about welding, ranging from the spectral lines of various particle types present in the arc plasma and electrodes to the black-body radiation spectrum lines of protective gases, molten metal, and other components. Optical spectrum emission has excellent precision and sensitivity.

- Visual Data Emission
  Visible light information is the primary source of welding visual data, which can accurately reflect the dynamic changes in the weld seam and welding pool. It contains information such as the welding pool condition, the arc form, the location of the weld seam, the type of joint, and so forth.
- Sound Emission
  It is possible to separate the sound signal into audible sound and acoustic emissions. When a material undergoes plastic deformation, it produces an elastic stress wave signal known as the acoustic emission signal [1], which can reach frequencies of millions of Hz. By using a sound sensor's vibrating membrane, the audible sound signal can be converted into a voltage signal for further analysis.
- Other Information
  Apart from the types of welding information mentioned above, there are several other crucial data forms necessary, including temperature information, ultrasonic information, and various other pertinent parameters. They convey information about welding quality both directly and indirectly by reflecting the dynamic welding process.

7.3 Welding Manufacture Based on IoT

The production model of the manufacturing sector for welding has undergone significant change as a result of the advent of internet of things (IoT) technology. The framework for the smart factory consists of four layers, namely, the physical resources layer, the industrial network layer, the cloud layer, and the layer designated for supervision and control terminals. The foundation of the physical resources layer is reliant on intelligent devices that have the capability to communicate with each other through an industrial network, as shown in Figure 7.2.

The cloud layer facilitates the collation of massive amounts of data from the physical resource layer through multiple information systems, which can then interact with users via different terminals like manufacturing

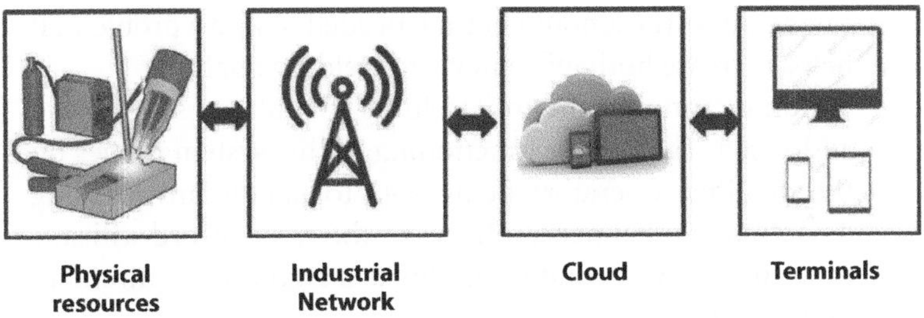

Figure 7.2 IoT-based smart factory—a typical framework.

execution systems (MES), enterprise resource planning (ERP), and many others. In reality, this creates a cyber-physical system (CPS) that is tightly connected with both physical objects and informational entities. Various examples of IoT-based welding are discussed below.

7.3.1 Example 1: Arc Quality Management with IoT

Figure 7.3 shows an example of the complete arc welding quality management system; the following areas show the impact of arc quality management on welding quality [1]:

- To guarantee that welding is performed by skilled, proficient, and capable welders, a detailed and comprehensive control system is implemented that identifies the welder's qualifications at the beginning of the welding process.
- All welding operations are kept in accordance with WPS standards. Welding data from all applications will be surveyed and compared to WPS-demanding data.
- A rigorous control mechanism is enforced to regulate the use of welding materials, requiring a comprehensive evaluation of the welding stick, welding materials, and process number before commencing the welding process. Additionally, ISO 3834 mandates traceability for spent materials to maintain a record of their usage.
- Implementing a management system for the pre-maintenance, usage conditions, and usage time of welding machines. It can give users and the inspection department access to all pre-use and post-use reports for welding machines.
- Delivering all complex welding parameters in real time while recording the entire welding operation. This approach

can decrease the amount of time needed to find a problem. It helps increase both efficiency and welding quality.

- Welding cannot begin until welding irregularities have been addressed. The proper functioning of this system hinges on the qualified operators being able to handle any welding deviation that happens; otherwise, the error record will stay in an unresolved condition. This is a rigorous requirement as per ISO 3834.
- Strict limits on who is authorized to operate a welding machine, including managers and technicians, in accordance with ISO 3834 requirements.
- Generation of quality reports. All welding parameters can be recorded in increments of time, generally in milliseconds, and the data are permanently preserved.
- Providing welding managers and technicians with qualification management and performance evaluation.

The self-explanatory Figure 7.4 shows how IoT works for an individual device. Various input sensors will be connected through a suitable network

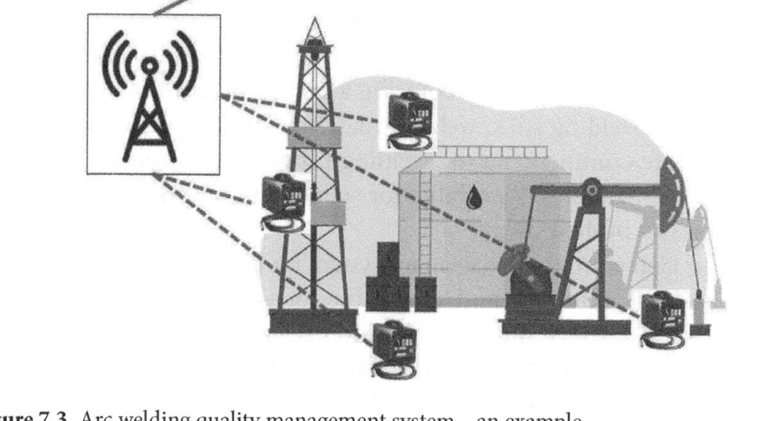

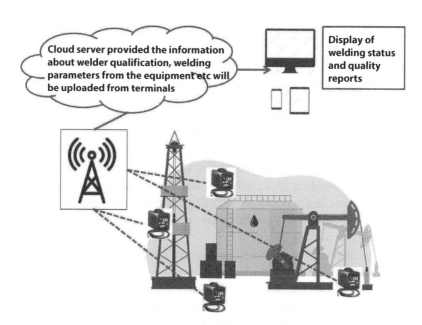

Figure 7.3 Arc welding quality management system—an example.

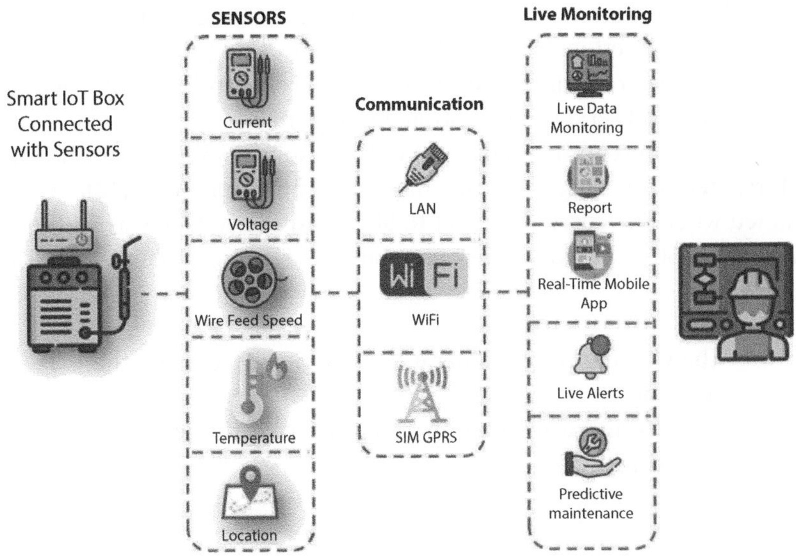

Figure 7.4 How IoT works—an example.

that is remotely monitored. The advantages of an IoT-based quality management system for arc welding are:

- Expanding and enhancing productivity
- Improving quality
- Enabling predictive maintenance
- Remote monitoring
- Managing part traceability
- Reducing welding costs
- Providing hourly/daily/weekly/monthly reports for better business development.

7.3.2 Example 2: Case Study on IoT-Enabled Molten Metal Temperature Sensing System for Welding

To maintain the quality of metal joints, welding temperature management is crucial [10]. The quality of the joint may be impacted by variations in the current and deviations made by the instruments. The influence of the microstructure may vary due to an excess of heat or a molten state. To solve this issue, a temperature measuring system that operates automatically is required. The utilization of temperature sensors based on the internet of things (IoT) to monitor molten metal during welding enables automatic temperature detection in the welding process. This process is enhanced through the use of temperature sensors, microcontrollers, LAN/wireless connections, and servers, as illustrated in Figure 7.5.

Figure 7.6 presents a comparison of the results obtained with the input factors, demonstrating that the highest temperature of 1,321 °C was attained when the current was set to 90 A and the voltage was within the range of 25–50 V. Based on the case study, the significant factors are listed below [10].

- The welding zone temperature was measured using the IoT concept.
- Sensors and a microcontroller improved the temperature-detecting procedure.

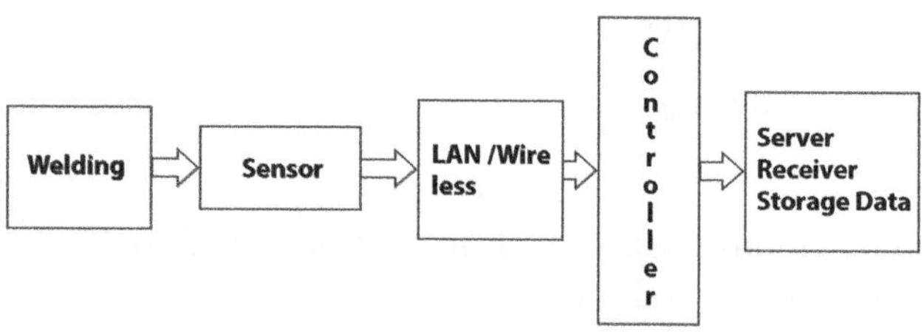

Figure 7.5 IoT-based temperature sensor for molten metal [11].

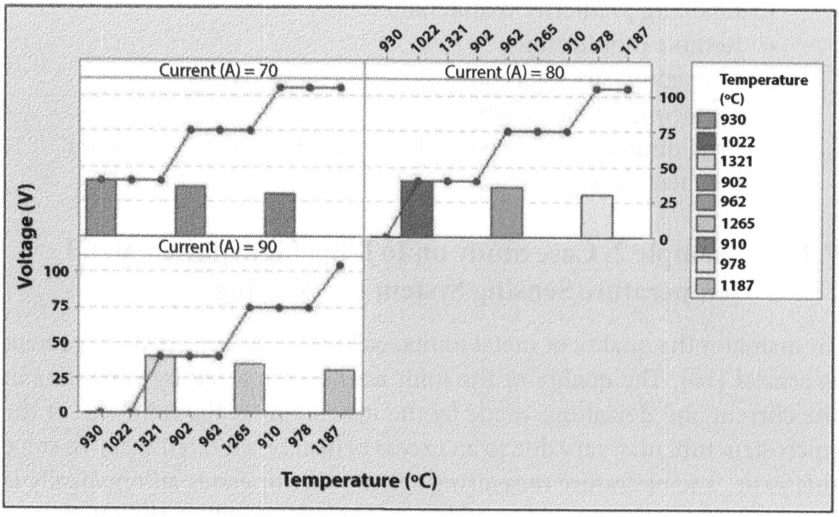

Figure 7.6 Comparison of results with input factors [11].

- The welding zone's temperature was calculated by varying input variables like current, voltage, and time. Taguchi optimization was used to assess the welding zone's ideal temperature. The process was accomplished by employing specific parameters, including a welding time of 50 seconds, a current of 90 A, and a voltage of 40 V.
- The current is the major factor that determines the temperature of the welding zone.

7.3.3 Example 3: IoT-Based Safety Monitoring System During Welding Operations

The latest ISO 3834 incorporates the safety of the welding operation. Typical hazards from welding operations are exposure to welding fumes related to electric welding, etc. However, there are other potential hazards to which welders are exposed due to work environmental conditions that can lead to fatalities or disasters in the workplace, such as confined spaces and hot work in process industries.

Recognizing confined space hazards is the first step in reducing fatalities because they can be found in almost any occupation. Confined spaces have potential atmospheric hazards such as being oxygen-deficient, toxic, or combustible. Welders in the majority of industries are expected to enter confined spaces to execute certain welding operations. Following are the major hazards that are encountered by welders during confined space entry operations [11], which are separate from the general welding hazards.

- Confined spaces can contain toxic fumes that, if inhaled by welders, can be fatal.
- If welders enter confined spaces where oxygen levels are low, it can be fatal.
- Flammable atmospheres due to flammable liquids, gases, etc., that can be ignited easily from welding sparks would lead to major disasters in chemical process industries, oil transport ships, etc.

Figure 7.7 shows an example of a confined-space welding safety management system. The following areas show the impact of an IoT-based confined space safety management system:

- Detailed and extensive control of confined space operators is required to ensure that the work is carried out by a correct, medically qualified, and capable person who is aware of the hazards of the confined space.

- Confined space entry permit requirements were compiled as per the local legal requirements.
- Atmospheric data from a multi-gas detector can be stored in the server and the online data transferred to the dashboards located at welding monitoring stations and fire rescue departments.
- If any flammable atmosphere is detected during welding operations, the power supply to the welding machine should stop automatically, and an alarm should sound to escape from the confined space. Also, the fire department should immediately get an alert along with the location for handling any emergencies.
- If any oxygen deficiency is detected, the power supply to the welding machine should stop automatically, and an alarm should sound to alert workers to warn people to escape from the confined space. A rescue team should also be immediately alerted along with the location for handling emergencies.
- If any toxic atmosphere is detected, the power supply to the welding machine should stop automatically, and an alarm

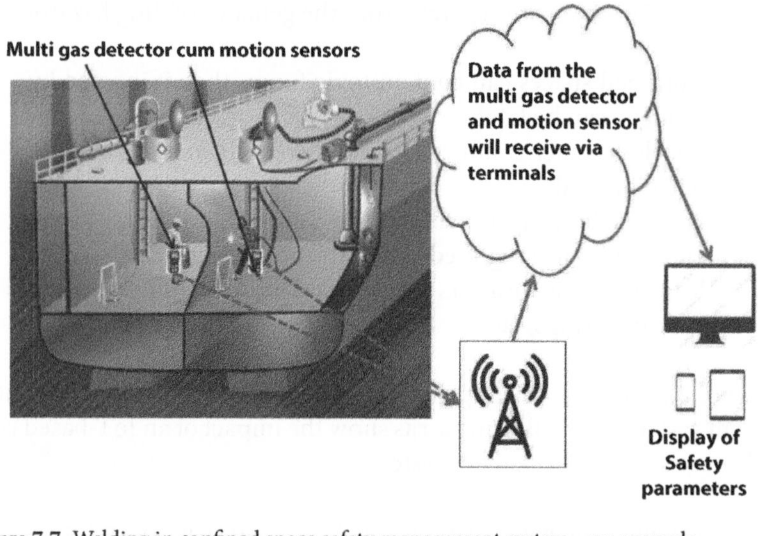

Figure 7.7 Welding in confined space safety management system—an example.

should sound to warn people to escape from the confined space. The rescue team should also immediately get an alert along with the location for handling any emergencies.

- If a welder becomes unconscious, motion detector signals should alert the rescue team, concerned supervisor, and manager for timely evacuation of the welder from the confined space.
- All minor deviations should be recorded and maintained for detailed investigation and corrective action to avoid future accidents or disasters.

Activities such as welding or other operations that produce sparks capable of igniting fires or explosions fall under the category of "hot work," as per the definition. Incidents of hot work accidents are widespread across several industrial sectors, such as food processing, pulp and paper manufacturing, oil production, fuel storage, waste treatment facilities, and others [12]. Those welders involved in hot work also suffer burn injuries or fatalities due to major fires and explosions.

Figure 7.8 shows an example of a hot work safety management system. The following areas show the impact of an IoT-based hot work safety management system:

- Detailed and extensive control of hot work to ensure that the work is carried out by a correct, qualified, and capable person who is aware of the hazards of hot work.
- Hot work permit requirements are compiled as per the local legal requirements.
- Atmospheric data from the multi-gas detector will be stored in a server and the online data will be transferred to the dashboards located at welding monitoring stations and fire rescue departments.
- If any flammable atmosphere is detected during welding operations, the power supply to the welding machine should stop automatically, and an alarm should sound to warn workers to escape from the worksite. The fire team should also immediately get an alert along with the location for handling emergencies.
- All minor deviations should be recorded and maintained for detailed investigation and corrective action to avoid future disasters due to hot work activities.

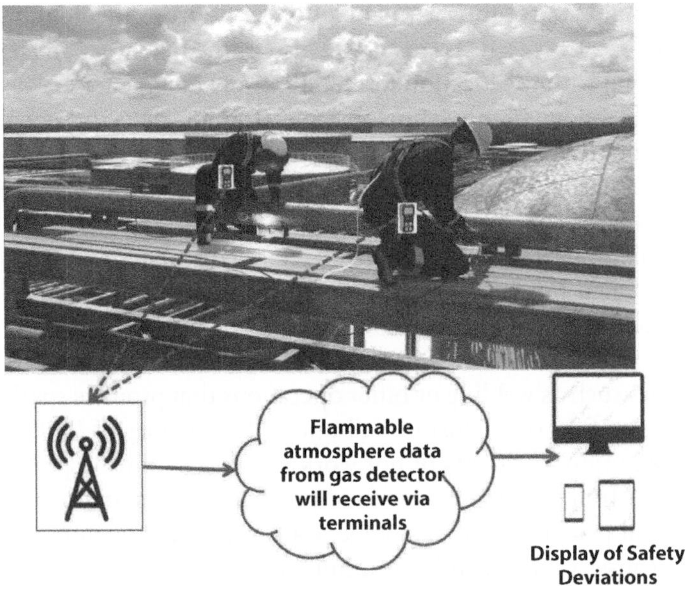

Figure 7.8 Hot work safety management system—an example.

7.3.4 Example 4: IoT-Based Monitoring of Submerged Arc Welding Process

Through the use of a bipolar stepping motor, submerged arc welding offers a high degree of control over the amount of metal transferred through the arc by allowing for the adjustment of the wire feed frequency step [13]. Weld bead geometry is more influenced by wire feed. Control of wire feed is an essential aspect of welding, which can be achieved by implementing a pulse wire feed mechanism in automatic submerged arc welding. This mechanism regulates the transfer of metal through the arc by adjusting the wire feed frequency and step using a bipolar stepping motor [13]. Weld bead diameters are more significantly influenced by travel speed. When the travel speed is increased, the width of the weld bead also grows while the depth of penetration decreases, and the opposite is true for welding speed values that are lower.

The linear magnetic Hall effect sensor used in the wire feed and welding speed measurement model detects the magnetic field of the magnets mounted on the carriage wheel and feed roller to measure speed in rpm. The Hall effect sensor detects magnetic pulses as the roller rotates. Studies conducted in a laboratory setting have demonstrated that the accuracy of

Hall effect sensor measurements can be improved by increasing the number of magnets utilized [13].

Upon receiving a signal from the sensor, the ESP32 microcontroller processes the data and utilizes an i2c module to detect wire feed and welding speed, which are then displayed on an LCD screen. To visualize real-time data on wire feed and welding speed, the IoT MQTT panel and HiveMQ open-source platforms are utilized on a mobile/computer dashboard. Furthermore, data may be stored on Google Sheets using the MQTT protocol via a Wi-Fi module in the microcontroller.

The model is shown schematically in Figure 7.9 and uses a Hall effect sensor to measure changes in capacitance to determine the speed of the welding trolley and wire feed. This signal is delivered to the ESP32 microcontroller as rpm; 3.3–5 V is used to power the ESP32 module. ESP32 can be connected to other systems and provide Wi-Fi and Bluetooth capability through its SPI/SDIO or I2C/UART interfaces. Using MQTT (MQ Telemetry Transport), the real-time data is tracked on LCD screens and Android smartphones and is also saved in Google Sheets. Batteries provide DC power for the sensor and microcontroller.

As illustrated in Figure 7.10, the microcontroller functions as the central processing unit of the system and transmits digital data to the MQTT platform before it is sent to the mobile application. Following the flowchart diagram, data is collected by the microcontroller and transmitted to the MQTT platform via an internet-connected microcontroller. The data

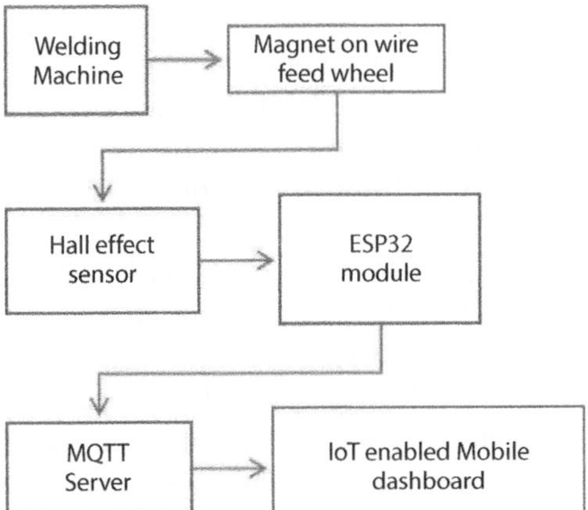

Figure 7.9 Wire feed and welding speed monitoring block diagram [13].

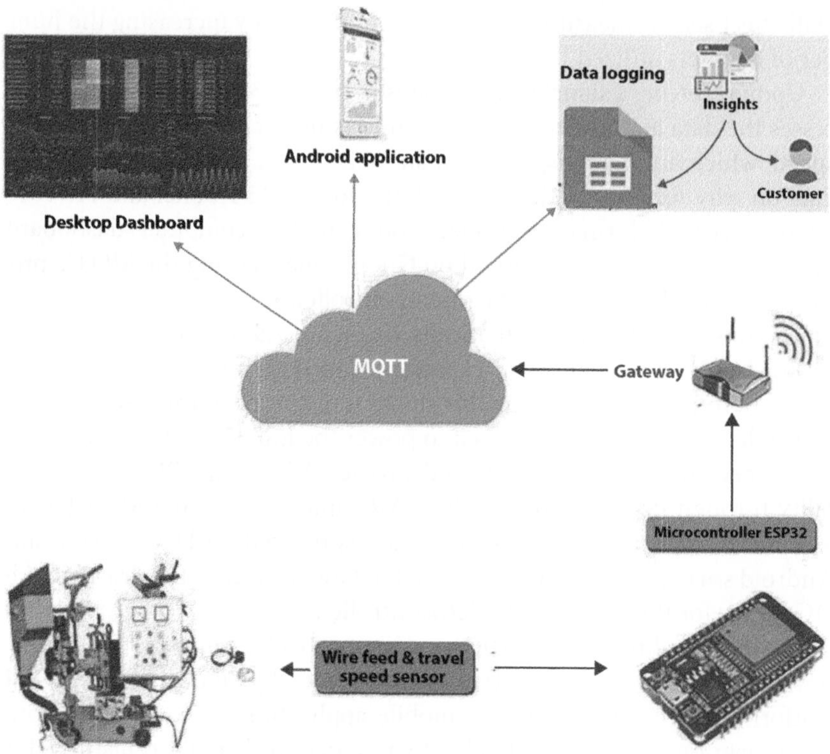

Figure 7.10 Process flow diagram for IoT-based submerged arc welding monitoring [13].

is then displayed on a mobile dashboard or application and stored in the cloud for future use.

Figure 7.11 demonstrates that an open-source IoT MQTT mobile application has been utilized to create the data logging system for the remote weld monitoring system dashboard. Using the MQTT protocol and the HiveMQ server, data is sent from the sensor to the mobile device or PC dashboard.

The mobile dashboard shown in Figures 7.11 and 7.12 has IoT-enabled SAW process monitoring and two-way communication capabilities, allowing for remote monitoring of welding conditions and providing process insight and precise control. The transformation of traditional welding into smart welding, as depicted in Figure 7.5, involves the use of the HTTP protocol to receive requests for two-way communication either on the welding work floor or through a remote monitoring device.

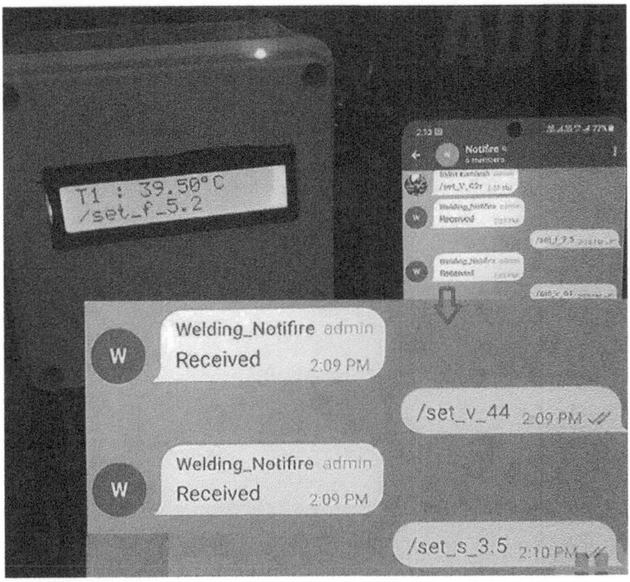

Figure 7.11 Monitoring of the weld process remotely in real time [13].

In addition to aiding in the delivery of live welding quality control, http protocol message alerts also facilitate the communication of corrective actions/messages to the operator supervisor. The collection of real-time welding data from sensors through microcontrollers, which is then monitored by the supervisor, further enhances the quality control of weld operations.

A comparison between the digital signal obtained from the smart welding IoT-enabled automation setup and the analog signal observed from analog meters for wire feed and welding speed is presented in Figures 7.13 and 7.14. The use of the smart welding IoT-enabled automation setup has resulted in significant improvements in the accuracy of the data readings; it also enables the establishment of a correlation between the performance and quality of the weld and the process parameters. Following are some of the advantages of this system:

- An IoT-based approach utilizing smart sensors provides a dependable means of remotely monitoring wire feed and welding trolley speed.

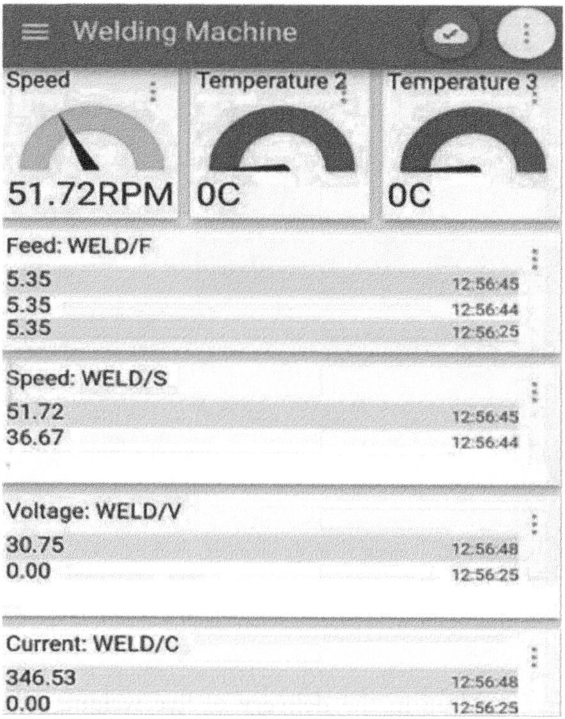

Figure 7.12 Dashboard for two-way communication using the HTTP protocol, HiveMQ server, and IoT MQQT protocol [13].

- The suggested welding process monitoring solution enabled by IoT technology provided welding automation that was economical, clever, and long-lasting.
- Another goal of this innovation is to track welding speed and live wire feed data from a distance, which controls the entire process system and enhances casting product quality with the least amount of work.
- The use of an IoT-enabled smart welding setup has facilitated real-time quality control of the welding speed and wire feed of the welding trolley in various scenarios.
- Human error does not occur during weld inspection with IoT-enabled smart welding.
- Reduction in the likelihood of defective components by analysis, improved welding quality, and elimination of the weld inspection process.

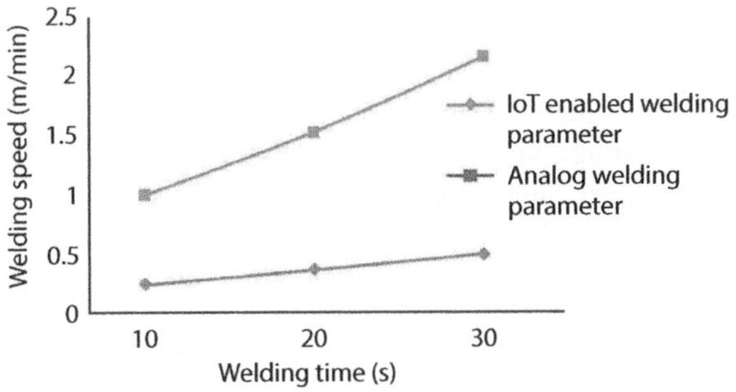

Figure 7.13 Comparison of real-time process monitoring using IoT and analogue measurement for SAW speed.

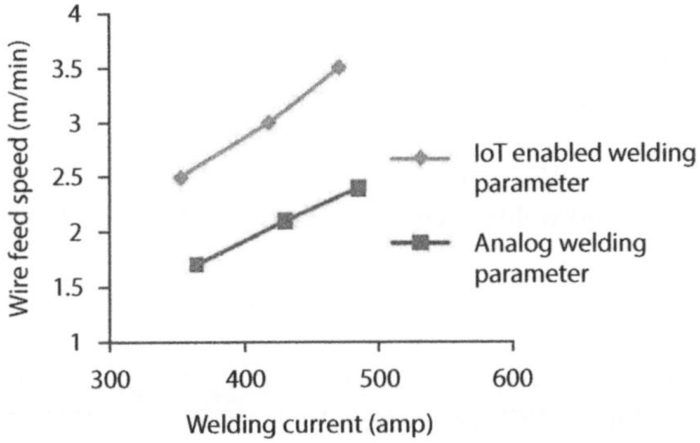

Figure 7.14 Comparison of real-time process monitoring using IoT and analogue measurement for SAW wire feed [13].

7.4 Conclusion

The welding manufacturing industry has witnessed significant technological advancements due to the continuous growth and development of the welding process. The IoT-enabled systems speed up the collection of data from various sensor networks and integrate it for necessary measures. This chapter presented various sensing methods for welding operations along with suitable examples of IoT-based systems for maintaining welding quality on par with ISO 3834 and monitoring the submerged arc welding process. The safety of the welder was also taken into consideration, and IoT-based solutions with examples described the safety management system for confined spaces and hot work operations in various industrial sectors.

References

1. Chen, C., Lv, N., Chen, S., Data-driven welding expert system structure based on internet of things, in: *Transactions on Intelligent Welding Manufacturing*, pp. 45–60, Springer, Singapore, 2018.
2. Tao, F., Zuo, Y., Xu, L.D., Zhang, L., IoT-based intelligent perception and access of manufacturing resource toward cloud manufacturing. *IEEE Trans. Industr. Inform.*, 10, 2, 1547–1557, 2014.
3. Jing, Q., Vasilakos, A.V., Wan, J., Lu, J., Qiu, D., Security of the Internet of Things: Perspectives and challenges. *Wirel. Netw.*, 20, 8, 2481–2501, 2014.
4. Chen, F., Deng, P., Wan, J., Zhang, D., Vasilakos, A.V., Rong, X., Data mining for the internet of things: Literature review and challenges. *Int. J. Distrib. Sens. Netw.*, 11, 8, 431047, 2015.
5. Liu, Q., Chen, C., Chen, S., Key technology of intelligentized welding manufacturing and systems based on the internet of things and multi-agent. *J. Manuf. Mater. Process.*, 6, 6, 135, 2022.
6. Xu, F., Xu, Y., Zhang, H., Chen, S., Application of sensing technology in intelligent robotic arc welding: A review. *J. Manuf. Process.*, 79, 854–880, 2022.
7. Wang, Q., Jiao, W., Wang, P., Zhang, Y., Digital twin for human-robot interactive welding and welder behavior analysis. *IEEE/CAA J. Autom. Sin.*, 8, 2, 334–343, 2020.
8. Madigan, R., Arc sensing for defects in constant-voltage gas metal arc welding. *Weld. J.*, 78, 322S–328S, 1999.
9. Koseeyaporn, P., Cook, G.E., Strauss, A.M., Adaptive voltage control in fusion arc welding. *IEEE Trans. Ind. Appl.*, 36, 5, 1300–1307, 2000.
10. Sanjith, S., Balaji, N., Anand, L.D.V., Anne, W.R., Shanmugapriya, P., Rani, S.S., IoT enabled temperature sensing system of molten metal in welding. *Mater. Today Proc.*, 45, 2514–2517, 2021.
11. Sakar, C., Buber, M., Koseoglu, B., Toz, A.C., Risk analysis for confined space accidents onboard ship using fuzzy bow-tie methodology. *Ocean Eng.*, 263, 112386, 2022.
12. Levine, S.P. and Thornton, J.R., LEL monitoring during hazard surveys for issuance of hot work permits. *Prof. Saf.*, 49, 2, 31, 2004.
13. Barot, R.S. and Patel, V.J., Development and investigations of IoT enabled wire feed and weld speed measurement for submerged arc welding. *MAPAN*, 37, 4, 741–751, 2022.

8

VR and AR in Welding Technologies

Veningston K. and Dinesh Kumar Rajendran*

National Institute of Technology Srinagar, Jammu and Kashmir, India

Abstract

Modern information technologies, including artificial intelligence, virtual reality, augmented reality, and extended reality, are revolutionizing welding systems. These technologies are being used in intelligent welding systems (IWS), which are attracting interest from the academic and industry communities. The use of intelligent systems to simulate, reinforce, and/or replace human operators in various operations is known as intelligent welding. This chapter's goal is to document the user's experience of augmented reality (AR) technology in welding instruction for further research and applications. Head-mounted displays (HMDs), a welding torch, and a portable device with peripherals and software for the simulation of the welding source, positioning system, and plate with the material foundation make up the indirect vision of the welding helmet used in AR welding technology. Augmented reality (AR), virtual reality (VR), and mixed reality (MR) are among the technologies useful in various welding operations, from the selection of welding parameters to checking quality assurance and quality control in welding industries.

***Keywords*:** AR, VR, MR, XR, Meta, intelligent manufacturing, welding, quality inspection

8.1 Introduction

In order to build a virtual world that might provide people with multisensory sensations in terms of sound, fragrance, wind, vibration, etc., a device called the Sensorama Simulator was developed and patented in 1962.

**Corresponding author*: rdinesh@nitsri.ac.in

Syed Quadir Moinuddin, Shaik Himam Saheb, Ashok Kumar Dewangan, Murali Mohan Cheepu and S. Balamurugan (eds.) Automation in Welding Industry: Incorporating Artificial Intelligence, Machine Learning and Other Technologies, (129–142) © 2024 Scrivener Publishing LLC

A few years later, Sutherland created the first head-mounted display system to address this issue. This device could provide an interactive visual based on a user's head position. Additionally, Krueger developed a virtual reality (VR) interactive environment where a computer could recognize a user's activities and reply in real time with visual and aural displays. Silicon Graphics created the VR modeling language in 1995, enabling individuals to quickly and easily construct and interact with a variety of virtual models. AR also comes in the form of mixed reality (MR). The idea of the "virtuality continuum" was initially put forth in 1994 by Milgram and Kishino, who explained that MR may offer a hybrid and continuous space that ranges from a wholly real world to a completely virtual one. The MR and AR technologies are similar in that they both emphasize the blending of real-world and virtual components.

8.1.1 Virtual Reality (VR)

Virtual reality (VR) is among the emerging technologies represented in Figure 8.1 that have been gaining interest among researchers. This technology can simulate three-dimensional, computer-generated surroundings that can be experienced with the help of a headset or other immersive display system. The user can relate to the virtual surroundings in a way that feels like they are there, often using specialized controllers or hand gestures. Virtual reality has been used in a variety of fields, including gaming,

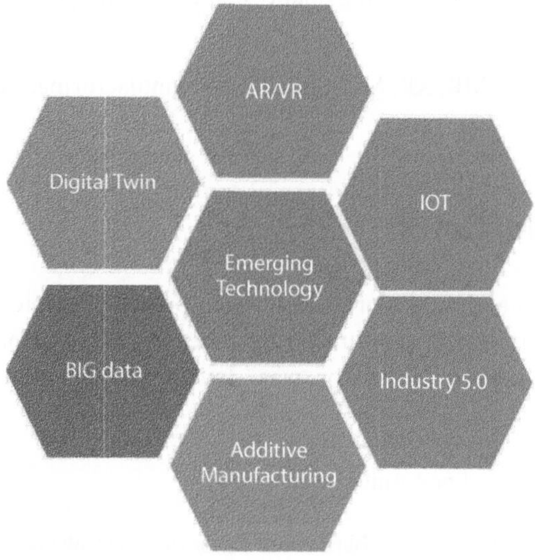

Figure 8.1 Emerging future technologies.

education, medicine, architecture, and entertainment. It has the potential to provide users with immersive, realistic experiences that can be used for training, education, and even therapy.

One of the benefits of virtual reality is that it allows users to experience situations or environments that might be difficult or dangerous, like medical procedures, fire and water robot trainings, or hazardous work environments. It can also be used to simulate social situations, such as job interviews or public speaking, to help users build confidence and skills. Virtual reality has the potential to transform the way we interact with technology and with each other, opening up new opportunities for learning, entertainment, and exploration [1].

8.1.2 Augmented Reality (AR)

The real world and computer-generated content are combined in augmented reality, an immersive experience. The content may include graphics and other visuals in addition to other modes. Augmented reality technology overlays digital data, like images, audio, and video, onto a person's view of the physical environment. It allows users to see virtual objects in real-world settings, making the objects appear as if they are part of the environment.

Augmented reality technology relies on devices such as smart phones, tablets, and head-mounted displays that are equipped with sensors and cameras to detect the physical environment and superimpose digital content onto it. AR applications can also be used to enhance productivity and efficiency in various industries, such as healthcare, manufacturing, and logistics [2].

8.1.3 Artificial Intelligence (AI)

Artificial intelligence is very hard to define. It is not really natural but man-made. It helps with reasoning and making decisions. Not all AI needs a robot to manifest. Similarly, not every robot manifests AI. A well-known AI system is known as an expert system, which works based on hand-coded rules in terms of if-then rules. Only when these rules are known can we infer other related rules. Typically, these rules are provided by domain experts. In cases where these rules are unknown, we need to depend on machine learning algorithms to infer the unknown rules from the data, and this process requires a huge volume of related data.

8.1.4 Machine Learning (ML)

Machine learning is the study of learning from data through unknown mathematical models. Initially, a random function/model would be tried, and it helps in learning the parameters of the function, which approximate the relation connecting the input and output. This has a very wide range of applications, including human resource management, tourism, weather forecasting, healthcare, finance, commerce, insurance, agriculture, and education domains. The real power of ML can be realized only when we have a sufficiently large amount of data describing the connection between input and output variables. The field of AI converges with ML when we attempt to analyze the data to know more about the hidden patterns that exist.

8.2 How Intelligent is AI When Coupled with VR/AR?

Currently, AI and VR are two of the most promising technologies in the world. Even though both technologies focus on different aspects, they allow human beings to have a deeper relationship with the digital space. Virtual reality uses a combination of software and hardware to immerse humans in the digital world, where numerous aspects can be modeled and visualized as if they physically exist. On the other hand, AI aids us in creating systems that can respond intelligently according to environments and situations. Therefore, AI coupled with VR/AR would open an interesting avenue for exploring mechanical aspects of macro- to micro-level tasks, such as welding and other tasks that require both humans and machines to coordinate [3, 4].

8.3 VR/AR Architecture

The fields of VR and AR essentially enable the transformation of models in digital design into realistic renderings and augmented reality visuals. This enables a deeper understanding of the system's processing. This could avoid the huge cost involved in physically testing a wide variety of micro-level tasks being performed.

The standard VR/AR architecture being followed in most of the successful systems is depicted in Figure 8.2 below.

8.4 Welding Processes

There are several welding simulators that have been developed by academics, professionals, and businesses. Some of these, such as the ARC+ and

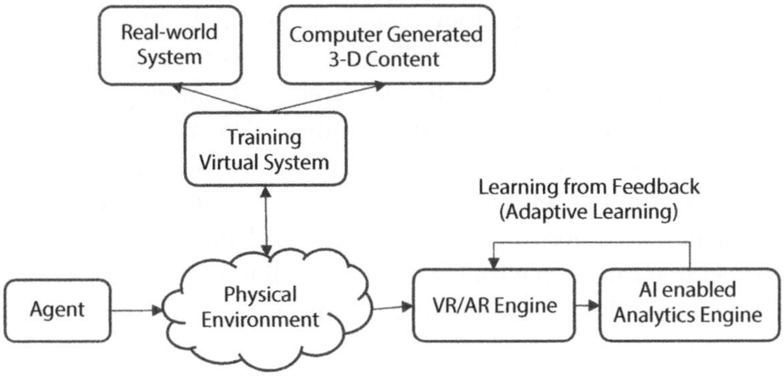

Figure 8.2 The standard VR/AR architecture.

Vertex systems, are extensively utilized and commercially accessible; the Army now uses the latter for trade training. The Edison Welding Institute has created the CS-WAVE technology in France. Unlike ARC Plus, it is a non-immersive welding simulator and does not employ a welding helmet. A welding simulator, which is the most crucial component of this product, is the form in the database that is composed of real-time assessed data from the gas metal arc weld bead. A helmet designed for welding assistance is one use of augmented reality that was created in Germany. A high-resolution HDR camera is built inside the helmet's visor, and the picture of the arc is altered to lessen glare and make the shape of the arc easier to perceive. Although its primary purpose is to improve weldability and welder output, it is also used as an adjunct to teaching.

8.5 Intelligent Welding Technology

Intelligent approaches and/or artificial intelligence are used in intelligent welding to duplicate, enhance, or even replace human intellect. These technologies are being used in intelligent welding systems (IWS), which are attracting interest from the academic and industry communities. The use of computers to replicate, reinforce, and/or replace human operators in sensing, learning, decision-making, monitoring and control, etc., is known as intelligent welding. This is achieved by incorporating human and physical system strengths into intelligent cybersystems [5–7]. Although there are some pilot implementations of intelligent welding in the industrial setting, a thorough examination of these applications, components, and future developments will assist in establishing a common definition of intelligent welding systems.

Intelligent welding technology related to the application of advanced technologies, such as artificial intelligence (AI), is used to optimize and automate the welding process. Intelligent welding technology can improve the quality and efficiency of welding, reduce defects, and rework, and increase productivity. One of the key applications of intelligent welding technology is robotic welding, where robots are used to perform welding tasks with high precision and speed. The use of AI and machine learning in robotic welding can enable robots to adapt to different welding conditions and optimize welding parameters in real time, resulting in more consistent and high-quality welds.

Intelligent welding technology can also be used for monitoring and quality control during the welding process. Sensors and cameras can be used to collect data on a variety of welding parameters, such as temperature, arc length, and wire speed, and AI algorithms can be used to analyze the data and detect any deviations from the desired parameters. This can help identify defects early on and prevent them from becoming more serious problems later.

In addition to improving the welding process, intelligent welding technology can also improve worker safety by reducing the need for human operators to be in close proximity to welding equipment. Overall, intelligent welding technology has the potential to revolutionize the welding industry and lead to significant improvements in productivity, quality, and safety.

8.6 Types of Intelligent Welding Processes

The welding techniques and procedures used in various welding processes vary. Arc welding methods, such as flux-cored arc welding (FCAW), gas tungsten arc welding, shielded metal arc welding, and gas metal arc welding, were the focus of the VR and AR welding training workshops. In addition to MIG and MAG welding, GMAW is sometimes referred to as metal inert gas (MIG) welding. An electrode is used during SMAW, which is also known as manual metal arc (MMA) welding. The term tungsten inert gas (TIG) welding can also be used to refer to GTAW.

According to investigations, GMAW was the most widely used welding technique. SMAW and GTAW, with twelve and seven studies, respectively, came next. With only three studies, FCAW received the least amount of attention from the research community. The specific welding process type was not mentioned in seven research studies.

8.6.1 Types of Welding Positions

Welding roles may be divided into several different categories. Two basic kinds of welding structures—plate welds and pipe welds—are based on welding certification. With research, we noticed that the level 1 welding position (1Fillet Weld (1F) and 1Groove Weld (1G)) was the subject of most studies for the plate weld structure. Levels 2 (2F and 2G) and 3 (3F and 3G) have each received 14 and 13 studies, respectively. Three investigations on pipe welding in horizontal fixed locations (2F and 2G) were conducted in comparison. The inclined pipe welding locations were documented by two research studies (6F and 6G).

8.7 Automated Welding Examples

8.7.1 Computer Interface of Automated Welding Processes

Automatic welding is a process using equipment that continues the welding task without any human operator intervention and runs the task continuously. The computer interface of an automated welding process is expected to have VR/AR-enabled visual capability to observe the statistics of the welding process [8, 9]. The system framework of a typical welding robot system is depicted in Figure 8.3.

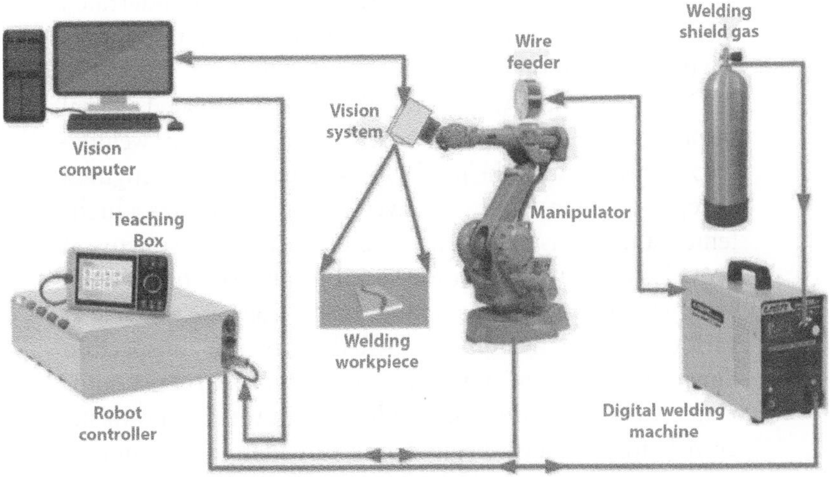

Figure 8.3 The system framework of a typical welding robot system.

Expected outcomes:

- High-precision welding
- Less human intervention in the welding process
- Effective utilization of weld equipment
- Power saving
- Potentials for optimizing the turnout time, welding wastes.

8.8 Applications of VR and AR in Automated Welding

It can be difficult to navigate what is real and what is possible when it comes to applying AI and ML to everyday business challenges. In this section, we focus on aiding the welding process to improve quality by using AI and ML for various aspects.

- **Automated Visual Inspection of welding**
  Visual inspection comes under the non-destructive testing (NDT) technique of weld precision checking. Typically, the welding job is examined visually by the eyes to determine surface discontinuities during the testing. Therefore, the process must be conducted only by an experienced welding inspector who has adequate skill in conducting the weld job. However, the precision of the welding cannot be assessed effectively. The manual visual inspection of weld quality assessment has been the most often misused and underrated method of welding quality inspection. The inspection results are purely based on the skill of the inspector.

  On the contrary, a VR/AR-based automated visual inspection method would enable high-precision welding inspection with the help of sophisticated analytic engines, as represented in Figure 8.4. Even though it requires a high-temperature resistance camera and other visual systems, it provides a robust system for visual inspection that is often error-free and quick to respond. Inspections are possible at various stages, including pre-weld inspection, inspection during welding, and post-weld inspection. A robust automated weld inspection tool could prevent welding problems even before the task begins. This provides an economical way of determining weld quality in terms of various factors, including surface discontinuities, weld depth, etc.

- **Weld Waste Inspection**
  Assessing the amount of weld equipment and raw materials required to accomplish a large-scale task is quite a challenging task. In this regard, a robust VR/AR-enabled visual system could provide a simulation environment in order to assess the weld requirement optimistically. This would aid in the pre-planning of the weld process.
- **Weld Job Assessment**
  The end-to-end assessment of a weld job is again a necessary task that is often ignored where welding is a prime job and consumes more time. In this respect, total quality management of the welding process could be effectively measured with the help of a VR/AR-enabled visual simulation system. Even the manpower requirement could be efficiently judged with the help of AI capabilities coupled with the welding system.
- **Potential Optimizations**
  The scope of optimization is open to minimize the cost involved and maximize the quality of the welding job quality. This is possible as it captures beneficial data and keeps it in a log, which can be further analyzed with the help of ML tools and algorithms. This could even aid in predetermining or predicting the manpower requirement for the task, weld equipment requirement, expected job quality, stability measurement of the weld job, etc.

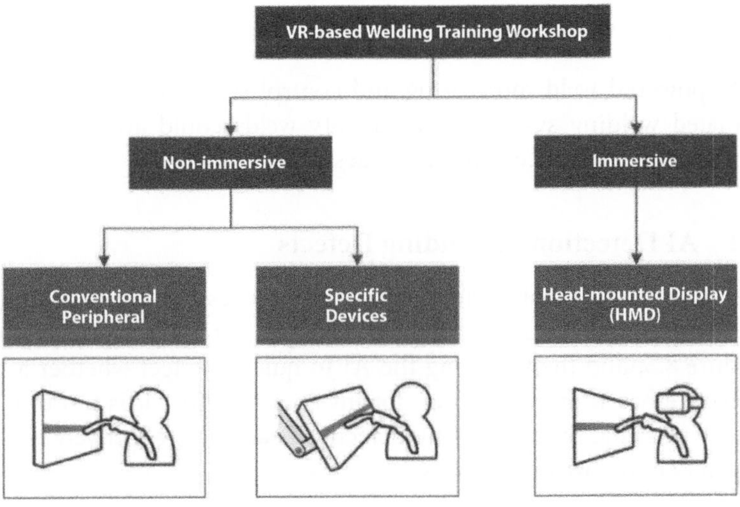

Figure 8.4 VR-based welding training.

8.9 AI and ML for Visual Inspection of Welds

Artificial intelligence (AI) and machine learning (ML) technologies are increasingly being used for the visual inspection of welds. Visual inspection is an important part of the welding process, as it helps to ensure that the welds are of high quality and free of defects. However, visual inspection can be time-consuming and subjective, and human inspectors can make errors or miss defects. Therefore, AI and ML can help to automate and improve the visual inspection of welds by analyzing images and videos of the welds and identifying defects with high accuracy. This can reduce the need for human inspectors and increase the speed and consistency of inspections. One of the key advantages of AI and ML for visual inspection of welds is that they can learn from data and improve their accuracy over time. The ML algorithms can be trained on large datasets of images and videos of welds to identify common defects such as porosity, cracks, and a lack of fusion. As the algorithms are exposed to more data, they can become more accurate and better at identifying defects.

Moreover, AI and ML can also be used for real-time monitoring of the welding process, allowing defects to be detected and corrected immediately. This can prevent defects from becoming more serious problems later on and can reduce the need for rework and repairs.

AI and ML technologies have the potential to revolutionize the visual inspection of welds by improving accuracy, reducing inspection time, and increasing productivity.

8.9.1 AI in Arc Welding

An AI-powered weld monitoring and control software would be a fully automated welding system. X-ray-quality welds could also be achieved with the help of advanced AI techniques.

8.9.2 AI Detection of Welding Defects

The system can automate welding inspection processes by learning the different shapes and features of weld beads from sample images, as shown in Figure 8.5, and then training the AI to quickly detect whether a bead is defective based on its features; for instance, whether it is too thin, too thick, or missing. By recognizing defective beads, this effectively controls the quality of the welding process.

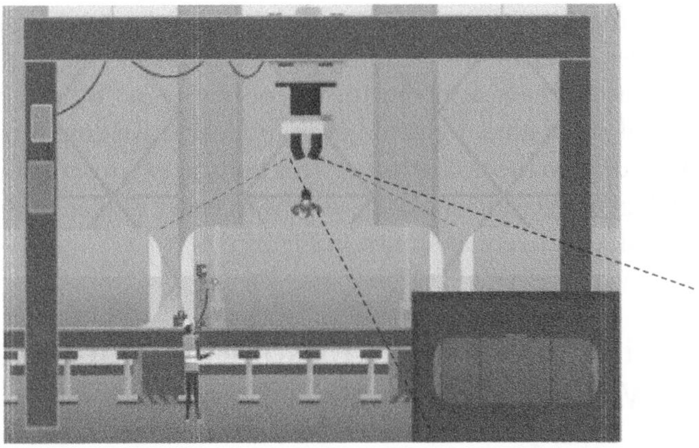

(a)

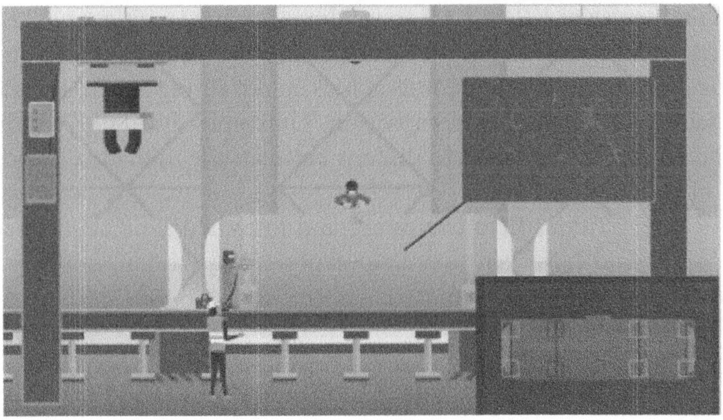

(b)

Figure 8.5 A camera visually detects any discontinuities in the weld and, simultaneously, the inkjet sprayer marks the car for rework: (a) before marking and (b) after marking.

8.9.3 VR/AR Welding Simulator

Several pioneering virtual welding simulators [10] are on the market. However, they are all lacking in terms of the intelligence and autonomous capabilities they possess. To address this deficiency, VR/AR blended with AI capabilities could even interact with virtual assistants/agents that can answer questions about the requirement well in advance. In the welding environment, a VR/AR system could deliver a promising experience for all the manpower deployed in a welding task. Despite its huge requirement for visual image capture devices and data-intensive analytic capabilities, it guarantees an error-free welding process by observing past errors and never repeating them again in the upcoming tasks. By using these VR/AR-enabled simulators, we could even model the welding process beforehand according to the task at hand. This holistic environment would facilitate intelligent decision-making systems in order to plan and execute the welding task effectively, as shown in Figure 8.6.

8.10 Limitations in the Existing State-of-the-Art Welding Techniques

A systematic review gathered information from several research studies to report on the use of VR and AR in welding training facilities [11, 12]. The potential for bias arises from the fact that different research studies use different subject populations, demographics, and training hours. The PICOS (Population, Intervention, Comparison, Outcomes and Study) indicates that the populace also failed to discern between the individuals' ages and levels of experience. Future research is advised to evaluate how well VR and AR interventions help beginning and intermediate students acquire motor skills and how well they help experienced welders improve their abilities.

8.10.1 Advantages of AR/VR

By utilizing AR/VR tools in training, qualified people may need less time to understand topics. Additionally, they will be less distracted, more confident and have a greater connection to the subject matter. Education, e-learning, and AR/VR learning are the three types of training available, as shown in Figure 8.6. There were several significant discoveries made during the processing of the data using several different methodologies:

- Employees with AR/VR training have demonstrated stronger resolve in putting what they have learned into practice.
- Scale-wise, AR/VR may be more cost-effective.
- The subjects of AR/VR training felt a strong connection to the subject matter.
- Compared to AR/VR workers, classroom personnel completed training three to four times more slowly.

Proposed VR/AR-Enabled Welding Architecture

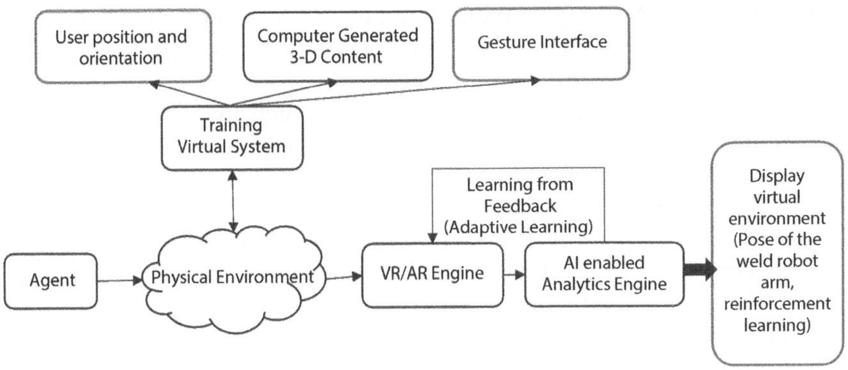

Figure 8.6 A holistic VR/AR architecture for welding evaluation.

8.11 Conclusions

The present VR and AR solutions for human-robot collaboration and interaction are summarized in this chapter. The implementation strategy, technology, and tools employed in various scenarios were the main topics of discussion. This chapter concluded with a brief examination of contemporary issues. It is noteworthy that the majority of collaborative robot applications have minimal payload limits and naturally safe designs. Additionally, case studies tended to emphasize the expansion of operator awareness as assistance. By 2030, augmented reality (AR) and virtual reality (VR) may contribute $1.5 trillion to the global economy, with setup costs as high as $294.2 billion. People who receive education through virtual reality will need less time to understand issues, will be less distracted and more productive, may have more confidence and a better emotional connection to the content, and may also need less time to understand the material. Both AR and VR have a noticeable impact on an industrial organization's output and productivity.

References

1. Cipresso, P., Giglioli, I.A.C., Raya, M.L.A., Riva, G., The past, present, and future of virtual and augmented reality research: A network and cluster analysis of the literature. *Front. Psychol.*, 9, 2086, December 7, 2011.

2. Wu, H.-K., Lee, S.W.-Y., Chang, H.-Y., Liang, J.-C., Current status, opportunities and challenges of augmented reality in education. *Comput. Educ.*, 62, 41–49, March 2013.
3. Yang, L., Liu, Y., Peng, J., Advances techniques of the structured light sensing in intelligent welding robots: A review. *Int. J. Adv. Manuf. Technol.*, 110, 1027–1046, Sept. 2020.
4. Huy, D.Q., Vietcheslav, I., Lee, G.S.G., See-through and spatial augmented reality–A novel framework for human-robot interaction, in: *Proceedings of the 3rd International Conference on Control, Automation and Robotics, ICCAR*, IEEE, pp. 719–726, 2017.
5. Bolano, G., Roennau, A., Dillmann, R., Transparent robot behavior by adding intuitive visual and acoustic feedback to motion replanning, in: *Proceedings of the 27th IEEE International Symposium on Robot and Human Interactive Communication, RO-MAN 2018*, IEEE, pp. 1075–1080, 2018.
6. Palmarini, R., del Amo, I.F., Bertolino, G., Dini, G., Erkoyuncu, J.A., Roy, R., Farnsworth, M. *et al.*, Designing an AR interface to improve trust in human-robots collaboration. *Proc. CIRP*, 70, 350–355, 2018.
7. Matsas, E., Vosniakos, G.C., Batras, D., Modelling simple human-robot collaborative manufacturing tasks in interactive virtual environments, in: *Proceedings of the 2016 International Conference on Virtual Reality, VRIC '16, ICPS Proceedings*, pp. 1–4, 2016.
8. Angel-Urdinola, D.F., Castillo-Castro, C., Hoyos, A., *Meta-analysis that assesses the effects of virtual reality training on students' learning and skills development*, The World Bank, World bank ELibrary Policy Research Working Papers 2021, https://doi.org/10.1596/ 1813-9450-9587.
9. Baglow, L. and Lovegrove, C., Virtual welders and their effectiveness in developing welding skills: Student perspectives, in: *Guidelines for Developing and Using e-Assessments with Vocational Learners Project Overview*, pp. 112–120, Ako Aotearoa, Wellington, New Zealand, 2019.
10. Baskoro, A.S. and Haryanto, I., Development of travel speed detection method in welding simulator using augmented reality, in: *2015 International Conference on Advanced Computer Science and Information Systems (ICACSIS)*, IEEE, pp. 269–273, 2015.
11. Okimoto, M.L.L.R., Okimoto, P.C., Goldbach, C.E., User experience in augmented reality applied to the welding education. *Procedia Manuf.*, 3, 6223–6227, 2015.
12. Kappler, W.D., *Smart driver training simulation: save money, prevent*, Springer-Verlag, Berlin Heidelberg, 2008.

9

Intelligent, Clean Cobot Arc Welding Cell

E. Schubert*, S. Rose, M. Bender, N. Spietz and T. Weber

Alexander Binzel Schweisstechnik GmbH & Co. KG, Buseck, Germany

Abstract

One goal of the project presented in this chapter was the development of a "clean" automated welding cell with a Cobot. The cell had to include a welding torch with integrated fume extraction and cell-integrated dust monitoring, as well as a gas-saving system to reduce shielding gas consumption. Other goals included the recording, storage, and visualization of all relevant process data and additional ambient data. For this purpose, the total energy consumption, including all auxiliary or secondary consumers, was determined, including the consumption data for wire and gas. With this, the user can get an overview of the productivity and can also monitor the ecological footprint (Life Cycle Assessment LCA/CO_2 footprint) of the production and thus the products—a combination that is an absolute novelty.

For data recording, collection, and processing, sensors were integrated at predefined places or fixed to the cell and connected to an edge computing PC, which processed the recorded data and transmitted it through a gateway to the cloud. The results are dashboards, directly accessible from the inside of the welding cell but also remotely via a cloud and thus independent from the location (e.g., to the office of the welding supervisor).

***Keywords*:** Arc welding, collaborative robots, data recording and processing, ecological footprint, fume extraction at source

9.1 Chances for SMEs

A lack of specialist experts, high productivity pressure, increasing customer demands, and compulsory health protection are just a few topics currently

**Corresponding author*: schubert@binzel-abicor.com

Syed Quadir Moinuddin, Shaik Himam Saheb, Ashok Kumar Dewangan, Murali Mohan Cheepu and S. Balamurugan (eds.) Automation in Welding Industry: Incorporating Artificial Intelligence, Machine Learning and Other Technologies, (143–156) © 2024 Scrivener Publishing LLC

forcing production companies to change their thinking. However, especially small- and medium-sized enterprises (SMEs) often consider the introduction of automation to be too high a hurdle, as it is always associated with very high investment and the necessary expert know-how in programming. Instead of directly investing in a fully automated robot cell, well-thought-out and designed welding cells incorporating a cobot (collaborative robot) are a comparatively cheap and, above all, user-friendly approach to a solution.

The automated "clean" arc welding cell solution developed by ABICOR BINZEL in the scope of this project minimizes the initial hurdle and is thus comprehensively helping SMEs enter the field of automation with all its challenges.

9.1.1 Introduction and Goals

One of the goals of this project was the development of a clean, automated welding cell with a Cobot. The cell had to include a welding torch with integrated fume extraction and cell-integrated dust monitoring as well as a gas-saving system to reduce the shielding gas consumption, as shown in Figure 9.1.

All welding tests were carried out with mild steel in the thickness range of 1 to 2 mm. The welding process was shielded gas metal arc welding (GMAW), also known as MIG/MAG welding. The filler metal used was G3Si1 (a chemical composition close to the base material). The welding

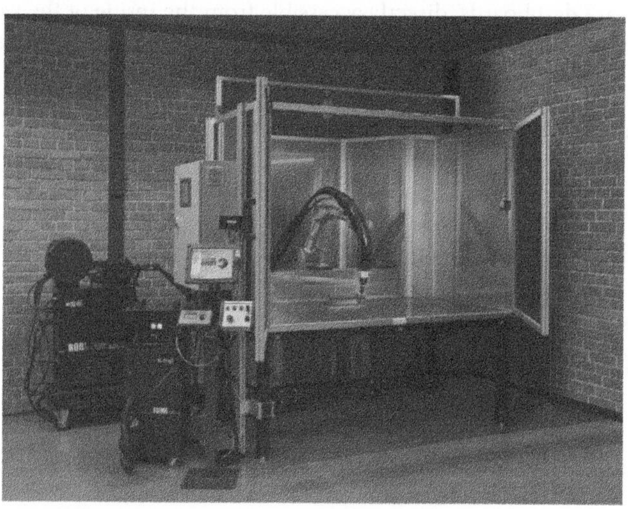

Figure 9.1 Cobot welding cell with sensors and data management.

fumes generated consist of particles and gases. As the welding fume comes mainly from the filler wire, the main components are iron, manganese, and the related oxides.

As the energy of the GMAW process is higher compared to gas tungsten arc welding (GTAW), more welding fume is produced.

Regarding the welded material, it can be stated that the most used materials are different kinds of steel and aluminum alloys. The amount of fume generated does not differ much between the different materials; it is mainly dominated by the welding process. The welding power source used allowed a maximum welding amperage of 450 A.

The fume was captured at the source by using a welding torch with integrated fume extraction. The fume extraction device was always running at maximum suction to generate a constant flow.

The welded samples were investigated after welding and showed no weld defects caused by a lack of shielding gas.

As collaborative robots are mainly used in small and medium-sized companies (SMEs) to keep costs under control, it must be stated that cobots are less accurate regarding welding path accuracy than industrial robots. This must be taken into consideration when choosing the right welding tasks for these cobot cells.

Regarding the size of the cobot cells, there are many possibilities to increase the limited reach of a cobot by adding linear or rotating axes, e.g., on rails.

The cobot welding system at this stage of development did not have any options for self-regulating, e.g., to react to increasing heat input.

Another goal was the recording, storage, and visualization of all relevant data. This included the measurement of all important process data and additional ambient data on one side. On the other side, all consumption data for wire and gas as well as the total energy consumption of the cell, including all auxiliary or secondary consumers, were determined. This extensive data recording gives the user an overview of the productivity but also information on the ecological footprint (CO_2 footprint) of the production and the products—a combination that is a novelty in this field.

The challenge of this project was to bundle all of today's customer demands regarding the recording and documentation of productivity indicators, extensive consumption key figures, and workplace conditions into one cell and one system.

For this purpose, all welding process parameters and consumption data (gas quantity, energy on the power supply, including all auxiliary consumers), as well as the inhalable dust concentration PM10 at the height of the head, were measured. This proved that it is possible to design a safe, clean welding cell while observing and documenting the limit values for welding fume exposure and—at the same time—giving the user detailed information on the consumption of energy, wire, and gas. It is a method to determine the ecological footprint of the welding cell and the goods produced.

9.2 Parameters and Consumption Data

Apart from the basic welding process key figures (process current and process amperage) shown on a live board, all other consumption data (wire quantity, gas quantity, energy of the power supply, including all auxiliary consumers and power losses) are recorded and aggregated.

The retrieval of detailed consumption data in the welding cell solutions of ABICOR BINZEL is a unique feature. So far, such have calculations only included the process data from the power source; some approaches have tried to integrate materials and filler metals, too. ABICOR BINZEL's cobot welding cell solution requires an extensive pool of data, especially for the accounting of the CO_2 footprint, and these data must include, in addition to the process data—representing the secondary side of the power source—all auxiliary users as well as the efficiency of the power source.

It should be mentioned that in this respect, for example, the power consumption of the fume extraction equipment. Even for compact central fume extraction devices for hoods and low welding power, this can be nearly as high as the power consumption of the power source itself—typical power consumptions in this field amount to 7.5 kW for volume flows of 6.000 m^2/h. For large-cell fume extraction systems, the energy consumption can be even higher than that of the welding process itself due to the post-flow times. For torch-integrated fume extraction, the power consumption amounts to less than 2 kW in general, due to volume flows that are one order of magnitude lower and correspondingly higher efficiency (e.g., xFUME Advanced 1.6 kW).

For the recording, collection, and processing of the dust exposure, welding fume sensors were installed at predefined places on the inside and beneath (as a reference) the cell at the head height of the operator. With these sensors, welding fume concentrations of 1.25 mg/m^3 (this corresponds to the inhalable fraction PM10) can be measured to monitor the occupational exposure limit value (AGW)) of 1.25 mg/m^3 valid in Germany.

All sensors are connected to an edge computing PC that processes the recorded data, transmits it through a gateway to the cloud, or visualizes it on-premises.

The result of this data recording and processing are dashboards, directly accessible in the inside of the welding cell but also remotely at a defined place (e.g., the office of the welding supervisor) via a cloud solution. Figure 9.2 shows an overview of the components included. Table 9.1 shows the data management.

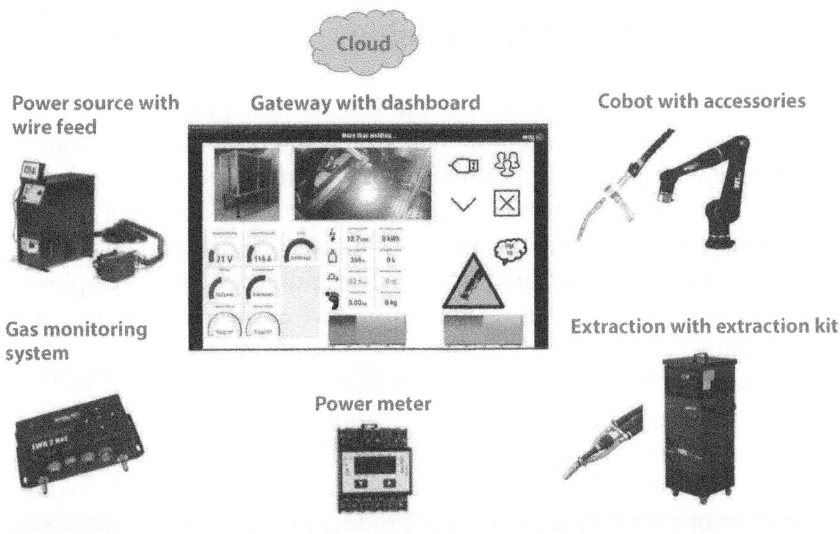

Figure 9.2 Overview of the components.

Table 9.1 Data recording and processing.

Data sources		Gateway		Visualization and analysis	
Device	**Communication**	**Hardware**	**Operating System**	**Hardware**	**Software**
Cobot	TCP/IP	Edge PC + Camera	Windows 10	Customer Network or Cloud	PostgreSQL
Power Source iROB	Ethernet				
Fume Extraction Device xFUME ADVANCED	RS485 to USB				Grafana
Gas Saving System EWR 2 Net	Ethernet				
Dust Sensor	Serial USB				OpenLCA
Power meter	ModBUS485-USB				

With the new ABICOR BINZEL welding cell concept, live data, aggregated data, and well-processed data can be determined, giving the user an overview of the consumption of energy, gas and wire, fume gas emissions, and environmental data. This allows for a comparison of different welding cells and an optimization of aggregated data with respect to the productivity of the welding cells.

9.3 CO_2 Footprint Methodology

Knowing your own CO_2 footprint and that of your products and being able to influence it is becoming an increasingly important topic for companies. Firstly, as regulations imposed by the legislation become stricter, and secondly, as more customers request data on the CO_2 footprint of the production steps in addition to the direct product data. Finally, potential qualified staff looking for a job are increasingly deciding in favor of employers and companies with a good reputation in environmental protection and sustainability.

To assess the life cycle, the Lifecycle Impact Analysis (LCIA) method from the EC-funded project "Product Environmental Footprint" (PEF) is used. This enables a comparably standardized evaluation but requires the use of the corresponding PEF database, which contains data on the ecological impact of a multitude of material production and material processing methods within the European industry.

In addition to the CO_2 footprint, further ecologically influencing factors, such as acidification of water bodies, ozone depletion, or toxicity, can be examined using the data provided by the database. As a result, and with the approach chosen, it is possible to respond to future requirements with suitable amendments.

Based on the available data, a "cradle-to-gate" analysis was carried out, i.e., the life cycle starting with the extraction of the resource up to the end of its own processing steps was examined.

Since the database does not yet contain any information on the production of shielding gases, this influence was left out in the first phase of the project or is balanced with zero.

The analysis of the influences was made with the open-source analysis tool OpenLCA, developed by GreenDelta. OpenLCA is freely available and can be addressed by external services via a JSONRPC API. GreenDelta provided a Python library for this purpose. This enables easy integration into existing software architectures and complete automation of the analyses.

The PEF database and the LCIA method can be directly integrated and used. For this purpose, a parameter-configurable process for a 1-m weld seam was defined with the inputs (type of current, shielding gas, and filler metal) and the outputs (shielding gas, weld fumes, carbon monoxide, ozone, and nitrogen oxides). In this context, it must be considered that all values are dependent on the actual process parameters, such as, e.g., welding voltage or wire feeding speed, and that shielding gas is appearing as input and output as the shielding gas is released into the atmosphere after welding, i.e., the filling and transportation of the gas are more relevant for the process than the gas itself. The input values are determined by the sensors installed, while the output values are calculated from the process data. The calculation of the output composition and quantities is based on the results of publicly funded research projects [1, 2].

Also, interfaces for direct input data are provided so that, e.g., the influence of a daily changeable power mix or a batch-dependent "CO_2 backpack" of materials can be taken into consideration.

This is where we must start, and for future improvement of the results, the quantity of available life cycle assessment data for welding wire and welding gas must be increased in the first place. There is a large potential for joint activities among material suppliers, equipment manufacturers, and users in this area.

9.4 Result Presentation

The challenge with respect to the data transmission and processing was to determine an acceptable data transmission rate and to provide a cloud solution (for this project, MS Azure Cloud), a database (Postgres), and a user surface or visualization tool for the dashboards (Grafana). The problem was solved successfully so that the user can log in from any internet connection via a secured link to the dashboards (provided on Grafana Cloud). The central compiling of a multitude of different measuring data is achieved without the data volume becoming too large, as this would result in considerable costs for local data storage or cloud storage.

Figure 9.3 shows an example of a dashboard with live data, in this case without fume extraction during and shortly after welding. The snapshot on the right side shows the highest short-time deflection measured for the dust values inside the cobot cell. Even in the case of small test workpieces, the German limit value of 1.250 mg/m^3 is temporarily exceeded. As the sensors are placed at a significant height above the process, it takes some

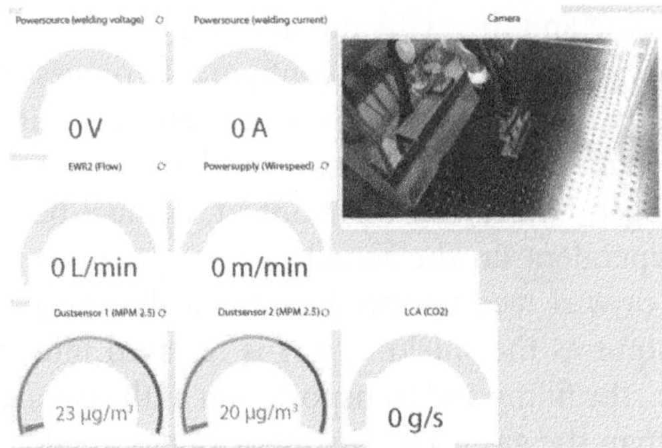

Figure 9.3 Live data cobot cell (dashboard, camera picture) without fume extraction during and after welding.

time for the welding fumes to reach the sensors; this is the reason for the time lag in the welding fume maxima measured. In this case, the welding process itself is already finished, so the actual (electrical) process parameters have already dropped to zero again.

Figure 9.4 shows the time-based welding data (current, voltage, gas consumption, and wire consumption), the total energy consumption of the cell (approximately 3 kW), as well as the CO_2 footprint in g/s. Here, too, the time lag in the peak of the welding fumes measured can be seen (note: sensor peaks are displayed in the dashboard slightly smoothed).

Figures 9.5 and 9.6 show the situation with switched-on fume extraction. Figure 9.5 shows the live data on the dashboard: on the left side during the welding process, including a live picture of the welding process, and on the right side at the same point in time after the welding as in Figure 9.3 on the right side. It shows that when using a welding fume extraction, nearly no increase in the welding fumes measured is happening, even after the welding. Figure 9.6 shows the values in chronological order and at no time during or after the welding can a significant increase in the welding fumes be seen.

In this connection, it is important that the maximum welding fume concentration amounts to 100 μg/m^3 (measured at head height); this is considerably below all limit values. Despite working with a mobile, compact fume extraction device, the additional energy consumption of approximately 1 kW is noticeable. As the fume extraction is done by spot extraction on the robotic torch, no large extraction hood with correspondingly large,

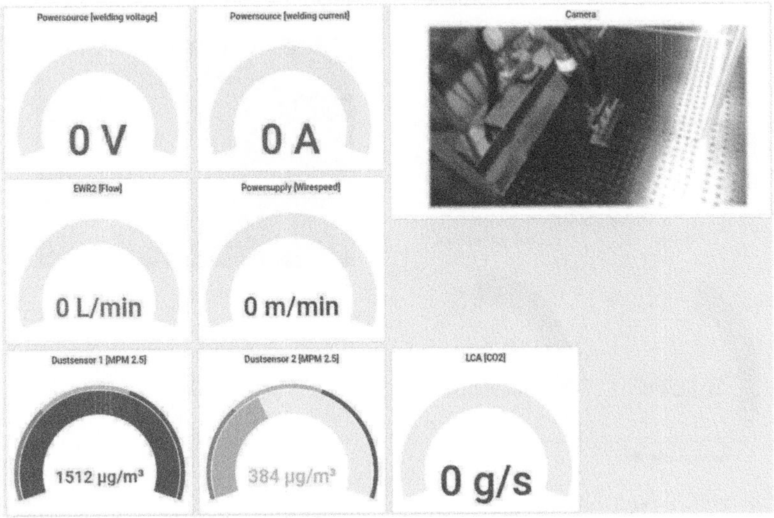

Figure 9.4 Aggregated data cobot cell without fume extraction.

stationary extraction equipment is needed. This saves several kW in power requirements and is a comparably easy way of increasing the efficiency of the whole equipment.

The power consumption of the fume extraction device has a measurable impact on the CO_2 footprint and cannot be neglected despite its high efficiency due to an efficient extraction close to the point of origin and integrated in the torch. The CO_2 footprint increases from approximately 5.6 g/s to 6.4 g/s.

Figure 9.7 compares the processes with and without fume extraction in a diagram. Without fume extraction, the welding fume remains inside the welding cell in a considerably higher concentration and over a longer period of time.

Finally, Figure 9.8 shows an overview dashboard enabling the selection of the cell as well as the display of live and consumption data. A special focus with respect to the design was the easy comprehension of the information.

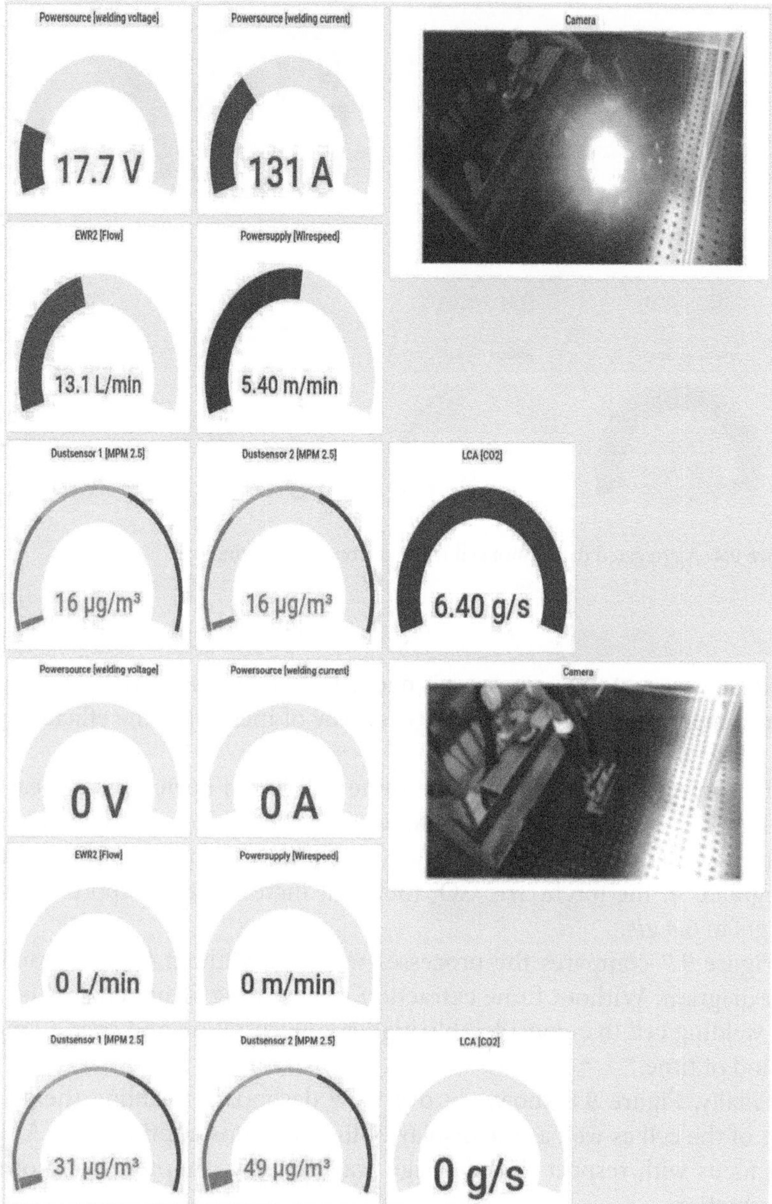

Figure 9.5 Live data cobot cell (dashboard, camera picture) with fume extraction.

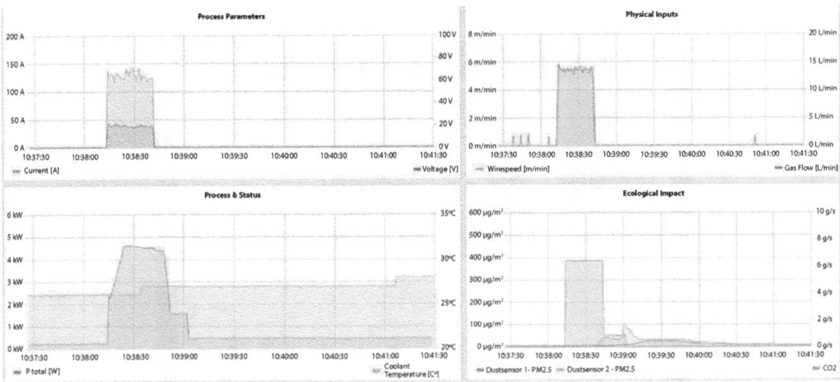

Figure 9.6 Aggregated data cobot cell with fume extraction.

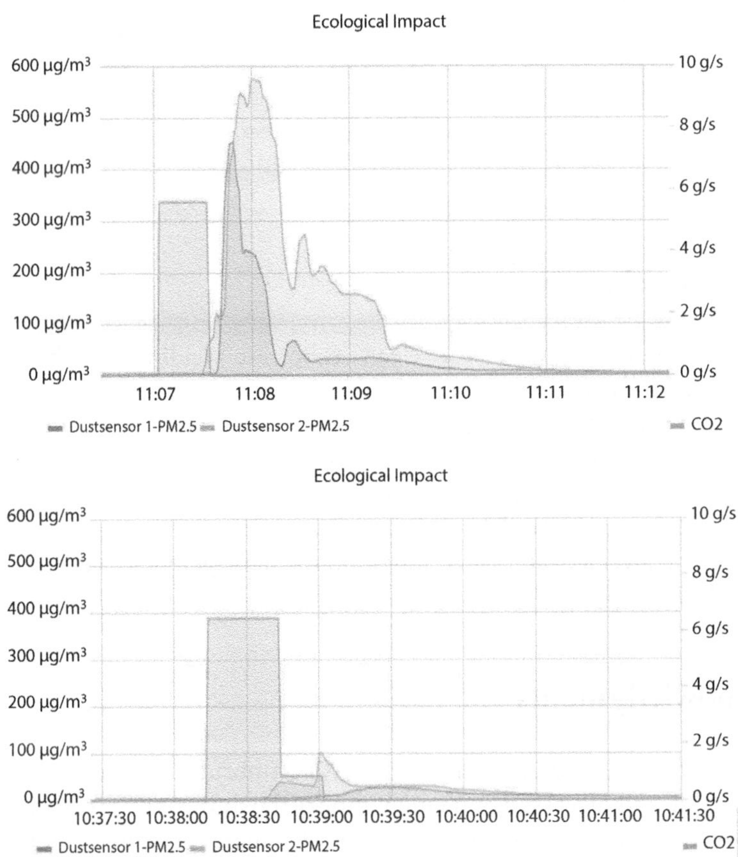

Figure 9.7 Comparison of the consumption data without (top) and with (bottom) fume extraction over a defined period of time.

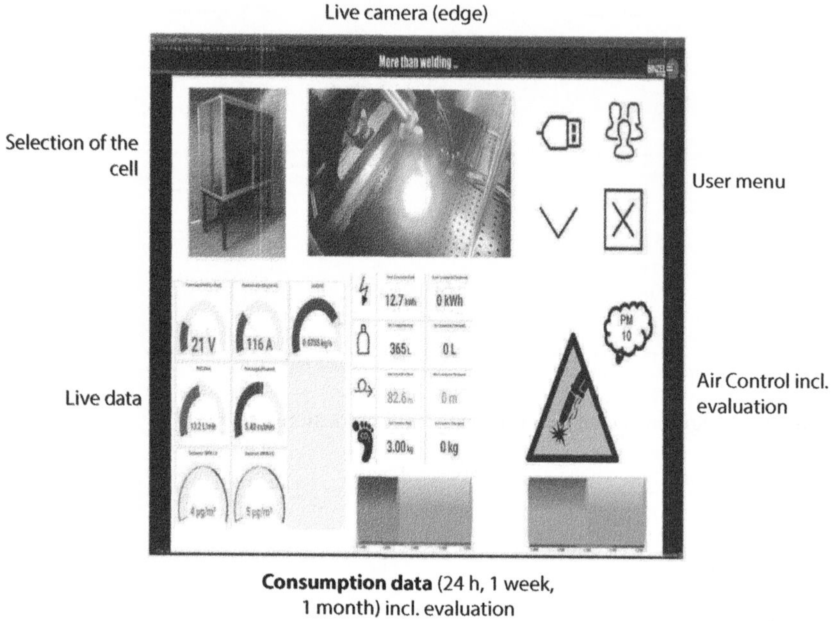

Figure 9.8 Example of an overview dashboard.

9.5 Conclusion

In summary, the concept of a "clean" robot arc welding cell shows the advantages of the use of flexible collaborative robots for SMCs in the fields of application and technology, as well as the potential of using additional sensor technology. The sensors can be used to collect additional information apart from the standard welding process data and to visualize or display live and aggregated data. This information can be used in the cells on the working level for fault detection or on the management level in a cloud for analysis purposes.

Acknowledgments

ABICOR BINZEL would like to thank TWI Cambridge for the cooperative partnership and successful implementation of the studies on the Clean Robot Arc Welding Cell Line as part of the project "Digital Dynamic Knowledge Platform for Welding in Manufacturing Industries" (WeldGalaxy) within the framework of the EU funding program for research and innovation "Horizon 2020" (grant number No. 822106).

References

1. Chang, Y.-J., Sproesser, G., Neugebauer, S., Wolf, K., Scheumann, R., Pittner, A., Rethmeier, M., Finkbeiner, M., Environmental and social life cycle assessment of welding technologies. *Proc. CIRP*, 26, 157–164, 2015. https://doi.org/10.1016/j.procir.2014.07.084.
2. Sproesser, G., *Umweltbewertung und Ökoeffizienz beim Metall-Schutzgasschweißen von Dickblechverbindungen*, Doctoral Thesis, Technical University Berlin, 2017, https://doi.org/10.14279/depositonce-5794.

10

Welding-Based 3D, 4D, 5D Printing

Suresh Goka[1], Satish Narayana Srirama[2], Divya Jyothi G.[3], Syed Quadir Moinuddin[4*] and Himam Saheb Shaik[4†]

[1]National Institute of Technology, Warangal, Telangana, India
[2]School of Computer and Information Sciences, University of Hyderabad, Hyderabad, India
[3]Centurion University, Paralakhemundi, India
[4]Department of Mechanical Engineering, College of Engineering, King Faisal University, Al-Hofuf, Kingdom of Saudi Arabia

Abstract

Many novel technologies are emerging on the market every day that improve the lifespan and quality of products. In the manufacturing field, the world rapidly adopts new technologies used for printing these products, viz., processes like three-dimensional printing (3DP), four-dimensional printing (4DP), and five-dimensional printing (5DP). Although many are still in the early stages of development, they already have a lot of promise.

The 3D and 4D printing technologies have opened new windows for a better future in various fields, especially in the production field. These new technologies, which are very successful at producing complex shapes, are being used in many sectors—from small-scale to large-scale industries. Although 5D printing is still a recent technological innovation, we are already familiar with the benefits of 3DP and 4DP and are not limited to printing only 3D objects. Therefore, the application of this technology continues to be an intriguing subject. Thus, our goal is to clarify these technologies and outline how they differ from the widely used 3D printing method for welding purposes across various fields.

***Keywords*:** Printing technologies, STL, additive manufacturing, direct energy deposition, hybrid layered manufacturing, functional gradient material, wire arc additive manufacturing, finite element analysis

**Corresponding author*: syedquadirmoinuddin@gmail.com
†*Corresponding author*: himamsaheb@ifheindia.org

Syed Quadir Moinuddin, Shaik Himam Saheb, Ashok Kumar Dewangan, Murali Mohan Cheepu and S. Balamurugan (eds.) Automation in Welding Industry: Incorporating Artificial Intelligence, Machine Learning and Other Technologies, (157–182) © 2024 Scrivener Publishing LLC

Nomenclature

3DP	Three-Dimensional Printing
STL	Standard Triangulation Language
4DP	Four-Dimensional Printing
AM	Additive Manufacturing
GMAW	Gas Metal Arc Welding
5DP	Five-Dimensional Printing
MIG	Metal Inert Gas
MAG	Metal Active Gas
TIG	Tungsten Inert Gas
FEA	Finite Element Analysis
HLM	Hybrid Layered Manufacturing
DED	Direct Energy Deposition
PBS	Powder Bed Fusion
HLA	Hybrid Laser Arc
ANN	Artificial Neural Network
WAAM	Wire-Arc Additive Manufacturing
FSP	Friction Stir Process
LENS	Laser Electron Beam Welding
DHC	Directionally Heat Conductive
FGM	Functionally Gradient Material
HAZ	Heat Affected Zone
SDM	Shaped Deposition Manufacturing
EBM	Electron Beam Welding

10.1 Introduction

Over the past two decades, everyone has become increasingly aware of 3D printing, a layer-by-layer technique used in manufacturing to transform an input CAD model format file into a concrete three-dimensional product. This cutting-edge technology, which is changing how products are made, has been adopted across the world in multiple sectors and a huge number of industries. The main reason for this is that the technology is unique in its methodology for building components, where the addition of material is carried out, whereas the deduction or subtraction of material takes place in old-fashioned methods.

The addition of material imparts the benefit of creating overhanging shapes and complex geometries that were not possible before the introduction of 3D printing. Moreover, as the material is added, the wastage of material is much less, thus reflecting the savings in cost. Furthermore, the overall cost and time can be reduced by incorporating software that develops new technology for topology optimization and generative designs.

In recent years, deposition using the direct energy deposition (DED) process has drawn attention across the world. DED is an additive manufacturing process in which concentrated thermal energy (heat) is used to fuse/melt the raw materials deposited layer upon layer. The thermal energy sources are laser, electron beam, plasma arc, etc., with hybrid laser arc (HLA) becoming increasingly popular. The HLA process increases the penetration of the welded material with the torch speed (travel speed of the thermal energy source) and lowers the width of the heat affected zone (HAZ), residual stress, distortion, and heat simultaneously. It is hard to do the process with an arc or laser individually. As a result of the hybridization of the thermal sources, the process capabilities are being improved. More importantly, productivity is increased, and hence the applicable areas are expanded [1].

In the construction field, 3DP is the process of constructing structural elements of an entire building using a printer that prints materials such as concrete, polymer, metal, or other materials layer-wise. Most of the process is carried out using a robotic arm that moves to and fro during concrete extrusion. In Amsterdam, additive manufacturing (AM) is demonstrated using a printing process for fully functioning metal bridges.

While 3D printing, there are several issues with the material system and the dynamic functionality of the product that need to be resolved. To get beyond 3D printing's limits, the rapid development of modeling and design (from a concept point of view) and smart materials (from a raw material point of view) became the foundations of 4D printing, which was developed by an MIT research team and has advantages over 3D printing.

Although 4D and 5D printing are not as well-known as 3D printing, they are quite intriguing. The 5D printing process is unique compared to 3D and 4D printing. Specifically, 5D printing refers to a five-axis printing process. The printing head in 5D printing has three axes of movement: X, Y, and Z directions, and the printing bed has two axes. During printing, both the printhead and the printing bed can move. As widely known, three linear axes (X, Y, and Z) are applied in 3D printing. Contrarily, in 5D printing, five axes enable rotation in the X and Y axes, enabling the creation of curved layers. The fourth dimension used in 4D printing is time, which causes the object to react by changing its shape.

The construction of several modules with customizable material properties is made possible by activating the bond interface in the modular 4DP process. Interestingly, modules' inherent dynamic nature allows for more customization of the fixed shapes. The researchers demonstrate the integration of various materials and geometric frameworks to produce shape transfer devices with geometry-determined functionality [2].

Although 3D printing offers a remedy, it is frequently constrained by the pace of manufacturing and/or the variety of materials. The benefit of 4D printing is that it uses speed to control the transformation of 3D from 2D shapes. However, the available shapes are constrained, and multiple material integrations are challenging. Here, we present an idea that, by fusing 4D printing and modular assembly, considerably broadens the technological horizon. Specifically, an interfacial bond exchange can be used to modularly create 4D photo-printed structures made of dynamically crosslinked polymers. The production of complex 3D objects with various customizable materials is possible afterwards. This makes it possible to create complex shape-memory devices.

In recent years, the quick advancement of 3DP technology has made it possible to manufacture mechanical metamaterials with intricate phenomena in significant quantities.

Additionally, the development of intelligent programmable mechanical metamaterials is being accelerated by the further fusion of 4DP-processed smart materials. Zhou *et al.* [3] presented an outline of current progress in the 3DP/4DP of mechanical metamaterials. Mechanical metamaterials are known to be a category of functional materials with design ability and exceptional mechanical properties. Chen *et al.* [4] used the electron beam freeform fabrication (EBFFF) method in contrast to conventional additive manufacturing methods, which are performed in a vacuum environment, demonstrating its supremacy in the production of element-based sensitive alloys.

10.2 Differences Among 3DP, 4DP and 5DP

The difference between the 3D and 4D printing processes is that 3D printing uses three axes, whereas 4D printing works with a 4th dimension, time. Therefore, 4D printing has an advantage over 3D printing due to its shape-shifting behavior. However, it cannot produce items with curved layers since they need more strength. Details of how 5D printing works and how it can be used are illustrated in Figure 10.1 [5]. The limitations of 3D and 5D printing processes are that they are not able to print structures or complex geometry products that demand more strength or have curvy layers. These limitations can be overcome using the 5DP process. Two extra axes, i.e., rotation of the print bed and rotation of the extruder head, are present in the case of 5D printing.

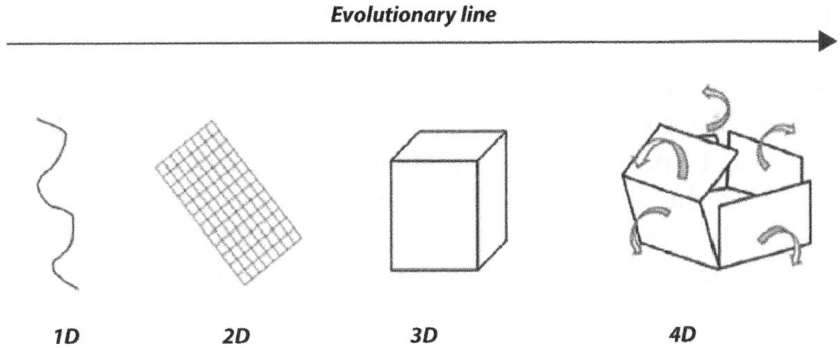

Figure 10.1 Illustration of concepts of various dimensional simple models [5].

A technique for producing three-dimensional objects is the 3DP process. It has control over the layer-by-layer installation of material (printable) to achieve the desired final product structure. Contrary to subtractive manufacturing fabrication techniques, additive manufacturing, also known as the 3DP process, is preferable in reducing material wastage because 3DP is layer upon layer sequential deposition of the required size and shape. Required 3D structure shapes are made using subtractive manufacturing techniques such as drilling, broaching, sawing, milling, and others.

Following are the many crucial benefits that the 3DP technique has over conventional manufacturing processes:

- **Time:** The structure can be made as requested in a matter of hours rather than days or weeks.
- **Efficiency:** The use of 3D printers makes the process of creating prototypes considerably simpler and quicker.
- **Quality:** It creates items with superb surface finishes to reach the highest quality.
- **Flexibility:** 3D models can use a variety of materials, which makes it more flexible to create prototypes or civil engineering models for industrial uses.
- **Cost-effective:** The cost of a building or other construction produced with 3D printing is shown to be much lower. The manufactured items are also strong and long-lasting.

The simplest way to understand the difference between 3D and 5D printing is that while 3D printers produce flat layers on a permanent platform, 5D printers can create curved layers by angling the printhead in five dimensions. The remaining steps are often the same. Identical 3D designs,

3D files, and 3D printing equipment and raw materials are used in both methods.

As a result of its reliance on various materials and 3D models, 4D printing is the most distinctive of the three techniques. With this technique, materials can be programmed to alter their behavior by adding hot water, light, or heat. The input is a "smart material," which differs from typical 3D printing materials in that it contains thermomechanical and additional material properties. These qualities allow for shape transformation.

Combining subtractive and additive processes is the essence of 5D printing. To create intricate patterns and constructions that need a lot of strength, 5D printing is the ideal option. The process is considered for specialized components, such as in the case of Mitsubishi, which uses 5D printing for the parts of its motorcycles, or those used by companies in the construction sector. These components must be sturdy to be used in industry because they must adhere to safety standards and industry rules.

10.3 Materials Used in 3DP, 4DP and 5DP Processes

Due to the fast-paced development of 3D printing (additive manufacturing) technology, a wide range of materials, including the most sophisticated and complicated multifunctional materials, are produced with these processes. With the use of additive manufacturing (AM), a wide range of materials, such as metals, polymers, composites, ceramics, cement, concrete, earth, salt, smart materials, and unique materials, can be used to create fully functional items [6].

Due to the involvement of nearly all the firms offering AM systems, metal AM shows amazing development potential. Most of the time, metals are utilized in 3D printing for research projects, component prototypes, cutting-edge applications, and more recently, short-span, and smart bridges. In metal 3DP, melting the metallic raw materials frequently involves the use of heating or temperature-raising sources.

For the 3D manufacturing of metallic materials, directed energy deposition (DED) and powder bed fusion (PBF) are the most often used AM technologies; however, more contemporary ones like cold spraying, friction stir welding, direct metal writing, diode-based approaches, and binder jetting can also be used. Polymers are the most widely used 3D-printed materials in AM technology because they work well with all commercially available AM printers and can be employed with a variety of printing processes. The industries with the most interest in 3D printing ceramic-based scaffolds for teeth, damaged bones, etc. include tissue engineering and biomaterial production. Ceramic material offers excellent durability, good resistance to temperature capabilities, and fluidization properties that enable it to take on a variety of desired shapes before setting and hardening. However, this material has two unique issues, namely a layer-by-layer look and a somewhat reduced printing resolution.

Polymers may be the most popular 3D-printed materials in additive manufacturing technology because they can be used with a wide range of printing techniques and have great compatibility with all commercially used AM printers. According to any trustworthy internet database search, concrete is the most extensively used construction material on Earth, followed by steel and wood in second and third place, respectively. Building and structure interior and exterior architectural design can be considerably improved using AM technology. Furthermore, construction costs can be reduced, and construction time can be reduced from months to days [7].

10.3.1 Additive Manufactured Metallic Components

Aluminum and its alloys, as well as titanium, are the most often utilized 3DP metals. Yet other metals, including gold, have also been effectively printed for use in the jewelry industry. The aerospace sector as well as isolated and dangerous environments have found use for 3DP nickel-based alloys because of their exceptional resistance to corrosive ions and high temperatures up to 1,200 °C. There are many techniques developed in AM to manufacture metal components. They are classified as direct and indirect layered manufacturing (LM) processes. The classification is shown in Figure 10.2, and several techniques, viz., DMD, SDM, LENs, 3D metal welding, electron beam melting (EBM), etc., have also been developed.

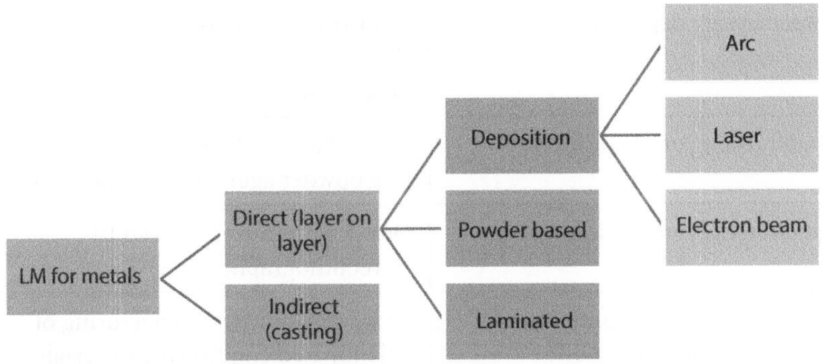

Figure 10.2 Layered manufacturing for metallic tools and components [8].

Some existing metal-based AM processes and cellular material manufacturing methods do not facilitate the micro- and macro-structures of parts and their material composition. Nevertheless, it is important to realize the conceptual design of manufacturing materials and parts [9]. In the metal deposition processes, the basic raw material, in the form of wire feedstock or powder, is melted and then solidified. The depositing head is a combination of a heat source, a powder/wire feed nozzle, and an inert gas passage.

With an emphasis on materials made of zirconia, Singh *et al.* [10] discussed the state of the art and the potential for the future of advanced material manufacturing technologies. Various additive manufacturing techniques are utilized to fabricate zirconia components using various heat sources, namely lasers, arcs, and electron beams. Table 10.1 illustrates the technologies.

Table 10.1 AM technologies producing zirconia components [11].

Additive manufacturing family	Technologies
Material jetting	Aerosol jet printing (Direct) inkjet printing
Fused Deposition Modeling (FDM)	Fused deposition of ceramic
Powder Bed Fusion	Slurry spraying Selective laser melting (SLM) Ring blade Powder Slurry coating Electrophoretic deposition Aerosol-assisted spray deposition Selective laser sintering (SLS)
Direct energy deposition	Hybrid-fused-deposition-modeling (FDM) (Traditional) direct energy deposition
Binder jetting or 3D printers	Slurry-based 3-Dimensional printing Dry powder agglomerate binder jetting
Vat photopolymerization	Direct light processing (DLP) Stereolithography (SLA)
Sheet lamination or laminated object modelling (LOM)	Computer-aided-manufacturing of laminated engineering materials (Traditional) sheet lamination

An open-sourced and low-cost MIG-based 3D printer is used [12] to produce a customized sprocket, as shown in Figure 10.3. Its properties are tabulated here. The printer is a combination of a delta robot from Reprap (Rostock) and a low-cost commercial MIG welder. The printer is controlled by an open-source microcontroller.

The development of robotics has increased tremendously in design and modeling, sensing ability and control systems. The present trends in robot-based arc welding are explained in detail in [13]. The robot-assisted MIG welding process is also used to produce complex and fully dense geometries at a low cost. All of the studies on weld bead geometry and overlapping of the beads concerning optimal process parameters can be understood with certain experiments and comparing the results with a simulated model [14]. A neural network and regression analysis have been done [15] to investigate these relationships among the process parameters of an integrated welding system by means of bead geometry, as shown in Figure 10.4. Wire feed speed, arc voltage, welding speed/travel speed, and standoff distance (nozzle-to-plate distance) are considered under procedure parameters; the height and width of the weld beads are output features. The modeling results have shown that both models produced good results; ANN gave slightly better results than regression due to its good capability of approximation in nonlinear processes. It has been noticed that heat accumulates during the layering process due to a small increase in bead width/breadth and a decrease in height.

The modified MIG welding technique, namely cold metal transfer (CMT), is a high-deposition-rated type of 3D printing process. This process

Figure 10.3 Reprap printer sprocket [12].

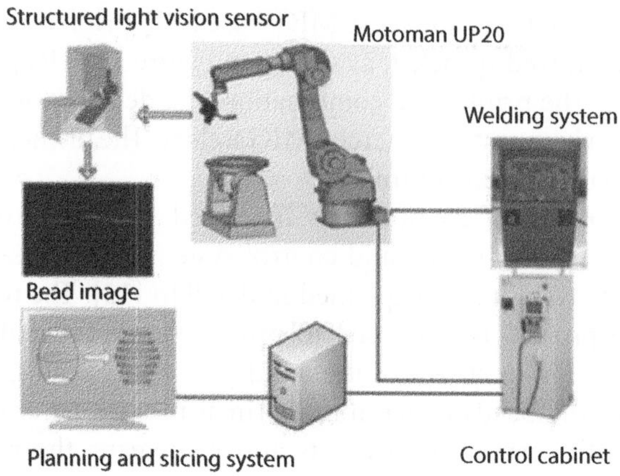

Figure 10.4 Integrated welding system [15].

exhibits greater control over droplet transfer and dilution. It can automatically adjust contact tips for work distance. Aluminum can also be used for additive layer processing. The CMT process provided benefits, such as surface tension transfer, zero spatters, automatic arc control, and lower heat input (30% less), over the other arc welding processes.

Four various types of arc modes, viz., CMT, CMT-P, CMT-ADV, and CMT-PADV, were used. Among them, CNT-PADV has developed proper thin walls with low heat input, no porosity, and effective cleaning of oxides. Pulsed advanced CMT welding has been used to prepare thin walls with ER2319 Al alloy. Furthermore, the strength can be increased by heat treatments and high-pressure interpass rolling. Using an AA2219 aluminum alloy, the porosity characteristic of the Al-6.3% Cu alloy was investigated [16].

The CMT process is useful to fabricate various geometrical structures [17] with carbon mild steel and aluminum. Various thin walls, viz., inclined, vertical, and overhang types, are produced. Here, the torch can be inclined in the direction of wall thickness to deposit the angled walls. The effective wall thickness is modified by the mixture of gases. From the observations, it was concluded that a torch speed of 0.2 m/min gave the best quality in terms of alloy efficiency and surface waviness. Figures 10.5 and 10.6 give the proper results of the CMT-deposited geometries fabricated by Kazanas *et al.*

The CMT process is used to produce large hanged structures, providing automated tool path planning [18]. A MATLAB code is generated for an automated tool path with inclined slicing so that large, hanged layers are deposited comfortably. A robust and automatic multi-direction slicing algorithm has been developed [19] to minimize the support structure.

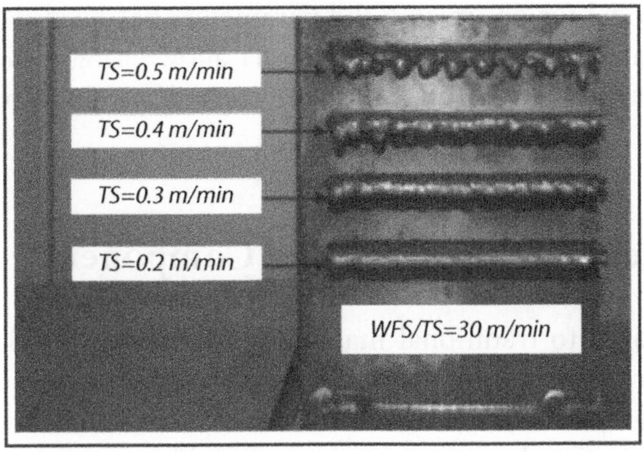

Figure 10.5 The deviation of wall quality [17].

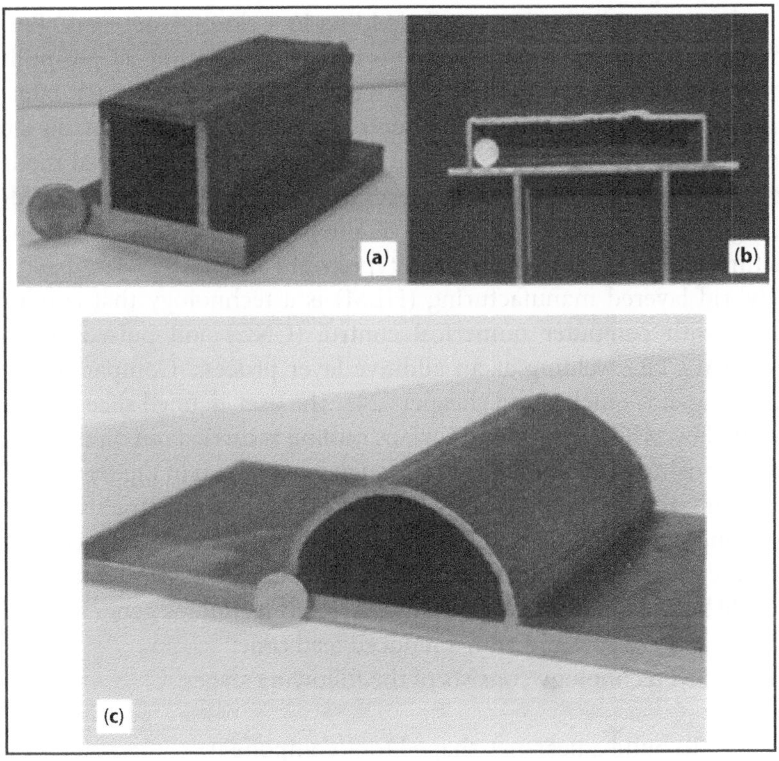

Figure 10.6 Closed sections such as (a) 50 mm square, (b) 200 mm overhang, and (c) 50 mm radius semicircle [17].

A process model for optimizing the parameters has been developed [20, 21] for manufacturing thin walls using Ti alloy. Using a fiber laser and MAG torch, deposits of HT780 HSS were created as a single bead-on-plate [1].

10.4 Machinability of Welded Components

When compared to traditional machining, the additive welding process and the subtractive milling method can offer some notable benefits. The additive manufacture of a near-net-form item offers an economical alternative to conventional processes if the material is tough to work with due to decreased tool wear [22, 23].

Moreover, utilizing the hybrid technique, characteristics that are either impossible or challenging to machine can be produced. Additionally, the deposition and machining processes can be completed in the same setup by combining additive and subtractive techniques. Each layer in these procedures is applied using metal cladding in a close-to-net form. Before moving on to the next layer, the layer is then sculpted using a CNC milling process into a net shape. These characteristics include arbitrary internal structures like conformal cooling ducts as well as deep and narrow slots. Furthermore, depending on the functional needs, the integrated method enables the fabrication of precise pieces using different materials. Welding is integrated with traditional milling as a new process called additive manufacturing to produce metallic prototypes right away.

Hybrid layered manufacturing (HLM) is a technology that combines milling with computer numerical control (CNC) and pulsed synergic MIG/MAG/TIG welding as an additive layer process. Compared to NC machining, it is quicker and cheaper [24]. The user-defined slice thickness is created by MIG welding, and surface milling is carried out on the deposited layer using CNC machining in sequence, as shown in Figure 10.7 [25]. As a result, the deposited layer is guaranteed to have an attractive surface smoothness and good dimensional accuracy. Additionally, the construction time, geometry hardness, and heat input to the beads are controlled by the weld bead geometry. Additionally, the HLM technique generates molds and dies at a low cost and with a reduced lead time.

The HLM technology consists of the following stages:

a. To build a near-net-shaped tool/component.
b. To machine the built tool till the rough final shape is obtained.

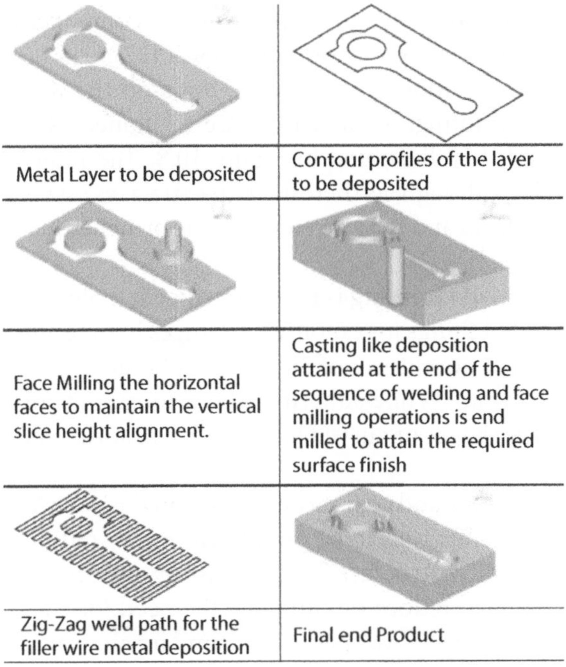

Metal Layer to be deposited
Contour profiles of the layer to be deposited
Face Milling the horizontal faces to maintain the vertical slice height alignment.
Casting like deposition attained at the end of the sequence of welding and face milling operations is end milled to attain the required surface finish
Zig-Zag weld path for the filler wire metal deposition
Final end Product

Figure 10.7 The sequence of HLM [25].

c. To perform heat treatment for strengthening.
d. To finish the tool/component until it has a good surface finish and dimensional accuracy.

10.5 Concept of 4D and 5D Printing

In comparison to manufacturing things, 3D printing technology is very cost-effective, and 4D printing, which combines smart materials and creates dynamic structures, is an evolution of 3D printing. Additionally, self-repair, self-assembly, and multifunctional qualities are possible with 4D-printed products. It is the most recent development in additive manufacturing, which is increasingly used in a wide range of engineering applications [26].

For the development of additive manufacturing, the advent of 4D printing technology considerably reduces the limitations that 3D-printed products have.

Additionally, in comparison to 5D printing, 4D printing has a relatively low modulus and is not very stable when taking the ambient temperature into account. When compared to 5D printing, the components of materials printed in four dimensions are not more robust [27].

In 3D printing technology, printing is done on the X, Y, and Z axes. When using 4D printing, 3D and time are combined as a function; the concept of 4DP [5] is illustrated in Figure 10.8. The same is not true in 5D printing (5DP), though, as there are two extra axes involved: the movement of the printhead and the movement of the print bed at a specific angle [28].

The idea behind 4D printing is to use intelligent materials that can alter the shape of printed things in response to changes in time and temperature. It is thought of as a novel form of 3D printing because the 5DP approach permits curved layers. While adhering to the constraints of the design, it produces concave shapes or curved layers with extraordinary accuracy and precision [29].

The multiple heating and cooling cycles used in the WAAM process cause the printed part's tempering to be out of uniformity [30]. Understanding the variation in microstructure brought on by process-related thermal events is necessary to reduce or eliminate the need for stress release heat treatment for printing WAAM parts with similar microstructure. Data on variations in cooling rates and remaining times as a function of part stature can be used to build computational models that can be tuned and optimized for certain processes [31].

The weld deposit torch can be inexpensively installed on an existing CNC machine without altering its fundamental operations [32]. Additionally,

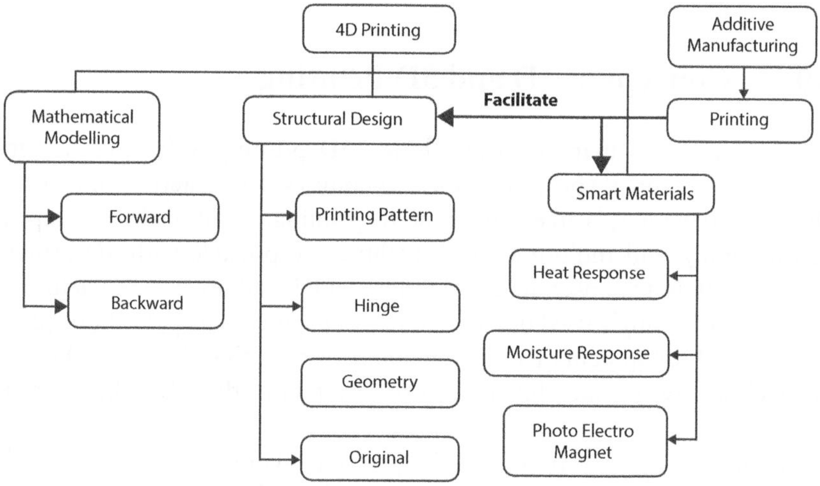

Figure 10.8 Concept of 4D printing [5].

it has clarified how functionally gradient materials, notably harder cores and dies, can be produced. They demonstrated how utilizing numerous torches may create a tougher surface.

Fabricating functionally gradient components using two separate methods is accomplished using the same process [33]. Steels with zinc and tin alloys, including mild steel, are the materials used. To deposit two distinct materials in a single layer using the first method, two separate guns are used. A single cannon is used to create the layer's boundary, while a second gun is used to fill the boundary's inside region. It is revealed in Figure 10.9.

The second approach is used to produce only the shell structure of the part. Later, it will be filled with low-melting alloys. Hence, it is declared that this method has the viability to manufacture rapid tools like injection molds and mold inserts. The thermal stress evaluation and residual stress distribution are investigated for single-pass multilayer (SPML)-manufactured parts. And an analysis [34] is done for the effect of deposition direction on residual strain and residual stress. The authors fabricated core and cavity inserts using the shell casting technique. The components are shown in Figure 10.10.

A statistical process design is implemented for the MIG/MAG hybrid layered manufacturing process [25, 35] to get the required contour profile of the deposited shape. Optimal weld parameters are found for minimum surface machining. The HLM process is also used to develop multilayer FGM of mild steel and Al alloy [36]. Realization of the FG object is done by directionally heat-conductive (DHC) objects. It is observed that as it goes down to the bottom layers, the hardness is reduced in the mild steel (MS) part, whereas there are negligible variations in the Al–Si alloy part. To improve the surface quality and dimensional accuracy, another new technique is introduced with the combination of weld deposition and milling, which is known as hybrid plasma deposition and milling (HPDM). From the results of this basic experimentation [37, 38], the characterization of

Figure 10.9 Filling of thin wall parts with a low melting alloy: (a) wall before filling, (b) wall after filling, and (c) wall after surface filling [33].

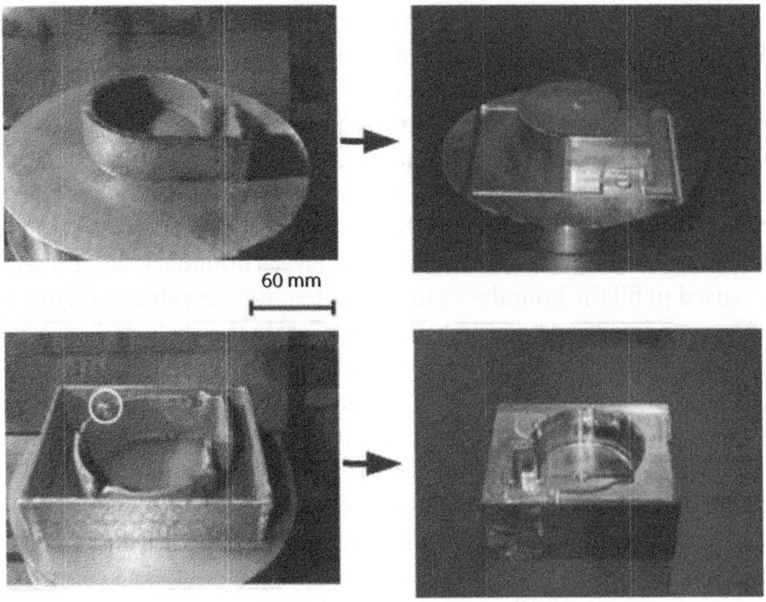

Figure 10.10 Shell casting technique: core and cavity inserts [34].

Table 10.2 Suitable milling parameters.

Parameter	Value
Milling speed V_m (m/min)	92.8
Feed per tooth f (mm)	0.0375
Amount of axis speed a_p (mm)	0.5
Amount of radial feed a_e (mm)	0.2

the fabricated part has been done in relation to its functionality. The optimized parameters mentioned in Table 10.2 have a surface roughness of 2.32 μm and a dimensional accuracy of ±0.05%.

10.6 FEM-Based Analysis

Finite element modeling considers some aspects, including thermal, fluid, metallurgical, and mechanical phenomena, concerning welding phenomena. Boundary conditions in mechanical and thermal aspects, material nonlinearities, and geometric discretization must all be considered. Then, only an appropriate FEM analysis for physically based weld models can be created [39, 40]. This is accomplished by discretizing models into individual elements or meshing.

The FEM model was used to investigate the mechanical structural implications of layered manufacturing-produced geometries. Thermal and structural impacts on the workpiece vary for different patterns, according to simulations [41] with a double ellipsoidal heat source. The parameters of the heat source are listed in Table 10.3. The arrangement that results in the least amount of structural warpage is the best. When the deposition began on the periphery and ended in the center, it is possible.

Tensile strains in the direction of the additional layer typically result in laminar tearing for components that are quickly fabricated via welding. It results from residual tension in the parts. Preheating the substrate is, therefore, necessary to avoid this issue and ensure higher-performing structures. Xu *et al.* [42] performed the corresponding temperature field and residual stress analyses, which revealed the refined ferrite grains and trace amounts of pearlite. For single-pass, multilayer produced parts, the evaluation of thermal stress and the distribution of residual stress are studied. Additionally, an analysis is done to determine the impact of deposition direction on residual strain and residual stress [34]. Thermo-elastic-plastic finite element analysis has been done for MS material to know the thermo-mechanical performances [43].

Table 10.3 Double ellipsoid heat source parameter [20].

Description	Value
Front ellipsoidal semi-axes length c_f (mm)	5
Rear ellipsoidal semi-length c_r (mm)	15
The half-width of arc a (mm)	5
Depth of arc b (mm)	4
Fraction of heat deposited in the front f_f	0.5
Fraction of heat deposited in the rear f_r	1.5
Voltage V (volts)	24
Welding current I (A)	232
Arc efficiency η (%)	75
Welding speed v (mm/s)	6.25

10.7 Applications

Three-dimensional printing is a revolutionary technology that has many applications across various industries. Here are some of the most common applications of 3D printing:

- **Rapid prototyping:** 3D printing is commonly used for rapid prototyping, allowing designers and engineers to quickly produce physical models of their designs, test them, and adjust before going into production.
- **Manufacturing:** 3D printing is increasingly being used in manufacturing to produce complex components. This can include anything from aerospace components to medical implants.
- **Architecture and construction:** 3D printing is used to create architectural models as well as large-scale construction components such as walls, columns, and beams.
- **Education:** 3D printing is increasingly being used in education to teach students about design, engineering, and manufacturing. It can also be used to create physical models of complex concepts such as molecules and cells.
- **Healthcare:** 3D printing is revolutionizing healthcare by enabling the production of custom prosthetics, implants, and medical devices. It can also be used to create models of organs and tissues for surgical planning and training.
- **Fashion and jewelry:** 3D printing can be used to produce customized jewelry and fashion accessories, as well as to intricate and unique designs that would be difficult to create using conventional methods [44].
- **Food:** 3D printing is being used to create edible food products, such as chocolates, candies, and even pizzas.
- **Art and design:** 3D printing is being used by artists and designers to create sculptures, installations, and other works of art. Overall, the applications of 3D printing are vast and varied, and the technology has the potential to transform many different industries.

10.7.1 4D Printing Applications

Four-dimensional printing is an advanced version of 3D printing technology that allows the printed object to change its shape or behavior over time. This is achieved by using materials that can be modified in response to external stimuli, such as heat, moisture, or light. Here are some of the potential applications of 4D printing:

- **Biomedical:** 4D printing can be used to create medical implants, such as stents or scaffolds, that can change shape or size over time as needed. This technology could also be used to create smart drug release systems that release drugs in response to specific stimuli.
- **Aerospace:** 4D printing could be used to create parts that can change shape in response to changes in temperature or pressure, making them more adaptable to the changing conditions in space.
- **Architecture:** 4D printing techniques are used to generate self-assembling structures that can adapt to different environmental conditions such as wind, rain, or temperature changes.
- **Fashion:** 4D printing can be used to create clothes that can change shape or color in reaction to different stimuli, such as light and variations in temperatures.
- **Robotics:** 4D printing can be used to create soft robots that can change shape or adapt to different environments, making them more versatile and adaptable.
- **Education:** 4D printing can be used as an educational tool to teach students about complex geometric shapes and how they can be manipulated over time.

Four-dimensional-printing has the potential to revolutionize a variety of industries, and we can expect to see more applications emerge as the technology continues to evolve.

10.7.2 3D Printing in the Aerospace Industry

Titanium alloys, nickel-base superalloys, high-strength steel alloys, and ultra-high temperature resistance ceramics are just a few examples of advanced and expensive materials that are frequently used in aerospace engineering. Manufacturing these ceramics is difficult and results in nearly 95% waste. To maintain the old parts during a plane's 30-year lifespan, large costs must be incurred. But, with additive manufacturing (AM), it is likely to produce the required parts as needed, with a correspondingly lower cost and shorter maintenance period [6]. To enjoy a lower shipping cost, aerospace components should be sturdy, lightweight, and have a good stiffness-to-mass ratio. The bearing bracket for an Alcoa airplane was topologically optimized using the topology optimization program ANSYS. This makes it feasible to boost the aircraft's efficiency and decrease weight through topology optimization, allowing for lower CO_2 emissions levels and fuel savings [45, 46].

10.7.3 3D Printing in Electronics

The flexible electronics business, as well as other industries, could undergo a revolution with the use of 3D printing technology, especially for printed electronic components. A basic review of 3DP processes has been provided [46], along with information on applications, classifications related to this cutting-edge technology in the electronics sector, and the most current developments in novel 3DP materials for the fabrication of electronic devices. The requirement for multimaterial 3D printing (MM3DP) would be a crucial factor when contemplating the use of 3D printing (3DP) to build printed circuit assemblies (PCAs) [47]. Most current electronic products contain them as standard components.

10.7.4 3D Printing in Electrochemical Industries

Batteries and supercapacitors are examples of electrochemical energy storage (EES) systems, which are increasingly being used as the primary power sources in efforts to shift away from the inefficient use of fossil fuels and towards sustainable and renewable energy sources [48].

10.7.5 5D Printing in Dentistry

The 5D printing process will outperform 3D and 4D printing in the field of healthcare, particularly dental surgery, as a cutting-edge manufacturing process for creating orthodontic braces, crowns, aligners, implants, bridges, and equipment [49]. It is used in the dental industry in various fields of dentistry. The 5DP method is made up of the same phases as 3D printing. A suitable dental scanner or design program is used to create a 3D image, which is then transformed into STL (standard triangulation language) or a printable format. For clinical dentistry purposes, this STL file only needs to be printed on the 5DP.

10.7.6 5D Printing in Orthopedics

In recent years, prospective applications of 3DP have been investigated in numerous dental specialties and other associated healthcare professions;

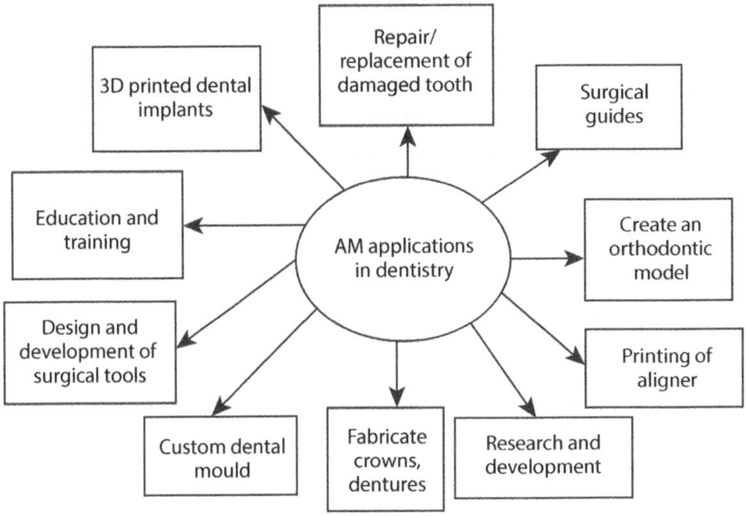

Figure 10.11 Applications of additive manufacturing in dentistry [10, 50].

therefore, the use of 5DP is anticipated for use in orthopedics [51]. The applications of additive manufacturing in dentistry is depicted in Figure 10.11. The model produced by 5D printing can be used to construct artificial bones for use in surgery. The surface of human bones is not flat; rather, it is curved. The 5D printing process is useful for printing artificial bones with good strength and high precision.

10.8 Conclusions

In the manufacturing and construction sectors, 3DP, 4DP, and 5DP have the potential to revolutionize the field with further investment in research and development. These technologies have various applications in different engineering and non-engineering fields. As 3D-printed buildings continue to advance and become more competitive, decision-makers will need to accept the trade-offs between traditional and 3D-printed civil construction technologies, as well as the anticipated impacts of their choice on human beings and cost-effectiveness. Multidimensional printing processes can use both subtractive and additive processes by nature. Before using 5D-printed items, it is important to analyze how they will be used. The processes of 3D and 4D printing are well known, and 3D printing has already become a global phenomenon in several industries, particularly manufacturing. However, complicated designs and structures that need a lot of strength are the best candidates for 5D printing.

References

1. Kapil, A., Suga, T., Tanaka, M., Sharma, A., Towards hybrid laser-arc based directed energy deposition: Understanding bead formation through mathematical modeling for additive manufacturing. *J. Manuf. Process.*, 76, 57–474, Apr. 2022.
2. Fang, Z. *et al.*, Modular 4D printing via interfacial welding of digital light-controllable dynamic covalent polymer networks. *Matter*, 2, 5, 1187–1197, May 2020.
3. Zhou, X. *et al.*, Advances in 3D/4D printing of mechanical metamaterials: From manufacturing to applications. *Compos. Part B Eng.*, 254, 110585, Apr. 2023.
4. Chen, G. *et al.*, Microstructure evolution and shape memory function mechanism of NiTi alloy by electron beam 4D printing. *Appl. Mater. Today*, 31, 101749, Apr. 2023.
5. Anas, S., Khan, M.Y., Rafey, M., Faheem, K., Concept of 5D printing technology and its applicability in the healthcare industry. *Mater. Today Proc.*, 56, 1726–1732, 2022.
6. G.H. and Ahmed, A review of '3D concrete printing': Materials and process characterization, economic considerations and environmental sustainability. *J. Build. Eng.*, 66, 105863, May 2023.
7. Schuldt, S.J., Jagoda, J.A., Hoisington, A.J., Delorit, J.D., A systematic review and analysis of the viability of 3D-printed construction in remote environments. *Autom. Constr.*, 125, 103642, May 2021.
8. Karunakaran, K.P., Suryakumar, S., Chandrasekhar, U., Bernard, A., Hybrid rapid manufacturing of metallic objects. *Int. J. Rapid Manuf.*, 1, 4, 433, 2010.
9. Williams, C.B., Mistree, F., Rosen, D.W., Towards the design of a layer-based additive manufacturing process for the realization of metal parts of designed mesostructure. *16th Solid Free. Fabr. Symp. SFF 2005*, pp. 217–230, January 2005.
10. Singh, R., Saxena, K.K., Singhal, P., Role of additive manufacturing in dental applications using ceramics: A review. *Mater. Today Proc.*, 56, 2359–2364, 2022.
11. Sun, J., Chen, X., Wade-Zhu, J., Binner, J., Bai, J., A comprehensive study of dense zirconia components fabricated by additive manufacturing. *Addit. Manuf.*, 43, 101994, Jul. 2021.
12. Nilsiam, Y., Sanders, P.G., Pearce, J.M., Applications of open source GMAW-based metal 3-D printing. *J. Manuf. Mater. Proc.*, 2, 1, 18, 2018.
13. Firdaus, and Shahril, A., Robotics application in arc welding–A review on current progress. *Int. J. Mech. Comput. Manuf. Res.*, 2, 1, 1–5, 2013.
14. Xiong, J., Zhang, G., Gao, H., Wu, L., Modeling of bead section profile and overlapping beads with experimental validation for robotic GMAW-based rapid manufacturing. *Robot. Comput. Integr. Manuf.*, 29, 2, 417–423, Apr. 2013.

15. Xiong, J., Zhang, G., Hu, J., Wu, L., Bead geometry prediction for robotic GMAW-based rapid manufacturing through a neural network and a second-order regression analysis. *J. Intell. Manuf.*, 25, 1, 157–163, 2014.
16. Cong, B., Ding, J., Williams, S., Effect of arc mode in cold metal transfer process on porosity of additively manufactured Al-6.3%Cu alloy. *Int. J. Adv. Manuf. Technol.*, 76, 9–12, 1593–1606, 2015.
17. Kazanas, P., Deherkar, P., Almeida, P., Lockett, H., Williams, S., Fabrication of geometrical features using wire and arc additive manufacture. *Proc. Inst. Mech. Eng. B J. Eng. Manuf.*, 226, 6, 1042–1051, 2012.
18. Panchagnula, J.S. and Simhambhatla, S., Inclined slicing and weld-deposition for additive manufacturing of metallic objects with large overhangs using higher order kinematics. *Virtual Phys. Prototyp.*, 11, 2, 99–108, 2016.
19. Ding, D., Pan, Z., Cuiuri, D., Li, H., Larkin, N., Van Duin, S., Automatic multi-direction slicing algorithms for wire based additive manufacturing. *Robot. Comput. Integr. Manuf.*, 37, 139–150, Feb. 2016.
20. Almeida, P.M.S. and Williams, S., Innovative process model of Ti-6Al-4V additive layer manufacturing using cold metal transfer (CMT). *21st Annu. Int. Solid Free. Fabr. Symp.-An Addit. Manuf. Conf. SFF 2010*, pp. 25–36, January 20102010.
21. Imam, M. *et al.*, Experimental study on improving the additively manufactured GMAW and TIG beads using FSP. *Mater. Today Proc.*, 56, 690–705, 2022.
22. Song, Y.A., Park, S., Choi, D., Jee, H., 3D welding and milling: Part I-A direct approach for freeform fabrication of metallic prototypes. *Int. J. Mach. Tools Manuf.*, 45, 9, 1057–1062, Jul. 2005.
23. Song, Y.-A., Park, S., Chae, S.-W., 3D welding and milling: Part II—Optimization of the 3D welding process using an experimental design approach. *Int. J. Mach. Tools Manuf.*, 45, 9, 1063–1069, Jul. 2005.
24. Karunakaran, K.P., Pushpa, V., Akula, S.B., Suryakumar, S., Techno-economic analysis of hybrid layered manufacturing. *Int. J. Intell. Syst. Technol. Appl.*, 4, 1–2, 161–176, 2008.
25. Sreenathbabu, A., Karunakaran, K.P., Amarnath, C., Statistical process design for hybrid adaptive layer manufacturing. *Rapid Prototyp. J.*, 11, 4, 235–248, 2005.
26. Tibbits, S., 4D printing: Multi-material shape change. *Archit. Des.*, 84, 1, 116–121, Jan. 2014.
27. Campbell, T.A., Tibbits, S., Garrett, B., *The Next Wave: 4D Printing-Programming the Material World*, pp. 1–15, Atlantic Council, United States, January 2014.
28. Kumar, L., Tanveer, Q., Kumar, V., Javaid, M., Haleem, A., Developing low cost 3 D printer. *Int. J. Appl. Sci. Eng. Res.*, 5, 6, 433–447, 2016.
29. Javaid, M. and Haleem, A., Current status and applications of additive manufacturing in dentistry: A literature-based review. *J. Oral. Biol. Craniofac. Res.*, 9, 3, 179–185, Jul. 2019.

30. Kulkarni, J.D., Goka, S.B., Parchuri, P.K., Yamamoto, H., Ito, K., Simhambhatla, S., Microstructure evolution along build direction for thin-wall components fabricated with wire-direct energy deposition. *Rapid Prototyp. J.*, 27, 7, 1289–1301, 2021.
31. Panicker, S., Nagarajan, H.P.N., Tuominen, J., Patnamsetty, M., Coatan, E., Haapala, K.R., Investigation of thermal influence on weld microstructure and mechanical properties in wire and arc additive manufacturing of steels. *Mater. Sci. Eng. A*, 853, 1–13, August 2022.
32. Karunakaran, K.P., Suryakumar, S., Pushpa, V., Akula, S., Low cost integration of additive and subtractive processes for hybrid layered manufacturing. *Robot. Comput. Integr. Manuf.*, 26, 5, 490–499, 2010.
33. Lee, P.-H., *Fabrication, Characterization and Modeling of Functionally Graded Materials*, pp. 1–180, ProQuest Diss. Theses, Columbia University, New York, 2013.
34. Zhao, H., Zhang, G., Yin, Z., Wu, L., Three-dimensional finite element analysis of thermal stress in single-pass multi-layer weld-based rapid prototyping. *J. Mater. Process. Technol.*, 212, 1, 276–285, 2012.
35. Kapil, S., Legesse, F., Kulkarni, P., Joshi, P., Desai, A., Karunakaran, K.P., Hybrid-layered manufacturing using tungsten inert gas cladding. *Prog. Addit. Manuf.*, 1, 1–2, 79–91, 2016.
36. Kapil, S., Kulkarni, P.M., Karunakaran, K.P., Joshi, P., Development and characterization of functionally graded materials using hybrid layered manufacturing. *AIMTDR*, pp. 1–6, 2014.
37. Xiong, X., A new method of direct metal prototyping: Hybrid plasma deposition and milling. *Rapid Prototyp. J.*, 14, 1, 53–56, 2008.
38. Xiong, X., Zhang, H., Wang, G., Metal direct prototyping by using hybrid plasma deposition and milling. *J. Mater. Process. Technol.*, 209, 1, 124–130, Jan. 2009.
39. Olabi, A.G. and Casalino, G., Mathematical modeling of weld phenomena, part 1, in: *Comprehensive Materials Processing*, pp. 101–109, 2014.
40. Olabi, A.G., Alaswad, A., Benyounis, K.Y., Mathematical modeling of weld phenomena, part 2: Design of experiments and optimization, in: *Comprehensive Materials Processing*, vol. 6, pp. 111–124, Jan. 2014.
41. Mughal, M.P., Mufti, R.A., Fawad, H., The mechanical effects of deposition patterns in welding-based layered manufacturing. *Proc. Inst. Mech. Eng. Part B J. Eng. Manuf.*, 221, 10, 1499–1509, Oct. 2007.
42. Xu, J., Zhang, H., Hu, R., Li, Y., Thermal process analysis in welding prototyping of metal structures, in: *Robotic Welding, Intelligence and Automation. Lecture Notes in Electrical Engineering*, Tarn, T.J.., Chen, S.B., Fang, G. (eds), vol. 88, pp. 383–390, Springer, Berlin, Heidelberg, 2011.
43. Ding, J. *et al.*, Thermo-mechanical analysis of wire and arc additive layer manufacturing process on large multi-layer parts. *Comput. Mater. Sci.*, 50, 12, 3315–3322, Dec. 2011.

44. Saheb, S.H., Durgam, V.K., Chandrashekhar, A., A review on metal powders in additive manufacturing. *AIP Conference Proceedings*, vol. 2281, AIP Publishing LLC, 2020.
45. Hanush, S.S. and Manjaiah, M., Topology optimization of aerospace part to enhance the performance by additive manufacturing process. *Mater. Today Proc.*, 62, 7373–7378, 2022.
46. Saheb, S.H. and Kumar, J.V., A comprehensive review on additive manufacturing applications. *AIP Conference Proceedings*, vol. 2281, AIP Publishing LLC, 2020.
47. Persad, J. and Rocke, S., Multi-material 3D printed electronic assemblies: A review. *Results Eng.*, 16, 100730, Dec. 2022.
48. Mubarak, S., Dhamodharan, D., Byun, H.-S., Recent advances in 3D printed electrode materials for electrochemical energy storage devices. *J. Energy Chem.*, 272–312, Feb. 2023.
49. Chawla, K. and Islamia, J.M., 3D bioprinting : Technology in dentistry. *Int. J. Dent. Res. Oral. Sci.*, 2, 2, 63–64, 2017.
50. Sharma, P., Sharma, N., Singh, P., Verma, M., Parihar, H.S., Examine the effect of setting time and compressive strength of cement mortar paste using iminodiacetic acid. *Mater. Today Proc.*, 32, 878–881, 2020.
51. Haleem, A., Javaid, M., Vaishya, R., 5D printing and its expected applications in orthopaedics. *J. Clin. Orthop. Trauma*, 10, 4, 809–810, Jul. 2019.

11

Welding and Joining of Novel Materials

Rajendra Goud[1], Poonam S. Deshmukh[1], Bhavesh Jain[1], G. Dan Sathiaraj[1*] and Kodli Basanth Kumar[2]

[1]*Department of Mechanical Engineering, IIT Indore, Simrol, India*
[2]*Department of Humanities and Sciences, Vardhaman College of Engineering, Hyderabad, Telangana, India*

Abstract
High-entropy alloys (HEAs) or multicomponent solid solution alloys are novel metallic alloys in which four or more elements are presented with at least 5% to 35% of each. Welding and joining of HEAs are key areas that will majorly impact future developments in these alloys. The types and selection of various welding processes are crucial to understanding the feasibility, future research, and engineering applications of HEAs. The study presented in this chapter discusses the critical research work on welding and joining of face-centered cubic (FCC) HEAs in detail for dissimilar welding methods. The structural and mechanical properties of welding zones, such as the stir zone (SZ) or the fusion zone (FZ), along with the heat-affected zone (HAZ) of various welding processes, are discussed and compared with those of conventional alloys. Laser and GMAW of FCC HEAs showed a low value of mechanical strength as compared to friction stir welding. The higher values of joint strength and appreciable ductility in tensile tests are observed in friction stir welding. Understanding the structure–property relationship of welding and the joining of HEAs may pave the way for future technological applications.

Keywords: Weldability, structure, mechanical property, welding methods, high-entropy alloys

**Corresponding author*: dansathiaraj@iiti.ac.in

Syed Quadir Moinuddin, Shaik Himam Saheb, Ashok Kumar Dewangan, Murali Mohan Cheepu and S. Balamurugan (eds.) Automation in Welding Industry: Incorporating Artificial Intelligence, Machine Learning and Other Technologies, (183–214) © 2024 Scrivener Publishing LLC

11.1 Introduction

11.1.1 Concept of High Entropy Alloys (HEAs)

High-entropy alloys are metallic materials with multiple elements in roughly equal proportions. Unlike conventional alloys that contain one or more dominant constituents with small amounts of other elements combined for specific properties, HEAs typically have five or more major elements in comparable amounts.

The unique proportions of HEAs result in extra configurational entropy, which refers to the large number of ways in which atoms can be arranged in the material's crystal structure. This high entropy makes HEAs inherently more stable and resistant to deformation than traditional alloys. Researchers have explored their potential applications, including energy, automotive, aerospace, and biomedical engineering. HEAs have shown promise for their high strength, excellent anti-corrosion properties, and ability to withstand high temperatures.

However, HEAs also pose several challenges, including difficulty processing and understanding their complex microstructures. Nevertheless, ongoing research in the field of HEAs is expected to reveal new ways of producing and utilizing these materials in the future. The conventional alloy system considers only one or two principal elements acting as a matrix. It limits the number of derivable alloys, admitting that the doping is performed with other elements for property enhancement [1, 2]. HEAs show very high configurational entropy, which leads to more stable single-solid solutions. The configurational entropy could be calculated following Boltzmann's hypothesis using the equation:

$$\Delta Sconf = -k \ln w = -R\left(\frac{1}{n}\ln\frac{1}{n} + \frac{1}{n}\ln\frac{1}{n} + \cdots + \frac{1}{n}\ln\frac{1}{n}\right) = -R \ln\frac{1}{n}$$

11.2 Core Effects

As shown in Figure 11.1(b), the four primary effects on the microstructure and phase formation, along with the characteristics of HEAs, are described below [3].

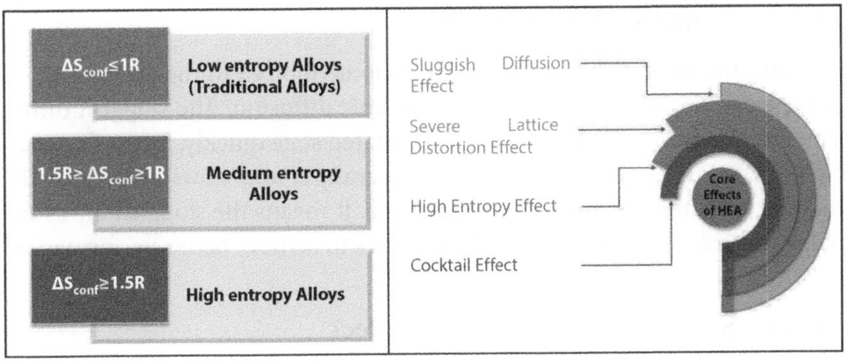

Figure 11.1 (a) Alloy classification based on configurational entropy; (b) Core effects of HEA.

11.2.1 High Entropy Effect

The HEE results encourage the development of solid solution phases and simpler microstructures. It is attributed to the medium ΔHmix, and high ΔSmix of HEAs, and Figure 11.2 compares the ΔHmix and ΔSmix to form solution phases, compounds, and elemental phases. A multi-principal element possesses a mixing enthalpy closer to or even highly competitive with the prepared state under the effect of excess mixing entropy. Thus, the solid mixture phases become dominant for the unlike atomic pairs with near-similar ΔHmix.

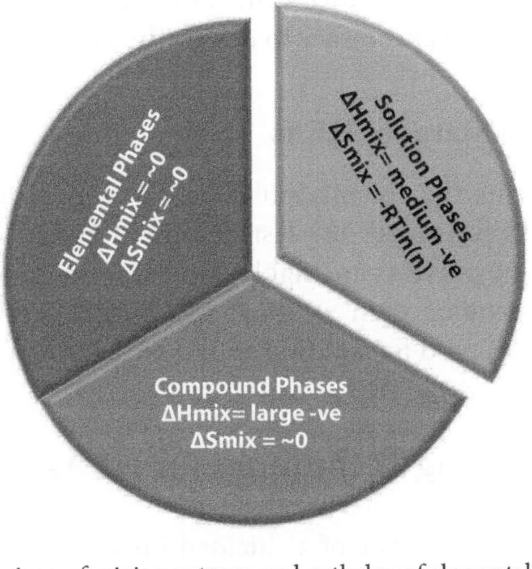

Figure 11.2 Comparison of mixing entropy and enthalpy of elemental phases, compound phases, and solid solution phases.

11.2.2 Sluggish Diffusion Effect

This effect of slow diffusion in the HEAs is attributred to the abundance of low-energy sites that hinder and trap atomic diffusion. The sluggish diffusion effect aids in reaching the super-saturated state quickly, forms fine precipitates, increases recrystallization temperature, and slows grain growth, thereby reducing the grain coarsening rate. It means the sluggish diffusion helps control microstructure and properties to achieve better performance.

11.2.3 Severe Lattice Distortion Effect

Each atom in HEAs is surrounded by atoms of different sizes from other elements since it is a whole-solute multi-element matrix. The atomic sizes, bonding energies, and crystal structures of HEAs differ, and this causes significant lattice distortions. Lattice distortions improve mechanical qualities like strength and hardness and lessen the impact of temperature on these qualities.

11.2.4 Cocktail Effect

Depending on the elemental work and processing technique, HEAs might exhibit only a single phase, two phases, or multiple phases. Each phase can be assumed to be an atomic-level composite, the properties of which are obtained from the basic properties of individual elements and their mutual interactions and the severe lattice distortions. Thus, an understanding of the underlying factors is necessary to design the alloy.

11.2.5 Current Status of HEAs

Figure 11.3 presents the recently published articles on the welding and cladding of HEAs from over the last decade. It could be observed that welding and joining of HEAs are highly popular, with cladding being more investigated and studied than welding. Subsequent sections present the different techniques used for welding and joining HEAs so far.

11.3 Arc Welding Techniques for HEAs

With or without the presence of a shielded inert gas atmosphere (argon, helium, etc.), arc welding techniques are those welding processes in which materials are melted with the aid of an electric arc formed between the

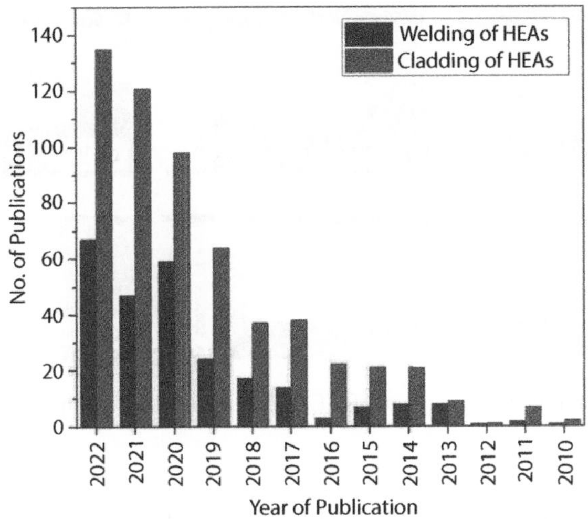

Figure 11.3 Number of published articles on welding of high-entropy alloys (source: Scopus database).

consumable and non-consumable electrodes and the workpiece. Gas tungsten arc (GTA) welding is the most popular arc welding method used for HEAs, in which an arc is created between the workpiece and a non-consumable tungsten electrode. To avoid atmospheric contamination, inert gases like argon, helium, etc. are poured into the weld area. HEA has also been joined using the gas metal arc (GMA) welding method, in which filler wire serves as the electrode.

There are other HEA compositions, but the majority of research focuses on the CoCrFeMnNi alloy, where each element is present in equal amounts. A face-centered cubic structure (FCC) is present in this alloy as a result of the system's high configurational entropy. Its outstanding cryogenic qualities and capacity to be employed as structural material are by far its greatest advantages [4–6]. To enhance the material's cryogenic and mechanical (namely tensile) qualities, further research is being done.

The weldability of rolled CoCrFeMnNi HEA using a GTAW process was investigated using two fillers: HEA and stainless steel (STS) 308L (see Figure 11.4). Filler materials are widely used in fusion-based welding processes to control and improve the constituents of welded joints to produce the desired microstructure and improve mechanical performance [7, 8]. This variation in hardness is due to the dissimilarity in grain size between BM (~6 μm) and WM (400–410 μm). The hardness distribution is related to the size of grains in various regions (BM/WM/HAZ). At the same time,

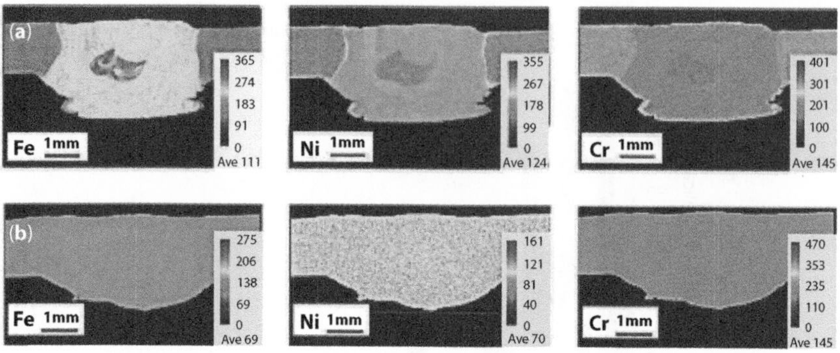

Figure 11.4 Component segregation of GTA welds using different fillers: (a) STS 308L and (b) HEA [9].

the hardness distribution behavior of welds produced using different fillers was almost the same. Hence, to improve the weldability of HEA, prevention of macrosegregation and enhancement of grains in the weld metals (WM) are necessary.

Nam *et al.* [9] then used Cu-replaced HEA filler to investigate the GTA weldability of rolled CoCrFeMnNi. The two fillers used were Co0·2Cr0·2Fe0 2Mn0 2Ni0.2 and Cu0·2Cr0 2Fe0 2Mn0 2Ni0.2. This aimed to confirm the phase separation by adding Cu, which improves the weld strength. Refined equiaxed grains were observed in rolled HEA BM, along with a small number of twins generated. However, the grains of HAZ were coarser because of the conduction of welding heat. There was also a partially melted zone near the FL with fine grains.

The Cu addition did not affect the grain refinement, as each WM revealed a similar grain size (353 μm for the Cu-replaced HEA filler and 365 μm for the HEA filler weld). However, due to Cu addition, there was phase separation in CuCrFeMnNi-based welds, confirming the Cu-rich phase formation. The XRD pattern is shown in Figure 11.5. This weld had better tensile properties and hardness than the CoCrFeMnNi-based weld (Figure 11.6) because of the Cu-rich phases. The tensile properties are shown in Figure 11.7.

The distribution of hardness is depicted in Figure 11.7. Because there were Cu-rich phases in the WM, the normal hardness of the CuCrFeMnNi-based weld was higher than that of the BM. So, it was further established that the existence of a Cu-rich stage had a greater impact on weld hardness than grain size.

In their subsequent study, Nam *et al.* [10] subjected the cold-rolled CoCrFeMnNi HEA to different post-weld heat treatment temperatures

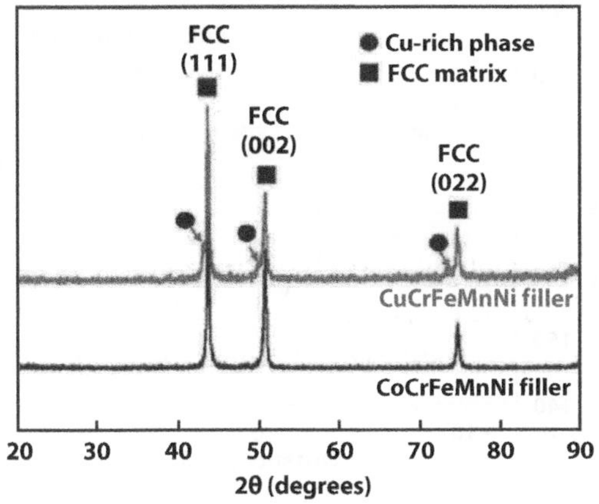

Figure 11.5 XRD patterns of GTA weld with Cu-replaced HEA filler and HEA [10].

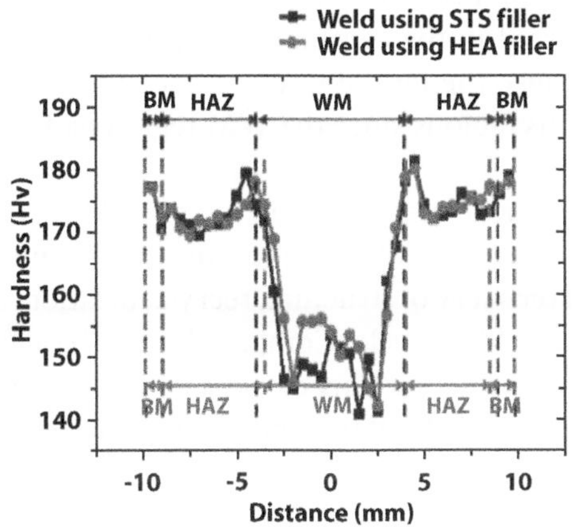

Figure 11.6 Hardness distribution behavior of welds using different fillers [9].

in the range of 973–1,173 K and investigated the Cu-coated HEA filler used to improve their weldability. The GTA weldability test was conducted under ideal conditions with complete penetration. The single-pass welding settings were as follows: 20 cm/min welding speed, 90 A welding current, Ar gas, and 1.5 F wire diameter.

The welds produced had no significant defects, like cracks or internal pores. All the PWHT-applied samples and the as-welded samples had FCC phases and slightly larger grain sizes. Hence, their tensile properties were poorer than those of BM subjected to annealing. As the PWHT temperature increased, the welds' elongation and tensile strength improved owing

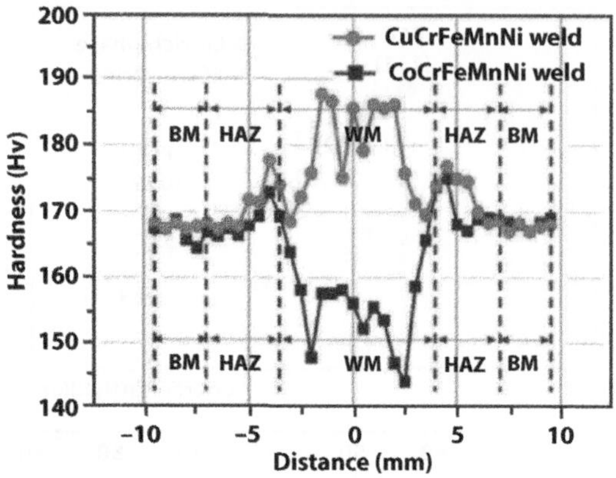

Figure 11.7 Hardness variation of GTA welds [10].

to the redissolution of inclusions, as shown in Figure 11.8. The fracture of all the welds occurred in the central portion of the welds despite PWHT temperatures, because the tensile fracture depends on the grain size and inclusions at various regions since the WM region had coarser grains than the BM.

Nam *et al.* [11] performed GTA welding of CrMnFeCoNi HEA sheets. Good weldability was observed without any significant welding defects. The HAZ suffered recovery of structure, recrystallization, and grain growth due to the thermal welding cycle. Compared to the base material, a deterioration in the strength and ductility of welded joints was reported. This can be linked to the presence of unfavorable microstructure in the FZ, such as

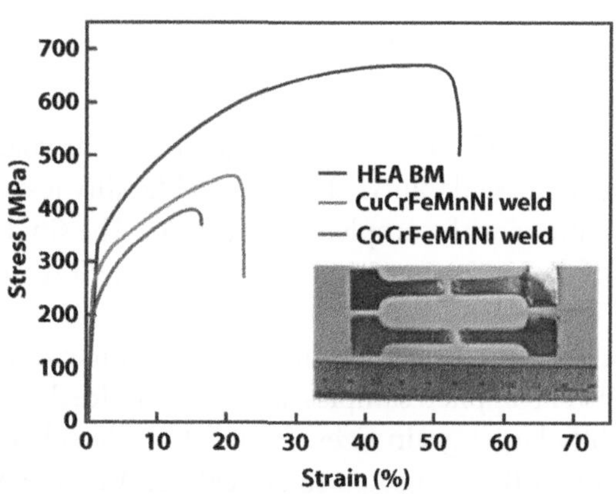

Figure 11.8 Tensile properties of GTA welds [10].

the presence of huge grains and important material softening phenomena. The yield strength for BM came to about 587 MPa, and for CoCrMnFeNi welds, it came to about 284 MPa. The tensile strength is compared with the GMA welded HEA (using ER410-NiMo stainless steel filler) in Figure 11.9.

In work by Shen *et al.* [7], GMA welding of CoCrFeMnNi HEA using ER410-NiMo SS filler wire was performed. The microhardness of all three regions (BM, HAZ, and FZ) was different, following a "U" shape trend, as shown in Figure 11.10. Since BM got strain hardening due to cold rolling,

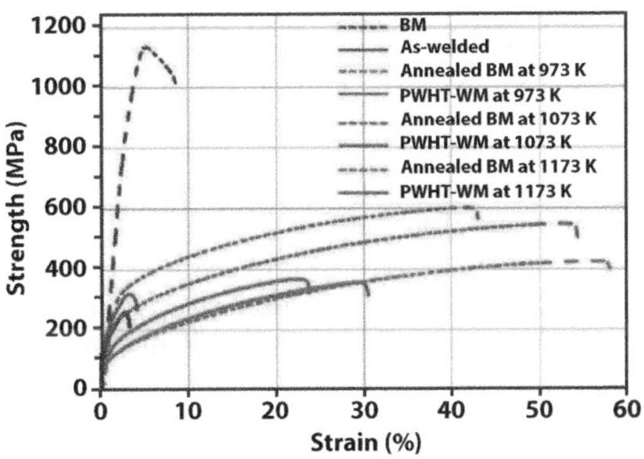

Figure 11.9 Tensile properties of GTA welds at different PWHT temperatures [11].

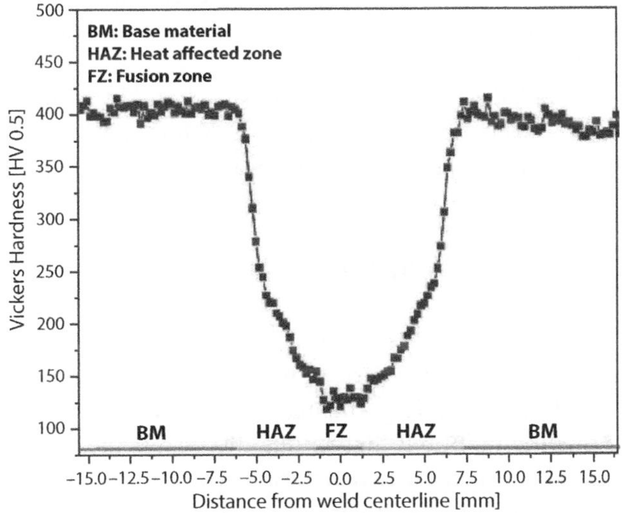

Figure 11.10 Microhardness profile at the middle of the joint [10].

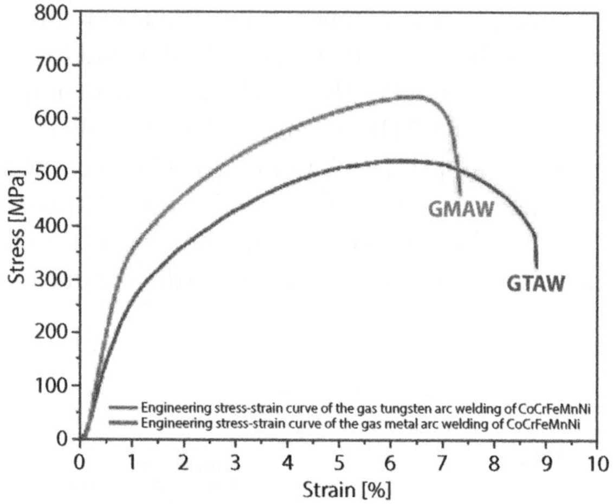

Figure 11.11 Engineering stress–strain curves of GTA-welded CoCrFeMnNi [7] and GMA-welded CoCrFeMnNi 410 SS filler [10].

it achieved the highest hardness. There was hardness decay in HAZ owing to the material exhibiting softening behavior due to the thermal cycle, which further induced grain growth and recrystallization. However, FZ achieved the lowest hardness, which could be attributed to the large grain size present in FZ. The addition of filler material did not help in increase FZ hardness. Compared with GTAW without filler material having a yield strength of 284 MPa and base material having a strength of 587 MPa, the addition of filler with the GMAW process achieved a strength of 355 MPa, as shown in Figure 11.11. This showed that adding raw filler material to join HEA is favorable.

A study by Sokkalingam *et al.* [12] consisted of Al0.5CoCrFeNi–HEA plates with homogeneous properties at 1,423 K for 24 h and subsequently subjected to cooling in a furnace, having a thickness of 2.5 mm.

11.4 Solid State Welding

A group of welding methods is referred to as solid-state welding (SSW), in which two metals are joined together without the use of a liquid or molten state. In solid-state welding, the materials are heated to a temperature below their melting point but high enough to enable the atoms to diffuse and form a bond between the two materials. These techniques are particularly useful when welding dissimilar materials, as they can provide a strong bond between materials with vastly different melting points.

One major advantage of solid-state welding is that it does not require the melting and solidification of the materials, which can lead to undesirable changes in the material's microstructure and properties. Solid-state welding also produces less distortion and residual stresses than traditional welding methods, making it particularly useful for precision applications. However, solid-state welding can be more challenging to execute than traditional welding techniques, as it requires precise control of the heating and cooling rates and the application of pressure to ensure proper bonding. Nevertheless, solid-state welding is an important technology with many potential applications in different industries.

Fusion-based welding approaches melt the welded metal and solidify it. Due to this solid–liquid–solid phase transformation, residual stresses develop, and joint distortion may happen. Furthermore, the higher width of HAZ and its softening may cause joint failure in a progressive environment. Though these issues can be curtailed by optimizing process variables, solid-state welding techniques can potentially eliminate them [13, 14].

11.4.1 Friction Stir Welding (FSW)

A more advanced type of solid-state joining than fusion welding is friction stir welding, or FSW. This solid-state welding method was created in the 1990s. It is a comparatively recent welding technique that is gaining acceptance in sectors like shipbuilding, automotive, and aerospace. The FSW process softens the workpiece material by applying frictional heat and plastic deformation, which allows for the fabrication of a weld using a revolving, non-consumable tool. The softened material is then forced to mix and bond together as the instrument is pushed along the joint line.

One of the main limitations of FSW is that it requires a significant amount of force to create the necessary frictional heat and plastic deformation. As a result, FSW is typically limited to materials that are relatively soft and ductile. However, ongoing research is aimed at expanding the range of materials that can be welded using FSW. The capability to limit solidification defects has led scientists to widely employ this welding technique in various materials [15, 16]. Researchers discovered that various similar and different materials might be joined effectively using FSW [17–21]. During this procedure, a spinning, non-consumable electrode by means of a shoulder and a threaded pin (probe) at the base is used to link the substrate. During welding, adequate contact is maintained between the shoulder and the top surface of the substrate. During welding, the material is moved from the tool's advancing side (AS) to its retreating side (RS), and the junction is then forged. The substrates, which must be linked, become heated by the tool's rapid rotation, and the plastic deformation fills the spaces [22]. The FSW procedure affects a significantly greater volume of material when compared to other fusion-based welding processes. Figure 11.12 shows a schematic of the FSW process [23].

The weld zone is frequently separated into four zones during the FSW process: the stir zone (SZ), thermo-mechanically impacted zone (TMAZ), HAZ, and BM. Figure 11.13 shows several heat zones that occur during an FSW procedure. Peak temperatures and extreme deformation are experienced in the SZ. In the SZ, a finer microstructure emerges in comparison to the BM microstructure. The SZ is strengthened by this grain refining during FSW. The TMAZ exhibits a heterogeneous microstructure with coarse and fine grains because of partial recrystallization [24].

Qin *et al.* [25] prepared the base material CoCrFeNi HEA by vacuum arc melting and conducted FSW at rotational speeds of 200, 300, 400, 500, and 600 rpm with a welding speed of 50 mm/min. The tool used was made of WC material. The shoulder and threadless pin diameters were 12 mm and

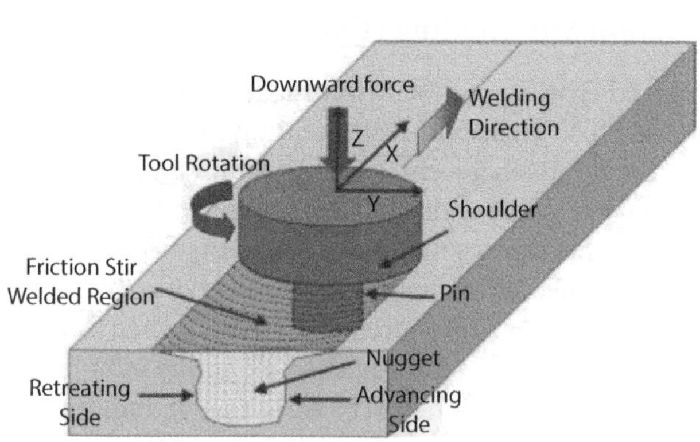

Figure 11.12 The FSW process [13].

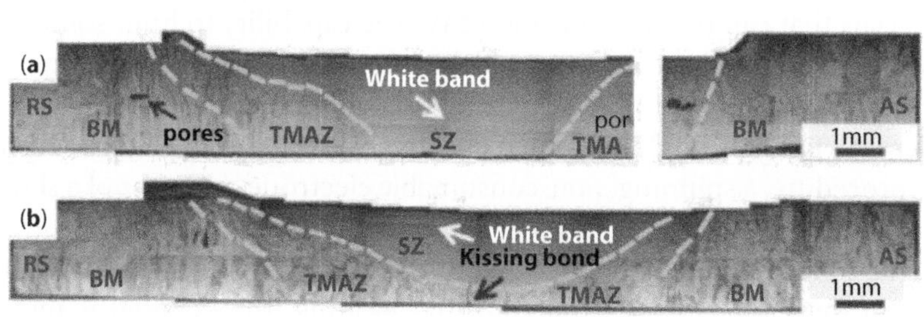

Figure 11.13 Various heat zones and its microstructures subsequent to welding at (a) 30 mm/min and (b) 50 mm/min [13].

4 mm, respectively. The authors observed that, keeping other parameters constant, the size of recrystallized grains in the SZ grew as the rotational speed of the welding tool increased. Onion-ring and fishbone structures were observed with varied parameters due to homogeneities in grain size and composition. Onion rings record the movement of the welding tool, while the alloy's turbulent flow due to the tool's higher rotational speed results in a fishbone structure. At 600 rpm, a greater tungsten particle concentration was discovered in the stir zone. These particles were thought to have developed from the wear debris of the weld tool. During the FSW process, the weld zone is typically divided into four zones: the stir zone (SZ), the thermo-mechanically affected zone (TMAZ), the HAZ, and the BM. Several heat zones that develop during an FSW operation are seen in Figure 11.13. In the SZ, temperatures reach their maximum, and deformations are extreme. In contrast to the BM microstructure, a finer microstructure appears in the SZ. This grain refinement during FSW strengthens the SZ. Due to partial recrystallization, the TMAZ has a heterogeneous microstructure with coarse and fine grains.

Nene *et al.* [26] joined Fe39Mn20Co20Cr15Si5Al1 HEA with Al-7050 using FSW, which demonstrated substantial mechanical mixing of sheared HEA particles in the nugget together with a defect-free weld cross section. Preliminary research on the weld microstructure and phase analyses showed no obvious sign of any intermetallic layer at the HEA/Al alloy contact. The joint efficiency in tensile testing was 80%, and the strength and ductility values were superior to those of the stainless steel/Al alloy butt welds.

Gupta *et al.* [27] explored the weldability of a Cu-HEA γ (FCC)-dominated metastable alloy using FSW. Fe38.5Mn20Co20Cr15Si5Cu1.5 HEA (Cu-HEA) was cast in a vacuum induction melting furnace, followed by rolling. The rolled sheet was homogenized for 8 h at 900 °C before quenching in water. FSW was carried out at 50.8 mm/min speed with a tool rotation of 350 rpm. The tool had a pin diameter of 5 mm, a length of 4 mm, a root diameter of 7.5 mm, and a shoulder diameter of 16 mm. The alloy resulted in a good blend of mechanical characteristics for all the zones, including improved nuggets and HAZ. In addition to the conventional transformation temperature, DSC was developed as a unique and practical method to explore the metastability and the transformation or twin-induced plasticity (TRIP or TWIP effect) impact in HEAs.

Lin *et al.* [28] butt-welded vacuum-arc-melted Al0.3CoCrCu0.3FeNi HEA by FSW and studied the weld's and the SZ's microstructure, mechanical, and metallurgical properties. Two HEA plates were butt-welded together using the FSW procedure at a plunge depth of 2 mm, a welding speed of 60 mm/min, and an anticlockwise rotational speed of 150 rpm. The transverse tensile properties of the SZ material were good, with YS: 920 MPa, UTS: 1037 MPa, and EL: 37%. The authors concluded that FSW is a cutting-edge processing method that improves mechanical and metallurgical properties to achieve strength-ductility synergy in a single phase.

Yao *et al.* [29] took Fe20Co20Cr20Ni20Mn20 equiatomic single-phase HEA and welded it using friction stir lap welding with pure aluminum (1,060 Al). These lap joints were created at a welding speed of 50 mm/min and a rotating speed of 1,500 rpm. The phase structures did not significantly alter due to the depletion of Cr and Mn. Stacking faults were commonly discovered in intermetallic compounds of the Al13Fe4 type and were correlated to STR II. STR III was observed as an orthorhombic Al5Fe2-type intermetallic compound.

Moghanni *et al.* [30] performed FSW with a pinless tool apparatus to weld thin sheets of the HEAs Al0.5CoCrFeNi in nine different sets of welding conditions, as mentioned in Table 11.1. The large quantity of AlNi phases (B2) that resulted from the optimal heat index also caused the pinning effect. They resulted in the tiny grain of the HAZ. As a result, the B2 phase was more critical for stopping HAZ's grain from growing. Higher hardness was achieved with a 10 mm/min speed due to the refined grains formed by high B2 precipitate. The ultimate tensile strength was also compared for different test specimens.

Table 11.1 Parameters of the joints.

No.	Specimen name	Rotation speed ω (rpm)	Welding speed v (mm/min)
1	A5	1200	5
2	A10	1200	10
3	A15	1200	15
4	B5	1400	5
5	B10	1400	10
6	B15	1400	15
7	C5	1700	5
8	C10	1700	10
9	C15	1700	15

Do *et al.* [31] investigated dissimilar joints of CoCrFeMnNi HEA and STS304 using FSW. The mechanism of dynamic recrystallization created fine-grain structures in the SZ and TMAZ. The SZ displayed a single-phase FCC. Slow atom diffusion in HEAs inhibited grain development in the treated zone.

Therefore, compared to the STS304 TMAZ, the HEA TMAZ would have a smooth grain structure. Grain refinement improved the hardness of the SZ. The cryogenic tensile performances of the FSW joint were better than their room-temperature tensile values. TRIP and TWIP processes were identified as the main strengthening mechanisms in tensile strength tests at cryogenic temperatures1.

11.5 Explosive Welding

In explosive welding (EW), two pieces of metal, identical or different, are forced together and joined using regulated explosives at extremely high pressure and velocity levels [32]. Explosive welding is a solid-state welding technique that involves the use of explosives to bond two metals together. It is a high-energy process that uses the energy of a detonation to create a metallurgical bond between the two materials. In the process of explosive welding, the two materials are arranged in a layered configuration and placed in close contact with each other. A layer of explosive material is then detonated, creating a shock wave that travels through the materials, causing them to collide and bond together. The resulting bond is very strong and can be used to join dissimilar metals, including aluminum, copper, steel, and titanium.

Explosive welding has several advantages over traditional welding techniques. First, it can be used to join metals with vastly different melting points and physical properties. Second, it does not require heat input, which can prevent distortion, oxidation, and other problems associated with traditional welding techniques. Finally, it can produce high-quality welds with minimal preparation and finishing. However, explosive welding also has some limitations. It requires specialized equipment, training, and safety precautions as it involves the use of explosives. It can also produce residual stresses, which can cause problems with the finished product. Additionally, the quality of the bond depends on several factors, including the material properties, the explosive charge, and the geometries of the materials being bonded.

Despite its limitations, explosive welding is an important welding technique in industries such as aerospace, defense, oil, and gas. It offers unique advantages for joining dissimilar metals and can produce strong and reliable bonds in a variety of applications. The impact velocity is good enough for diffusion, which links the initial atomic layers of each substance. As a result of the impact, impurities and flaws between the two materials are eliminated, leaving behind a single metal piece with perfect bonding [14]. Despite the interface generating much heat, the heat transfer to the substrate is only tiny due to the rapid EW. The microstructure developed at the interface strongly affects the strength of the EW. A schematic of the EW process is presented in Figure 11.14 [13].

Arab *et al.* used explosives to weld together AlCoCrFeNi and Al-6061 plates [33]. Base plates were made of round AlCoCrFeNi plates with a 2 mm thickness, and flyer plates were made of circular Al-6061 plates with a 3 mm thickness. To support the base plate, a 10 mm-thick Al-6061 plate was chosen. The explosive material selected was ANFO, which had a density of 0.65 g/cm^3 and a detonation velocity of 2,100 m/s. To test at various collision velocities, the standoff distance was changed from 1 mm to 3 mm. After EW, they saw that the samples with standoff distances of 2 mm and 3 mm exhibited interface cracks that spread throughout the AlCoCrFeNi alloy. The sample with a standoff distance of 3 mm experienced some cracking on the AlCoCrFeNi alloy's reverse side as a result of the reflected wave. There were no cracks visible at the welding contact in the sample with a 1 mm standoff distance. The HRTEM investigation showed the existence of the 1.8-m transition layer between the two alloys, and the diffraction patterns demonstrated grain refinement in this region. The findings of the microhardness test demonstrated that the AlCoCrFeNi microstructure after welding was unaffected by the explosion shock wave. However, the artificial intelligence's hardness increased close to the contact as a result of plastic deformation and grain refinement.

Tian *et al.* [34] studied explosive welding of FeCoNiCrAl0.1 HEA and pure copper. The copper plate was 1 mm thick and was used as a flyer plate, while the HEA plate was 2 mm thick and was used as the base plate. The emulsion explosive was made up of 75% emulsified matrix and 25% hollow glass microspheres. The explosion velocity was around 2,500 m/s,

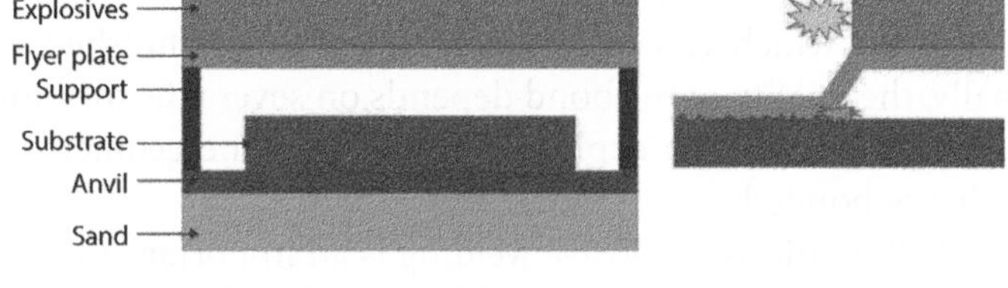

Figure 11.14 Schematic of EW process (permission required [13]).

and the density was roughly 0.8 g/cm^3. The authors reported that near the interface, there was a noticeable increase in hardness, which was attributed to plastic deformation and grain refinement. This hardness decreased with the distance from the interface. It was observed that the microstructures at the interface were elongated, and the superior thermal conductivity (K) of the copper material enhanced the rate of cooling, resulting in refined columnar grains. With increased standoff distance, more energy was consumed, and the flyer plate's high-velocity impact increased the interface's hardness.

11.5.1 Soldering and Brazing

Soldering and brazing are two similar but distinct processes used to join two metals. Both processes employ the use of a filler metal that is heated to a liquid state and then allowed to flow between the surfaces of the metals being joined. Soldering is a process in which a lower-melting-point metal alloy, called solder, is used to join two metals together. The solder is heated to its melting point, typically around 200–300 °C, and then applied to the joint between the two metals. As the solder cools, it solidifies and forms a bond between the two metals. Soldering is typically used to join thin or delicate materials, such as electronic components, jewelry, and plumbing fixtures.

Brazing, on the other hand, uses a higher-melting-point metal alloy called brazing filler to join two metals together. In the brazing process, filler metal is heated to a temperature above 450 °C, which is greater than the melting region of the metals being joined but below their melting point. As the brazing protective material melts, it flows into the metal joint and creates a strong, permanent bond between the two metals. Brazing is typically used for joining thicker materials, such as pipes, automotive components, and heat exchangers. Both soldering and brazing have several advantages over traditional welding techniques. They require lower temperatures and less heat input, which can prevent damage to delicate materials and reduce distortion and warping in the finished product. They also provide a strong, durable bond that can withstand a range of temperatures and stresses.

However, soldering and brazing also have limitations. They are not suitable for joining materials with high melting points or high strength requirements, and they can be affected by the quality of the joint preparation and cleanliness. Additionally, the choice of solder or brazing filler metal depends on the specific application and material being joined, and it can be challenging to select the right material for a given application.

Using a Ni-based filler, Li *et al.* [35] brazed AlCoCrFeNi HEA and examined its microstructure and mechanical characteristics. The authors succeeded in creating an AlCoCrFeNi HEA brazed joint that resembles the base metal and contains Ni. The CrB, (Cr, W)5B3, Ni(s,s), Al-rich BCC, and Al-depleted FCC phases were found to make up the fusion zone. Using different processing conditions, a microstructure approximating the base metal was achieved at 1,300 °C for 15 min. The strongest average joint strength was found in the near-homogeneous joint that was brazed at 1,300 °C for 15 min. It was 687.223.2 MPa. Liu *et al.* [36] soldered Au80Sn20 with CrMnFeCoNi in a vacuum and found a joint interface that was composed of Au5Sn bright phases, Co3Fe7 dark nanoparticles, and (Au, Ni, Co)Sn films. From a sample made at 370 °C to a sample made at 450 °C, the intermetallic compound layer increased steadily with temperature from 3.07 μm to 5.38 μm. A thin AuSn layer was reported at the contact region between the high-entropy and Au80Sn20 alloys. A higher Vickers hardness was reported for the intermetallic layer compared to the HEA and Au80Sn20. The average shear strength initially increased from 42.89 MPa for the 370 °C prepared solder joint to 67.52 MPa for the 410 °C prepared solder and then decreased to 39.75 MPa at 450 °C.

11.6 EBW and EBC of HEAs

Sokkalingam *et al.* [37] performed experimental investigations on the microstructure and mechanical properties of electron beam-welded Al0.1CoCrFeNi HEA to AISI 304 SS. Welded joints were defect-free without brittle intermetallic phases, thus showing good weldability. The microstructure of the weld metal was composed entirely of austenitic columnar dendrites. These were attributed to the rapid cooling rates and lower Cr/Ni equivalent ratio. The weld metal exhibited YS and UTS of 310 ± 10 MPa and 560 ± 15 MPa, which was higher than the Al0.1CoCrFeNi HEA. It ensured the suitability of EBW to join the HEA and stainless steel.

For the first time, Li *et al.* [38] successfully performed EBW to join the TiZrNbTa refractory HEA (RHEA) and obtained a defect-free welded joint. The fusion zone possessed a fine microstructure with a reduction in porosities compared to the as-casted RHEA. The hardness of the fusion zone was uniform without any significant increase. The welded joint showed a tensile stress of 940 MPa and a welding joint strength efficiency of 90%.

Yin *et al.* [39] deployed EBW to obtain a high entropic weld to join Mo and Kovar alloy with the welding interlayer of CoCrCuFeNi HEA. The weld joint was composed of the pro-eutectic fcc phase in combination with the eutectic fcc + laves phases, as seen in Figure 11.15. The border of α-Mo in the interface consisted of the continuous brittle σ(FeMo) phase, which

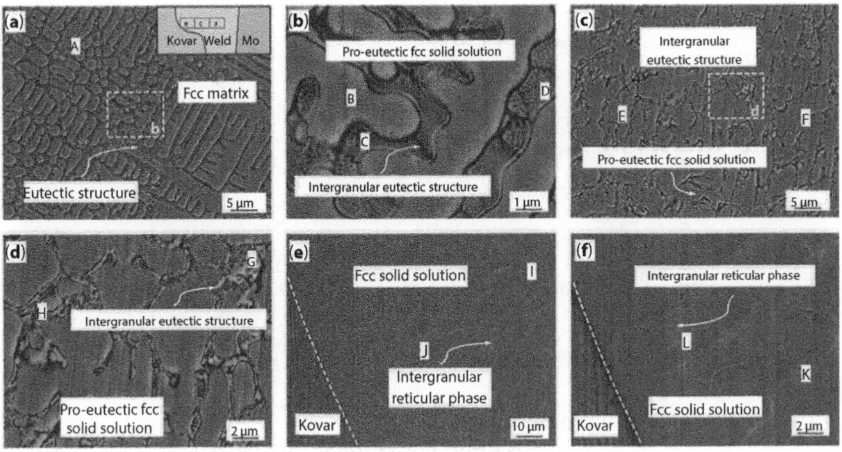

Figure 11.15 SEM micrographs of the weld metal with a 1-mm thick HEA interlayer: (a–b) Mo side and magnified view; (c–d) Kovar side and magnified view; (e–f) Fusion line at Kovar side and magnified view [39].

was gradually reduced and replaced by the irregular fine σ(FeCr) phase with the increase in HEA interlayer thickness. This transformation is considered a significant factor in the optimization of weld metal properties. When compared, the tensile strength of weld metal with an HEA interlayer was 87% higher than the joint without an HEA interlayer. This was ascribed to the arrangement of fine σ(FeCr) phases due to the superior affinity of Cr to Fe.

Since HEAs are new materials, they are being studied for use in the field of surface protection. Yu *et al.* [40] performed experimental studies on a coating of AlCrTiNbMo HEA on Ti600 alloy using the electron beam cladding (EBC) technique. The HEA coating showed bonding with the Ti600 substrate, with BCC solid solutions composed of disordered A2 phases in dendrites and ordered B2 phases in interdendritic regions. The same group [5] further extended studies to investigate the feasibility of the EBC to produce coatings of RHEA. The Mo20Nb20Co20Cr20(Ti8Al8Si4) RHEA was coated on the Ti600 substrate without any cracks or pores. The coating was composed of: BCC1 phase: Mo, Nb, Al-richA2/B2 + BCC2 phase: Co, Cr, Ti-rich-B2 + IMC1: Laves phase-CoTi + IMC2: (Ti, Nb, Zr)5Si3, as shown in Figure 11.16. The coefficient of friction of the HEA coating was 2.16 times less than that of the substrate. However, the current cladding needs were optimized since microhardness reduces with the increase in current,

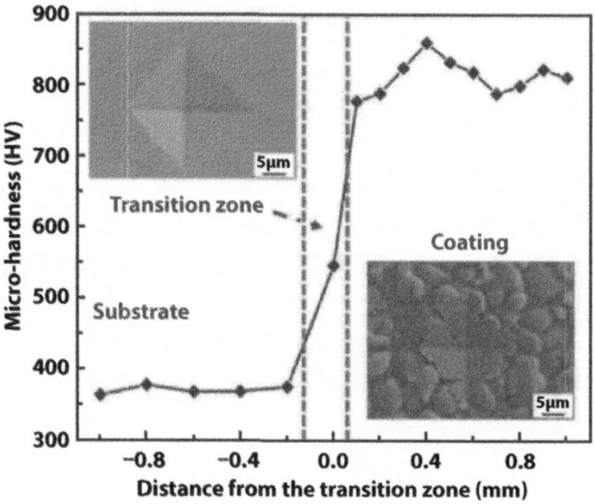

Figure 11.16 Microhardness distribution of the coating [40].

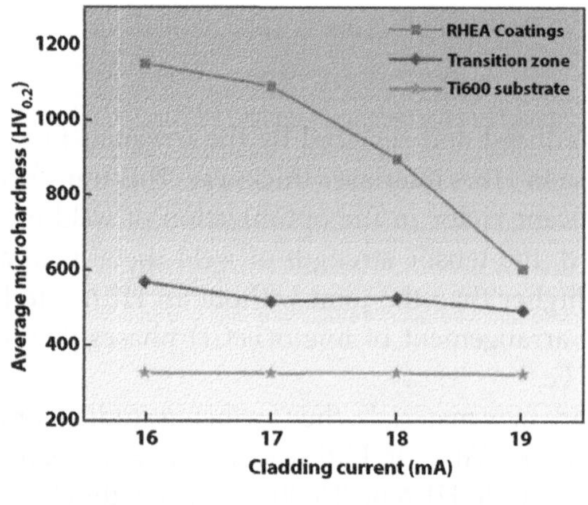

Figure 11.17 Effect of cladding current on microhardness [41].

as seen in Figure 11.17. It was attributed to the increased Ti diffusion at higher currents, which caused larger BCC1, IMC1, and IMC2, leading to hardness reduction [41].

11.7 Laser Welding of HEAs

Many research groups have worked on the laser welding of HEAs in different configurations, such as welding HEA to HEA, welding HEA to metal/

conventional alloy, and using HEA as filler material to join conventional alloys. Several of the latest studies on these configurations are discussed in this section. Laser welding of HEAs offers several advantages over traditional welding techniques. First, it is a high-precision process that allows for precise control of the heat input, resulting in a smaller HAZ and reduced distortion and residual stresses. Second, laser welding can create high-quality welding joints with minimal defects and excellent mechanical properties. Third, laser welding can be used to join dissimilar materials, including HEAs and other alloys.

Despite its advantages, laser welding of HEAs also has some limitations. One of the main challenges is the high reflectivity and thermal conductivity of some HEAs, which can make it difficult to achieve adequate melting and bonding. Additionally, the process requires specialized equipment and expertise, which can be costly and time-consuming. Overall, laser welding is a promising technique for joining HEAs, and ongoing research is aimed at improving the process and expanding its applications in various industries, including aerospace, automotive, and biomedical.

Verma *et al.* [42] carried out LBW of CoCrFeNi and CoCrCuFeNi with microstructure studies and mechanical properties. The fcc-phase CoCrFeNi alloy remained fcc even after welding, while the single-phase fcc CoCrCuFeNi alloy was composed of fcc-Cu and fcc-HEA phases after welding. On the other hand, Cu-containing alloys showed almost a 50% reduction in tensile strength from 315 MPa to 666 MPa. This drastic reduction in tensile strength was attributed to the grain growth and reduction in Cu content during welding. The experimental investigations on LBW of CoCrCuFeNi were successfully performed by Fiocchi *et al.* [43]. The average hardness of the fusion zone was higher than the base metal HEA at about 187.8 HV. The weld zone's increased hardness was caused by the creation of finer grains as a result of its quick solidification. CoCrCuFeNi has good weldability, as evidenced by the fact that the tensile strength of the welded connection was roughly equivalent to that of the base metal alloys and that failure occurred outside the welded region. Zhang *et al.* [44] performed the LBW of the Al-containing AlCoCrFeNi2.1 eutectic HEA, and Figure 11.18(a) displays the optical picture of the weld cross section. The fusion zone (FZ) consisted of refined eutectic columnar grains with preferential orientation along <111>. Fine eutectic columnar grains contained fcc(L1) and bcc(B2) solid solution phases. The base metal alloy consisted of mesh-like, well-aligned, and radical emanating lamellar structures. The heat-affected zone was composed of lamellar structures (Figure 11.18). The welded joint showed appreciable tensile strength, attributed to grain refinement and high dislocation densities. Thus, the study suggested that the LBW can be potentially used in engineering applications to join the HEAs.

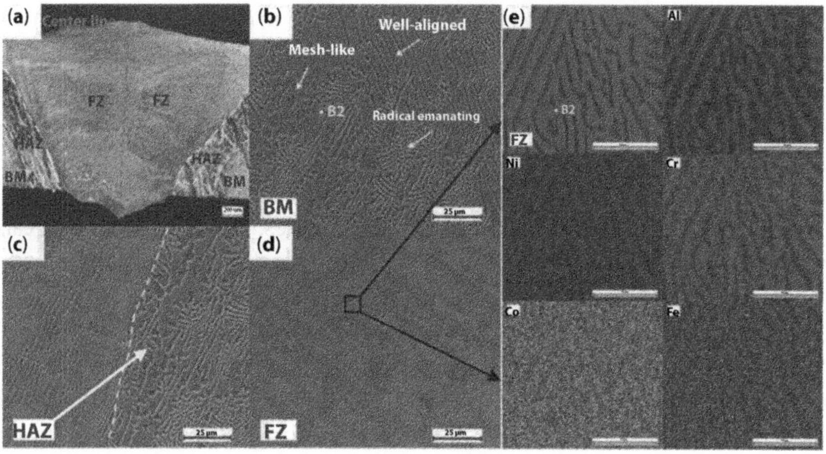

Figure 11.18 (a) Optical microscopic images of the weld joint cross section; (b–d) SEM micrographs of BM, HAZ, and FZ; (e) elemental mapping of FZ.

Shan *et al.* [45] utilized LBW of FeCoCrNiMnAlx with different content of Al (x = 0, 0.75). The Al promoted the phase transformation of the fcc-base material and the welded joints into the bcc-phase. In each case, the hardness of materials and tensile strength increased while the ductility of weld joints decreased after welding in each case. This was due to the grain modification and increased dislocation density promoted by Al content. In addition, the weld pool width and heat-affected zone increased with the increase in Al content.

Dissimilar laser welding of HEA and the conventional alloy followed by post-weld heat treatment (PWHT) was experimentally investigated by Adomako *et al.* [46]. The sound weld joint was produced without defects between CoCrFeMnNi HEA and duplex SS. Recrystallization and grain growth are the major contributing factors to hardness reduction. The weld joint exhibited comparable strength to the welded HEA, but low ductility was observed.

Furthermore, the ductility was increased by 20% after PWHT without any significant reduction in strength. The dominant deformation mechanism of the as-welded joint changed from dislocation to twinning after PWHT. Thus, the study suggested laser welding followed by heat treatment as a feasible technique to join dissimilar materials.

Oliveira *et al.* [47] carried out dissimilar LBW of cold-rolled CoCrFeMnNi HEA (Cantor alloy) to SS316, and defect-free weld joints were obtained. The fusion zone possessed a single fcc phase with large columnar grains. The solid solution strengthening of the weld zone was caused by the carbon incorporation in the weld zone from the SS316. This led to higher hardness and tensile strength, with a comparatively lower ductility of 5%. However, the welded joint failed at the fusion zone, which could be due to the large grains and microstructure developed at the failure location. The ductility in this study was much lower since the alloy was rolled. Oliveira *et al.* [48] further extended their study to increase the ductility of various welded joints. The coarse lamellar microstructure was evident in the fusion zone of the weld. The ductility increased to 10% from 5%, with tensile strength maintained at ~450 MPa and a more uniform hardness distribution in the fusion zone. Despite the single fcc-phase weld zone, the fractured zone presented mixed ductile and brittle failure features.

Mohan *et al.* [49] attempted laser welding of duplex SS (UNS S33207) and AA6061 alloy with Fe5Co20Ni20Mn35Cu20 HEA as a filler material. HEA, with its sluggish kinetic diffusion and high entropy, was used as a filler material that encourages the formation of solid solutions. The HEA filler restricted the interaction of Fe–Al and hindered the formation of Fe-Al intermetallics. The study on LBW of conventional alloys with HEA interlayer was carried out by Wang *et al.* [50]. The base metals used were NiTi and 304 SS with a CoCrFeNiMn HEA interlayer. The HEA suppressed the formation of Fe–Ti intermetallics. Therefore, the interlayer consisted of Fe and Ni, a solid solution with minor Fe–Ti intermetallics, and a B2 phase. The hardness of the welded joint with HEA interlayers decreased by 70% compared to the joint without HEA interlayer, albeit the tensile shear strength of the weld with HEA interlayer was six times greater than the weld without HEA interlayer.

Hussain *et al.* [51] successfully laser welded Ti-22Al-27Nb with the interlayer of Ti–Hf–Zr–Cu–Ni HEA. The fusion zone of the weld joint

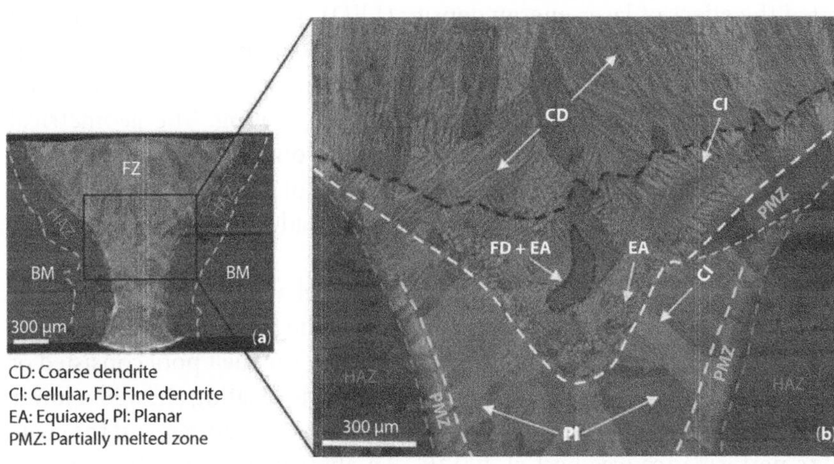

Figure 11.19 Microstructure of the fusion zone.

consists of a fine-grained B2 phase with dominant high-angle grain boundaries due to heterogeneous nucleation owing to the distinct base material and filler material. The fusion zone of the HEA interlayer was composed of columnar + planar + cellular + equiaxed dendritic grains, as depicted in Figure 11.19. The hardness, tensile strength, and ductility of the HEA interlayer joint were compatible with those of the base metal. The better mechanical performance was attributed to the refined grains and a higher misorientation angle between grain boundaries.

11.8 Laser Cladding of HEAs

Chong *et al.* [52] carried out the high-speed laser cladding (HLC) of AlCoCrFeNi HEA on SS and compared the cladding efficiency and quality with the conventional laser cladding (CLC). The HLC samples showed a ~40% lower surface roughness and a three-time lower dilution ratio than the CLC samples. This contributed to grain refinement and a decrease in the heat-affected zone. The HLC samples consisted of a single-phase BCC/B2 phase with fine columnar and equiaxed dendrites. HLC showed more potential to reduce the friction coefficient and improve wear and corrosion resistance. The same research group [53] further extended studies to investigate the effect of laser remelting on HLC coating properties. It was observed that several liquid phase separation zones were formed after HLC coating owing to rapid cooling rates, which were eliminated after remelting. The study suggested that remelting could be incorporated to enhance the service properties of the coatings. Rui *et al.* [54] investigated the effect of laser energy density (LED) on the microstructure and corrosion resistance of a FeCrNiMnAl HEA coating on 17-4PH SS. It was suggested that the laser process parameters are major contributing factors to optimizing the performance of the coating. The geometrical characteristics of the coating were dependent on the LED. Günen *et al.* [55] performed an experimental investigation of the effect of the boride environment on the wear properties of laser cladding AlCoCrFeNi HEA coatings on AISI 316L SS.

Zhang *et al.* [56] examined the wear behavior of laser cladding AlCrFeMnNi HEA at elevated temperatures. The coating showed a single bcc phase with a homogeneous microstructure. The melt pool consisted of a columnar-to-equiaxed transition structure. The Coating showed a lower coefficient of friction and wear rates at elevated temperatures, and the coating's performance was best at 400 °C. An abrasive wear mechanism was observed at room temperature, which changed to wear at temperatures of

200 °C to 400 °C. The same strengthening mechanisms with temperature dependence of hardness, wear resistance, and corrosion resistance were observed for laser cladding CoCrFeNiMo0.2 performed by Deng *et al.* [57].

Zhu *et al.* [58] laser-cladded CoCrFeNi HEA on AISI 1045 SS and annealed it after cladding. A single-phase fcc structure with columnar grains and cell substructures was observed. Cell walls showed Cr enrichment, while cell interiors were enriched with the remaining elements. However, post-annealing resulted in equiaxed grain structures due to recrystallization and eliminated segregation. Thus, a homogeneous microstructure was obtained, which showed improved corrosion resistance. Li *et al.* [59] and Wu *et al.* [60] discussed the results of Mo addition on the microstructure and corrosion resistance of CoCrFeNi laser-aided coating. The randomly oriented dendritic grain structure was observed in the laser-cladded CoCrFeNiMo (x = 0, 0.15, 0.2, 0.25) alloy. HEA with Mo0.25 showed finer grains, the highest hardness, and the lowest wear rate. Wang *et al.* [61] and Wu *et al.* [62] studied the effect of Nbx (x = 0, 0.1, 0.2, 0.3) addition on the microstructure, phases, and corrosion resistance of CoCrFeNiNbx laser-aided coating. The microhardness increased with the increase in Nb content. The HEA coating with x = 0.3 exhibited excellent corrosion resistance with a two-time larger passivation region than the 316 SS.

Laser cladding of NiCoCrMnFe HEA without any microcracks was carried out by Shi *et al.* [63]. The coating showed a single fcc phase and a hardness of 2.5 times that of the H13 die steel substrate. The wear rate was reduced by 63.2%, and the coating showed superior hot erosion resistance to liquid Al alloy. In a subsequent study, Sun *et al.* [64] laser-cladded TiC-reinforced NiCoCrMnFe HEA and investigated its oxidation and wear properties at a high temperature of 600 °C. The coating was composed of a fcc phase with micro-TiC particles. The size of TiC particles tended to increase as the TiC content increased. TiC particles encouraged oxidation under the short-circuit diffusion effect owing to higher dislocations and grain boundaries.

At elevated temperatures, uneven layers of Mn2O3 and Cr2O3 oxides were twisted on the coating surface, which enhanced the wear resistance of the coating. The coating exhibited low hardness and a high friction coefficient, attributed to the protective film of the hard particles and oxides.

Apart from Cantor alloy and its derivative alloys, few researchers have reported studies on laser-aided coatings of refractory HEAs (RHEAs). Lou *et al.* [65] deployed laser cladding to produce a coating of lightweight Al0.2CrNbTiV RHEA on a TC4 substrate. Laser power density and specific energy density parameters were realized as contributing factors to dilution. The high-speed laser cladding coatings possessed a single fcc phase and a fine columnar grain structure. The finer grain structure was due to the high-temperature gradient and sluggish diffusion. AlxMoNbTa (x = 0.5, 1.0, and 1.5) RHEA coating was produced by Hong *et al.* [66] using laser cladding. These coatings are composed of a single-phase bcc matrix with Ti2AlNb second-phase particles. The coating showed an increase in hardness and a reduction in wear rate with the increase in Al content. Moreover, a balance of wear resistance and elevated high-temperature corrosion resistance was achieved at x = 1.0.

11.9 Conclusion and Summary

The current review study provides an introduction to the various joining and welding techniques used for HEAs, such as friction stir welding (FSW), explosive welding, soldering, and brazing. The impact of various welding parameters on the development of the microstructure and the mechanical characteristics of HEAs has been examined. The analysis of numerous articles led to the conclusion that HEAs had good welding properties. The various welding techniques were shown to be effective for joining HEAs with fewer flaws and cracks. In addition, the intended weldability varied according to the compositional group of HEAs. The studies on dissimilar HEA joints were few or absent. All in all, currently, further investigations on welding and joining of HEAs are in very early stages. Hence, the welding and joining of these novel alloys need to expand their application in various fields of structural engineering, marine, nuclear, automobile, and so on.

References

1. Yeh, J.W., Chen, S.K., Lin, S.J., Gan, J.Y., Chin, T.S., Shun, T.T., Tsau, C.H., Chang, S.Y., Nanostructured high-entropy alloys with multiple principal elements: Novel alloy design concepts and outcomes. *Adv. Eng. Mater.*, 6, 5, 299–303, 2004.
2. Zhang, Y., Yang, X., Liaw, P.K., Alloy design and properties optimization of high-entropy alloys. *JOM*, 64, 7, 830–838, 2012.
3. Yeh, J.W., Alloy design strategies and future trends in high-entropy alloys. *JOM*, 65, 12, 1759–1771, 2013.
4. Guo, J., Tang, C., Rothwell, G., Li, L., Wang, Y.C., Yang, Q., Ren, X., Welding of high entropy alloys—A review. *Entropy*, 21, 4, 431, 2019.

5. Moon, J., Qi, Y., Tabachnikova, E., Estrin, Y., Choi, W.M., Joo, S.H., Lee, B.J., Podolskiy, A., Tikhonovsky, M., Kim, H.S., Microstructure and mechanical properties of high-entropy alloy Co20Cr26Fe20Mn20Ni14 processed by high-pressure torsion at 77 K and 300 K. *Sci. Rep.*, 8, 1, 1–12, 2018.
6. Tirunilai, A.S., Sas, J., Weiss, K.P., Chen, H., Szabó, D.V., Schlabach, S., Haas, S., Geissler, D., Freudenberger, J., Heilmaier, M., Kauffmann, A., Peculiarities of deformation of CoCrFeMnNi at cryogenic temperatures. *J. Mater. Res.*, 33, 19, 3287–3300, 2018.
7. Shen, J., Gonçalves, R., Choi, Y.T., Lopes, J.G., Yang, J., Schell, N., Kim, H.S., Oliveira, J.P., Microstructure and mechanical properties of gas metal arc welded CoCrFeMnNi joints using a 410 stainless steel filler metal. *Mater. Sci. Eng. A*, 857, 144025, 2022.
8. Oliveira, J.P., Curado, T.M., Zeng, Z., Lopes, J.G., Rossinyol, E., Park, J.M., Schell, N., Fernandes, F.B., Kim, H.S., Gas tungsten arc welding of as-rolled CrMnFeCoNi high entropy alloy. *Mater. Des.*, 189, 108505, 2020.
9. Nam, H., Yoo, S., Lee, J., Na, Y., Park, N., Kang, N., GTA weldability of rolled high-entropy alloys using various filler metals. *Materials*, 10, 10, 1371, 2020.
10. Nam, H., Park, S., Kim, S.W., Shim, S.H., Na, Y., Him, N., Song, S., Hong, S.I., Kang, Ny., Enhancement of tensile properties applying phase separation with Cu addition in gas tungsten arc welds of CoCrFeMnNi high entropy alloys. *Scr. Mater.*, 220, 114897, 2022.
11. Nam, H., Yoo, S., Ha, J.W., Lee, B.J., Song, S., Na, Y., Kang, N., Enhancement of tensile properties of gas tungsten arc welds using Cu-coated CoCrFeMnNi filler and post–weld heat treatment. *J. Mater. Res. Technol.*, 19, 4857–4866, 2022.
12. Sokkalingam, R., Mishra, S., Cheethirala, S.R., Muthupandi, V., Sivaprasad, K., Enhanced relative slip distance in gas-tungsten-arc-welded Al0. 5CoCrFeNi high-entropy alloy. *Mater. Sci. Eng. A*, 48, 8, 3630–3634, 2017.
13. John, M., Diaz, O., Esparza, A., Fliegler, A., Ocenosak, D., Van Dorn, C., Bhat K, U., Menezes, P.L., Welding techniques for high entropy alloys: Processes, properties, characterization, and challenges. *Materials*, 15, 6, 2273, 2022.
14. Li, J., Meng, X., Wan, L., Huang, Y., Welding of high entropy alloys: Progresses, challenges and perspectives. *J. Manuf. Process.*, 68, 293–331, 2021.
15. Mishra, R.S. and Ma, Z.Y., Friction stir welding and processing. *Mater. Sci. Eng., R Rep.*, 50, 1-2, 1–78, 2005.
16. Fujii, H., Sun, Y., Kato, H., Nakata, K., Investigation of welding parameter dependent microstructure and mechanical properties in friction stir welded pure Ti joints. *Mater. Sci. Eng. A*, 527, 15, 3386–3391, 2010.
17. Zhang, S., Chen, G., Liu, Q., Li, H., Zhang, G., Wang, G., Shi, Q., Numerical analysis and analytical modeling of the spatial distribution of heat flux during friction stir welding. *J. Manuf. Process.*, 33, 245–255, 2018.
18. Li, P., Sun, H., Wang, S., Hao, X., Dong, H., Rotary friction welding of AlCoCrFeNi2. 1 eutectic high entropy alloy. *J. Alloys Compd.*, 814, 152322, 2020.

19. Shaysultanov, D., Stepanov, N., Malopheyev, S., Vysotskiy, I., Sanin, V., Mironov, S., Kaibyshev, R., Salishchev, G., Zherebtsov, S., Friction stir welding of a carbon-doped CoCrFeNiMn high-entropy alloy. *Mater. Charact.*, 145, 353–361, 2018.
20. Çam, G., Friction stir welded structural materials: Beyond Al-alloys. *Int. Mater. Rev.*, 56, 1, 1–48, 2011.
21. Ralls, A.M., Kasar, A.K., Menezes, P.L., Friction stir processing on the tribological, corrosion, and erosion properties of steel: A review. *J. Manuf. Mater. Process.*, 5, 3, 97, 2021.
22. Kumar Rajak, D., Pagar, D.D., Menezes, P.L., Eyvazian, A., Friction-based welding processes: Friction welding and friction stir welding. *J. Adhes. Sci. Technol.*, 34, 24, 2613–2637, 2020.
23. Nandan, R., DebRoy, T., Bhadeshia, H.K.D.H., Recent advances in friction-stir welding–process, weldment structure and properties. *Prog. Mater Sci.*, 53, 6, 980–1023, 2008.
24. Zhu, Z.G., Sun, Y.F., Ng, F.L., Goh, M.H., Liaw, P.K., Fujii, H., Nguyen, Q.B., Xu, Y., Shek, C.H., Nai, S.M.L., Wei, J., Friction-stir welding of a ductile high entropy alloy: Microstructural evolution and weld strength. *Mater. Sci. Eng. A*, 711, 524–532, 2018.
25. Qin, X., Xu, Y., Sun, Y., Fujii, H., Zhu, Z., Shek, C.H., Effect of process parameters on microstructure and mechanical properties of friction stir welded CoCrFeNi high entropy alloy. *Mater. Sci. Eng. A*, 782, 139277, 2020.
26. Nene, S.S., Gupta, S., Morphew, C., Mishra, R.S., Friction stir butt welding of a high strength Al-7050 alloy with a metastable transformative high entropy alloy. *Materialia*, 11, 100740, 2020.
27. Gupta, S., Agrawal, P., Nene, S.S., Mishra, R.S., Friction stir welding of γ-fcc dominated metastable high entropy alloy: Microstructural evolution and strength. *Scr. Mater.*, 204, 114161, 2021.
28. Lin, P.T., Liu, H.C., Hsieh, P.Y., Wei, C.Y., Tsai, C.W., Sato, Y.S., Chen, S.C., Yen, H.W., Lu, N.H., Chen, C.H., Heterogeneous structure-induced strength-ductility synergy by partial recrystallization during friction stir welding of a high-entropy alloy. *Mater. Des.*, 197, 109238, 2021.
29. Yao, H., Wen, H., Chen, K., Jiang, M., Reddy, K.M., Kondoh, K., Wang, M., Hua, X., Shan, A., Interfacial phases formed in friction stir lap welding high entropy alloy to Al alloy. *Scr. Mater.*, 201, 113972, 2021.
30. Moghanni, H., Dehghani, K., Shafiei, A., Effects of process parameters on microstructure and mechanical properties of Al0. 5CoCrFeNi high entropy alloy thin sheets using pinless friction stir welding. *J. Mater. Res. Technol.*, 16, 1069–1089, 2022.
31. Do, H., Asadi, S., Park, N., Microstructural and mechanical properties of dissimilar friction stir welded CoCrFeMnNi high entropy alloy to STS304 stainless steel. *Mater. Sci. Eng. A*, 840, 142979, 2022.

32. Zhou, Q., Liu, R., Ran, C., Fan, K., Xie, J., Chen, P., Effect of microstructure on mechanical properties of titanium-steel explosive welding interface. *Mater. Sci. Eng. A*, 830, 142260, 2022.
33. Arab, A., Guo, Y., Zhou, Q., Chen, P., Joining AlCoCrFeNi high entropy alloys and Al-6061 by explosive welding method. *Vacuum*, 174, 109221, 2020.
34. Tian, Q., Liang, H., Zhao, Y., Ma, H., Shen, Z., Sun, Y., Yang, M., Interfacial microstructure of FeCoNiCrAl0. 1 high entropy alloy and pure copper prepared by explosive welding. *Coatings*, 10, 12, 1197, 2020.
35. Li, H., Shen, W., Chen, W., Wang, W., Liu, G., Lu, C., Zheng, W., Ma, Y., Yang, J., Ding, Z., Zou, H., Microstructural evolution and mechanical properties of AlCoCrFeNi high-entropy alloy joints brazed using a novel Ni-based filler. *J. Alloys Compd.*, 860, 157926, 2021.
36. Liu, X., Chen, B., Wu, S., Lin, P., Ma, Y., Tang, S., Huang, Y., Liu, W., Formation of nano-phase Co3Fe7 intermetallic and its strengthening in Au80Sn20/CrMnFeCoNi solder interface. *J. Alloys Compd.*, 843, 155924, 2020.
37. Sokkalingam, R., Mastanaiah, P., Muthupandi, V., Sivaprasad, K., Prashanth, K.G., Electron-beam welding of high-entropy alloy and stainless steel: Microstructure and mechanical properties. *Mater. Manuf. Processes.*, 35, 16, 1885–1894, 2020.
38. Li, N., Wang, R.X., Zhao, H.B., Tang, Y., Xue, P., Ni, D.R., Xiao, B.L., Ma, Z.Y., Wu, L.H., Microstructure and mechanical properties of electron beam welded TiZrNbTa refractory high entropy alloy. *Mater. Today Commun.*, 32, 103847, 2022.
39. Yin, Q., Chen, G., Ma, Y., Zhang, B., Huang, Y., Dong, Z., Cao, J., Strengthening mechanism for high-entropic weld of molybdenum/Kovar alloy electron beam welded joint. *Mater. Sci. Eng. A*, 851, 143619, 2022.
40. Yu, T., Wang, H., Han, K., Zhang, B., Microstructure and wear behavior of AlCrTiNbMo high-entropy alloy coating prepared by electron beam cladding on Ti600 substrate. *Vacuum*, 199, 110928, 2022.
41. Yu, T., Wang, H., Han, K., Wang, Y., Qiu, Y., Zhang, B., Mo20Nb20Co20Cr20(Ti8Al8Si4) refractory high-entropy alloy coatings fabricated by electron beam cladding: Microstructure and wear resistance. *Intermetallics*, 149, 107669, 2022.
42. Verma, A., Natu, H., Balasundar., I., Chelvane, A., Niranjani, V.L., Mohape, M., Mahanta, G., Gowtam, S., Shanmugasundaram, T., Effect of copper on microstructural evolution and mechanical properties of laser-welded CoCrFeNi high entropy alloy. *Sci. Technol. Weld. Join.*, 27, 197–203, 2022.
43. Fiocchi, J., Casati, R., Tuissi, A., Biffi, C.A., Laser beam welding of CoCuFeMnNi high entropy alloy: Processing, microstructure, and mechanical properties. *Adv. Eng. Mater.*, 24, 10, 2200523, 2022.
44. Zhang, M., Wang, D., He, L., Ye, X., Zhang, W., Laser beam welding of AlCoCrFeNi2.1 eutectic high-entropy alloy. *Mater. Lett.*, 308, 131137, 2022.

45. Shan, M., Wang, S., Cai, Y., Gao, F., Manladan, S.M., Zhu, L., Sun, D., Han, J., Laser welding of FeCoCrNiMnAl x (x = 0, 0.75) high-entropy alloys fabricated by additive manufacturing. *Mater. Sci. Technol.*, 38, 18, 1617–1624, 2022.
46. Adomako, N.K., Shin, G., Park, N., Park, K., Kim, J.H., Laser dissimilar welding of CoCrFeMnNi-high entropy alloy and duplex stainless steel. *J. Mater. Sci. Technol.*, 85, 95–105, 2021.
47. Oliveira, J.P., Shen, J., Zeng, Z., Park, J.M., Choi, Y.T., Schell, N., Maawad, E., Zhou, N., Kim, H.S., Dissimilar laser welding of a CoCrFeMnNi high entropy alloy to 316 stainless steel. *Scr. Mater.*, 206, 114219, 2022.
48. Oliveira, J.P., Shamsolhodaei, A., Shen, J., Lopes, J.G., Gonçalves, R.M., Brito, M., de, F., Piçarra, L., Zeng, Z., Schell, N., Zhou, N., Kim, H.S., Improving the ductility in laser welded joints of CoCrFeMnNi high entropy alloy to 316 stainless steel. *Mater. Des.*, 219, 110717, 2022.
49. Mohan, D.G., Tomków, J., Karganroudi, S.S., Laser welding of UNS S33207 hyper-duplex stainless steel to 6061 aluminum alloy using high entropy alloy as a filler material. *Appl. Sci.*, 12, 2849, 2022.
50. Wang, H., Xie, J., Chen, Y., Liu, W., Zhong, W., Effect of CoCrFeNiMn high entropy alloy interlayer on microstructure and mechanical properties of laser-welded NiTi/304 SS joint. *J. Mater. Res. Technol.*, 18, 1028–1037, 2022.
51. Hussain, M.Z., Jiangtao, X., Jinglong, L., Siddique, F., Zhang, L.J., Yajie, D., Zhou, X.R., Effect of Ti-Hf-Zr-Cu-Ni high entropy alloy addition on laser beam welded joint of Ti2AlNb based intermetallic alloy. *J. Mater. Sci. Technol.*, 120, 214–216, 2022.
52. Chong, Z., Sun, Y., Cheng, W., Han, C., Huang, L., Su, C., Jiang, L., Enhanced wear and corrosion resistances of AlCoCrFeNi high-entropy alloy coatings via high-speed laser cladding. *SSRN Electron. J.*, 33, 104417, 2022.
53. Chong, Z., Sun, Y., Cheng, W., Huang, L., Han, C., Ma, X., Meng, A., Laser remelting induces grain refinement and properties enhancement in high-speed laser cladding AlCoCrFeNi high-entropy alloy coatings. *Intermetallics*, 150, 107686, 2022.
54. Rui, H., Meiping, W., Chen, C., Xiaojin, M., YuLing, G., Effects of laser energy density on microstructure and corrosion resistance of FeCrNiMnAl high entropy alloy coating. *Opt. Laser Technol.*, 152, 108188, 2022.
55. Günen, A., Lindner, T., Karakaş, M.S., Kanca, E., Töberling, G., Vogt, S., Gök, M.S., Lampke, T., Effect of the boriding environment on the wear response of laser-clad AlCoCrFeNi high entropy alloy coatings. *Surf. Coatings Technol.*, 447, 128830, 2022.
56. Zhang, M., Wang, D., He, L., Ye, X., Ouyang, W., Xu, Z., Zhang, W., Zhou, X., Microstructure and elevated temperature wear behavior of laser-cladded AlCrFeMnNi high-entropy alloy coating. *Opt. Laser Technol.*, 149, 107845, 2022.

57. Deng, C., Wang, C., Chai, L., Wang, T., Luo, J., Mechanical and chemical properties of CoCrFeNiMo0.2 high entropy alloy coating fabricated on Ti6Al4V by laser cladding. *Intermetallics*, 144, 107504, 2022.
58. Zhu, Q., Liu, Y., Zhang, C., Laser cladding of CoCrFeNi high-entropy alloy coatings: Compositional homogeneity towards improved corrosion resistance. *Mater. Lett.*, 318, 132133, 2022.
59. Zhang, H., Li, W., Xu, H., Chen, L., Zeng, J., Ding, Z., Guo, W., Liu, B., Microstructure and corrosion behavior of laser cladding FeCoNiCrBSi based high-entropy alloy coatings. *Coatings*, 12, 628, 2022.
60. Wu, H., Zhang, S., Wang, Z.Y., Zhang, C.H., Chen, H.T., Chen, J., New studies on wear and corrosion behavior of laser cladding FeNiCoCrMox high entropy alloy coating: The role of Mo. *Int. J. Refract. Met. Hard Mater.*, 102, 105721, 2022.
61. Wang, T., Wang, C., Li, J., Chai, L., Deng, C., Luo, J., Materials characterization microstructure and properties of laser-clad high entropy alloy coating on Inconel 718 alloy. *Mater. Charact.*, 193, 112314, 2022.
62. Wu, H., Zhang, S., Wang, Z.Y., Zhang, C.H., Zhang, D.X., Chen, H.T., Wu, C.L., Phase evolution, microstructure, microhardness and corrosion performance of CoCrFeNiNb x high entropy alloy coatings on 316 stainless steel fabricated by laser cladding. *Corros. Eng. Sci. Technol.*, 57, 301–310, 2022.
63. Shi, F.K., Zhang, Q.K., Xu, C., Hu, F.Q., Yang, L.J., Zheng, B.Z., Song, Z.L., *In-situ* synthesis of NiCoCrMnFe high entropy alloy coating by laser cladding. *Opt. Laser Technol.*, 151, 108020, 2022.
64. Sun, D., Cai, Y., Zhu, L., Gao, F., Shan, M., Manladan, S.M., Geng, K., Han, J., Jiang, Z., High-temperature oxidation and wear properties of TiC-reinforced CrMnFeCoNi high entropy alloy composite coatings produced by laser cladding. *Surf. Coat. Technol.*, 438, 128407, 2022.
65. Lou, L.Y., Liu, K.C., Jia, Y.J., Ji, G., Wang, W., Li, C.J., Li, C.X., Microstructure and properties of lightweight Al0.2CrNbTiV refractory high entropy alloy coating with different dilutions deposited by high speed laser cladding. *Surf. Coat. Technol.*, 447, 128873, 2022.
66. Hong, S., Li, J., Zhao, P., Xu, Y., Li, W., Evolution in wear and high-temperature oxidation resistance of laser-clad AlxMoNbTa refractory high-entropy alloys coatings with Al addition content. *Coatings*, 12, 121, 2022.

12

Sustainability in Welding Industries

Y.G. Bala[1], Santhi B.[2] and Dinesh Kumar R.[3]*

[1]Department of Mechanical Engineering, Motilal Nehru National Institute of Technology (MNNIT) Allahabad, Uttar Pradesh, India
[2]Department of Mechanical Engineering, National Institute of Technology Goa, Farmagudi, Ponda, Goa, India
[3]Department of Mechanical Engineering, National Institute of Technology Srinagar, Srinagar, India

Abstract
Welding is one of the primary metal joining processes in which two or more materials, usually metals, are fused together with or without the application of pressure. Sustainability is an essential requirement of the welding process because welding applications have a considerable impact on various aspects of the environment, economy, society, and physical performance. These impacts of the welding process are studied in detail in this chapter, which provides direction on having environmentally friendly welding processes. The study includes factors that affect the sustainability of the welding process, such as sustainable welding practices and using various control measures for various welding processes. The information provided in this chapter will help researchers as well as business experts make the welding process more sustainable.

Keywords: Sustainability, welding, Industry 5.0

12.1 Introduction

Sustainability is a dynamic factor in any manufacturing technology and has an environmental impact on customer product raw materials, end product utilization by the consumer, service life, and cost-effectiveness. It is a

**Corresponding author*: rdinesh@nitsri.ac.in

Syed Quadir Moinuddin, Shaik Himam Saheb, Ashok Kumar Dewangan, Murali Mohan Cheepu and S. Balamurugan (eds.) Automation in Welding Industry: Incorporating Artificial Intelligence, Machine Learning and Other Technologies, (215–228) © 2024 Scrivener Publishing LLC

common business factor increasingly being considered nowadays across most competitive industries for improving productivity and efficiency through adapting the best possible techniques and practices. Also, sustainability is a growing idea that will guarantee society's faith in industries operating properly within the environmental limits when processing parts; therefore, industries will continue to move towards a holistic approach to development and assessment.

Sustainable welding technology has the combined effect of technological, economic, and ecological advantages over society [1]. Welding technology and its noteworthy applications intend to address the global need to move towards a green economy and aim to stop debasing the environment through methods of substantial quality and ease of application. It is highly important to adapt sustainable welding to the growing economy, as welding technology plays a large role in many manufacturing economies and meets end consumers' needs. The general trend in sustainability is to design end products to last longer with replaceable spare parts. As welding parts are used in major applications in the construction, automotive, transportation industries, etc., the increasing demand for high strength in lighter structures requires more attention to sustainability.

Sustainable production is achieved by the extensive utilization of modern and sophisticated tools in welding technology with good welding speed to maintain consistent high quality. High-quality products are required to be efficient and cost-effective for long-term use by consumers, which is the benchmark for the sustainability of production. The combination of welding speed and a correct welding process decreases rework and increases the role of sustainable welding in industrial production. Conscious use of energy and resources is also highly important in sustainable welding technology.

12.2 Critical Factors for Sustainability of Welding

Welding technology is an important technology for many production processes. Therefore, a sensible approach is required that uses resources and energy to increase sustainable manufacturing to produce goods [2]. This approach should not only adhere to energy laws and eco-friendly design but also be considered cost-effective while leaving a green footprint. The exact choice of consumable resources and proper training of the welder are critical factors [3] in assessing the sustainability of the welding practice and welding industries. Sustainability of welding processes and practices depends upon a whole range of factors and the entire process chain, such as raw materials, filler materials, auxiliary materials, processing time, welding speed, seam quality, and system costs. The procurement of raw materials and production of individual components of the welding system highly influence the sustainability of the welding and welding industries.

The use of modern and sophisticated welding techniques is equally important for more reliable, versatile, and efficient manufacturing, which is highly significant in achieving sustainable production processes in welding. Cost-effective and high-quality welds for maintaining ideal conditions help reduce the use of energy and the possible production of raw materials such as filler materials and other auxiliary essentials with entire production cells. The negative impact on sustainability would come across, especially during the fusion welding process, due to the poor practice of depending on the inefficient skills and knowledge of the worker or welder. Corrective maintenance could be incorporated to make the process more efficient or maximize production with proper utilization of the power source, such as changing the rod electrode and cleaning the bead by the welder during the welding cycle time, to make the system more sustainable. Though most fusion welding has proven to be the most sustainable welding, it must be combined with eco-friendly, clean, fast, precise, and flexible practices. High-speed welding practice, automation, and boosting the efficiency of special welding processes with low rework and rejection rates also advance the sustainability of welding for the next generation. Another aspect of the sustainability of the welding process is the environmental impact caused by the detrimental products of toxic emissions, process heat, and the emission of minute particles of metal oxides and gases like carbon monoxide, ozone, and various nitrogen oxides, which affect the immediate environment of the welders and the surroundings of the welding plant. These by-products generate environmental damage and have a negative impact on sustainability. Proper selection of power sources, consumable electrodes, shielding gases, and filler materials has less obvious environmental costs. Further pollution of the environment can be prevented by proper disposal of slag and electrode stubs during the welding process to alleviate the effects of welding.

Basic training of welders on virtual reality (VR) and virtual welding simulation systems enables users to learn about the practice of welding using different welding processes that positively contribute to sustainability. Manual arc welding, gas metal arc welding (MIG/MAG), and tungsten inert gas welding procedures are available to novice welders (TIG) to complete virtual training in basic skills on selecting the right welding system and exact torch control.

12.3 Adoptability of Sustainable Welding

There are different ways to sustain welding practice and technology to gain benefits [4]. Among the important ways are cutting down on the wastage of raw materials, using energy resources in an optimal manner, and disposing of fumes occurring during welding processes in a proper manner. To reduce production waste and recycle the scrap material of sustainable welding, recycling waste should be managed, and the waste that cannot be recycled must be efficiently disposed of in a sustainable manner. Irrespective of the manufacturing and industrial sectors, recycling is the most popular and resourceful way of reducing environmental costs with environmentally friendly options. Moreover, new sustainable welding techniques should be introduced, such as diffusion welding, magnetic pulse welding, friction stir welding, vacuum soldering, underwater welding, etc. [5], to improve the quality of the weld while reducing the operational cost. The use of a repairable and recyclable welding system with a long service life is a significant contribution to sustainability. Welding spatter results in the waste of filler metals and energy, along with time-consuming rework in terms of fettling and cleaning. Several techniques are observed to reduce spatter, including exact handling and the ideal selection of a welding system that cuts down on spatter by as much as 75%. Furthermore, sustainability of the welding practice with increased service life of the product with good quality imparts reduced wear and low repairable or disposable parts with proper selection of process parameters. Another sustainable welding practice involves training new employees or welders with modern virtual tools and a virtual simulator that enables them to choose their career. Well-trained trainees can improve production efficiency by reducing material waste.

12.4 New Welding Standards for Sustainability

Though best practices in welding techniques have been available in recent decades with improved facilities, there still remains the issue of encountering reduced weld quality during the process, which leads to an economic loss for the end users and manufacturing industries. Also, a potentially fatal consequence of the use of unskilled labor in the welding process is that the safety of the workers is not guaranteed, as is that of the end user of the final product. Various kinds of pollutants are generated by different welding techniques, which have a detrimental impact on the environment. Creating new techniques like friction stir welding and magnetic pulse welding reduces pollution by eliminating the need for fillers or fluxes that are responsible for producing dangerous flames [5]. Several standards govern the productivity of the welded parts in the factories, operator safety, and transportation, like ISO 3834, EN1090, and 5S. The 5S methodology is highly recommended for welding practice standards to minimize risks and improve workplace cleanliness, organization, workplace safety, part quality, and productivity with various degrees of assessability and implementation. Furthermore, implementation of 5S impacts the improvement of material handling and storage practices for the manufacturing of welded parts, reduces the incidence of critical issues like cracks, which lead to joint failures, and maintains required levels of ergonomics, safety, and quality. Other sustainability assessments include life cycle assessments (LCA), an ISO-standardized method to estimate the possible impact of the product and process over their entire life cycle. Similarly, social life cycle assessments (SLCA) also review the critical issues according to ISO 14040/44 and DIN/TS 35235 for production processes in improving workplace health and safety, as well as continuously optimizing processes from an ecological and economic point of view. Regarding the requirement of eco-design in welding manufacturing, the European Commission (EU) forwarded the latest step to the new law taking effect in which manufacturers are obliged to have parts to repair their products for 10 years after the product is no longer manufactured. Furthermore, the new welding procedure test standard, EN-ISO 15614-1:2017, provides recommendations for the measurement and calculation of heat input for MIG/MAG welding during practice. The welder or user can use heat input or arc energy calculated in accordance with ISO/TR 18491 and 17671-1. True sustainable welding involves optimal health and safety standards for users and values for humankind. The welding process releases welding fumes, UV radiation, flash burns, heat, and flames; therefore, fresh air filtration systems, fume extraction torches, and air filtering devices are crucial for protection against harmful gases. High-quality and practical protection gear, such as welding gloves and protective shoes, guards against extreme heat and welding splatter and contributes to the welding techniques' unwavering durability.

12.5 Resource-Conserving Techniques

Sustainability in the welding process is impacted by a wide range of variables. The speed of welding, system charges, raw materials, processing time, filler metals, and seam quality are a few of them, although they are not all inclusive. It is important to consider the complete process chain in order to acquire a comprehensive view. After all, the production of auxiliary materials as well as the welding of filler metals and the extraction of the raw materials for parent materials require energy. Therefore, the manufacturing of the different components of a welding system is just as vital as resource acquisition.

12.5.1 Sustainable Welding in Practice

Using cutting-edge welding technologies is equally important to achieving sustainable production processes. Depending on how flexible the welding system is, the more productive the manufacturing processes are. Operators can speed up welding with the correct technology while continuing to maintain good quality and ideal circumstances. This implies that cells capable of complete output might not be essential. It helps reduce the consumption of energy and production materials, such as supplementary as well as filler materials.

12.5.2 Boosting Efficiency with Special Welding Processes

Since it is particularly efficient, immaculate, rapid, precise, and versatile when in use, laser-gas metal arc welding is an environmentally responsible welding technique. This method has the advantage of a fast speed while also requiring relatively little filler material. However, using one of these welding techniques does not imply that you are performing particularly sustainably. It is crucial to consider which application process is best before submitting it. Welding is only deemed sustainable when the system design effort is balanced against resource consumption, quality, and cost-effectiveness.

12.6 Sustainability in Welding Training

Utilizing the right materials will help in welder training by instilling long-lasting habits from the start. A product in Fronius' portfolio called the virtual welding simulation system allows beginning welders to become totally immersed in virtual instruction in fundamental tasks and torch control. Different welding techniques can be learned and subsequently practiced using virtual reality (VR). The processes available to novice welders are MIG/MAG and tungsten inert gas welding (TIG). Since no consumables are needed, virtual training conserves resources and reduces expenses. As a result, this kind of training greatly benefits sustainability.

A variety of components must come together for sustained action in welding technology, including the appropriate welding technique for the application, a greater welding speed, a low rework and rejection rate, and others. But picking the proper welding system is the first and most important step.

12.6.1 Sustainable Technologies for Thick Metal Plate Welding

Welding makes up a significant portion of the manufacturing expenses and resource consumption in the steel construction industry, such as when producing the sections for windmills. Additionally, societal problems associated with welding include working in hazardous situations. This feature has sadly been ignored so far due to a predominant focus on economics and a lack of appropriate assessment methodologies. This section provides examples of effective welding techniques that lessen the negative effects of thick metal plate welding on the environment and society. Welding's social and environmental effects are expressed and examined using social and environmental life cycle assessments for thick metal plate joints. Compared to conventional technologies, welding with modified spray arcs and laser arc-hybrid welding improves social and environmental performance, and as a result, they have a great deal of potential for sustainable manufacturing.

12.7 5S Lean Strategy for a Sustainable Welding Process

The durability of products during their useful lives is thought to depend heavily on the proper operation of the welding procedures used to combine metal components or structural elements. An operator can carry out these tasks successfully in a safe setting thanks to effective workstation design. A number of standards have been developed to ensure the quality of welding seams, which are used to join metal parts and structural components. These standards set requirements to ensure the proper performance of welding procedures and the inspection of the metal welds produced.

The 5S technique is a cornerstone methodology for businesses that use lean production approaches since it has been demonstrated to be a reliable instrument for enhancing workplaces in industrial and service operations. The framework for using the 5S methodology in metal welding workplaces is presented in Figure 12.1. It outlines an index to measure the extent of 5S approach implementation and the use of the crucial performance analysis technique. Many evaluation indicators are suggested to handle the vagueness of evaluating using the fuzzy logic approach. This structure is utilized in a

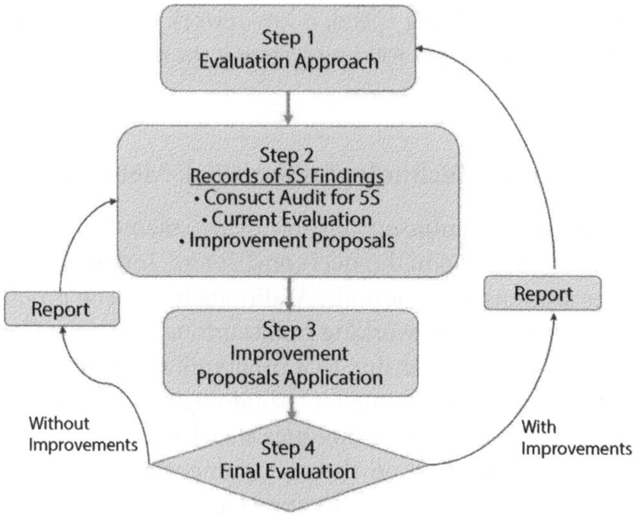

Figure 12.1 The 5S approach in process of effective joining.

real-world application to show how it can be used to create good industrial production practices that guarantee adherence to welding principles and ensure the proper handling and storage of the materials and tools used in welding processes to produce welded parts and structural elements.

12.7.1 Sustainability Assessment of Shielded Metal Arc Welding (SMAW) Process

One of the most popular techniques for joining materials is SMAW-shielded metal arc welding, which finds use in a number of industrial sectors, such as petrochemicals, aeronautical, automobile, and marine applications. The manufacturing sector is under increasing pressure to make the welding process environmentally friendly. Multiple input and output stream types are used in the SMAW process. Concerns about sustainability are associated with the SMAW process's numerous inputs and output channels, which include the conditions for electric power, input material use, slag and fume generation, and potentially dangerous working circumstances, as they pertain to occupational safety as well as human health. The SMAW welding process [6] needs to be described as sustainable within the larger definition of sustainability in order to improve its environmental performance. The majority of the material that is currently in print focuses on the technical and financial elements of welding, with little attention paid to its social and environmental implications. The paper examines the

SMAW process in light of the sustainability strategy that emphasizes the triple bottom line (economic, environmental, and social). Finally, the study offers suggestions for developing a cost-effective and long-lasting SMAW technique.

12.8 A-TIG Welding: A Small Step Towards Sustainable Manufacturing

Sustainable manufacturing is essential in today's society to reduce negative environmental effects and protect natural resources. Due to the superior quality and aesthetic appearance of the joint, conventional tungsten inert gas (TIG) welding is the most adaptable procedure used to combine various comparable and dissimilar materials. This method's only drawback is its limited production as a result of shallow penetration. Thus far, many researchers have attempted to use various TIG welding techniques to increase the depth of penetration. The activated tungsten inert gas (A-TIG) process is the best method for joining various comparable and dissimilar materials since it requires no filler metal, uses less energy, and boosts productivity. In spite of these advantages, this approach is not frequently used in industrial applications.

12.8.1 Weight Space Partitions-Based Sustainable Welding

Regarding the sustainability of part manufacturing, it is essential to choose the right welding procedure for a particular application. Unfortunately, preferences for one or the other welding method may conflict because there are several criteria used to evaluate welding procedures. The common practice of assigning weights to each criterion, however, is arbitrary and does not reveal information about the whole solution space. The ability to evaluate every conceivable weight and determine which welding technique is best for each set of weights is crucial from the viewpoint of a decision-maker. Using a weighted space partitioning approach, this problem is investigated. Three parameters that measure the performance of two welding methods from an economic and environmental standpoint are taken into account.

12.8.2 Sustainability Assessment of Welding Processes

Recently, the idea of "sustainability" has emerged to advance the traditional idea of being "green." The most favorable welding technique for a given application was then determined by adapting these to calculate and assess the sustainability of welding processes through the construction of a comprehensive framework. In order to use this methodology, information regarding welding processes would be gathered and divided into four categories: physical performance, social impact, economic effect, and

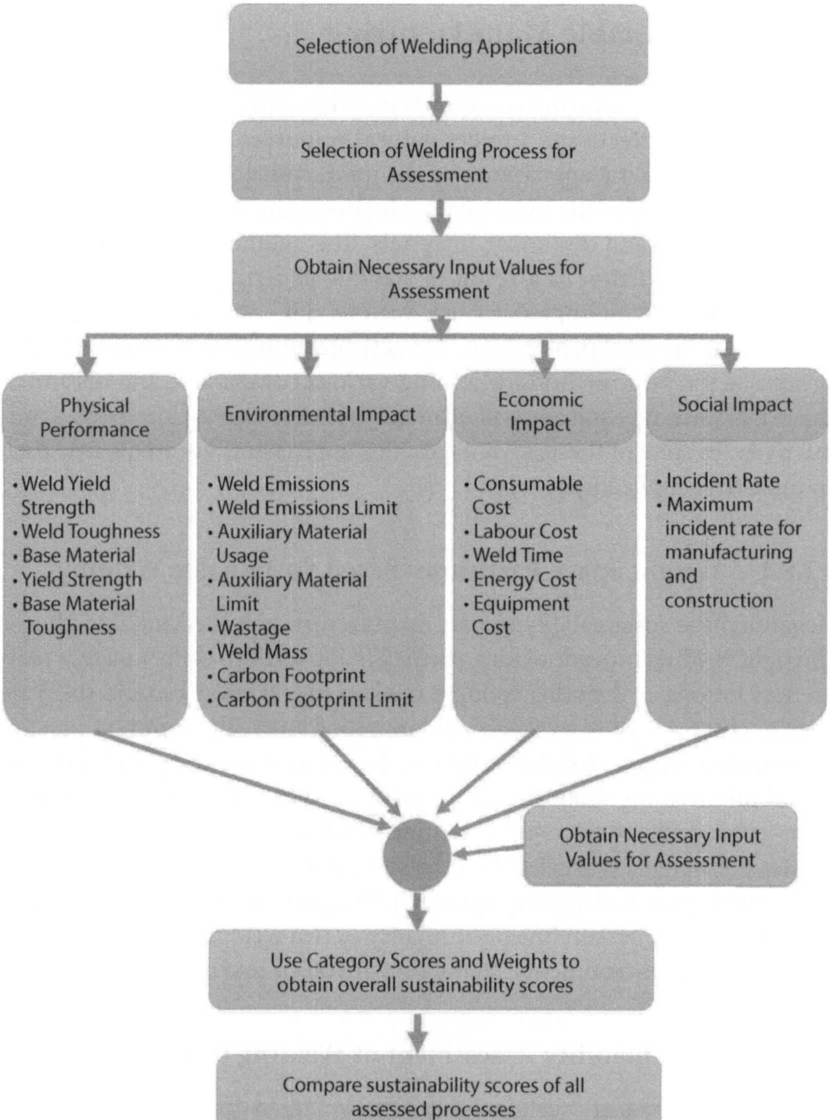

Figure 12.2 Sustainability assessment flowchart.

environmental impact, as shown in Figure 12.2. The results of each category's presentation would then be combined to create a single sustainability score. Three different welding procedures were the subjects of case studies to show the effectiveness of this methodology. Compared to GMAW and GTAW, friction stir welding [7, 8] received the highest overall sustainability grade.

Welding processes can have a significant impact on the environment and society in terms of energy consumption, air and water pollution, waste generation, and worker health and safety. Therefore, a sustainability assessment of welding processes is necessary to identify potential environmental and social impacts and develop strategies to mitigate them. Following are some factors that should be considered in a sustainability assessment of welding processes:

- **Energy Consumption:** The energy required to power welding equipment [9] and other supporting systems, such as ventilation and cooling, can contribute to greenhouse gas emissions and increase energy costs. Therefore, assessing the energy efficiency of welding processes and identifying ways to reduce energy consumption can improve the sustainability of the process.
- **Material Use:** Welding processes can generate a significant amount of waste material, such as consumables, slag, and fumes. Minimizing material waste and promoting the use of sustainable materials [10], such as recycled or biodegradable consumables, can reduce the environmental impact of welding processes.
- **Air and Water Pollution:** Welding processes can release hazardous air pollutants and wastewater, which can negatively impact air and water quality. Implementing pollution control technologies and properly disposing of hazardous waste can help reduce the environmental impact of welding processes.
- **Worker Health and Safety:** Welding processes can expose workers to hazardous fumes [11], radiation, and other health and safety risks. Implementing appropriate safety measures, such as ventilation systems, protective clothing, and training programs, can improve worker health and safety.
- **Social Impact:** Welding processes can have social impacts such as noise pollution, disruptions to local communities, and potential conflicts with indigenous or traditional knowledge.

Addressing these impacts through stakeholder engagement, community consultation, and respecting local traditions can help ensure that the welding process is socially sustainable.

12.8.3 Sustainability in Manufacturing

Researchers and business leaders have been debating sustainable manufacturing for the past few years. Manufacturing operations have been identified as one of the most significant elements that have seriously harmed the environment. A study was created that seeks to scientifically create a framework for world-class sustainable manufacturing (WCSM). The study makes use of a structured questionnaire that was created using previously published research and pretested for content validity. To enhance the quality of the responses, the data were gathered using a modified version of Dillman's comprehensive design method. Confirmatory factor analysis, multiple regression analysis, and the partial least squares approach were used to evaluate the psychometric aspects of the test, including reliability and concept validity. The results of the multiple regression analysis indicate that all of our assumptions are supported, which adds to the body of existing research. In terms of scope and its contribution to supply chain management theory and practice, our current study is exceptional. The research calls made by different academics have been empirically tested in this study. They have also been expanded to include WCSM activities, and a scale for measuring the framework has been further created.

Sustainability in manufacturing refers to the practice of creating products in a way that minimizes environmental impact and promotes long-term economic viability. This includes reducing waste, conserving natural resources, minimizing energy consumption [9], and ensuring worker safety. There are several key ways in which sustainability can be integrated into the manufacturing process:

- **Material Selection:** Choosing sustainable materials [10], such as recycled or bio-based materials, and reducing the use of harmful chemicals and substances
- **Energy Efficiency:** Implementing energy-efficient processes and equipment, such as using renewable energy sources [9] like solar and wind power and optimizing production schedules to minimize energy use
- **Waste Reduction:** Implementing processes that minimize waste production, such as recycling, reusing, or repurposing materials, and reducing packaging

- **Worker Safety:** Ensuring that workers are provided with safe working conditions and that they are not exposed to hazardous substances [11]
- **Supply Chain Management:** Engaging with suppliers to ensure that they follow sustainable practices and adhere to environmental and social standards. By integrating sustainable practices into the manufacturing process, companies can reduce their environmental impact, minimize waste, and create products that are environmentally friendly and economically viable in the long term. This can also help companies build a positive reputation and brand image and attract customers who prioritize sustainability in their purchase decisions.

12.9 Sustainability Indices

There are published standardized sustainability indices and measurements, and using them for a given application is reliable. The selection of the index to employ is a very important step since it must be appropriate for the process or product being evaluated. If not, it is likely that some components of a procedure or a product may be missed. This can lead to an incomplete study, which would cast doubt on the validity of the entire study. These include:

1. Global Reporting Initiative
2. Dow Jones Sustainability Index
3. General Motors Sustainability Index
4. Organization for Economic Co-operation and Development
5. Ford's Product Sustainability Index
6. EU Eco-Management and Audit Scheme (EMAS).

12.10 Conclusion

Cost-cutting, downsizing, and mass layoffs have been popular methods used around the world to address recent economic crises and partially offset losses. This has not, however, ensured a continual degree of effectiveness and quality. Additionally, the crises gave people who were already hesitant a stronger justification for omitting measures for reducing environmental damage from their plans for expansion. This might wreak havoc on ecology on a worldwide scale. To provide a better, more comprehensive approach to the evaluation of products, firms, processes, etc., a new paradigm is therefore necessary. Sustainability is a notion that ensures that businesses, goods, and processes operate effectively while respecting environmental constraints, maximizing revenues, and ensuring the satisfaction of society. It offers a more comprehensive method of development and evaluation. This is the reason why sustainability has recently attracted a lot of interest and support. This study offered a broad framework for evaluating sustainability, which was later modified to offer a tool for precisely evaluating the sustainability performance of welding processes.

References

1. Jamal, J., Darras, B., Kishawy, H., A study on sustainability assessment of welding processes. *J. Eng. Manuf.*, 234, 3, 501–512, 2020.
2. Rauch, E., Dallinger, M., Dallasega, P. *et al.*, Sustainability in manufacturing through distributed manufacturing systems (DMS). *Procedia CIRP*, 29, 544–549, 2015.
3. https://www.fronius.com/en/welding-technology/info-centre/magazine/2018/sustainable-welding
4. https://www.nationalskillsnetwork.in/5-ways-to-adopt-sustainable-welding/
5. Cary, H.B. and Helzer, S.C., Welding background, in: *Modern Welding Technology*, Pearson Education, Upper Saddle River, New Jersey, 2005.
6. Integrated Publishing, *Master Chart of Welding and Allied Processes Arc Welding*, Integrated Publishing, USA, 2016. [Online]. Available: http://www.tpub.com/steelworker1/14.htm, [Accessed 31 December 2016].
7. Schwartz, M., Friction stir welding and related processes, in: *Innovations in Materials Manufacturing, Fabrication, and Environmental Safety*, p. 300, CRC Press, New York, 2011.
8. Mishra, R. and Ma, Z., Friction stir welding and processing. *Mater. Sci. Eng.*, 50, 1–2, 1–78, 2005.
9. ASM, Energy sources of fusion welding, in: *ASM Handbook*, vol. 6.
10. Sarila, V.K., Moinuddin, S.Q., Cheepu, M.M., Rajendran, H., Kantumuchu, V.C., Characterization of microstructural anisotropy in 17-4PH stainless steel fabricated by DMLS additive manufacturing and laser shot peening. *Trans. Indian Inst. Met.*, 76, 2, 403–410, 2022.
11. BOC, *MIG Welding*, Linde Group, New Zealand, 2022. [Online]. Available: http://www.bocgas.co.nz/en/sheq/welding-cutting-hazards/mig-welding/mig-welding.html.

13

Global Welding Market Growth

Y.G. Bala[1] and Dinesh Kumar Rajendran[2*]

[1]*Motilal Nehru National Institute of Technology Allahabad, Uttar Pradesh, India*
[2]*National Institute of Technology Srinagar, Jammu & Kashmir, India*

Abstract
Welding has been one of the prime technologies that has contributed to the wealth of many countries across the world in the past and will continue to do so the in upcoming decades. Increased adoption of technological advancements with AI-based robotic welding and automation will assure this continued fast growth in the welding products market globally. Demand by different growing manufacturing sectors of construction, automation, transportation, aerospace, shipbuilding, renewable power, and other modern industries is highly dependent on different welding techniques, which has led welding products to drive the global growth of the welding market. The quality of this large volume of diverse metallic and non-metallic materials processed through welding techniques is the underlying reason for the attention paid to the growth of the global welding market.

Keywords: Welding technologies, global market, global growth, weld market dynamics and opportunities

13.1 Introduction

Welding is a fabrication technique used for joining similar and dissimilar materials with the application of heat and without the pressure causing fusion. The sturdy and quality joints of a wide range of industrial and end-user products are made by welding consumables. Welding is a key factor for many industries, which has enabled them to grow substantially till now and will continue to do so in the next generation of modern society. The large

**Corresponding author*: rdinesh@nitsri.net

Syed Quadir Moinuddin, Shaik Himam Saheb, Ashok Kumar Dewangan, Murali Mohan Cheepu and S. Balamurugan (eds.) Automation in Welding Industry: Incorporating Artificial Intelligence, Machine Learning and Other Technologies, (229–244) © 2024 Scrivener Publishing LLC

volume and variety of the end-user products depends on the fabrication or assembly of parts or products, which are highly influenced by the welding techniques. The increasing need for technological adoption is likely to drive the development of welding technology, its processing, and its products to ensure future demand throughout the forecast period. Though technological transfer happens over a period, the demand for welding technology has never wavered due to the implementation of changes in all the safety standards. Welding technology has greater flexibility towards technology transfer due to newer materials, newer manufacturing techniques, and automation, which enables it to grow in the right direction across the global market in terms of quantity, quality, and commercial viability.

The key growth factor for welding products in the global market is advanced technology producing quality products with long-term sustainability that have a wide range of material suitability in diverse environmental applications. The welding market has grown massively over the past few decades, and its continued growth is surprising, though there is an unexpected technology transfer. The market strategy for welding processes is to adapt to changes toward modernization and innovation. The welding market continues to develop steadily towards increased industrialization and infrastructure expansion. For increased flexibility of the welding technology, the welding technologist is a key player in developing welded products with improved mechanical, micromechanical, and tribological properties to meet the overall industrial requirements with the expected outlook. The expected market growth of welding always shows increasing demands as compared to the preceding year. This projected demand is based on the growth of modern industries, including automotive, oil and gas, building and construction, industrial machinery and equipment, and all other miscellaneous fabrication industries across the world. Apart from this, there is an increasing demand and need for lightweight, high-strength materials for end-users, which is another driving factor for the growing demand for welding materials in the welding market. Welding consumables and welding equipment are also the primary factors that are anticipated to boost the development of the welding market. The worldwide distribution of welding products across North America, Europe, Asia Pacific, South America, the Middle East, and Africa is expected to grow to account for USD million from 2021 to 2028, as shown in Figure 13.1(b). Figure 13.1(a) shows the Asia Pacific welding market for the years 2017–2028, which is considered to own the diverse prime manufacturing sectors [1].

The growth of welding technology in the global market is analyzed according to the market size of the welding products in global segments, the growth of the major key players and drivers of the global market, and

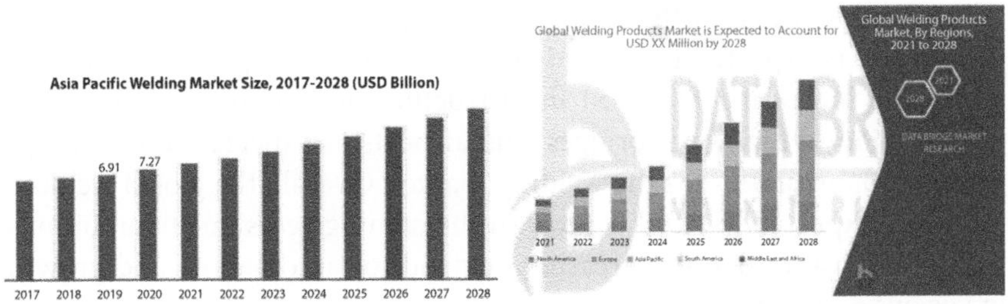

(a) (b)

Figure 13.1 (a) Asia Pacific Welding Market 2017–2028 and (b) Worldwide welding products market 2021–2028 (source: Data Bridge Market Research [1]).

sales of the welding products by entities like organizations, sole traders, partnerships, and market competitors across geographical scale [2].

13.1.1 Overview of Global Welding Products Market

On a geographical basis, the worldwide welding materials market is divided into Europe, Asia Pacific, North America, and the rest of the world. The foremost global welding materials market by geography is Europe due to the rising necessity for different types of welding materials and welding products from manufacturing sectors like construction, transportation, automotive, maritime activities, heavy machinery, and robotic energy-efficient equipment in the European market.

Welding is the process of joining two or more metals or thermoplastics by melting the materials and adding a filler material to form a strong bond. It is widely used in various industries, such as construction, automotive, aerospace, and manufacturing. The global welding market is projected to grow at a CAGR of around 5% during the forecast period (2021–2026) [3], according to various market reports.

One of the key drivers of growth in the welding market is the increasing demand for welding automation technologies. With advancements in robotics and artificial intelligence, welding automation has become more sophisticated, efficient, and cost-effective. This has led to increased adoption of automated welding systems, especially in industries such as automotive and aerospace, where precision and quality are critical. Another factor driving the growth of the welding market is the increasing demand for lightweight materials such as aluminum and titanium in various industries. These materials require specialized welding techniques, which are driving the demand for advanced welding equipment and technologies.

In addition, the growth of the welding industry, especially in advanced economies, is expected to drive demand for welding equipment and services. The increasing focus on infrastructure development, such as the construction of highways, bridges, and airports, is expected to create significant opportunities for the welding market. Overall, the global welding market is expected to steadily grow in the coming years due to ambitious technical advancements, increasing demand for automation, and growth in various end-use industries.

The rapidly growing demand for welding products and techniques from different industrial sectors is of paramount importance to the global welding materials market. Industrial sectors, such as automobiles, civil and structural, aerospace, railways, shipbuilding, and power sectors, require fabrication operations that propel welding market growth. The rapid growth of these mentioned industrial sectors, especially the automobile sector, is due to the rising demand for middle-class income in emerging economies. The increasing investments of the government in renovation and refurbishing activities also drive the comprehensive welding materials market's growth. The infrastructural progress across developed and developing countries, along with the governmental proposals, also influence the need for the welding market to grow globally. As part of their 14th Five-Year Plan 2025, the Chinese discussed how the welding equipment used to join steel beams, footers, columns, and trusses in the construction sector is likely to drive and expand the welding equipment for the forecast period. The different processing procedures and techniques of welding, such as rotary friction welding, resistance seam welding, and spot welding, are frequently used for the quality building of the applications, which tends to drive the global growth of the welding market.

The increasing trend in new design in construction, automobiles, and other sectors is the shift from manual to automated machines, which will likely ensure the nonstop use of welding products by end users. Other important progress in the renewable energy sector is its expected growth in capacity due to its being coupled with welding products to address the required essentials for specifically providing wind and solar energy around the world. The overdistribution of the welding materials market by different end users, such as automotive and transportation, building and construction, marine, aerospace, oil and gas, power, and other sectors, is shown in Figure 13.2.

Another ample opportunity for growth in welding products is the continuous improvement and espousal of new innovations and automation in welding techniques, such as robotic welding [5, 6], robotic laser welding, and oxy-fuel welding, which is intent on becoming cost-sensitive in emerging economies to improve the welding market. However, only a few restraints,

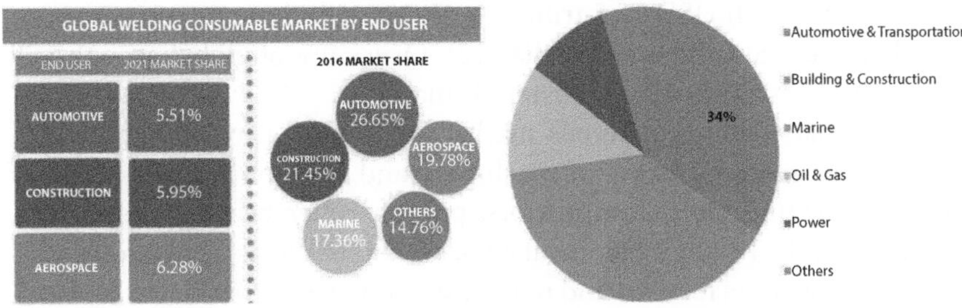

Figure 13.2 Distribution of welding products market according to end user [2–4].

such as the threat from substitutes for joining metals like rivets, adhesives, and clinching, and the high cost of advanced welding technology equipment, would sensitize the growth of welding technologies in the global market.

13.2 Patrons of Global Welding Market

For the professional partners and key players in the global welding market, analysis provides an insight into financial statements along with their benchmarking. The modest landscape section also includes key growth strategies, market share, and market ranking analysis for the welding materials market.

Population growth across the world, including in China, the United States, India, and Indonesia, is expected to propel the growth of the welding market due to the rise of rapidly expanding construction industries that build residential and non-residential constructions, in addition to large modern constructions, such as multi-story buildings, skyscrapers, or bridges, that are highly cherished by welding organizations. According to a forecast survey, the Asia-Pacific region is projected to hold the largest share in the welding materials market [7–11]. APAC will record the highest population and economic growth rates and percent of the world's consumption of products over the next two decades. Welding material applications in the building and construction industry, especially in emerging economic countries like India, China, and Brazil, are growing at a steady rate, with new infrastructural development projects likely to drive the welding materials market. Construction and infrastructure development have led to crucial growth in the welding market in the past and will continue to do so in the upcoming years.

From a global construction perspective based on Oxford economics, the growing demand for residential and commercial buildings is expected to grow 85% to reach USD 15.5 trillion by 2030, with three important countries like the US, China, and India [12]. Over 50% of global growth will positively impact the welding materials market.

The global welding materials market for industrial machinery, which includes the manufacturing of machinery and components consisting of presses, machine tools, compressors, pumps, roller bearings, escalators, pollution control equipment, insulators, and other metal fabrications, provides a region-level forecast and market size along with broad market landscape coverage, including the key drivers and restraints.

Another candidate for global welding market growth is the fast-growing, wide-ranging automotive industry, which has been a major contributor for the past several decades and continues to have a high demand for welding equipment across many industries. Extensive use of welding processes and equipment is necessary to develop different vehicles and parts. If the needs of the automotive industry persist, the demand for the primary use of welding tools, materials, and techniques in the global market will be a long-term trend. This is made evident by the rapid urban growth in developing countries like China, India, Brazil, and Russia, leading to increased demand for automobiles globally.

Germany is one of the leading drivers of welding equipment in the automobile sector for a broad range of applications, including wheel welding, frame and fender welding, and exhaust system welding, throughout the forecast period. Various principal beneficiaries of the global welding products market are shown in Figure 13.3. Internationally, welding techniques are widely used

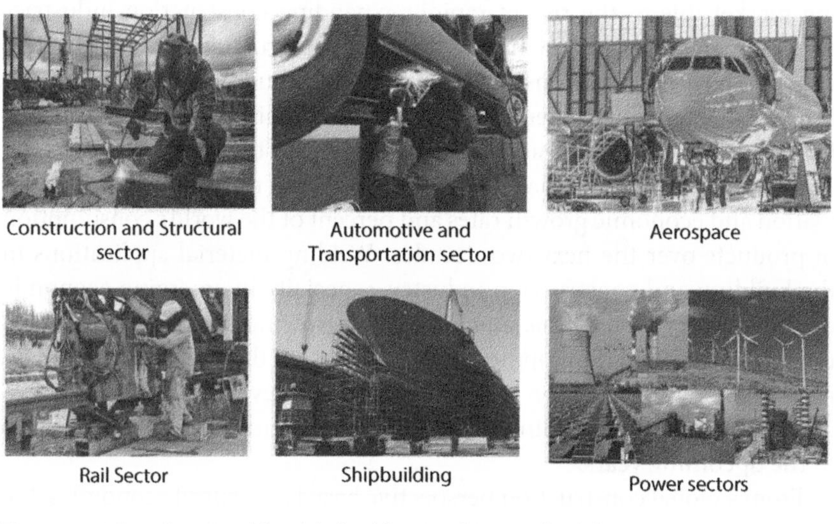

Figure 13.3 Beneficiaries of the global welding products market [3].

in manufacturing various body components of vehicles with sufficient joint strength as the base material. According to the records of the International Organization of Motor Vehicle Manufacturers, the transportation end user constitutes 34.42% of the total welding materials market. Still, there is a great opportunity for the welding materials market to grow in this industry. It is predicted for the forecast period that technological advancements and innovations in the transportation and automobile sectors will provide the expected customer satisfaction to create a high demand for welding materials [10]. Strong domestic demand and expansion of the end user are projected to enhance the production of vehicles in the upcoming years, which is expected to push the demand for welding products, which is evident by the projected 5.4% increase in the North America market from 2017 to 2025.

Another milestone in welding market growth is the wide use of welding products by the railroad industry. Though steel rails were introduced more than a century ago, the welding being the important factor to link them together, the worldwide connectivity of the railroad sector paves the way for crucial development of the welding market. However, welding technology for the rail sector is not only used to build or expand new pathways; it also involves repairing and reconstructing, which supports the sustainability of the technology for future use.

Next, the focus shifts to the reliance of the aircraft industry on welding techniques. In fact, aerospace engineers utilized welding to build the first commercial aircraft. There is an increasing need for lightweight, high-strength structures in the aircraft industry, and the construction of different aircraft components for long-term use is best suited for the welding process. As advancements in the aircraft sector progress, so too does the demand for welding techniques and equipment. Specialized aerospace welding is used to assemble, repair, and inspect the parts of airplanes, helicopters, spacecraft, and satellites. Aerospace welding is a multitasking function in which the work involved requires a controlled environment using special equipment that is highly sensitive and involves structural metal joining, inert gas welding, and erosion-resistant welds for thermoplastic components. Undeniably, the aerospace industry expands the upcoming market size of welding materials universally, as expected.

In addition, shipbuilding also extends the influence of the welding materials market. Most ships—from cruise ships to large tankers to cargo ships—are built with welding. Particularly, the underwater welding technique is highly used for the refurbishment of ships, thereby increasing the demand for welding materials.

Welding represents an essential element in the process of power plant equipment fabrication and maintenance. In particular, the manpower/

welders used for nuclear welding are highly valued for their specialized knowledge. Adding to the progress being made in the welding products market, the significant demand for other power plants is also expanding, necessitated by the belief that aging power plants create global warming.

13.3 Welding Technologies in the Global Welding Market

There are various categories of welding technologies in the marketplace, such as arc welding, friction welding, resistance welding, etc. These techniques include all machines and tools that can be used to perform the welding process, such as stick, gas, laser-beam welding, TIG and MIG welding, and other welders. It also includes soldering irons, torches, solder, filler metals, and electrodes. Arc welding technology is the main welding technique, which has the advantage of producing a high heat concentration during the welding process that makes a sturdy joint on large surfaces by providing a better depth of penetration. Arc welding is an ideal welding technology for a variety of applications on a wide range of metal surfaces. Also, according to major users of the welding market, it is an ideal technique due to its low cost, reduced welding time, and safe utilization. The heavy use of various resistance welding processes, such as projection welding, seam welding, and spot welding, in the automotive industry has had a high impact on the welding market globally. The stability of arc welding and the flexibility of a wide range of metal thicknesses, have caused a surge in the growth of the welding market across the world. Figure 13.4 shows the expected value analysis of different welding technologies for the years 2014–2025 and 2019–2029 according to different research resources. The unique welding technique grabbing the global welding market is friction stir welding, which is becoming increasingly popular in the automotive sector.

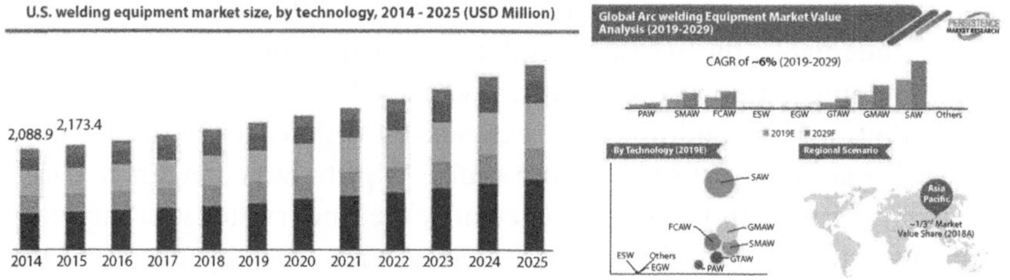

Figure 13.4 Welding technologies in global market (2014–2025) and (2019–2029) (source: Persistence Market Research [4]).

The Asia-Pacific region (APAC), which is home to an enormous manufacturing industry, accounts for over 42% of the global friction stir welding market revenue due to the impact it has on the overall positive demand in the region globally. Inert gas welding, such as metal inert gas welding (MIG) and tungsten inert gas welding (TIG), is used in the mass production of a wide range of products due to its speed and cost-effectiveness for high-volume production. Metal inert gas welding is especially responsible for over 60% of all welding jobs. Aluminum sheets are ideally joined by the MIG welding technique to create a super bond, even in thin metals. Greater penetration and cost-effectiveness in vehicle manufacturing require thousands of welds recognized by MIG welding. This factor will lead to a rise in the global welding market in the near future.

13.4 Fluxes, Wires, Electrodes, and Fillers

The welding market is characterized by its products segmented into fluxes, flux-cored wires, stick electrodes, solid wires, fillers, and others [12]. The leading product shared by welding is the stick electrodes and extensive use of filler materials that highly favor good mechanical properties like strength and corrosion resistance of the base metal. The fluxes and wires are commonly used, predominantly in the welding processes. Generally, flux is a purifying agent used to clean the surface, which usually dissolves the oxides by releasing gases that are trapped on the surfaces. Also, fluxes remove the impurities from the base metal surface and provide good blending between the filler material and the base metal. The increase in flux materials is also the reason for the highest growth in the welding materials market. Other paramount materials that play a vital role in the welding processes are the filler materials used in welding metals like aluminum, stainless steel, copper alloys, nickel, cobalt, and titanium alloys. A wide range of these consumables are used across a wide range of industries for the finished products, which highly inspire welding materials products universally. Figure 13.5 shows the prediction of the welding element demand rise for the years 2021 and 2028.

The welding operation widely uses welding wires for joining the two pieces of metal, which is projected to grow marginally. The wires are used for solid electrode welding such as gas metal, gas tungsten, arc welding, and submerged arc welding. Generally, wires are made from parent metals to be welded, which contain a continuous chain of atoms in the weld wire, which means the joining processes will progress without interruption during the process.

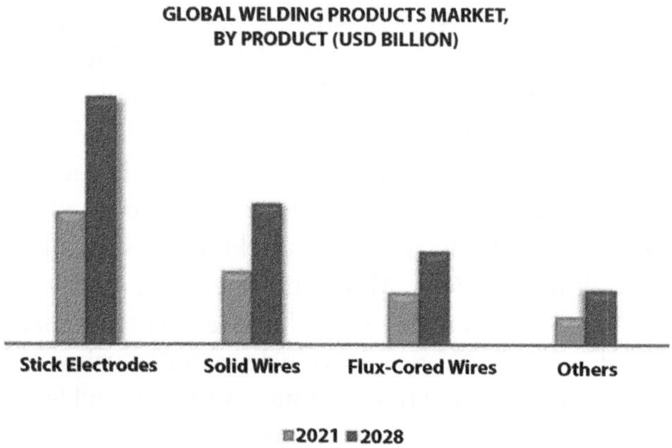

Figure 13.5 Welding products market by elementary product (2021 and 2028) [6, 12].

13.5 Welding Market Dynamics

The global welding materials market is characterized by the type of application, manufacturing sector, and region. The welding industry is growing due to the intensifying demand for welders from various welding-related merchandise in the construction, manufacturing, and automotive industries. The welding market has steadily grown over the past decades and is expected to experience rapid growth of USD 6.7 billion within four to five years between 2021 and 2025. The global welding market in 2020 was worth USD 20.23 billion and is expected to grow to USD 28.66 billion by 2028. The global welding-related products market is expected to grow at a CARG of 5.1% by the year 2025. For equipment used in different welding techniques, such as friction stir welding equipment, the market is expected to reach USD 433.23 Mn by 2027, at a CAGR of 6.34%, and is assured of continued progress in future decades even if not estimated exactly.

Welding in the transportation sector to manufacture different vehicle parts constitutes 34.42% of the total welding materials market. Technological innovations in the transportation sector amount to USD 67.14 million in the production of passenger cars. The application of welding products in new infrastructure construction, as per a global construction perspective, is expected to grow by 85% and reach USD 15.5 trillion by 2030 [12]. The rapid expansion of construction is expected to fuel a 6.7% compound annual growth rate (CAGR) in the welding products market in the coming forecast period. Furthermore, the growing population of emerging economic countries like Brazil, China, and India has discovered that steady growth in the construction sector leads to growth in the welding materials market.

New project development is likely to drive the consumption of steel, which mainly relies on the welding sector in several end-use industries such as construction, automotive and transportation, and marine industries, which, according to future market insight, is expected to grow from $US 15.36 billion at 5.7% over the forecast period of 2030 [12]. The welding materials market can grow at 3% of the compound annual growth rate (CAGR) for the coming forecast period. The estimated cost in 2020 is about USD 11948.0 million and is expected to reach USD 13449.2 million in the next 5 years, and USD 20.99 billion in 2021 to reach USD 28.66 billion at 4.6% in 2028.Certain well-known companies dominate the welding materials industry, including Lincoln Electric Holdings (US), Tianjin Bridge Welding Materials Group (China), Kobe Steel (Japan), Air Products & Chemicals (US), Illinois Tool Works (US), Linde plc (UK), and Colfax Corporation (US). The welding goods market is predicted to increase from USD 14.79 billion in 2022 by 11.1% at a compound annual growth rate (CAGR) during the following few years, according to a global industry analysis by Business Research. By the end of 2026, it is anticipated that the global market for welding equipment will reach USD 15,210 million [11], growing at a rate of 4.8%.

13.6 Manpower and Labor Challenges in Global Market

The growth of any technology is not possible without the involvement of manpower. The global labor market faces a range of challenges, including a shortage of skilled workers in some industries, the rise of automation and artificial intelligence, and changing workforce demographics. One of the major challenges facing the labor market is a lack of skilled workers in certain industries, such as human healthcare, technology, and manufacturing. This scarcity is partly due to a lack of investment in training and education, as well as demographic shifts such as an aging workforce and declining birth rates.

Another challenge is the rise of automation and artificial intelligence, which is expected to lead to significant changes in the types of jobs available and the skills required to perform them. While automation may increase productivity and efficiency, it may also displace workers in certain industries and require significant retraining and upskilling for those seeking new job opportunities. In addition, changing workforce demographics, such as an aging population, are creating challenges for employers in terms of attracting and retaining skilled workers. Younger generations have different expectations around work-life balance and job security, which may require employers to adjust their practices and policies to remain competitive.

The welding industry is highly dependent on the human resources of expert welders in countries across the world. It is expected to act as a major challenge for the growth of the welding materials market. Also, a shortage of skilled labor tends to increase labor costs in countries like America, Europe, China, Russia, and India. The workforce of certified, experienced welders is essential to the effective completion of all significant projects throughout the world relating to infrastructure, bridges, ports, railways, roadways, and power sectors. The welding industry in aerospace is rewarding and successful. There is an increasing need for competent welders as the aerospace industry develops. There is a need for 1.2 million welding specialists, including welders, cutters, fitters, equipment operators, engineers, and inspectors, according to the Indian Institute of Welding (IIW). The IIW has filed a petition with the Union Ministry for Skill Development due to the shortage brought on by growth-related increases in job opportunities and replacing the workforce that is retiring. A labor shortage in the welding professions is sure to increase the demand for the welding market globally by millions in the coming years.

13.7 COVID-19's Impact on Global Welding Materials Market

The impact of COVID-19 across the world resulted in a huge amount of ruin to the health and wealth of common people. The welding industry was also greatly impacted by COVID-19. The initial stage of COVID-19 forced the shutdown of factories in several countries, with strict implementation by governments to stop the spread of the virus. Later, with several rules and regulations, manufacturers of welding materials manufacturers were allowed to resume factory operations at a limited capacity. In addition to the reduction in demand related to the end-use industries, the demand for welding materials was also reduced, which left many welders facing difficulties during this pandemic. Due to this lockdown, many construction activities, including government infrastructure projects underway, came to a complete halt. Mass unemployment in the construction industry caused widespread panic among the workforce and led many workers to return to their homelands to sit out the pandemic. There was a delay in delivering projects due to reduced finances, labor, and working hours, which disturbed the welding materials market in 2020. A similar adverse effect on the automobile sector in this pandemic led to disruption in the export of Chinese parts, the shutdown of assembly plants in the US, and big manufacturing problems across Europe and other countries, creating intense pressure to cope with the downshift in global demand. Although unexpected fluctuations are expected to occur in the market size due to natural events, the welding materials market could substantially benefit from this disturbance in demand by using advanced, robust automation techniques.

13.8 New Opportunity in the Welding Market and Advanced Applications

The increasing adoption of the latest welding techniques, such as robotics [5, 6] and automation in welding, acts as a propellant in the welding materials market. Numerous applications at a faster rate are due to the several advantages and greater efficiency of the modern tools used in welding. Most of the electrical appliances, robotic appliances [5, 6], and moving automotive parts that are of great importance in the precision and accuracy of the joints are popularly induced by welding technology. Welding technology has proven its potential importance in space and under water, which makes it the only technique for making joints. Underwater welding is also emerging as an evolving technique in various marine applications. Welding techniques are used to carry out the refurbishment and restoration of ships, pipelines in the oil industry, and other important end-use industries and support their maintenance. The lightweight, high-strength materials of modern manufacturing are utilized for advanced steel materials with sufficient mechanical properties that are efficiently processed and fabricated by welding processing technologies. Advanced steel materials have a potential application in the automotive and transportation industries, which translate into greater investment in the growth of the welding materials market globally.

13.9 Conclusions

Based on its past record, welding is a prime technology that will continue to be the driving force for the economies of many countries across the world for decades to come. Increased adoption of technological advancements with AI-based robotic welding and automation will assure fast growth in global demand for welding products throughout the year. The demands of different growing manufacturing sectors, such as construction, automation, transportation, aerospace, shipbuilding, the renewable power sector, and other modern industries, are highly dependent on different welding techniques, which has led to welding products driving the global growth of the welding market. The quality of the large volume of wide-ranging metallic and non-metallic materials processed through welding techniques underlies the growth of the global welding products market.

References

1. *Global Welding Products Market–Industry Trends and Forecast to 2028*, Data Bridge Market Size Publisher, USA, 2021, https://www.databridgemarketresearch.com.
2. *Global Welding Products Market Size, Forecasts, and Opportunities – Welding Mission Industry*, Business Research Company, USA, April 27, 2022. https://blog.tbrc.info.
3. *Welding Equipment, Accessories, and Consumables Global Market Report 2022–By Technology (Arc Welding, Oxy-Fuel Welding), by Application (Automotive, Building and Construction, Heavy Engineering, Railway & Shipbuilding, Oil & Gas), by Equipment Type (Welding Electrode, Filler Metal, Oxy-Fuel Gas)–Market Size, Trends, and Global Forecast 2022-2026*, The Business Research Company, USA, 2023. https://www.thebusinessresearchcompany.com/.
4. *Global Welding Products Market Size by Product (Stick Electrodes, Solid Wires, Flux-Cored Wires), by Technology (Arc-Welding, Resistance-Welding, Laser-Beam Welding), by Geographic Scope and Forecast*, Verified Market Research Company, USA, 2022. https://www.verifiedmarketresearch.com.
5. *Robotic Welding Market: Global Industry Trends, Share, Size, Growth, Opportunity and Forecast 2022-2027*, Global Information, USA, 2023. https://www.giiresearch.com.
6. *Global Welding Robots Market 2022–Industry Trends, Size, Share, Forecast 2030 and SWOT Analysis*, Market Watch, USA, 2023. https://www.marketwatch.com.
7. *Global Explosion Welding Market 2021 Recent Trends, In-depth Analysis, Size and Forecast to 2028*, Global Market Vision, USA, 2021. https://globalmarketvision.com.
8. *Welding Consumables Market: Global Industry Trends, Share, Size, Growth, Opportunity and Forecast 2022-2027*, Research and Markets, Ireland, 2023. https://www.researchandmarkets.com.

9. *Global Welding Equipment Market-Trends, Growth, Outlook to 2022*, Modor Intelligence, India, 2022. https://www.mordorintelligence.com.
10. Sarila, V.K., Moinuddin, S.Q., Cheepu, M.M., Rajendran, H., Kantumuchu, V.C., Characterization of microstructural anisotropy in 17-4PH stainless steel fabricated by DMLS additive manufacturing and laser shot peening. *Trans. Ind. Inst. Met.*, 76, 403–410, 2022.
11. *Global Welding Market Trends 2021 Market Size Estimates, Share, Top Manufacturers, latest Trends, Growth Factor and Forecast to 2026*, MENAFN, USA, 2023. https://menafn.com.
12. *Welding Products Market Size, Share & Trends Analysis Report by Technology, by Product (Stick Electrodes, Solid Wires, Flux-cored Wires, Saw Wires, and Fluxes, Others), by Region, and Segment Forecasts, 2022–2030*, Grand View Research, USA, 2023. https://www.grandviewresearch.com.

14

Quality Assurance and Control in Welding and Additive Manufacturing

Venkata Charan Kantumchu[1]*, Syed Quadir Moinuddin[2], Ashok Kumar Dewangan[3] and Muralimohan Cheepu[4]

[1]Bradley University, Department of Manufacturing Engineering, Bradley University, Peoria, Illinois, USA
[2]Department of Mechanical Engineering, College of Engineering, King Faisal University, Al-Hofuf, Kingdom of Saudi Arabia
[3]Department of Mechanical Engineering, National Institute of Technology, Delhi, India
[4]STARWELDS Inc., Busan, South Korea

Abstract

Welding is one of the oldest and most traditional methods of joining metals. It is used in a variety of applications like automotive, aerospace, construction, infrastructure, shipping, locomotives, and other applications. We also have additive manufacturing (AM), which, as the name suggests, involves adding material (in layers) in the desired dimensions and shapes to create the required parts. Like welding, AM has several applications, such as aerospace, automotive, medical implants, machinery, and various custom parts. Welding and additive manufacturing may have as many challenges as several other applications. There could be several issues and quality defects in the process of welding and AM. Some common quality issues with welding are incomplete penetration, incomplete fusion, cracks, undercutting, porosity, spatter, slug inclusions, and longitudinal cracking; for AM there are other issues such as strength of the part, brittleness, precision, repeatability, and impurities. Modern technology has answers to some of these problems since automated processes are more consistent and precise. The quality of the product in production is so important that it could cost an organization anywhere from 25% to 40% of its operating expenses. In 2021 alone, the AM market was estimated to be worth $16.86 billion globally. This would mean the cost

**Corresponding author*: vkantumuchu@mail.bradley.edu

Syed Quadir Moinuddin, Shaik Himam Saheb, Ashok Kumar Dewangan, Murali Mohan Cheepu and S. Balamurugan (eds.) Automation in Welding Industry: Incorporating Artificial Intelligence, Machine Learning and Other Technologies, (245–262) © 2024 Scrivener Publishing LLC

of poor quality could be several billion dollars for additive manufacturing, and when welding quality costs are considered, this number would only get bigger. If the inputs for welding like temperature and voltage are kept in check, it is easier to control factors such as welding speed, wire feed speed, and nozzle-to-metal distance through automation. Similarly, for AM, if variables like temperature and feeding material are taken care of, then automation could handle other factors like speed, feed, and layer thickness. However, even with technological advances, such as Industry 5.0, where there is minimum human intervention and IoT plays a major role, there could still be challenges that need to be addressed, and this chapter specifically focuses on the challenges that Industry 5.0 can address, the challenges that might remain, and any new challenges that might arise with the use of such technology.

Keywords: Welding, additive manufacturing, quality, artificial intelligence, Industry 5.0, IoT, machine learning, challenges

14.1 Introduction

Welding is all about heat—using heat to melt separate pieces of metal so they will flow together and fuse to form a single, seamless piece [1]. It is used in a variety of applications, such as automotive, aerospace, energy, and construction. According to Wallis, "Welding is the most common method used to join metal parts in large structures and equipment due to its strength [2]." There are various types of welding [3], which may be broadly classified into gas metal arc welding, gas tungsten arc welding, shielded metal arc welding, and flux-cored arc welding. Depending on the application and other factors, such as cost, time, and strength requirements, different welding techniques may be used. The welding industry is so big [4] that manufacturing (of which welding is a big part) contributes to 12% of the US GDP. There is a high demand for qualified welders in the industry, and a shortage of welders [5] could have a moderate to extensive productivity impact. The global welding market is projected to grow from $21 billion in 2021 to $29 billion by 2028. This rapid increase is because of the exponential growth in the manufacturing industries. Similarly, a relatively newer technology that is paving the way for astounding results is additive manufacturing. According to Linke, "Additive manufacturing is the process of creating an object by building it one layer at a time. It is the opposite of subtractive manufacturing, in which an object is created by cutting away at a solid block of material until the final product is complete [6]." This is often referred to as 3D printing as well. 3D printing has various applications [7], such as manufacturing, automotive, aerospace, medicine, and the arts as well. The use of 3D printers has even entered space. NASA entered into a contract [8] with a company that helped them make a 3D printer for the international space station to print the parts that were mission critical. Just like welding, the 3D printing market is growing rapidly. According to Fan *et al.*, the 3D printing market in 2018 was $9.9 billion and is expected to grow to $34.8 billion in 2024 [9]. This is an exponential growth rate considering the short period. With such growth comes the question of quality and the various challenges that arise both with the 3D printers and the parts that are printed using these 3D printers. Through the rest of this chapter, we will discuss the various quality challenges that have been uncovered in both welding and additive manufacturing.

14.2 Quality Issues in Welding

There are various issues that arise due to poor welds. Some of the quality defects in welding are:

- Lack of Root Fusion

This is a root bead fully penetrating but not fusing to the root face, as shown in Figure 14.1. This occurs for various reasons, some of which are misplaced welds, energy input that is too low, using an electrode that has a large diameter, or a root gap that is too small [10].

This is a serious failure and can cause property damage or even injuries depending on where the weld is done. In an analysis performed by E. J. France on the Alexander L. Kielland disaster in Norway [11], as shown in Figure 14.2, the author has stressed the importance of not including a weld engineer in the disaster investigation and how such an engineer would have discovered that the true root cause of the incident was not the design of the platform but rather a case of improper weld penetration or a case of "lack of root fusion." This disaster that took place in Norway in 1980

Figure 14.1 Lack of fusion due to the filler metal not fusing with the base metal completely.

Figure 14.2 Damaged platform from the Alexander L. Kielland disaster [13].

is one of the worst industrial accidents that claimed 123 lives [12]. So, the challenge is to prevent and detect these failures so that disasters such as the one discussed earlier can be prevented, saving hundreds of lives.

Lack of fusion is mainly caused by not providing enough heat at the point of contact or the root of the weld. This can be addressed by employing newer technologies such as IoT, where the devices are connected to each other and insufficient heat may be promptly detected and real-time adjustments may be made, preventing such failures. Such a setup would almost be foolproof and provide almost zero errors. This is possible through Industry 5.0, as humans can teach the systems through AI the right balance of parameters to be chosen. Though the efficiency and the accuracy of the weld may be controlled through the disciplined approach of Industry 5.0 technology, there may be other challenges, such as environmental issues. According to Adel, "As large smart devices are connected, energy management is an issue for industry 5.0." So, energy management could be an issue that needs to be managed with many smart devices trying to feed data that needs to be analyzed for real-time adjustments that need to be made [14].

- **Lack of Penetration (Figure 14.3)**

This is another welding defect that is about not attaining the penetration of the weld as specified by design. There are various reasons why this could happen, such as an incorrect torch angle, a travel speed that is too high, or improper weld preparation.

Just as lack of fusion, lack of penetration may cause severe damage as well. Welding, being an older technology, holds a much bigger share of the market than additive manufacturing, and defects, such as a lack of

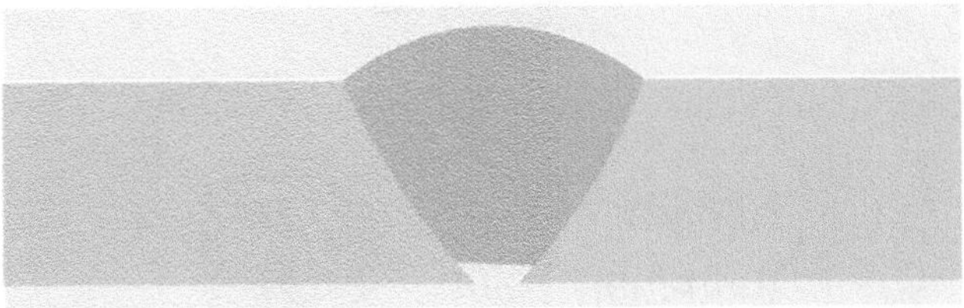

Figure 14.3 Improper penetration caused by the filler material not completely penetrating to the base of the welded joints.

penetration, could cause millions of dollars in cost due to poor quality. It is estimated that the welding market share will grow from $20.99 billion in 2021 to $28.66 billion in 2028 [15]. At a moderate 10% cost of poor quality, there have been losses in excess of $2.1 billion because of welding defects, and with a mere 15% of these defects being lack of penetration, there have been quality costs of at least $315 million in 2021 alone. Just as discussed in the poor fusion section, poor penetration is also considered to be a cause for the Alexander L. Kielland platform disaster. Lack of penetration may mainly cause serious accidents in aerospace and the construction industry. Travel speed, which is one of the causes of the lack of penetration, may also be controlled by the application of a technology like machine learning, which is a part of AI. However, just as in the case of a lack of fusion, a lack of penetration will have to be managed for energy conservation to minimize the effect on the environment.

- **Inclusions**

Inclusions are a simple yet damaging defect that is seen in welding. Inclusion is a process in which impurities are trapped in the weld and may weaken the weld joint. Such joints will quickly fail due to fatigue.

In an accident caused by a weld failure at an automotive plant, a 52-year-old contractor was crushed under a conveyer carriage weighing nearly 4 tons.

In the accident, which happened in December 2014, a temporary support safety pin failed to engage on an assembly line conveyor carriage at the Ford Kansas City Assembly Plant in Claycomo, Missouri (see Figure 14.4) because of a weld failure [16]. Though it was not clear as to which weld defect was the cause of the failure, inclusion is one of the potential causes that might have been detected during an ultrasonic test.

This defect may occur because of slag that is trapped in the bead along with bits of rust or other materials such as tungsten (see Figure 14.5). This may even happen when the molten metal cools too fast, allowing the slag to settle in the bead of the weld. This defect may be avoided by thoroughly

Figure 14.4 Assembly plant at which an accident happened due to weld failure (image source: KMBC.com).

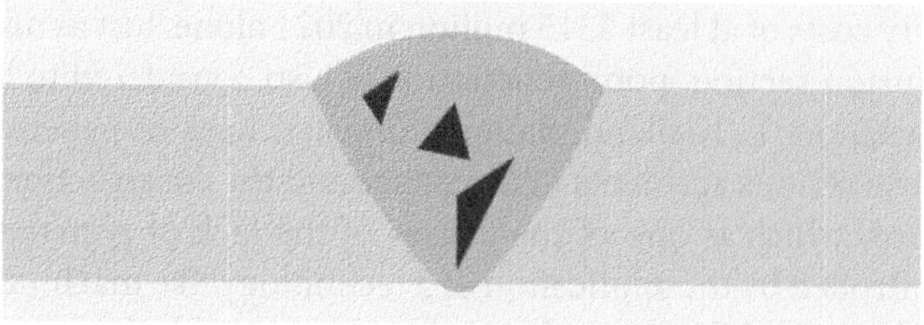

Figure 14.5 Inclusion, otherwise referred to as trapped impurities inside a weld.

cleaning the base metal, maintaining the right speed and angle of the torch, and cooling temperatures. All of these may be achieved by integrating AI to monitor slag inclusion and impurities and checking the weld strength at regular intervals. This may be achieved through the implementation of Industry 5.0. The challenge with such implementation would be the time and costs involved in developing such models and then checking their effectiveness.

- **Cracks**

Cracks (see Figure 14.6) are another common failure in welding that are caused by internal stresses exceeding the strength of the weld metal or base metal, and, in some cases, it could be both. Cracking is the most serious welding defect of all. The issue with cracks is that sometimes they are microscopic and sometimes not. When they are microscopic, they may be hard to identify and fix. In such cases, they propagate and turn into bigger cracks that may cause catastrophic failures.

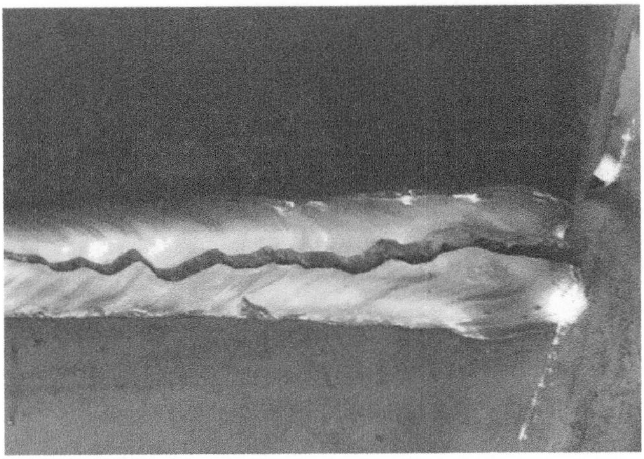

Figure 14.6 A deep crack caused by potential cooling issues.

A fracture found in a 900-foot steel beam is suspected to be caused by a crack. On the I-40 Hernando de Soto Bridge on the Mississippi River connecting both Arkansas and Tennessee (see Figure 14.7), a steel beam was found to have a fracture, and the inspectors closed the bridge for the safety of the public. This was caused by a crack, which may have happened because of shrinkage strains that may have occurred during the cooling of the metal. This caused a traffic diversion and other logistics issues. This type of crack is typically detected through inspections performed annually or every other year. It is estimated that rerouting costs the trucking industry $2.4 million per day [17]. The incident reported in May 2021 is an example of how expensive welding issues can be in practical applications such as construction and infrastructure.

There are several ways to prevent cracks. They can be prevented by just doing these or a combination of them. Consider preheating the joints to normalize any temperature differential between the base metal and the welding temperature. Ensure the base metal is defect-free. Inclusions are one of the reasons for cracks and can be the origin of a propagating crack. Another concern that can initiate cracks is low currents combined with high travel speeds. Finally, allowing enough time for the weld to expand and contract during the cooling of the weld may also prevent cracks. It is recommended to follow these steps either stand-alone or in combination to minimize cracks. These are mostly human-driven processes and deploying AI to handle these processes could alleviate the cracks. For example, as discussed previously, currents and speeds may be controlled using AI. By using sensors and a vision system, the feedback is instantaneous, and

Figure 14.7 The I-40 Bridge over the Mississippi River with a significant crack.

corrections may be made by the AI system in real time to minimize the defects and any failures that may be caused by these defects. According to Sassi *et al.*, deep learning techniques may be used to train networks with about seven million parameters to obtain an accuracy of 97.22% [18]. This is impressive based on the approximately 3% defect rate caused by human welding. With more technology and deeper learning techniques, it could be possible to increase the accuracy rate to closer to 99%. The challenges with implementing AI or other Industry 5.0 techniques are beyond technical abilities. According to Gyasi *et al.*, automation will displace people and create unemployment [19]. General Motors was given a loan by the Obama administration to stop them from closing their factory in the US and moving it to Mexico to minimize unemployment. However, despite this loan being awarded, half of the people were still replaced using robots and automation, which is a real problem, regardless of the improvement in throughput and efficiency.

- **Porosity**

Another common defect that is often reported in welding is porosity. Porosity happens when the gas bubbles released from the weld pool are trapped in the weld, making the weld weaker (see Figure 14.8). These gases could be hydrogen, carbon dioxide, or simply steam that is released. When the welds are porous, they lose their strength and, depending on the application, could cause catastrophic failures. Sometimes these accidents involve fatalities. Usually, this defect can be caught visually, and, in some cases, it could be hard to see it with the naked eye. There are different ways to avoid this failure. The operator needs to check the current to make sure it does not get too high. Making sure the correct electrode is used and

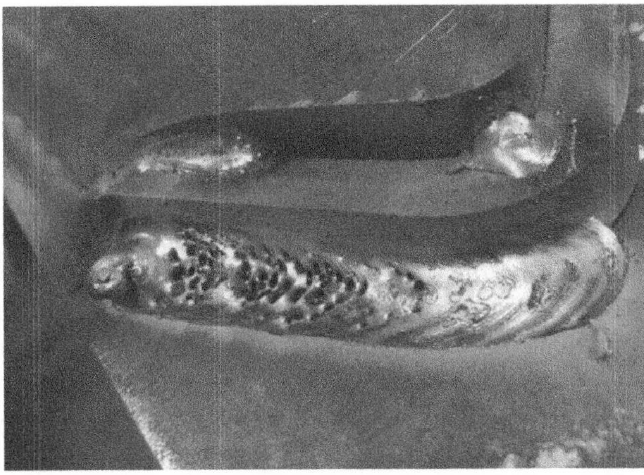

Figure 14.8 A weld joint with cavities caused by porosity (source: Arc Helmets).

that the coating is not damaged will ensure that this defect is minimized. Another important thing to do could be to clean the base metal thoroughly. By following the precautions, the porosity of the welds could be avoided or at least minimized.

In a tragic accident that took place in San Bruno, California, in September 2010, porous welds were claimed to be one of the perpetrators. The accident took place when a 30-inch-diameter pipe buried in 1948 three feet below ground, exploded, killing eight people and damaging about 40 houses [20]. The pipe owned by Pacific Gas and Electric Company was found to have various weld defects, including porosity and improper fusion. This accident triggered an investigation into the strength of the pipe to handle the gas pressure [20]. Using AI, sensors, and vision detection systems, such defects may be avoided. According to Gyasi *et al.*, despite the use of sensors and monitoring devices, common challenges such as arc instability, distortion, porosity, joint position errors, microstructure deterioration, and cracks still exist [19].

- **Spatter**

Spatter is the last welding defect that will be discussed in this chapter. Though there are several other welding defects, such as undercut, burn-through, overlap, and whiskers, the chapter intends to cover some of the more common failures and not focus on all of them. Spatter defects are relatively less concerning because of the nature of the failure. Spatter defects do not necessarily cause weld failures, but they are a major safety concern as the molten metal balls flying through the air could cause eye injuries or sometimes even explosions. They make the weld look aesthetically unpleasing (see Figure 14.9).

In an accident reported by OSHA, a 48-year-old male was killed in an explosion caused by welding. In the incident reported on June 15, 2022 [21], an employee was MIG welding nipples onto the top of a fuel tank truck. The accident happened in an indoor bay of a building when the employee was welding the tank that exploded, blowing him through the roof of the building. The employee was killed because of blunt force trauma to his head and torso. As discussed earlier, spatters could even cause explosions. Though the cause of death was not narrowed down to spatter, such accidents may be minimized by robotic welding and using AI systems to automate the welding process [21].

Spatter may be caused by the voltage being too low or the current being too high for the application it is used for. Spatter makes welds look unprofessional and unsafe, and hence it is important to minimize it to reduce rejections from customers. A few safeguards may be used to minimize spatter failure in welds. Shortening the arc is one way to minimize the spatter. Setting the polarity correctly is another way of reducing spatter. Using the correct voltage and amperage settings is almost guaranteed to reduce spatter. Cleaning the base metal well is one of the options that is always considered reliable. Much of this may be attained by using AI and vision systems. Vision systems may easily detect such failures, and using IoT, they may communicate with the systems that control the critical parameters such as voltage and current and help reduce the spatter. Though AI systems

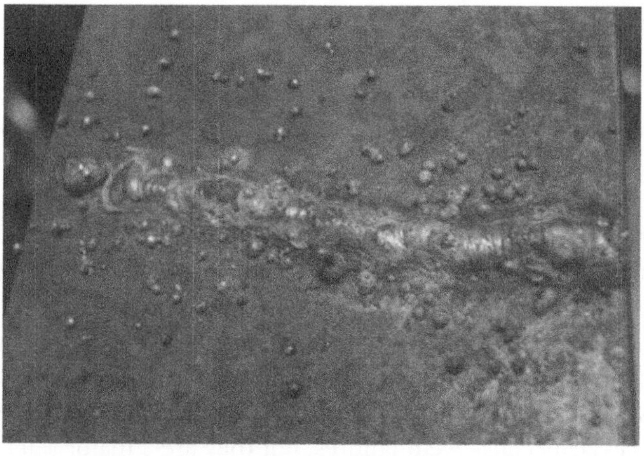

Figure 14.9 Spatter produced during the welding process.

may be successful in reducing the spatter to a great extent, eliminating the failure completely may still be a longshot.

14.3 Quality Issues in 3D Printing

Just as in welding, there are various quality issues that are caused by 3D printing as well. In this section, we will discuss some of the quality issues caused during the 3D printing process and how using newer technologies such as AI and IoT may alleviate some of these issues.

- **Excess Heating**

Excess heating may cause the material/plastic to deform (see Figure 14.10). This not only affects the print quality, but also compromises the dimensions, aesthetics, and strength of the 3D-printed part. There are various reasons that cause this failure. Excess heating may be caused by printing too fast, printing multiple parts at the same time, the extruder temperature being too high, or not cooling fast enough. Of these, the most common cause is the plastic not being cooled fast enough. This causes it to deform and lose its geometry.

Figure 14.10 The deformation of a 3D-printed part caused by slow cooling (source: Simplify3D).

There are some obvious solutions that can fix this problem. Regulating the speed of printing can minimize the problem by giving the printer enough time to cool the layers before adding more. Adjusting the temperature of the extruder and the bed may be another way of eliminating this problem. Some studies may be required, such as the design of experiments or a box and whisker plot, to understand the right temperatures required for the print to not have heating issues. This may be perfectly achieved through deep learning of the parameters required to maintain the temperatures. Most modern 3D printers can connect to other devices and share data. This enables the system to maintain and control the temperature at the right levels, which would allow enough cooling. There are almost no limitations on the use of AI in this application, although there may be issues, such as the time and costs involved in training such a system.

- **Layer Misalignment**

Layer misalignment is a result of layers not being aligned properly (see Figure 14.11) on each other, mostly due to mechanical or moving parts of the 3D printer. The major issue with such misalignment is that the mechanical properties of the outcome may not be within the specs and may be susceptible to failure depending on the application and the loads that they are subjected to. The causes for such failure could be the speed of the toolhead, loose belts and pulleys, an unsecured bed, and others. When unintended movements occur due to such issues, the layers do not stack on top of each other linearly.

This problem may be solved by making a few adjustments. The first solution to try would be to check the slack on the belts and pulleys and make sure they have the right tension. The second thing to try would be

Figure 14.11 Misaligned layer printed object (source: Merlin—Stack Exchange).

to calibrate the printer and make sure the bed is properly aligned, as are the printing head and the shafts that support the movement of the printing head. The third and most obvious solution is to adjust the print speed to allow the layers to bond properly.

These solutions may be achieved through the application of AI and sensors. The speed of the toolhead may be adjusted. According to Zewe, researchers at MIT have trained a machine-learning model to monitor and adjust the 3D printing process to adjust and correct the issues in real time [22]. Such breakthrough technology can certainly enable the reduction or elimination of layer shifting because of toolhead speed. Similarly, once a 3D printer is calibrated, you can rest assured that the calibration will ensure that the layers are aligned. This can be achieved using sensors that can accurately calibrate the 3D printer. The same is applicable for loose belts and pulleys as well. The tension in the pulleys and the belts may be accurately gauged and adjusted by sensors controlled through AI. The drawback involved with the use of such technology is again the time and money involved in training such an agile system.

- **Warping**

Warping is a different but still common quality failure in 3D printing. Warping occurs due to material shrinkage during the printing process, and this causes the corners of the print to slightly lift and separate from the bed (see Figure 14.12). Warping caused by excess heating causes the parts to deform, causes aesthetic concerns, and compromises the strength of the part, rendering it useless in many cases. The most probable causes for warping to occur are print bed alignment issues and the filament cooling too quickly on the bed, causing shrinkage. This problem could cause the part to separate from the bed because of the imbalance caused by the curling on the edges. Though it is more likely

Figure 14.12 A warped 3D printed part (source: dddrop.com).

to happen in bigger models, it could happen with medium- and smaller-sized parts as well.

In an experiment conducted on ABS-printed cuboids, it was found that the length of the models affected the warping. As the length of the model increased, the warping increased with it [23]. Warping is a critical problem that may be solved in different ways. The first would be to regulate the temperature of the plate or the bed since an incorrect temperature could be a cause for the warping. The second solution would be to ensure the plate is leveled. This is important since an uneven plate surface could cause the model to be warped. Cooling is another solution to the warping problem, as cooling too quickly may also cause warping and needs to be monitored for proper cooling settings. Finally, adjusting the primary layer may improve the adhesion between the layers. These adjustments could include both the speed and temperature of the initial layer. All the discussed solutions could be implemented with the aid of AI. With its deep learning ability, AI can regulate the temperature of the plate and hence also the cooling of the layers for better adhesion between the layers and the plate. Uneven surfaces may be adjusted through sensors and motors that may be controlled through IoT and AI as well. Just as in the case of the misaligned layers, the drawback of such a system is mainly the time and resources involved in training it.

- **Over Extrusion**

The last quality defect that will be discussed in this section is overextrusion. Overextrusion is the process in which too much filament is released from the nozzle onto the build bed (see Figure 14.13). Overextrusion could cause quality problems that may make the printed objects useless. It may

Figure 14.13 An over-extruded 3D printed object (source: reddit.com).

lead to other problems, such as oozing or stringing, that can create dimensional issues as well.

The first cause of overextrusion could be the size of the nozzle. Often, oversized nozzles could ooze out too much filament, which would cause overextrusion. A second cause of overextrusion is incorrect settings, such as those of the feed rate and nozzle head speed, that may cause an inappropriate amount of filament to be released. The two obvious solutions are to first adjust the settings for extrusion so that the speed and the feed rate can be regulated to prevent too much filament from being extruded. The second solution would be to choose the right nozzle size. Choosing the right nozzle size may be tricky since fine printing is desired, but at the same time, if the right size is not chosen, it may affect the speed of the printing and cause underextrusion, making the model appear incomplete. These issues may be addressed by employing AI, which can quickly learn the required settings depending on the application, the type of filament used, the temperature of the head, the ambient temperature, the temperature of the bed, and the nozzle size. The limitations of AI implementation in such cases are almost negligible, except for the resources and time involved in developing such systems.

14.4 Conclusion

Quality in fabrication is an important element, and as explained at the beginning of the chapter, quality costs in welding and additive manufacturing could cost billions of dollars if not addressed. With the help of AI and advanced technology, such as sensors and IoT, it is possible to achieve high-quality products in these applications. The use of AI will minimize and, in some cases, eliminate the quality errors, reduce the costs, reduce the labor, and reduce the time required to finish the models with high accuracy and precision. Though some drawbacks have been discussed here, they may be addressed with more research.

References

1. Ruth, K., *Welding Basics: An Introduction to Practical & Ornamental Welding*, Creative Publishing International, Minnesota, 2004.
2. Wallis, L., *Welding–Beyond the Sparks and the Arc*, June 9, 2021, Go to. Retrieved January 15, United States of America, 2023, from https://www.qualityinfo.org/-/welding-beyond-the-sparks-and-the-arc.

3. Stoltz, R., 4 different types of welding processes. *NEIT*, November 23, 2021. Retrieved January 15, 2023, from https://www.neit.edu/blog/types-of-welding-processes#:~:text=The%20four%20main%20types%20of,Cored%20Arc%20Welding%20(FCAW).&text=Earn%20your%20degree%20in%20Welding,your%20new%20career%20path%20today.
4. Plaza, C., *Welding: The Driving Force of the Economy*, American Welding Society Education, United States of America, June 30, 2016, Online. Retrieved January 15, 2023, from https://awo.aws.org/2016/06/welding-the-driving-force-of-our-economy/.
5. *Welding-Related Expenditures and Productivity Measurement in U.S. Manufacturing, Construction, and Mining Industries*, Documents. United States of America, May 2002, Retrieved January 15, 2023, from https://www.bis.doc.gov/index.php/documents.
6. Linke, R., Additive Manufacturing, explained. *MIT Sloan*, December 7, 2017. Retrieved January 15, 2023, from https://mitsloan.mit.edu/ideas-made-to-matter/additive-manufacturing-explained#:~:text=What%20is%20additive%20manufacturing%3F,the%20final%20product%20is%20complete.
7. Kantumuchu, V.C., Additive manufacturing for industrial applications and potential quality challenges, in: *Advances in Additive Manufacturing Processes*, Bentham Science Publishers, Bussum, The Netherlands, 216-239, 2021. https://doi.org/10.2174/9789815036336121010016.
8. Doolittle, H., *3D Printers for Woodworkers a Short Introduction*, Linden Publishing, United States of America, 2020.
9. Fan, D., Li, Y., Wang, X., Zhu, T., Wang, Q., Cai, H., Li, W., Tian, Y., Liu, Z., Progressive 3D printing technology and its application in medical materials. *Front. Pharmacol.*, 11, 122, 2020, doi: 10.3389/fphar.2020.00122.
10. *Lack of Penetration & Root Fusion*, BOC online, UK, Retrieved January 15, 2023, from https://www.boconline.co.uk/en/processes/welding/welding-defects/penetration-root-fusion.html.
11. France, E.J., The Alexander L. Kielland disaster revisited: A review by an experienced welding engineer of the catastrophic north sea platform collapse. *J. Fail. Anal. Prev.*, 19, 875–881, 2019. https://doi.org/10.1007/s11668-019-00680-4.
12. Nikel, D., Stephen, R., Jackie, A., Nelson, K.J., Walker, L., Remembering the Alexander L. Kielland disaster of 1980. *Life Norway*, May 24, 2022. Retrieved January 15, 2023, from https://www.lifeinnorway.net/alexander-l-kielland-disaster/.
13. Alexander L Kielland accommodation platform. *TWI*. Retrieved January 15, 2023, from https://www.twi-global.com/media-and-events/insights/alexander-l-kielland-accommodation-platform.
14. Adel, A., Future of industry 5.0 in society: Human-centric solutions, challenges and prospective research areas. *J. Cloud Comput. (Heidelb)*, 11, 1, 40,

2022. doi: 10.1186/s13677-022-00314-5. Epub 2022 Sep 8. PMID: 36101900; PMCID: PMC9454409.

15. *Welding Market Size, Share: Global Industry Growth, 2021-2028*, USA, August 2021, Retrieved January 15, 2023, from https://www.fortunebusinessinsights.com/industry-reports/welding-market-101657.
16. Department of Labor Logo United States Department of Labor, 7,600-pound conveyor crushes worker after weld failure-a preventable death, says OSHA. Occupational Safety and Health Administration, USA, June 11, 2015. Retrieved January 15, 2023, from https://www.osha.gov/news/newsreleases/region7/06122015.
17. Oman, N., Faulty Weld suspected for I-40 bridge fracture. *Arkansas*, May 27, 2021. Online. Retrieved January 15, 2023, from https://www.arkansasonline.com/news/2021/may/27/faulty-weld-suspected-for-i-40-bridge-fracture/.
18. Sassi, P., Tripicchio, P., Avizzano, C.A., A smart monitoring system for automatic welding defect detection. *IEEE Trans. Ind. Electron.*, 66, 12, 9641–9650, Dec. 2019, doi: 10.1109/TIE.2019.2896165.
19. Gyasi, E.A., Handroos, H., Kah, P., Survey on artificial intelligence (AI) applied in welding: A future scenario of the influence of AI on technological, economic, educational and social changes. *Procedia Manuf.*, 38, 702–714, 2019. https://doi.org/10.1016/j.promfg.2020.01.095.
20. Wald, M.L., Weld flaws found on gas pipe in blast. *New York Times*, January 22, 2011. Retrieved January 15, 2023, from https://www.nytimes.com/2011/01/22/science/earth/22pipe.html.
21. United States Department of Labor, *Accident Report Detail | Occupational Safety and Health Administration*, USA, June 15, 2022, osha.gov Retrieved January 15, 2023, from https://www.osha.gov/ords/imis/accidentsearch.accident_detail?id=146989.015.
22. Zewe, A., Using artificial intelligence to control digital manufacturing. *Massachusetts Institute Technol.*, August 2, 2022. Retrieved January 15, 2023, from https://news.mit.edu/2022/artificial-intelligence-3-d-printing-0802.
23. Ramian, J., Ramian, J., Dziob, D., Thermal deformations of thermoplast during 3D printing: Warping in the case of ABS. *Mater. (Basel, Switzerland)*, November 21, 2021. Retrieved January 15, 2023, from https://www.ncbi.nlm.nih.gov/pmc/articles/PMC8620654.

15

Welding Practices in Industry 5.0: Opportunities, Challenges, and Applications

Suresh Goka[1], Syed Quadir Moinuddin[2]*, Muralimohan Cheepu[3] and Ashok Kumar Dewangan[4]

[1]*Department of Mechanical Engineering, National Institute of Technology Warangal, Warangal, India*
[2]*Department of Mechanical Engineering, College of Engineering, King Faisal University, Al-Hofuf, Kingdom of Saudi Arabia*
[3]*STARWELDS Inc., Busan, South Korea*
[4]*Department of Mechanical Engineering, National Institute of Technology, Delhi, India*

Abstract
In the present automated industrial environment of Industry 5.0, automated manufacturing is moving towards mass customization using collaborative automation of humans and robots. Because there are so many manufacturing technologies in welding that concern various industries, it is important that any new trends be noted for various applications. In addition, relevant research should be analyzed with certain case studies. The objective of this review chapter is to make the reader aware of the current challenges, opportunities, and applications in welding with regard to an automated industrial environment.

Keywords: Welding, arc welding, metal additive manufacturing, Industry 5.0, opportunities, challenges, and applications

**Corresponding author*: syedquadirmoinuddin@gmail.com

Syed Quadir Moinuddin, Shaik Himam Saheb, Ashok Kumar Dewangan, Murali Mohan Cheepu and S. Balamurugan (eds.) Automation in Welding Industry: Incorporating Artificial Intelligence, Machine Learning and Other Technologies, (263–280) © 2024 Scrivener Publishing LLC

15.1 Introduction

Manufacturing has entered a new era known as "Industry 5.0". The current production process should be changed to enable man and machine to collaborate, combining the distinct intellectual abilities of humans with the exact technical abilities of robots to foster an inventive work environment. Industry 5.0, which is the evolution of the manufacturing sector, may be the catalyst for the subsequent industrial revolution.

The Fourth Industrial Revolution (FIR), also known as Industry 4.0, revolutionized industrial manufacturing, making it easier to integrate new techniques and trends. In a word, the idea of Industry 4.0 embodies how the production system evolved from a labor-intensive mass production model to a seamless, automated factory. The entire product value chain is being digitalized, production procedures are being optimized, and networked communication systems are being integrated as part of this dynamic shift toward mechanization along the assembly line.

15.2 Manufacturing Trends

The manufacturing industry serves as the main engine of growth for the diverse economies in Southeast Asia. Manufacturers have realized the increased demand for more complicated skill sets with a wider range of applications to increase productivity in high-mix, low-volume production scenarios. Companies will be forced to create more creative solutions to address changing production needs because of changes in market trends and consumer preferences.

The International Federation of Robotics (IFR) estimates that 139,300 industry robots were sold in Asia in 2014, which was the region with the largest robot market. The use of industrial robots is currently expanding across many industries, with Asia, specifically countries such as China and Taiwan, Korea, India, and other Southeast Asian economies, being recognized as a significant region for growth in the upcoming years. Manufacturers looking for automation solutions to familiarize themselves with the dynamics of the upgraded fabrication field can notice the expansion of the robot industry.

Today, product manufacturers have been facing various challenges in every kind of manufacturing method as well as technique. Some of the challenges are quality and consistency, the safety of workers, market competition, complex geometries, keeping low overheads, etc. Consequently, the first industrial robot was developed to handle and carry out challenging and dangerous jobs, save manufacturing lead time, investment, and maintenance costs, and protect workers and managers from health risks.

15.3 Welding Technology

Over the past years, welding technology has quickly evolved, and hence the advancements in the technology have led to new welding equipment with enhanced components and devices like DAC setup, *in-situ* monitoring, online monitoring, etc. Up until the 1980s, the equipment consisted of big transformers and bulky machinery as power sources for the welding process, which needed a lot of maintenance. Later, the bulky power sources were replaced with generators, which would give DC as an output, even though the maintenance was extensive. Then rectifiers were introduced into the setup. After the 1980s, the inverter was introduced into welding technology by Fronius. After that, huge changes occurred in the last 20 years. Portable and low-size equipment were introduced. Therefore, inverters can be considered the initial cause of the revolution. After a few years, inverters became programmable machines, which brought many advantages to users and led to the digital revolution in technology. The intelligent revolution evolved in a big way with the programmable machines currently being used by many industries and academic institutes, the so-called REF technology.

Welding is the process of joining similar or dissimilar metals or non-metals with or without heat addition, and with or without the application of pressure, and with or without the melting of the parent material. The welding phenomenon leads to a permanent joint. From a strength point of view, the joint should have strength as high as that related to the base metal/parent material that undergoes the joining phenomenon. The perfect weld joint reflects the continuously formed joint provided by the homogeneous nature of bonding. Practically, it is a difficult task to obtain homogeneous properties across the deposited material and the parent material. The mechanical properties and the microstructural behavior will not be identical. Thus, welding is a complex method that includes:

- Heat transfer and liquid metal transfer
- Coalescence or chemical reactions
- Melting, solidification, re-melting, and re-solidification
- Metallurgical transformation, etc.

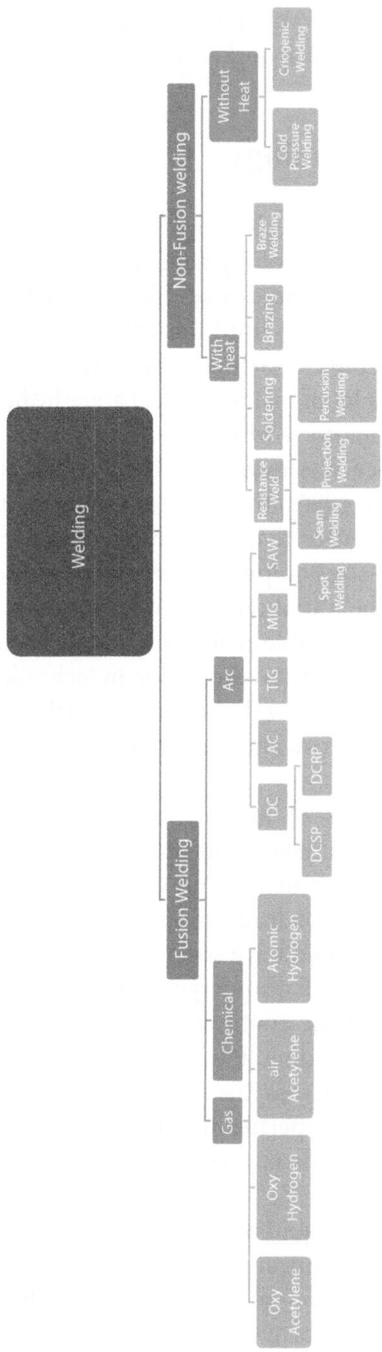

Figure 15.1 Classification of welding.

15.3.1 Classification of Welding

The flowchart shown in Figure 15.1 represents the classification of welding.

15.4 Variety of Materials Used by Welding for Industry 5.0

In this section, the broader classification of materials that are used in the welding process is represented in Figure 15.2. The most common materials used in construction are steel and aluminum. They are common in nature, which is why they are so prevalent in today's world. Steel is the least common metal on Earth, while aluminum is the most commonly used alloy. Although they are used similarly, their applications are very different from each other; both materials possess characteristics that allow for their use in industrial environments. Steel is robust and has a great strength-to-weight ratio compared to aluminum. The two crucial factors are a good ratio and corrosion resistance, which are critical in the automotive industry. Additionally, containers used in cryogenic and chemical plants, maritime craft, and aircraft use steel and aluminum alloys.

However, integrating steel and aluminum to get the advantages of both materials in a single piece has long been uncharted territory. Fusion welding aluminum to steel has a variety of inherent difficulties, including a lack of joint strength, because it produces hard and brittle intermetallic compounds. Due to this, research scholars are increasingly focusing on hybrid methods [1].

Friction stir welding (FSW) is one of the generalized processes to join dissimilar materials. The process parameters vary for each alloy system, and different rpm result in different joint strengths [2–4]. However, one pattern in the data indicates that as rpm increases, the thickness of the intermetallic compound (IMC) layer also increases, and as a result, tensile strength decreases. Numerous investigations have been conducted to determine the FSW tool's ideal revolutions. However, it is noted that not every metal grade or even every sheet thickness can achieve an ideal rpm. Therefore, it may be fairly concluded that an ideal rpm rather than thinning the IMC layer is necessary for successful joining in friction stir welding [5].

Ultrasonic welding (UW) has been utilized with a variety of materials for more than 60 years, overcoming many of the metallurgical, environmental, and energy-use restrictions of other joining techniques used at the time. However, a thorough understanding of the underlying workings of the welding techniques utilized in ReBCO-based superconductors and

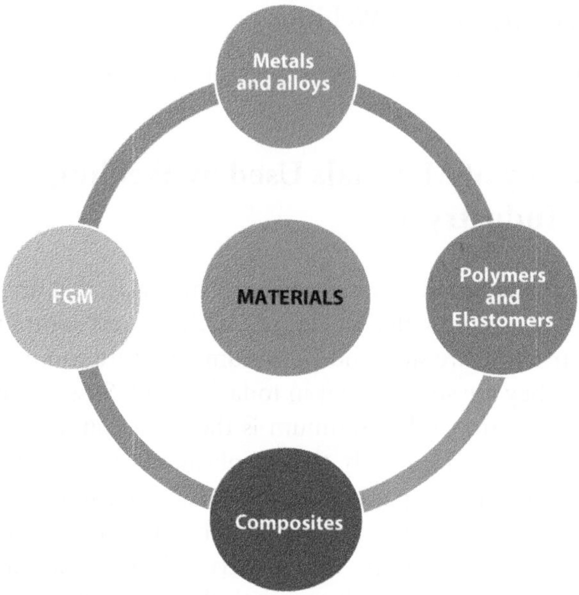

Figure 15.2 Materials used for welding.

electric car batteries is still lacking. Further research is needed, namely on the combining of aluminum and copper alloys often used in lithium-ion batteries and second-generation high-temperature superconducting tapes. Numerous investigations have concentrated on the use of ultrasonic welding in wires and polymers, and fewer on ultrasonic welding with metal sheets that have concentrated on adjusting parameters to provide the highest weld strength and quality. To better comprehend the procedure, weld mechanics employ their understanding of the weld temperature distribution at the interface and the connection between weld strength and quality, given its implications for different fracture types.

In recent years, functionally gradient materials (FGM) applications have developed further, and there is a rising need for FGM applications. The majority of the advantages of FGMs come from their potential for customization to satisfy the needs of various properties at various locations within a single component. These materials were initially utilized in the aerospace industry, but their use has now spread to other industries. Engineering difficulties are always being addressed by researchers, and they are successful in developing functionally graded materials (FGM). Engineering materials having a specialized chemical composition and (sometimes) microstructure are referred to as FGM. A compositional gradient from one material to another defines FGM. These gradients can either be smooth with homogeneous mixtures or sharp with heterogeneous blends of two different components.

A revolutionary method to vigorously mix metallic elements or change the composition/microstructure inside a three-dimensional volume is involved in the process of additive manufacturing of functionally graded materials (AM-FGM). With the use of AM technology, a metallic FGM with a range of qualities is intended to be produced. In another way, AM-FGM refers to the process of gradually combining materials to create a component with a near-net shape and changeable properties. AM-FGM can profit from both the AM and the FGM advantages simultaneously.

15.4.1 Advantages of Welding

- A permanent joint can be formed.
- Welding process equipment is not very expensive.
- All the joining processes are not involved in melting the strong base material.
- Dissimilar metals and non-metals can also be joined.
- Many of the welding processes offer less effort and require fewer investments.

15.4.2 Applications

Many industries are coming up with different products to fulfill different purposes. Towards the industrial revolution, the welding of the parts could be done with the lowest possible manufacturing lead time, minimal cost, and an improvement in the quality of the products. Because of the above-mentioned advantages, the applications of welding technology have expanded across various fields. The services of the welding phenomenon have especially been extended through the aircraft industries, automobile sector, shipping industries, railway tracks and bridges, piping factories, fabrication of cylinders and pressure vessels, thermal power plants and nuclear plants, and civil works. Figure 15.3 depicts some of the applications of welding.

15.4.3 Automation

In manufacturing industries and production environments, robots are commonplace and serve as reliable tools to help employees with their

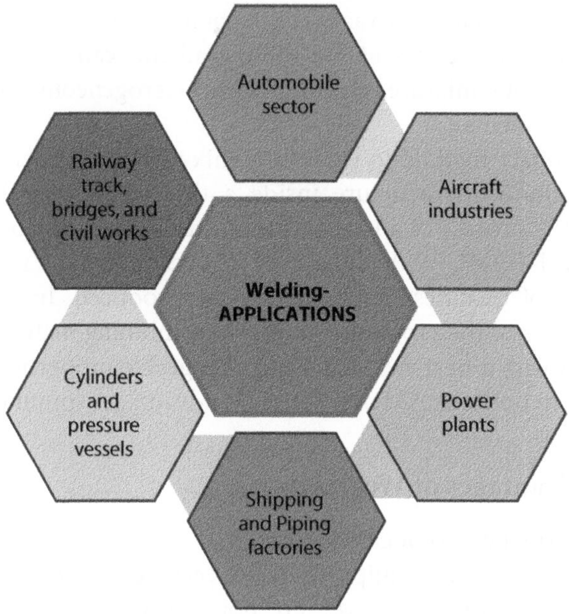

Figure 15.3 Welding applications.

regular tasks. The basic operations for a robot, such as picking, placing, palletizing, moving, turning, even welding, and any other kind of activity, can be performed easily if it is programmed to do so. Only programming and implementing it on the robot interface platform fall under the purview of the working operator. The ability of coworkers to use their imagination and ingenuity to take production to the next level is the key to realizing the maximum potential of automation. A new generation of industrial robots called collaborative robots (Co-bots) was created to work cooperatively with their teammates in confined locations to improve the fabrication process.

For instance, the worker is responsible for writing a program for the co-bot to carry out a specific operation, such as distributing liquids or joining metal components. The worker can monitor the entire process, quickly address any possible problems, and visually verify the finished products while each item is being created. With this collaborative approach in place, staff members can be empowered to manage additional projects concurrently or enhance existing processes to increase performance.

Modern manufacturing companies have several chances to streamline their production processes because of the superior technologies and skilled labor force that are available today. Even with the advent of industrial robots like co-bots, factory workers will continue to play a critical role as collaborative employers to supervise and ensure that work is completed safely, compassionately, and efficiently. Business owners that have already begun to construct smart factories will rapidly understand the necessity of making future plans. Companies must constantly innovate their products or modernize their processes to stay on top of their game in today's rapidly changing manufacturing environment. Today's factories and industries are beginning to implement Industry 5.0, and the interaction among machines and workers will indeed continue.

15.4.4 Welding-Based AM

In recent years, welding has realized its potential in Industry 5.0 because of its ability to produce parts directly from a CAD model to the final finished product with reduced manufacturing lead time and fewer production steps. In this way, AM technology has been witnessed in producing complex design parts, overhanging components, composite materials, functionally gradient materials, etc. Nowadays, attention to metal component welding has shifted to AM as the manufacturing of metallic parts meets the demands of various industries like aerospace and automotive. There are various sources like arc, laser, and electron beams used for the metal welding process, where the deposition rate and investment cost are prominent to differentiate the processes.

The use of electron beams and lasers helped in producing certain quality products but was limited to the size of the components. In addition, the capital investment and maintenance costs are huge. Alternatively, the arc is an energy source with a high deposition rate.

15.4.5 Welding Trends in Aeronautic Industry

There are exciting developments in the aeronautic industry employing welding technology. Various new trends in this area were explored in detail by the Massachusetts Institute of Technology in Cambridge, Massachusetts. Mendez has narrated their innovations concerning different welding methods [6], an exploration of which follows.

Friction welding is the process in which the joining of metals happens through mechanical deformation without melting. Hence, the joint formed is as strong as the base material, and the joint is also free of defects that occur during the regular process of melting and solidification. This process is useful in joining Al landing gear components (with a relatively simple cross section). This linear friction welding is being examined by General Electric and Pratt & Whitney as a substitute for creating and mending high-temperature alloy blisks (bladed disks) for jet engines. Solid-state welding, known as friction stir welding (FSW), connects the material by mechanically deforming it. Even non-weldable aluminum alloy series, such as the 2xxx and 7xxx utilized in airplane structures, can be welded. To use FSW to weld the booster core tanks for the Delta line of space launch vehicles, Boeing invested $15 million. It was the country's inaugural FSW. Next, the fuel and oxidizer tanks for the Saturn V rocket using AA2219 were mostly built using gas metal arc welding (GMAW). For Patriot missiles, the vanes are also welded using the same process. Gas tungsten arc welding (GTAW) is used for welding SS vanes in jet engines. The space shuttle's external fuel tank is constructed using plasma arc welding. Lastly, diffusion welding, a solid-state welding process, is useful in the aeronautic industry for welding titanium alloys and aluminum alloys with superplastic forming.

15.4.6 Robotic and Automated Welding

The first robot ever created was utilized by General Motors as an automated welder in the industrial sector in 1962. Because it is still expanding, especially in the aluminum industry, and because computing costs are falling, automated welding is becoming even more affordable. By the end of 2021, there will be over 3.8 million active industrial robots, up almost 80% from the previous five years, according to the International Federation of Robotics (IFR). By the end of 2023, it is projected that the global market for robotic welding will be worth $5.95 billion, growing at a compound annual growth rate (CAGR) of 8.9%. Other nations, including India, China, Japan, and South Korea, are among those with the largest markets expected to expand in the Asia-Pacific region.

By making knowledge and workflow feasible, human-robot collaboration (HRC) can provide many opportunities while avoiding the difficulties of existing research advances, regardless of the working sectors or industries [7]. HRC is a crucial approach that may be used in a variety of manufacturing industries since it produces effective resource utilization by embracing new technology. The robots also contribute to the system's accuracy, precision, time efficiency, and repeatability. Figure 15.4(a) depicts the robot's function [8].

Due to potential risks and hazards associated with the communication gap between people and robots, the exclusive benefits provided by HRC are now restricted. The role of identifying tasks and executing them with human teammates, bidirectional intent recognition, estimation at trade-off to attain optimality, and other issues are the main hurdles to extending

HRC, as shown in Figure 15.4(b). During a period, the fulfillment of raised requirements and HRC technologies are evaluated, as represented in Figure 15.4(c). In addition, the timeline of milestones and revolutions in industries through robots is explored in the schematic in Figure 15.4(d).

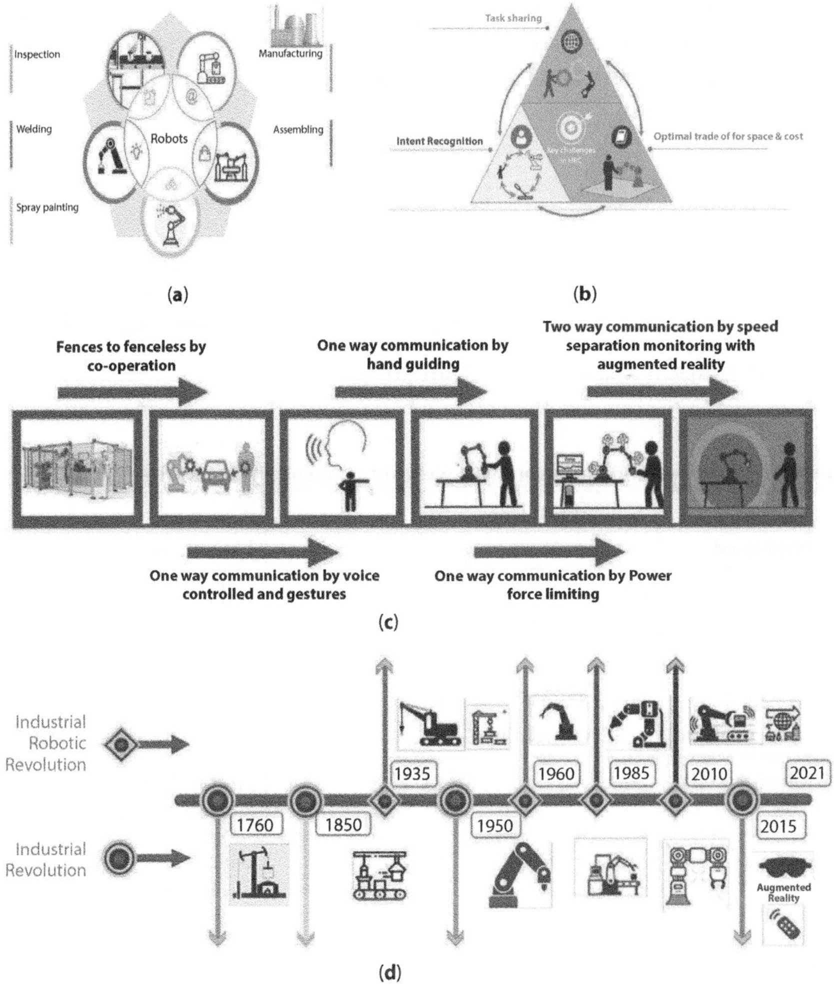

Figure 15.4 Human–robot collaboration towards the industrial revolution [7]: (a) Role of industrial robots in the manufacturing field; (b) Key challenges of HRC; (c) Evaluation of HRC technologies; (d) Industrial robot revaluation.

15.5 Virtual Reality (VR) for Welders

Virtual reality (VR), which is mostly related to video games, uses a headset to completely immerse a viewer in a digital world. However, it might also be used in a variety of fields, such as skyscraper construction, shipbuilding, and welding. With the use of VR, designers may swiftly create virtual prototypes and evaluate them more physically. As a result, this will dramatically accelerate the construction of the project by streamlining and prototyping the process. In the welding area, VR may be useful for training, workplace safety, and instructing welders on the basics (Table 15.1). VR offers new perspectives on the world to learners and welders, and it can be

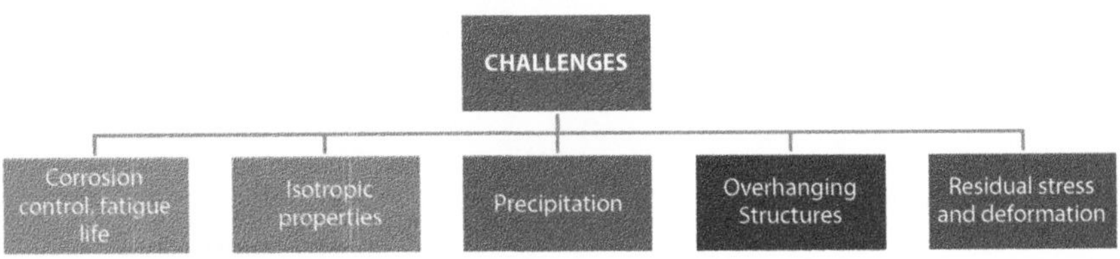

Figure 15.5 Challenges in welding in Industry 5.0.

Table 15.1 Robot collaboration with welding applications across the world.

Robot used	Type of welding used	Reference	University
Kuka	GMAW Twin wire type	[9–12]	Indian Institute of Technology Hyderabad
OTC (Daihen Corporation)	Hybrid laser-MAG welding	[13]	KU Leuven University
Motorman UP 20	GMAW	[14, 15]	Harbin Institute of Technology
Motoman	Hybrid (MIG)	[16]	Huazhong University of Science and Technology
Fronius	GMAW	[17, 18]	University of Wollongong
Kuka	Friction stir welding	www.coeamt.com [16]	Indian Institute of Technology Kharagpur

extremely helpful for a variety of training needs. However, with the help of AI, ML, and Digital Twin, various challenges could be addressed, as shown in Figure 15.5, wherein VR and AR facilitate prototypes rather than actual welding that leads to material waste.

15.6 Challenges and Opportunities in Nuclear Reactor

According to a perspective on the challenges and opportunities of welding treatment in the nuclear sector [19], the following issues are addressed:

- Relative magnetic field
- Creating vacuums for substantial components
- Vacuum preheating
- Terminations of welds.

Residual magnetism can cause the electron beam (EB) to deflect to the point where it misses the weld seam over a portion of the thickness when welding thick sections of steel. De-magnetization is therefore crucial. In some circumstances, reaching that level will be difficult. Large pressure vessels must be positioned in a vacuum, which is a very difficult task. The existing technology is more affordable. Additionally, TWI and collaborators developed localized vacuums and close-up systems when welding at lower pressures as opposed to high vacuums. If a vessel is positioned in a vacuum chamber, preheating and applying it could be challenging. By rastering a defocused beam over the surface, heating can be achieved.

According to past research, troublesome cavities and craters can be avoided by using a tapered weld finish (namely slope out) that gradually reduces the beam current rather than stopping it all at once (according to the Electric Power Research Institute 2021 report).

Opportunities

- Studies in multiple physics on transitory keyholes.
- The development of vacuum-assisted laser welding.
- Normalizing and tempering procedures are applied after welding.
- Weld performance after irradiation.
- Weldable steels with extremely high strength.

15.7 Challenges of AM-Based Functionally Graded Materials Through LDED

Numerous possible uses for metallic FGMs exist, and their advancement can be facilitated by AM. Given that AM-FGM is a new idea, there is still much to learn about the various difficulties it may cause. This section discusses some of the difficulties that come with using LDED to implement AM-FGM [20].

- Alloy Incompatibility

When mixing multiple materials, the efficacy of the heat input is influenced by the varying melting temperatures of each component, since each component requires a different amount of heat to be sufficiently melted. This might lead to some elements that have a lower melting point vaporizing more frequently [21]. Furthermore, segregation, dimensional inaccuracy, porosity creation, and partially melted or unmelted particles may emerge from changes in density and surface tension (liquid) between the ingredients [22].

- Process Modeling

Process modeling is a useful technique for managing the AM-FGMs' characteristics and microstructure. Due to the various intrinsic features of the elements, modeling is still difficult. Data on the thermophysical characteristics of various compositions rely on temperature and are not readily available. In addition, the local composition is constantly changing as new metals and alloys are added to the melt pool. If available, the data for all ingredients can be tailored into a polynomial to forecast the thermophysical characteristics of a gradient. If not, the compositional dependency and effective qualities, which must be approximated using a rule of mixes, should be considered using a more complicated methodology. Programs using thermodynamics can also predict thermophysical characteristics.

The path strategies with significant composition fluctuation values, however, displayed a high level of inaccuracy. Powder mixing in the LDED system needs to be managed as well. Segregation inside the powder injection system is possible as a result of the varied densities, shapes, and sizes of the particles. One hopper/nozzle can be used to transport pre-mixed powders.

- Thermodynamic Modeling

The development of multicomponent phase diagrams by thermodynamic modeling can assist in forecasting and preventing the onset of undesirable brittle phases. Phase changes and thermophysical characteristics can both be modeled using thermodynamics. It should be emphasized that these diagrams are primarily designed for equilibrium processes, like casting, and that they may not accurately forecast non-equilibrium processes like LDED. To quickly establish whether a specific gradient is experimentally achievable, however, this approach might be useful.

15.8 Conclusion

To completely comprehend the microstructural evolution, *in-situ* observation and monitoring of microstructure and the formation of phases are also required. The successful application of welded FGMs can be aided by non-destructive real-time characterization methods, particularly those with *in-situ* implementation capabilities. Another difficult issue is the absence of technical industry-wide standards for welding. The use of welding for Industry 5.0 applications may be hampered by this absence. Even though they could be of utmost significance in practical applications, some crucial features of welding advanced materials, including post-processing, machining, thermomechanical responses under various conditions, and other attributes of the printed parts, have not yet been well researched. To close the gaps, additional research and advanced studies are required in this developing area.

References

1. Kaushik, P. and Dwivedi, D.K., Al-steel dissimilar joining: Challenges and opportunities. *Mater. Today Proc.*, 62, 6884–6899, 2022, doi: 10.1016/j.matpr.2022.05.211.
2. Kundu, S., Roy, D., Bhola, R., Bhattacharjee, D., Mishra, B., Chatterjee, S., Microstructure and tensile strength of friction stir welded joints between interstitial free steel and commercially pure aluminium. *Mater. Des.*, 50, 370–375, Sep. 2013, doi: 10.1016/j.matdes.2013.02.017.
3. Watanabe, T., Takayama, H., Yanagisawa, A., Joining of aluminum alloy to steel by friction stir welding. *J. Mater. Process. Technol.*, 178, 1–3, 342–349, Sep. 2006, doi: 10.1016/j.jmatprotec.2006.04.117.
4. Dong, H., Liao, C., Yang, L., Dong, C., Effects of post-weld heat treatment on dissimilar metal joint between aluminum alloy and stainless steel. *Mater. Sci. Eng. A*, 550, 423–428, Jul. 2012, doi: 10.1016/j.msea.2012.04.110.
5. Sarila, V.K., Moinuddin, S.Q., Cheepu, M.M., Rajendran, H., Kantumuchu, V.C., Characterization of microstructural anisotropy in 17-4PH stainless

steel fabricated by DMLS additive manufacturing and laser shot peening. *Trans. Ind. Inst. Met.*, 76, 2, 403–410, 2022.

6. Mendez, P.F., Welding processes used in the aeronautic industry friction welding (FRW), in: *New Trends in Welding in the Aeronautic Industry*, pp. 21–38, 2000.
7. Inkulu, A.K., Bahubalendruni, M.V.A.R., Dara, A., SankaranarayanaSamy, K., Challenges and opportunities in human robot collaboration context of industry 4.0-a state of the art review. *Ind. Rob.*, 49, 2, 226–239, 2022, doi: 10.1108/IR-04-2021-0077.
8. Gibbs, A. and Ohshima, K., Potyviruses and the digital revolution. *Annu. Rev. Phytopathol.*, 48, 1, 205–223, Jul. 2010, doi: 10.1146/annurev-phyto-073009-114404.
9. Adinarayanappa, S.M. and Simhambhatla, S., *Determination of Process Parameter for Twin-Wire Weld-Deposition Based Additive Manufacturing*, American Society of Mechanical Engineers, United States of America, Aug. 2014, doi: 10.1115/DETC2014-34658.
10. Moinuddin, S.Q. and Sharma, A., Arc stability and its impact on weld properties and microstructure in anti-phase synchronized twin-wire gas metal arc welding. *Mater. Des.*, 67, 293–302, 2015.
11. Moinuddin, S.Q., Kapil, A., Kohama, K., Sharma, A., Ito, K., Tanaka, M., On processstructure- property interconnection in anti-phase synchronized twin-wire GMAW of low carbon steel. *Sci. Technol. Weld. Join.*, 21, 6, 452–459, 2016.
12. Kumar, M., Moinuddin, S.Q., Surya, S., Sharma, A., Discrete wavelet analysis of mutually interfering co-existing welding signals in twin-wire robotic welding. *J. Manuf. Process.*, 63, 139– 151, 2020.
13. Kapil, A., Suga, T., Tanaka, M., Sharma, A., Towards hybrid laser-arc based directed energy deposition: Understanding bead formation through mathematical modeling for additive manufacturing. *J. Manuf. Process.*, 76, 457–474, Apr. 2022, doi: 10.1016/j.jmapro.2022.02.027.
14. Xiong, J., Zhang, G., Hu, J., Wu, L., Bead geometry prediction for robotic GMAW-based rapid manufacturing through a neural network and a second-order regression analysis. *J. Intell. Manuf.*, 25, 1, 157–163, 2014, doi: 10.1007/s10845-012-0682-1.
15. Xiong, J., Zhang, G., Gao, H., Wu, L., Modeling of bead section profile and overlapping beads with experimental validation for robotic GMAW-based rapid manufacturing. *Robot. Comput. Integr. Manuf.*, 29, 2, 417–423, Apr. 2013, doi: 10.1016/j.rcim.2012.09.011.
16. Haribabu, S., Cheepu, M., Devuri, V., Kantumuchu, V.C., Optimization of welding parameters for friction welding of 304 stainless steel to D3Tool steel using response surface methodology. *Techno-Societal 2018*, pp. 427–437, 2019, https://doi.org/10.1007/978-3-030-16962-6_44.
17. Sarila, V.K., Koneru, H.P., Pathapalli, V.R., Cheepu, M., Kantumuchu, V.C., Wear and microstructural characteristics of colmonoy-4 and stellite-6

additive layer deposits on En19 steel by laser cladding. *Trans. Ind. Inst. Met.*, 76, 2, 457–464, 2022, https://doi.org/10.1007/s12666-022-02769-1.

18. Kavitha, C., Malini, P.S.G., Kantumuchu, V.C., Kumar, N.M., Verma, A., Boopathi, S., An experimental study on the hardness and wear rate of carbonitride coated stainless steel. *Mater. Today Proc.*, 74, 595–601, 2022, https://doi.org/10.1016/j.matpr.2022.09.524.
19. Francis, A., A perspective on welding technology challenges in the nuclear sector. *Sci. Technol. Weld. Join.*, 27, 4, 309–317, 2022, doi: 10.1080/13621718.2022.2047407.
20. Dewangan, A.K. and Sajjan, S.K., Chapter 3 Boiling behavior of isobutane on a horizontal plain tube, in: *Advances in Thermal Engineering, Manufacturing, and Production Management, Lecture Notes in Mechanical Engineering*, Springer, Singapore, ISBN: 978-981-16-2346-2, 2021, doi: 10.1007/978-981-16-2347-9.
21. Mukherjee, T., Zuback, J.S., De, A., DebRoy, T., Printability of alloys for additive manufacturing. *Sci. Rep.*, 6, 1, 19717, Apr. 2016, doi: 10.1038/srep19717.
22. DebRoy, T. *et al.*, Additive manufacturing of metallic components–process, structure and properties. *Prog. Mater. Sci.*, 92, 112–224, Mar. 2018, doi: 10.1016/j.pmatsci.2017.10.001.

Index

3D printing, 157, 159, 162
4D printing, 157
4D printing applications, 174
5D printing in dentistry, 176
5D printing in orthopedics, 176, 177
5S lean strategy, 221

Activated tungsten inert gas, 224
Aggregated data, 146, 148, 151, 153, 154
AI detection of welding defects, 138
AI-based robotic welding, 229, 242
AlCrFeMnNi HEA, 206
Alloy incompatibility, 276
ANN, 86, 87
Application, 245, 246, 249, 251, 252, 254, 256, 257, 259, 260
Arc welding, 45, 143–145, 154
  MIG welding, 45
Artificial intelligence, 131, 245, 246, 261
Asia-Pacific region, 237
Automatic welding types, 39
Automation, 271
Autonomous robots, 112

Benefits of automatic welding, 40
  quality control, 41
  weld-fault diagnostics, 41
Big data analytics, 8
Boltzmann's hypothesis, 185
Brittleness, 245

Case studies, 86
CFRTP, 88
Challenges, 245–248, 252, 253, 260
CLIP, 105
CNC milling, 169
CO_2 footprint, 143, 145, 146, 148, 150, 151
Cobot, 143–147, 149–153
Cocktail effect, 186
Cold metal transfer, 166
Computer interface of automated welding processes, 136
Consumption data, 143, 145, 146, 151, 153, 154
Conventional laser cladding, 206
Cracks, 245, 250–253
CS-WAVE technology, 133
Cyber security, 112
Cyber-physical systems, 91

Dashboard, 147, 149–152, 154
DED, 163
Digital twin, 91, 95, 105
Direct light processing, 164
Dissimilar materials, 267
Doubled pulsed GMAW, 23
DT for FSW, 99
DT for laser welding, 105

EBW, 93, 200
Ecological impact, 148
Effect of pulse parameters,
  weld bead geometry, 19
  weld dilution, 20
  weld microstructure, 20
Electric arc welding, 4

Electrical process tests, 51
acoustic measurement, 58
measurement of displacement and velocity, 59
measurement of force, 59
optical measurement, 56
thermal measurement, 54
voltage and current for welding, 51
Emerging economies, 232
EN1090, 219
Energy consumption, 143, 145, 146, 150
EU eco-management and audit scheme, 227
Explosive welding, 197

Failure, 247–250, 252–257, 261
FCAW, 135
Flammable atmospheres, 120
Ford's product sustainability index, 227
Fourth industrial revolution, 264
Fracture, 251, 261
Friction stir welding, 73, 87
FSW parameters, 94
Fume extraction, 143–147, 149–154
Functionally gradient materials, 268

Gateway, 143, 146, 147
Global growth of welding, 233
Global welding market, 240
GMAW, 144, 145
GMAW of FCC HEAs, 184
GMAW shielding gas flow, 27

Hall effect sensor, 122
HEAs, 184, 185, 200, 204, 205
Heat conduction welding, 103
High-entropy alloys, 184
HLM technique, 169
HPDM, 171
HRC technologies, 273
Hybrid laser arc, 159

Industrial revolution, 2
Industry 4.0, 9, 79, 84
predictive maintenance, 9
quality control, 9
remote monitoring, 9
welding automation, 9
Industry 5.0, 10
automated welding, 10
collaborative welding, 10
virtual welding, 10
welding process optimization, 10
welding quality control, 10
In-situ observation, 277
Intelligent manufacturing, 129
Intelligent welding systems, 133
IoT, 3, 76, 246, 248, 254, 255, 258, 259
IoT MQTT panel, 123
IoT-based safety monitoring system, 119
IoT-based solutions, 111
ISO 3834, 116, 219

Joint line remnants, 97

Keyhole welding, 103

Laser beam welding, 92
Laser cladding, 207
Laser welding, 44, 102
Laser welding of HEAs, 204, 205
Layered manufacturing, 163
LDED, 276
Lightweight materials, 231
LOM, 164

Machine learning, 73, 131
Machine learning algorithm types, 80
MAG torch, 166
Measurement of oxygen concentration, 31
MES, 115
Microcomputer control, 26
Microhardness, 191
MIG-based 3D printer, 165, 171

Mining industry, 84

Normalizing and tempering, 275

Optical spectrum emissions, 113

Parameters, 248, 252, 254, 256
Particle image velocimetry (PIV), 27
PBF, 163
Peak temperatures, 194
Permanent joint, 20
P-GMAW numeric simulation,
  approach I, 32
  approach II, 33
P-GMAW process stability factors, 18
Plasma welding, 42
Porosity, 245, 252, 253
Process monitoring applications, 61–67
  acoustic measurement, 65
  EMF measurement, 67
  measurement of displacement and velocity, 66
  measurement of force, 67
  optical measurement, 64
  thermal measurement, 63
  voltage and current for welding, 61
Production monitoring, 41
  programming of automation systems, 42
  welding advancements, 42
Pulsed current GMAW, 16
Pulsed current GMAW advances, 22

Quality of weld joint, 15

Railroad industry, 235
Random forest, 86
ReBCO-based superconductors, 267
REF technology, 265
Relation between AI, ML, and DL, 75
Relative magnetic field, 275
Resistance welding, 46
Resource-conserving techniques, 219, 220
RHEA coating, 208
RLW, 105
Robot, 252, 254
Robotic welding, 6, 76
Root flaw, 98

Self-regulating control, 25
Sensing technology, 113
SLCA, 219
Slug, 245
Sluggish diffusion effect, 186
SMAW, 93, 135
SMAW process, 222
Soldering and brazing, 199
Sound emission, 114
Spatter, 245, 253–255
Spectroscopic measurements of plasma temperature, 31
Spool welding robots, 75, 78
STL, 157
Subtractive and additive processes, 162
Suitable pulsed parameters of selection, 18
Supply chain management, 227
Sustainability, 215
Synergic control, 24

Techniques for process monitoring, 51–61
Technology, 245, 246, 248, 249, 252, 257, 259, 260
Temperature, 246, 250, 251, 255, 256, 258, 259
Thermodynamic modeling, 276
Thermo-mechanically affected zone, 195
Tool tilt angle, 96
Tungsten inert gas welding, 220

UTS, 96

Virtual reality, 77
Virtuality continuum, 130
Vision, 251, 253, 254
Visual data emission, 114

Voids, 96
Voltage, 246, 254
VR/AR architecture, 132
VR/AR welding simulator, 139

W/V ratio, 95
WAAM parts, 170
Weld defects, 82
Weld job assessment, 137
Weld quality, 83
Weld waste inspection, 137
Weldability, 183
Welding automation, 38
Welding market dynamics, 238
World-class sustainable
manufacturing, 226

Printed and bound by CPI Group (UK) Ltd, Croydon, CR0 4YY
27/10/2024
14580127-0001